Accounting

FOR

DUMMIES

A Wiley Brand

5TH EDITION

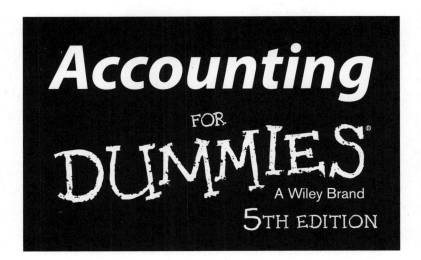

Accounting FOR DUMMIES®
A Wiley Brand
5TH EDITION

by John A. Tracy, CPA

Accounting For Dummies®, 5th Edition

Published by
John Wiley & Sons, Inc.
111 River St.
Hoboken, NJ 07030-5774
www.wiley.com

About the Author

John A. Tracy (Boulder, Colorado) is Professor of Accounting, Emeritus, at the University of Colorado in Boulder. Before his 35-year tenure at Boulder, he was on the business faculty for four years at the University of California in Berkeley. Early in his career he was a staff accountant with Ernst & Young. John is the author of several books on accounting and finance, including *How To Read a Financial Report*, *The Fast Forward MBA in Finance*, and *Cash Flow For Dummies* and *Small Business Financial Management Kit For Dummies* with his son Tage C. Tracy. John received his BSC degree from Creighton University. He earned his MBA and PhD degrees at the University of Wisconsin in Madison. He is a CPA (inactive status) in Colorado.

Dedication

For our twelve grandchildren — Alexander, Ryan, Mitchel, Paige, Katrina, Claire, Eric, MacKenzie, Madison, Tanner, Karsen, and Brody.

Author's Acknowledgments

I'm deeply grateful to everyone at Wiley Publishing who helped produce this book. Their professionalism, courtesy, and good humor were much appreciated. It has been a pleasure working with everyone.

I got a call in 1996 from Kathy Welton, then Vice President and Publisher for the Consumer Publishing Group of the For Dummies books. Kathy asked if I'd be interested in doing this book. It didn't take me very long to say yes. Thank you again, Kathy!

I can't say enough nice things about Pam Mourouzis, who as project editor on the first edition of the book had to teach me the Dummies ways. The book is immensely better for her insights and advice. The two copyeditors on the book — Diane Giangrossi and Joe Jansen — did a wonderful job. Mary Metcalfe provided valuable suggestions on the manuscript. Thanks to Holly McGuire and Jill Alexander who encouraged me to revise the book. The second edition benefited from the editing by Norm Crampton and Ben Nussbaum.

I owe a special thanks to Stacy Kennedy, acquisitions editor, for asking me to do this and previous revisions. Joan Friedman was the project editor on the two previous editions. Joan was a delight to work with, and it goes without saying that she made the book much better. Susan Hobbs (or Suz, as she prefers) was the project editor for this revision. She had the thankless task of keeping me in line — and she did a very good job. Suz didn't let any sloppy sentences slip through, and she made many helpful suggestions. Thank you most sincerely Suz, and I hope to work with you again on the next edition. Also, thanks to Carla Su DeWitt, the technical editor on this edition, who made several good suggestions.

I've been very fortunate to see five editions of this book. But I'm getting older. I have convinced my son Tage to come on as coauthor for the next edition. We are already coauthors on three books, and you will notice in this edition I refer to our books several times. This is not just fatherly pride. Tage is a very successful business and financial consultant with a wealth of experience. You could say that I'm the "academic" and he's the practitioner. It is my great joy that we work together so well. A chip off the old block, as they say.

Publisher's Acknowledgments

We're proud of this book; please send us your comments at http://dummies.custhelp.com. For other comments, please contact our Customer Care Department within the U.S. at 877-762-2974, outside the U.S. at 317-572-3993, or fax 317-572-4002.

Some of the people who helped bring this book to market include the following:

Acquisitions, Editorial, and Media Development

Project Editor: Susan Hobbs
  (*Previous Editions: Joan Friedman, Norm Crampton*)

Acquisitions Editor: Stacy Kennedy

Copy Editor: Susan Hobbs
  (*Previous Edition: Joan Friedman*)

Assistant Editor: David Lutton

Editorial Program Coordinator: Joe Niesen

Technical Editor: Carla Su DeWitt

Editorial Manager: Carmen Krikorian

Editorial Assistant: Rachelle Amick

Art Coordinator: Alicia B. South

Cover Photo: © Yue Wang / iStock Images

Cartoons: Rich Tennant
  (www.the5thwave.com)

Composition Services

Project Coordinator: Katie Crocker

Layout and Graphics: Carl Byers, Joyce Haughey

Proofreaders: Lindsay Amones, Evelyn Wellborn

Indexer: Potomac Indexing, LLC

Publishing and Editorial for Consumer Dummies

  Kathleen Nebenhaus, Vice President and Executive Publisher

  Ensley Eikenburg, Associate Publisher, Travel

  Kelly Regan, Editorial Director, Travel

Publishing for Technology Dummies

  Andy Cummings, Vice President and Publisher

Composition Services

  Debbie Stailey, Director of Composition Services

Contents at a Glance

Table of Contents

Chapter 13: How Lenders and Investors Read a Financial Report 291

Chapter 14: Filling Out the Financial Statements for Business Managers 319

Introduction

*Y*ou may know individuals who make their living as accountants. You may be thankful that they're the accountants and you're not. You may prefer to leave accounting to the accountants, and think that you don't need to know anything about accounting. This attitude reminds me of the old Greyhound Bus advertising slogan *"Leave the Driving to Us."* Well, if you could get around everywhere you wanted to go on the bus, that would be no problem. But if you have to drive most places, you'd better know something about cars. Throughout your life you do a lot of "financial driving," so you should know something about accounting.

Sure, accounting involves numbers. So does watching your car mileage, knowing your blood pressure, keeping track of your bank balance, negotiating the interest rate on your home mortgage, monitoring your retirement fund, and bragging about your kid's grade point average. You deal with numbers all the time. Accountants provide *financial numbers.* These numbers are very important in your financial life. Knowing nothing about financial numbers puts you at a serious disadvantage. In short, financial literacy requires a working knowledge of accounting, which this book provides.

About This Book

This book, like all *For Dummies* books, consists of freestanding chapters, like boats tied up to a dock. Each chapter floats on its own but the boats are all tied to the same dock. You can read the chapters in any order you please. You can tailor your reading plan to give priority to the chapters of most interest to you, and read other chapters as time permits. Of course, you could start on page 1 and continue straight through until the last page. The choice is yours.

I've written this book for a wide audience. You may be a small business manager who has experience with financial statements, for example, but you need to know more about how to use accounting information in analyzing your profit performance and cash flow. Or, you may be an investor who needs to know more about financial statements, so your chief interest probably will be the chapters that explain those statements. You could be an accounting student who needs shorter and clearer explanations of topics than in your textbook. (Unfortunately accounting textbooks, even introductory texts, tend to be excessively technical and convoluted.)

This book offers several advantages:

- ✔ I explain accounting in plain English and I keep jargon and technical details to a minimum.
- ✔ I carefully follow a step-by-step approach in explaining topics.
- ✔ I include only topics that non-accountants should understand; I avoid topics that only practicing accountants have to know.
- ✔ I include frank discussions of certain sensitive accounting topics, which go unmentioned in many books.

I should mention one thing: This book is *not* an accounting textbook. Introductory accounting textbooks are ponderous, dry as dust, and overly detailed (in my judgment). However, textbooks have one useful feature: They include exercises and problems. You can learn much by reading this book without doing problems. If you have the time, you can gain additional insights and test your understanding of accounting by working the exercises and short problems in my *Accounting Workbook For Dummies* (Wiley).

Conventions Used in This Book

Learning accounting means learning about *financial statements*, because these reports are how accountants communicate to the managers and stakeholders of a business, the insiders and the outsiders. Accountants don't present the actual accounting journals and accounts of the business to its managers, lenders, and investors. Rather the accounting records are summarized in the form of financial statements. Financial statements are the nexus between accountants and the users of these accounting reports. Financial statements are designed for non-accountants. But here's a Catch 22: To know how to read financial statements, you need a basic working knowledge of accounting. One of my main goals in writing this book is to provide you with this basic working knowledge to make you a savvy user of financial statements.

Financial statements are presented according to established (one could say *entrenched*) conventions. Uniform styles and formats for reporting financial statements have evolved over the years and have become generally accepted. The conventions for financial statement reporting can be compared to the design rules for highway signs and traffic signals. Without standardization there would be a lot of accidents.

I present financial statement examples throughout the book. Therefore, I take a moment now to explain the conventions for presenting financial statements. To illustrate these points I use the following example of an *income statement* for a business, which summarizes its sales revenue, expenses, and bottom-line profit for a period. See the following figure.

Income Statement for Year	
Sales Revenue	$5,236,000
Cost of Goods Sold Expense	$3,143,000
Gross Margin	$2,093,000
Selling, General and Administrative Expenses	$1,346,000
Operating Earnings	$747,000
Interest Expense	$152,000
Income tax Expense	$226,000
Net Income	$369,000

Income Statement Illustrative Example

Here are several conventions and customs in reporting financial statements to keep in mind:

✔ It may be obvious, but you read the income statement from the top down. *Sales revenue* is listed first, which is the total income from the sale of products and services during the period before different expenses in the period are deducted. If the main revenue stream of the business is from selling products, the first expense deducted from sales revenue is *cost of goods sold expense,* as in this income statement example.

Deducting the cost of goods sold expense from sales revenue gives *gross margin* (also called *gross profit*). The number of other expense lines in an income statement varies from business to business. In the example, three expenses are given in addition to cost of goods sold expense. A common practice is to show *operating earnings* (or a similar title), which equals profit before interest income tax expense.

✔ An amount that is deducted from another amount — such as the cost of goods sold expense — may be placed in parentheses to indicate that it is being subtracted from the amount above it. Alternatively, the accountant who prepares the financial statement may assume that readers know that expenses are deducted from sales revenue, so no parentheses are put around the number. You see expenses presented both ways in financial reports, but you hardly ever see a minus (negative) sign in front of expenses. With rare exceptions, the color red is not used to report negative items; financial statements are in black and white.

✔ Notice the use of dollar signs in the income statement example. In this illustrative example all amounts have a dollar sign prefix. However, financial reporting practices vary quite a bit on this matter. The first number in a column always has a dollar sign, but from here down it's a matter of personal preference.

✔ To indicate that a calculation is being done, a single underline is drawn under a number, as you see under the $\underline{3,143,000}$ cost of goods sold expense number in the example. This means that the expense amount is being subtracted from sales revenue. The number below the underline is a *calculated* amount. Calculated amounts, such as gross profit and operating earnings, are not accounts. Sales revenue and the four expenses in the illustrative example are the accounts.

Note that there are three calculated amounts in the example: $2,093,000 gross margin; $747,000 operating earnings; and, $369,000 net income.

✔ Dollar amounts in a column are always aligned to the right, as you see in the income statement example. Trying to read down a jagged column of numbers that are not right-aligned would be asking too much; the reader might develop vertigo.

✔ In the income statement example, dollar amounts are rounded to the nearest thousand for ease of reading, which is why you see zeros in the last three places of each number. Really big businesses round off to the nearest million. Instead of including a lot of zeros in a financial statement the accountant could chop off the last three digits and include a notation that dollar amounts are in thousands (or millions, as the case may be).

Some accountants don't like rounding off amounts reported in a financial statement, so you see every amount carried out to the last dollar, and sometimes even to the last penny. However, this gives a false sense of precision. Accounting for business transactions cannot be accurate down to the last dollar; this is nonsense. The late Kenneth Boulding, a well-known economist, once quipped that accountants would rather be precisely wrong than approximately correct. Ouch! That stings because there's a strong element of truth behind the comment.

✔ The final number in a column typically is double underlined, as you see for the $\underline{369,000}$ bottom-line profit number in the income statement. This is about as carried away as accountants get in their work — a double underline. Instead of a double underline for a bottom-line number, it may appear in **bold.** For an accountant this is rather a bold thing to do (pun intended).

What You're Not to Read

While you're reading, I assume you're on the edge of your seat and can hardly wait to get to the next exciting sentence. Well, perhaps I get more pumped up about accounting than you. So, one question you may have is this: Do I really have to read every sentence in the book? To be honest, you can skip the paragraphs marked with the Technical Stuff icon. You can simply leapfrog over these sections without missing a beat. If you have time, you can return to these topics later. Also, the sidebars in the chapters are interesting, but not absolutely essential for understanding the topics at hand. Sidebars are like in a conversation when you say, "By the way, did you know . . . ?"

There's reading, and then there's remembering what you read. You should read the examples I use throughout the book, but you don't have to remember the numbers in each example. For instance, consider the income statement example in the previous section. You should understand that the bottom-line profit is the amount remaining after all expenses are deducted from sales revenue. But, of course, you don't need to remember the specific amount of the bottom-line profit in the example.

Foolish Assumptions

I assume that you have a basic familiarity with the business world, but I take nothing for granted regarding how much accounting you know. I start at the beginning. Even if you have some knowledge of accounting and financial statements, I think you'll find this book useful. The book should provide insights you haven't thought of before. I gained many new insights about accounting while writing this book, that's for sure.

I have written this book with a wide audience in mind. You should find yourself more than once in the following list of potential readers:

- ✔ **Accountants to be:** This book is a good first step for anyone considering a career in professional accounting. If the content turns you off, you might want to look for another vocation.

- ✔ **Active investors:** Investors in marketable securities, real estate, and other ventures need to know how to read financial statements, both to stay informed about their investments and to spot any signs of trouble.

- ✔ **Passive investors:** Many people let the pros manage their money by investing in mutual funds or using investment advisors to handle their money; even so, they need to understand the investment performance reports they get, which use plenty of accounting terms and measures.

- ✔ **People who want to take control of their personal finances:** Many aspects of managing your personal finances involve the accounting vocabulary and accounting-based calculation methods.

- ✔ **Business managers (at all levels):** Trying to manage a business without a good grip on financial statements can lead to disaster. How can you manage the financial performance of your business if you don't understand the financial statements of your business?

- ✔ **Anyone interested in following economic, business, and financial news:** Articles in *The Wall Street Journal* and other financial news sources are heavy with accounting terms and measures.

- ✔ **Administrators and managers of government and not-for-profit entities:** Although making profit is not the goal of these entities, they have to stay within their revenue limits and keep on a sound financial footing.

- ✔ **Politicians at local, state, and federal levels:** These men and women pass many laws having significant financial consequences, and the better they understand accounting, the better informed their votes should be (we hope).

- ✔ **Bookkeepers:** Strengthening their knowledge of accounting should improve their effectiveness and value to the organization and advance their careers.

- ✔ **Entrepreneurs:** As budding business managers, they need a solid grasp of accounting basics.

- ✔ **Business buyers and sellers:** Anyone thinking of buying or selling a business should know how to read its financial statements and how to "true up" these accounting reports that serve as a key point of reference for setting a market value on the business.

- ✔ **Investment bankers, institutional lenders, and loan officers:** I don't really have to tell these folks that they need to understand accounting; they already know.

- ✔ **Business and finance professionals:** This includes lawyers and financial advisors, of course, but even clergy counsel their flock on financial matters occasionally.

I could put others in the above list. But I think you get the idea that many different people need to understand the basics of accounting. Perhaps someone who leads an isolated contemplative life and renounces all earthly possessions does not need to know anything about accounting. But, then again, I don't know.

How This Book Is Organized

This book is divided into parts, and each part is further divided into chapters. The following sections describe what you can find in each part.

Part 1: Opening the Books on Accounting

In Chapters 1 and 2, I introduce the business financial statements *gradually,* one step at a time. Rather than throwing you in the deep end of the pool, hoping that you learn to swim before drowning in too many details, I make sure you first learn to float and then move on to some basic strokes. The information source for financial statements is the bookkeeping system of the entity (also called the *recordkeeping system*). The financial statements of an entity are no more reliable and accurate than the reliability and accuracy of its bookkeeping system — and the integrity of the company's managers, of course. So, in Chapter 3, I offer a brief overview of bookkeeping and accounting systems. You could jump over this chapter, if you must. But I recommend at least a quick read.

Part 11: Exploring Financial Statements

In Part II, I complete the explanations of the financial statements of businesses (see Chapters 4, 5, and 6). In Chapter 7, I explain that businesses are not put in a straitjacket when it comes to deciding which accounting methods to use for recording their revenue and expenses. They can select from alternative methods for recording certain revenues and expenses. The choices of accounting methods affects the values recorded for assets and liabilities and, most importantly, directly affect the amount of profit recorded for the period.

Part 111: Accounting in Managing a Business

To start a business and begin operations, its founders must first decide on which legal structure to use. Chapter 8 explains the different types of legal entities for carrying on business activities. Each has certain advantages and disadvantages and each is treated differently under the income tax law, which is always an important factor to consider.

Chapter 9 explains a very important topic: designing a profit performance report for business managers that serves not only as a good digest of profit performance but also serves as a good profit model, one that focuses on the chief variables that drive profit and changes in profit. A hands-on profit model is essential for management decision-making. A manager depends on the profit model to determine the effects of changes in sales prices, sales volume, product costs, and the other fundamental factors that drive profit.

In Chapter 10, I discuss accounting-based planning and control techniques, through the lens of *budgeting*. Managers in manufacturing businesses should clearly understand how their product costs are determined, as Chapter 11 explains. Compared with retailers, the product costs of manufacturers are much more complicated and arbitrary. The chapter also explains other economic and accounting cost concepts relevant to business managers.

Part IV: Preparing and Using Financial Reports

In Part IV, I first explain how a financial report is made ready for release outside the business (see Chapter 12). Next I discuss how investors and lenders read financial statements (see Chapter 13). Business managers need more information than is included in an external financial report to investors and lenders. In Chapter 14, I survey the additional information that managers need.

Part V: The Part of Tens

In the *For Dummies* style, I close the book with a pair of chapters in "The Part of Tens." I condense the main lessons from the book's chapters into two lists of ten vital points each. Chapter 15 reviews ten important ways business managers should manage the accounting system of their business and how to use accounting information. Chapter 16 gives business investors handy tips for getting the most out of reading a financial report — tips on how to be efficient in reading a financial report and the key factors to focus on.

Glossary

The accounting terminology in financial statements is a mixed bag. Many terms are straightforward, but accountants also use esoteric terms that you don't see outside of financial statements. Sometimes it must seem like accountants are speaking a foreign language. I must admit that accountants use jargon more than they should. In some situations accountants resort to arcane terminology to be technically correct, much like lawyers use arcane terminology in filing lawsuits and drawing up contracts.

Where I use jargon in the book, I pause and clarify what the terms mean in plain English, using street language where I can. Also, I present a helpful glossary at the end of the book that can assist you on your accounting safari. This glossary provides succinct definitions of key accounting and financial terms, with relevant commentary and an occasional editorial remark. This is better than your average glossary.

Icons Used in This Book

This icon points out especially important accounting ideas and concepts that are particularly deserving of your attention. The material marked by this icon describes concepts that are the undergirding and building blocks of accounting — concepts that you should be very clear about and that clarify your understanding of accounting principles in general.

I use this icon sparingly; it refers to very specialized accounting stuff that is heavy going, which only a CPA could get really excited about. However, you may find these topics important enough to return to when you have the time. Feel free to skip over these points the first time through and stay with the main discussion.

This icon calls your attention to useful advice on practical financial topics. It saves you the cost of buying a yellow highlighter pen.

This icon is like a caution sign that warns you about speed bumps and pot-holes on the accounting highway. Taking special note of this material can steer you around a financial road hazard and keep you from blowing a fiscal tire. In short — watch out!

Where to Go from Here

There's no law against you starting on page 1 and reading through to the last page. However, you may first want to scan the book's Contents at a Glance and see which chapters pique your interest.

Perhaps you're an investor who is very interested in learning more about financial statements and the key financial statement ratios for investors. You might start with Chapters 4, 5, and 6, which explain the three primary financial statements of businesses, and finish with Chapter 13 on reading a financial report. (And don't overlook Chapter 16.)

Perhaps you're a small business owner/manager with a basic understanding of your financial statements, but you need to improve how you use accounting information for making your key profit decisions, and for planning and controlling your cash flow. You might jump right into Chapters 9 and 10, which explain analyzing profit behavior and budgeting cash flows.

The book is not like a five-course dinner in which you have to eat in the order the food is served to you. It's more like a buffet line from which you can pick and choose, and eat in whatever order you like.

Part I
Opening the Books on Accounting

The 5th Wave   By Rich Tennant

"Numbers to an accountant are like notes to a
composer, and Janet, these accounts are not
music to my ears."

In this part . . .

Accounting is indispensable in the worlds of business, investing, finance, and taxes. In this part, you find out why.

Accountants are the "information gatekeepers" in the economy. Without accounting, a business couldn't function, wouldn't know whether it's making a profit, and would be ignorant of its financial situation. Accounting is equally vital in managing the business affairs of not-for-profit and governmental entities.

From its accounting records, a business prepares its financial statements, its tax returns, and the reports to its managers. Accounting methods used to prepare financial statements conform to established standards. If not, the financial reports of a business probably would be misleading and possibly fraudulent, which could have dire consequences.

Bookkeeping — the record-keeping part of accounting — must be done well to ensure that the financial information of a business is timely, complete, accurate, and reliable — especially the numbers reported in its financial statements and tax returns. Wrong numbers in financial reports and tax returns can cause all sorts of trouble.

Chapter 1

Accounting: The Language of Business, Investing, Finance, and Taxes

1 had a captive audience when I taught Accounting 101 because, then as well as now, all business school students have to take this course. In contrast very few arts and science students elect the course, which is their loss. Accounting 101 teaches about business, including the nature of profit (which most people don't understand) and the fundamentals of capitalism. The course is a very good training ground for becoming *financially literate*. These days there is a big push to improve financial literacy, and a basic accounting course offers a useful framework for understanding and thinking about financial issues.

In one sense this book is the accounting course you never took. For business grads the book presents an opportune review of topics you've gotten rusty on. I dare say that even accounting majors can glean a lot of insights from this book. You don't need a college education to gain from this book, however. Like all the *For Dummies* books, this book delivers useful information in a plain-talking manner, with a light touch to keep it interesting.

As you go through life, you come face to face with a torrent of accounting information — more than you would ever imagine. Regretfully, much of this information is not inherently intuitive, and it does not come with a user's manual. In short, most of the accounting information you encounter is not readily transparent.

One main reason for learning some accounting is to understand its vocabulary and valuation methods, so you can make more intelligent use of the information. Accountants are financial scorekeepers. In playing or watching any game, you need to know how the score is kept. The purpose of this book is to make you a knowledgeable spectator of the accounting game.

Let me point out another reason you should know accounting basics — I call it the *defensive* reason. A lot of people in the cold, cruel financial world are on the prowl to take advantage of your lack of savvy about accounting. These unscrupulous characters treat you as a lamb waiting to be fleeced. The best defense against such tactics is to know some accounting, which helps you ask the right questions and understand the crucial points about which con artists want to keep you in the dark.

Accounting's Main Jobs: Providing Vital Information to Non-Accountants

In a nutshell, accountants "keep the books" of a business, and for not-for profit and government entities also, by following systematic methods to record all the financial activities and prepare *summaries*. Accountants then communicate this summary information to *non-accountants*, such as business owners, lenders, and investors. In particular, accounting information is presented in the form of *financial statements* that are packaged with other information such as explanatory footnotes and a letter from top management in what is called a *financial report*.

Financial statements are sent to people who have a stake in the outcomes of the activities. If you own stock in General Electric, for example, or you have money in a mutual fund, you receive regular financial reports. If you invest your hard-earned money in a private business or a real estate venture, or you save money in a credit union, you receive regular financial reports. If you are a member of a nonprofit association or organization, you're entitled to receive regular financial reports. I hope you carefully read these financial reports, but if you don't — or if you do yet don't understand what you're reading — it could be that you don't understand the language of accounting.

In summary, one important reason for studying accounting is to make sense of the financial statements in the financial reports you get. I guarantee that Warren Buffett knows accounting and how to read financial statements. I sent him a copy of my *How To Read A Financial Report* (John Wiley & Sons). In his reply, he said he planned to recommend it to his "accounting challenged" friends.

Distinguishing among different users of accounting information

People who use accounting information fall into two broad groups: *insiders* and *outsiders*. Business managers are insiders; they have the authority and responsibility to run a business. They need a good understanding of accounting terms and the methods used to measure profit and put values on assets and liabilities. Accounting information is indispensable for planning and controlling the financial performance and condition of the business. Likewise, administrators of nonprofit and governmental entities need to understand the accounting terminology and measurement methods in their financial statements.

The rest of us are outsiders. We are not privy to the day-to-day details of a business or organization. We have to rely on financial reports from the entity to know what's going on. Therefore, we need to have a good grip on the financial statements included in the financial reports. For all practical purposes, financial reports are the only source of financial information we get directly from a business or other organization.

By the way, the employees of a business — even though they obviously have a stake in the success of the business — do not necessarily receive its financial reports. Only the investors in the business and its lenders are entitled to receive the financial reports. Of course, a business *could* provide this information to those of its employees who are not shareowners, but generally speaking most businesses do not. The financial reports of public businesses are in the public domain, so their employees can easily secure a copy. However, financial reports are not automatically mailed to all employees of a public business.

In our personal financial lives, a little accounting knowledge is a big help for understanding investing in general, how investment performance is measured, and many other important financial topics. With some basic accounting knowledge, you'll sound much more sophisticated when speaking with your banker or broker. I can't promise you that learning accounting will save you big bucks on your income taxes, but it can't hurt and will definitely help you understand what your tax preparer is talking about.

Keep in mind that this is *not* a book on bookkeeping and recordkeeping systems. I offer a brief explanation of procedures for capturing, processing, and storing accounting information in Chapter 3. Even experienced bookkeepers and accountants should find some useful nuggets in that chapter. However, this book is directed to *users* of accounting information. I focus on the end products of accounting, particularly financial statements, and not on how information is accumulated. When buying a new car, you're interested in the finished product, not details of the manufacturing process that produced it.

Overcoming the stereotypes of accountants

I recently saw a cartoon in which the young son of clowns is standing in a circus tent and is dressed as a clown, but he is holding a business briefcase. He is telling his clown parents that he is running away to join a CPA firm. This cartoon has a touch of humor because it plays off the stereotype of a CPA (certified public accountant) as a boring "bean counter" who wears a green eyeshade, has no sense of humor, and possesses the personality of an undertaker (no offense to morticians). Maybe you've heard the joke that an accountant with a personality is one who looks at *your* shoes when he is talking to you, instead his own shoes.

Like most stereotypes, there's an element of truth in the preconceived image of accountants. As a CPA and accounting professor for more than 40 years, I have met and known a large number of accountants. Most accountants are not as gregarious as used-car sales people (though some are). Accountants certainly are more detail-oriented than your average person, and maybe a little more math-focused. However, you don't have to be a mathematics whiz to be a good accountant because accountants use very little math (no calculus and only simple algebra). Accountants are very good at one thing: They want to see both sides of financial transactions — the give and take. Accountants know better than anyone that, as economists are fond of saying, there's no such thing as a free lunch.

If you walked down a busy street in Chicago, New York, or Los Angeles, I doubt that you could pick out the accountants. I have no idea whether accountants have higher or lower divorce rates, whether they go to church more frequently, whether most are Republicans or Democrats, or if they generally sleep well at night. I do think overall that accountants are more honest in paying their income taxes than other people, although I have no proof of this. (And, yes, I know of a couple of accountants who tried to cheat on their federal income tax returns.)

Making good use of accounting in your personal financial life

I'm sure you know the value of learning personal finance and investing fundamentals. (Given the big push these days on improving financial literacy I recommend *Personal Finance For Dummies* and *Investing For Dummies* by Eric Tyson, MBA, both published by Wiley.) Well, a great deal of the information you use in making personal finance and investing decisions is *accounting information*. I do have one knock on books in these areas: They don't make clear that you need a basic understanding of accounting terminology and valuation methods in order to make good use of the financial information.

I have noticed that a sizable percent of the populace bash the profit motive and seem to think businesses should not make a profit. I would remind you, however, that you have a stake in the financial performance of the business you work for, the government entities you pay taxes to, the churches and charitable organizations you donate money to, the retirement plan you participate in, the businesses you buy from, and the healthcare providers you depend on. The financial performance and viability of these entities has a direct bearing on your personal financial life and well-being.

We're all affected by the profit performance of businesses, even though we may not be fully aware of just how their profit performance affects our jobs, investments, and taxes. For example, as an employee your job security and your next raise depend on the business making a profit. If the business suffers a loss, you may be laid off or asked to take a reduction in pay or benefits. Business managers get paid to make profit happen. If the business fails to meet its profit objectives or suffers a loss, its managers may be replaced (or at least not get their bonuses). As an author, I hope my publisher continues to make a profit so I can keep receiving my royalty checks.

Your investments in businesses, whether direct or through retirement accounts and mutual funds, suffer if the businesses don't turn a profit. I hope the stores I trade with make profit and continue in business. The federal government and many states depend on businesses making profit so they can collect income taxes from them.

Recognizing the Broad Sweep of Accounting Everywhere You Look

Accounting extends into many nooks and crannies of your life. You're doing accounting when you make entries in your checkbook and when you fill out your federal income tax return. When you sign a mortgage on your home, you should understand the accounting method the lender uses to calculate the interest amount charged on your loan each period. Individual investors need to understand accounting basics in order to figure their return on invested capital. And it goes without saying that every organization, profit-motivated or not, needs to know how it stands financially.

Here's a quick sweep to give you an idea of the broad range accounting covers:

- ✔ Accounting for organizations and accounting for individuals
- ✔ Accounting for profit-motivated businesses and accounting for nonprofit organizations (such as hospitals, homeowners' associations, churches, credit unions, and colleges)

✔ Income tax accounting while you're living and estate tax accounting when you die

✔ Accounting for farmers who grow their products, accounting for miners who extract their products from the earth, accounting for producers who manufacture products, and accounting for retailers who sell products that others make

✔ Accounting for businesses and professional firms that sell services rather than products, such as the entertainment, transportation, and healthcare industries

✔ Past-historical-based accounting and future-forecast-oriented accounting (budgeting and financial planning)

✔ Accounting where periodic financial statements are legally mandated (public companies are the primary example) and accounting where such formal accounting reports are not legally required

✔ Accounting that adheres to historical cost mainly (businesses) and accounting that records changes in market value (mutual funds, for example)

✔ Accounting in the private sector of the economy and accounting in the public (government) sector

✔ Accounting for going-concern businesses that will be around for some time and accounting for businesses in bankruptcy that may not be around tomorrow

Accounting is necessary in a free-market, capitalist economic system. It's equally necessary in a centralized, government-controlled, socialist economic system. All economic activity requires information. The more developed the economic system, the more the system depends on information. Much of the information comes from the accounting systems used by the businesses, institutions, individuals, and other players in the economic system.

Some of the earliest records of history are the accounts of wealth and trading activity. The need for accounting information was a main incentive in the development of the numbering system we use today. The history of accounting is quite interesting (but beyond the scope of this book).

Taking a Peek Behind the Scenes

Every business and not-for-profit entity needs a reliable bookkeeping system (see Chapter 3). Keep in mind that *accounting* is a much broader term than *bookkeeping*. For one thing, accounting encompasses the problems in measuring the financial effects of economic activity. Furthermore, accounting includes the function of *financial reporting* of values and performance measures to those that need the information. Business managers and investors, and many other people, depend on financial reports for information about the performance and condition of the entity.

Bookkeeping refers to the process of accumulating, organizing, storing, protecting, and accessing the financial information base of an entity, which is needed for two broad purposes:

- ✔ Facilitating the day-to-day operations of the entity
- ✔ Preparing financial statements, tax returns, and internal reports to managers

Bookkeeping (also called *recordkeeping*) can be thought of as the financial information infrastructure of an entity. Of course the financial information base should be complete, accurate, and timely. Every recordkeeping system needs quality controls built into it, which are called *internal controls* or *internal accounting controls*. When an error creeps into the system it can be difficult to root out and correct. Data entry controls are particularly important. The security of online and computer-based accounting systems has become a top priority of both for-profit businesses and not-for-profit entities.

Accountants design the internal controls for the bookkeeping system, which serve to minimize errors in recording the large number of activities that an entity engages in over a specific time period. The internal controls that accountants design are also relied on to detect and deter theft, embezzlement, fraud, and dishonest behavior of all kinds. In accounting, internal controls are the ounce of prevention that is worth a pound of cure.

I explain internal controls in Chapter 3. Here, I want to stress the importance of the bookkeeping system in operating a business or any other entity. These back-office functions are essential for keeping operations running smoothly, efficiently, and without delays and errors. This is a tall order, to say the least.

Most people don't realize the importance of the accounting department in keeping a business operating without hitches and delays. That's probably because accountants oversee many of the back-office functions in a business — as opposed to sales, for example, which is front-line activity, out in the open and in the line of fire. Go into any retail store, and you're in the thick of sales activities. But have you ever seen a company's accounting department in action?

Folks may not think much about these back-office activities, but they would sure notice if those activities didn't get done. On payday, a business had better not tell its employees, "Sorry, but the accounting department is running a little late this month; you'll get your checks later." And when a customer insists on up-to-date information about how much he or she owes to the business, the accounting department can't very well say, "Oh, don't worry, just wait a week or so, and we'll get the information to you then."

Typically, the accounting department is responsible for the following:

- **Payroll:** The total wages and salaries earned by every employee every pay period, which are called *gross wages* or *gross earnings,* have to be calculated. Based on detailed private information in personnel files and earnings-to-date information, the correct amounts of income tax, social security tax, and several other deductions from gross wages have to be determined.

  Stubs, which report various information to employees each pay period, have to be attached to payroll checks, or prepared separately if net pay is sent electronically to the employee's bank account. The total amounts of withheld income tax and social security taxes, plus the employment taxes imposed on the employer, have to be paid to federal and state government agencies on time. Retirement, vacation, sick pay, and other benefits earned by the employees have to be updated every pay period.

  In short, payroll is a complex and critical function that the accounting department performs. *Note:* Many businesses outsource payroll functions to companies that specialize in this area.

- **Cash collections:** All cash received from sales and from all other sources has to be carefully identified and recorded, not only in the cash account but also in the appropriate account for the source of the cash received. The accounting department makes sure that the cash is deposited in the appropriate checking accounts of the business and that an adequate amount of coin and currency is kept on hand for making change for customers. Accountants balance the checkbook of the business and control which persons have access to incoming cash receipts. (In larger organizations, the *treasurer* may be responsible for some of these cash flow and cash-handling functions.)

- **Cash payments (disbursements):** In addition to payroll checks, a business writes many other checks during the course of a year — to pay for a wide variety of purchases, to pay property taxes, to pay on loans, and to distribute some of its profit to the owners of the business, for example. The accounting department prepares all these checks for the signatures of the business officers who are authorized to sign checks. The accounting department keeps all the supporting business documents and files to know when the checks should be paid, makes sure that the amount to be paid is correct, and forwards the checks for signature.

- **Procurement and inventory:** Accounting departments usually are responsible for keeping track of all purchase orders that have been placed for *inventory* (products to be sold by the business) and all other assets and services that the business buys — from postage stamps to forklifts. A typical business makes many purchases during the course of a year, many of them on credit, which means that the items bought are received today but paid for later. So this area of responsibility includes keeping files on all liabilities that arise from purchases on credit so that cash payments can be processed on time. The accounting department also keeps detailed records on all products held for sale by the business and, when the products are sold, records the cost of the goods sold.

✔ **Costing:** Costs are not as obvious as they look. Tell someone that the cost of a new car is so many dollars and most people accept the amount without question. Business owners and managers know better. Many decisions have to be made regarding what factors to include in the manufacturing cost of a product, and in the purchase costs of products sold by retailers such as Costco and Wal-Mart. Tracking costs is a major function of accounting in all businesses.

✔ **Property accounting:** A typical business owns many different substantial long-term assets that go under the generic names *property, plant, and equipment* — including office furniture and equipment, retail display cabinets, computers, machinery and tools, vehicles (autos and trucks), buildings, and land. Except for relatively small-cost items, such as screwdrivers and pencil sharpeners, a business maintains detailed records of its property, both for controlling the use of the assets and for determining personal property and real estate taxes. The accounting department keeps these property records.

In most businesses and other entities, the accounting department is assigned other functions as well, but this list gives you a pretty clear idea of the back-office functions that the accounting department performs. Quite literally, a business could not operate if the accounting department did not do these functions efficiently and on time. And to repeat one point: To do these back-office functions well, the accounting department must design a good bookkeeping system and make sure that it is accurate, complete, and timely.

Focusing on Transactions

The recordkeeping function of accounting focuses on *transactions*, which are economic exchanges between a business or other entity and the parties with which the entity interacts and makes deals. A good accounting system captures and records every transaction that takes place without missing a beat. Transactions are the lifeblood of every business, the heartbeat of activity that keeps it going. Understanding accounting, to a large extent, means understanding how accountants record the financial effects of transactions.

The financial effects of many transactions are clear-cut and immediate. On the other hand, figuring out the financial effects of some transactions is puzzling and dependent on future developments. The financial effects of some transactions can be difficult to determine at the time of the original transaction because the outcome depends on future events that are difficult to predict. I bring this point because most people seem to think that accounting for transactions is a cut-and-dried process. Frankly, recording some transactions is more in the nature of "let's make our best assessment, cross our fingers, and wait and see what happens." The point is that recording the financial effects of some transactions is tentative and conditional on future events.

A business is a whirlpool of transactions; accountants categorize transactions into three basic types:

- **Profit-making transactions,** which consist of *revenue* and *expenses*. Profit is the sum total of revenue for the period minus all expenses for the period. *Note*: Profit is not a transaction but rather a calculated amount that depends on how revenue and expenses are recorded.

- **Investing transactions,** which refer to the acquisition (and eventual disposal) of *long-term operating assets* such as buildings, heavy machinery, trucks, office furniture, and so on. Some businesses also invest in *financial assets*, (bonds, for example). These are not used directly in the operations of the business; the business could get along without these assets. These assets generate investment income for the business. Investments in financial assets are included in this category of transactions.

- **Financing transactions,** which refer to raising capital and paying for the use of the capital. Every business needs assets to carry on its operations, such as a working balance of cash, inventory of products held for sale, long-term operating assets (as described in the previous *investing transactions* bullet point), and so on. Broadly speaking, the capital to buy these assets comes from two sources — *debt* and *equity*. Debt is borrowed money, on which interest is paid. Equity is ownership capital. The payment for using equity capital depends on the ability of the business to earn profit and have the cash flow to distribute some or all of the profit to its equity shareholders.

Profit-making transactions, also called *operating activities*, are high frequency. During the course of a year even a small business has thousands of revenue and expense transactions. (How many cups of coffee, for example, does your local coffee store sell each year? Each sale is a transaction.) In contrast, investing and financing transactions are generally low frequency. A business does not have a high volume of these types of transactions, except in very unusual circumstances.

Figure 1-1 gives you some idea of the range of persons and entities that a business deals with, such as engages in economic exchanges with. A business is the hub of transactions involving the following persons and entities:

- Its **customers,** who buy the products and services that the business sells. Also, a business may have other sources of income, such as from investments in financial assets (bonds, for example).

✔ Its **employees,** who provide services to the business and are paid wages and salaries and provided with benefits, such as a retirement plan, medical insurance, workers' compensation, and unemployment insurance.

✔ **Independent contractors**, who are hired on a contract basis to perform certain services for the business. These services can be everything from hauling away trash and repairing plumbing problems to high-priced consultants who advise the business on technical issues to audits by a CPA firm.

✔ Its **vendors and suppliers,** who sell a wide range of things to the business, such as products for resale, electricity and gas, insurance coverage, telephone and Internet services, and so on.

✔ **Government entities,** which are the federal, state, and local agencies that collect income taxes, sales taxes, payroll taxes, and property taxes from or through the business.

✔ **Sellers of the various long-term operating assets** used by the business, including building contractors, machinery and equipment manufacturers, and auto and truck dealers.

✔ Its **debt sources of capital,** who loan money to the business, charge interest on the amount loaned, and are due to be repaid at definite dates in the future.

✔ Its **equity sources of capital,** the individuals and financial institutions that invest money in the business as owners and who expect the business to earn profit on the capital they invest.

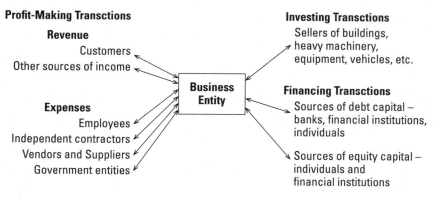

Figure 1-1:
Transactions between a business and the parties it deals with.

Even a relatively small business generates a surprisingly large number of transactions, and all transactions have to be recorded. Certain other events that have a financial impact on the business have to be recorded as well. These are called *events* because they're not based on give-and-take bargaining — unlike the something-given-for-something-received nature of economic exchanges.

Events such as the following have an economic impact on a business and are recorded:

- ✔ A business may lose a lawsuit and be ordered to pay damages. The liability to pay the damages is recorded.

- ✔ A business may suffer a flood loss that is uninsured. The waterlogged assets may have to be written down, meaning that the recorded values of the assets are reduced to zero if they no longer have any value to the business. For example, products that were being held for sale to customers (until they floated down the river) must be removed from the inventory asset account.

- ✔ A business may decide to abandon a major product line and downsize its workforce, requiring that severance compensation be paid to the laid-off employees.

As I explain in more detail in Chapter 3, at the end of the year the accountant conducts a special survey to ensure that all events and developments during the year that should be recorded have been recorded, so that the financial statements and tax returns for the year are complete and correct.

Taking the Pulse of a Business: Financial Statements

I devote a good deal of space in this book to discussing financial statements. In Chapter 2, I explain the fundamental information components of financial statements, and then Part II gets into the nitty-gritty details. Here, I simply want to introduce you to the three primary kinds of financial statements so you know from the get-go what they are and why they're so crucial.

Financial statements are prepared at the end of each accounting period. A period may be one month, one quarter (three calendar months), or one year. Financial statements report *summary amounts,* or *totals.* Accountants seldom prepare a complete listing of the details of all the activities that took place during a period, or the individual items making up a total amount. Business managers may need to search through a detailed list of all the specific transactions that make up a total amount. When they want to drill down into the details, they ask the accountant for the more detailed information. But this sort of detailed listing is *not* a financial statement —although it may be very useful to managers.

The outside, nonmanager investors in a business receive summary-level financial statements. For example, investors see the total amount of sales revenue for the period but not how much was sold to each and every customer. Financial statements are based on the assumption that you, the reader, are not a manager of the business (see "Distinguishing different users of accounting information" earlier in this chapter.) The managers of the business should make good use of their financial statements, but they also need more detailed information beyond what's in the business's financial statements.

Meeting the balance sheet and the accounting equation

One type of financial statement is a "Where do we stand at the end of the period?" type of report. This is called the *statement of financial condition* or, more commonly, the *balance sheet.* The date of preparation is given in the header, or title, above this financial statement.

A balance sheet shows two sides of the business, which I suppose you could think of as the financial yin and yang of the business:

✔ **Assets:** On one side of the balance sheet the *assets* of the business are listed, which are the economic resources owned and being used in the business. The asset *values* reported in the balance sheet are the amounts recorded when the assets were originally acquired — although I should mention that an asset is written down below its historical cost when the asset has suffered a loss in value. (And to complicate matters, some assets are written up to their current fair values.) Some assets have been on the books only a few weeks or a few months, so their reported historical values are current. The values for other assets, on the other hand, are their costs when they were acquired many years ago.

✔ **Sources of assets:** On the other side of the balance sheet is a breakdown of where the assets came from, or their *sources.* Assets do not materialize out of thin air. Assets arise from two basically different sources: *creditors* and *owners.* First, the *creditors*: Businesses borrow money in the form of interest-bearing loans that have to be paid back at a later date, and they buy things on credit that are paid for later. So, part of total assets can be traced to creditors, which are the *liabilities* of a business. Second are the *owners*: Every business needs to have owners invest capital (usually money) in the business. In addition, businesses retain part or all of the annual profits they make, and profit increases the total assets of the business. The total of invested capital and retained profit is labeled *owners' equity.*

To help visualize the two-sided nature of the balance sheet let's put all assets on the left tray of a balance scale and put liabilities and owners' equity on the right tray (see Figure 1-2). The total weight of all assets equals the total weight of liabilities and owners' equity. One side cannot be heavier than the other side. An imbalance signals accounting errors in recording the transactions of the business. This fundamental axiom of accounting is also summarized in the *accounting equation*, as follows:

Figure 1-2:
The fundamental balance, or equality of assets and sources of the assets.

Suppose a business reports $2.5 million total assets (without going into the details of which particular assets the business holds). Knowing that total assets are on the books at $2.5 million, we also know that the total of its liabilities, plus the capital invested by its owners, plus its retained profit, adds up to $2.5 million.

Continuing with this example, suppose that the total amount of the liabilities of the business is $1.0 million. This means that the total amount of *owners' equity* in the business is $1.5 million, which equals total assets less total liabilities. This amount is also called the *net worth* of the business; to be more accurate should be called the *recorded net worth* of the business (which does not necessarily equal the present market value of the business). Without more information we don't know how much of total owners' equity is traceable to capital invested by the owners in the business and how much is the result of profit retained in the business. But we do know that the total of these two sources of owners' equity is $1.5 million.

The financial condition of the business in this example is summarized in the following *accounting equation* (in millions):

$2.5 assets = $1.0 liabilities + $1.5 owners' equity

Looking at the accounting equation, you can see why the statement of financial condition is called the *balance sheet*; the equal sign means the two sides balance or are equal in amount.

A pop quiz

Here's a teaser for you. If a business's total assets equal $2.5 million and its total liabilities equal $1.0 million, we know that its total owners' equity is $1.5 million. *Question*: Could the owners have invested more than $1.5 million in the business? *Answer*: Yes. One possibility is that the owners invested $2.5 million, but the business has so far accumulated $1.0 million of losses instead of making profit. The accumulated loss offsets the amount invested, so the owners' equity is only $1.5 million net of its cumulative loss of $1.0 million. The $1.0 million of cumulative loss is down the rat hole. The owners bear the risk that the business may be unable to make a profit. A loss falls on the owners and, accordingly, causes a decrease in the owners' equity amount reported in the balance sheet.

Double-entry bookkeeping is based on the accounting equation — the fact that the total of assets on the one side is counterbalanced by the total of liabilities, invested capital, and retained profit on the other side. I discuss double-entry bookkeeping in Chapter 3. Basically, double-entry bookkeeping simply means that both sides of transactions are recorded. For example, if one asset goes up, another asset goes down — or, alternatively, either a liability or owners' equity goes up. This is due to the economic nature of transactions. In accounting double-entry means *two-sided,* not that the transactions are recorded twice.

Reporting profit and loss, and cash flows

Other financial statements are regularly prepared, and they are fundamentally different from the balance sheet: They summarize the *flows* of activities over the period. (An example of a *flow number* is the total attendance at Colorado Rockies baseball games over its entire 82 home game regular season; the cumulative count of spectators passing through the turnstiles over the season is the flow.) Accountants prepare two types of flow reports for a business:

✔ The **income statement** summarizes the inflows from sales revenue and other income, which are offset by the outflows for expenses during the period. Deducting expenses from revenue and income leads down to the well-known *bottom line,* which is the final net profit or loss for the period and is called *net income* or *net loss* (or some variation of these terms). Alternative titles for this financial statement are the *statement of operations* and the *statement of earnings.* Inside a business, but not in its external financial reports, the income statement is commonly called the *profit and loss statement,* or *P&L* report.

⌐ The **statement of cash flows** summarizes the business's cash inflows and outflows during the period. The accounting profession has adopted a three-way classification of cash flows for external financial reporting matching the three basic type of business transactions I discuss in the above section *Focusing on Transactions*: cash flows from making sales and incurring expenses; cash flows from investing in assets and selling assets; and cash flows from raising capital from debt and equity sources, returning capital to these sources, and making distributions from profit to owners.

Respecting the importance of this troika

I explain more about the three primary financial statements (balance sheet, income statement, and statement of cash flows) in Chapter 2. They constitute the hard core of a financial report to those persons outside a business who need to stay informed about the business's financial affairs. These individuals have invested capital in the business, or the business owes them money; therefore, they have a financial interest in how well the business is doing.

The managers of a business, to keep informed about what's going on and the financial position of the business, also use these three key financial statements. The three financial statements are essential in helping managers control the performance of a business, identify problems as they come up, and plan the future course of a business. Managers also need other information that is not reported in the three basic financial statements. (In Part III of this book, I explain these additional reports.)

The three primary financial statements constitute a business's financial center of gravity. The president and chief executive officer of a business (plus other top-level officers) are responsible for seeing that the financial statements are prepared according to applicable financial reporting standards and according to established accounting principles and methods.

If a business's financial statements are later discovered to be seriously in error or deliberately misleading, the business and its top executives can be sued for damages suffered by lenders and investors who relied on the financial statements. For this reason, business managers should understand their responsibility for the financial statements and the accounting methods used to prepare the statements. In a court of law, they can't plead ignorance.

I have met more than one business manager who doesn't have a clue about his or her financial statements. This situation is a little scary; a manager who doesn't understand financial statements is like an airplane pilot who doesn't understand the instrument readouts in the cockpit. Such a manager *could* run the business and "land the plane safely," but knowing how to read the vital signs along the way is much more prudent.

Business managers at all levels need to understand financial statements and the accounting methods used to prepare them. Also, lenders to a business, investors in a business, business lawyers, government regulators of business, entrepreneurs, anyone thinking of becoming an entrepreneur and starting a business, and, yes, even economists should know the basics of financial statement accounting. I've noticed that even experienced business journalists, who ought to know better, sometimes refer to the balance sheet when they're talking about profit performance. The bottom line is found in the income statement, not the balance sheet!

Mapping Accounting Careers

In our highly developed economy, many people make their living as accountants — and here I'm using the term *accountant* in the broadest possible sense. If you look in the *Statistical Abstract of the United States* you'll see that upwards of 2 million people make their living as bookkeepers, accountants, and auditors. They work as independent practitioners, or they work for businesses, government agencies, nonprofit organizations, and other organizations and associations.

Because accountants work with numbers and details, you hear references to accountants as bean counters, digit heads, number nerds, and other names I don't dare mention here. Accountants take these snide references in stride and with good humor. Actually, accountants rank among the most respected professionals in many polls.

Certified public accountant (CPA) and specialties

In the accounting profession, the mark of distinction is to be a *CPA*, which stands for *certified public accountant*. The term *public* means that the person has had some experience working for a CPA firm, or other qualifying experience depending on the state in which the person lives. The CPA credential does not indicate whether that person is presently in public practice (as an individual CPA or as an employee or partner in a CPA firm that offers services to the public at large) rather than working for one organization. For example, I have a CPA certificate in Colorado, but I'm on inactive status because I have retired and do not offer my services to the public.

To become a CPA, you go to college, graduate with an accounting major in a five-year program (in most states), and pass the national, computer-based

CPA exam. You also must satisfy professional employment experience; this requirement varies from state to state but generally is one or two years. After satisfying the education, exam, and experience requirements, you get a CPA certificate to hang on your wall. More important, you get a permit from your state to practice as a CPA and offer your services to the public. States require continuing education hours to maintain an active CPA permit.

As a person gains experience in public accounting he or she may decide to qualify for one of the specialization designations offered by the American Institute of Certified Public Accountants (AICPA). For example, you could qualify as a personal financial consultant, or as a forensic expert. (I don't list all the specializations or their requirements here.) The idea is to better "advertise" your special qualifications in a particular area of practice. Keep in mind one critical point: The CPA license is regulated by the state. Each state has specific requirements regarding how to become a CPA; the specializations, on the other hand, are created and regulated by the AICPA, which is a private organization.

Introducing a new kid on the block: Chartered Global Management Accountant (CGMA)

Over the years certified public accountants have worn three hats: as independent auditors, as tax experts, and as management accountants. The first two hats rest on the heads of CPAs very well. Most people you meet probably know the auditing and tax roles of CPAs. I bet you did. But the third hat doesn't fit so well on the head of a CPA who has joined the management team of a business. As an auditor and tax professional a CPA needs *independence*, to be in a position to stand back and judge impartially whether the accounting methods used by a business conform to established accounting standards and tax laws. However, once a CPA becomes a member of management, he or she no longer is independent from the business. (I should mention in passing that CPAs also serve as independent business consultants, in addition to their auditing and tax functions.)

Taking a job with a business does not strip the CPA designation from a person. As the Controller of a business, for example, you can still refer to yourself as a CPA. (But you are not independent of the business.) Over the years various organizations have developed credentials that management accountants can earn by additional education or experience (or some of both). The two primary purposes of these credentialing programs are to improve the abilities of professional management accountants, and, second, to create an acronym or "brand" that is widely known. See the sidebar *The CPA as a brand*.

The CPA as a brand

The CPA title has gained broad recognition and respect. When I mention to people that I'm a CPA I don't have to explain what a CPA is. It's generally understood what a CPA is. Now I certainly don't mean to sound critical here, but the blunt truth of the matter is that accountants don't have the status and recognition without the CPA after their name. Many highly qualified accountants work for businesses, non-profit organizations, and government entities. They may have other designations after their names, which attest to their qualifications. The problem is that these particular qualifications are not widely understood. In contrast the CPA is a "brand" that people understand.

Recently the American Institute of CPAs (AICPA) and the Chartered Institute of Management Accountants (CIMA) in the United Kingdom and the Republic of Ireland joined forces to sponsor and promote a new professional designation called the *Chartered Global Management Accountant*, or *CGMA* for short. A member in good standing of the AICPA can gain the CGMA designation by meeting experience requirements in the fields of internal auditing, management accounting (both in profit and non-profit entities), and business consulting. Starting in 2015 a qualifying examination will be required. The CGMA initiative has just gotten off the ground at the time of revising this book. It's too early to tell how successful it will be. But you probably want me to make a bold (and reckless) prediction, don't you? Let's just say I have my doubts.

The controller: The chief accountant in an organization

The top-level accounting officer in a business organization is usually called the *controller*. The controller designs the entire accounting system of the business and keeps it up-to-date with changes in the tax laws and changes in the accounting rules that govern reporting financial statements to outside lenders and owners. Controllers are responsible for hiring, training, evaluating, promoting, and sometimes firing the persons who hold the various bookkeeping and accounting positions in an organization — which range from payroll functions to the several different types of tax returns that have to be filed on time with different government agencies.

The controller is the lead person in the financial planning and budgeting process of the business organization. Furthermore, the controller designs the accounting reports that all the managers in the organization receive — from the sales and marketing managers to the purchasing and procurement managers. These internal reports should be designed to fit the authority and responsibility of each manager; they should provide information for managers' decision-making analysis needs and the information they need to exercise effective control. The controller also designs and monitors the accounting reports that go to the business's top-level vice presidents, the chief financial officer, the president, the chief executive officer, and the board of directors. All the tough accounting questions and problems get referred to the controller although he or she may not make the final decision.

Smaller businesses may employ only one accountant. In many cases a small company's full-time bookkeeper or office manager carries out many of the duties that would be done by the controller in a larger organization. Smaller businesses often call in a CPA for advice and help. The CPA may function more or less as a part-time controller for a small business, preparing its annual income tax returns and helping to prepare the business's external financial reports.

State incorporation laws typically require that someone in the business be designated the *treasurer,* who has fiduciary responsibilities. Also, these laws usually require that someone be designated the *secretary.* The organizational charts of larger businesses usually put their controller under their *vice president for finance, or chief financial officer (CFO).* The accounting functions in a business are integrated with and work in close coordination with its financial, treasury, and secretary functions.

A springboard to other careers

Many CPAs move on to other careers. A recent article in the *Journal of Accountancy* featured former CPAs who moved on to other interesting careers. One became a Harley-Davidson dealer, another a high school teacher, another an auto racing track owner, another a physical fitness coaching business owner, and one even became a stand-up comedian whose stage name is "Debitman." Serving time with a CPA firm is a good springboard to many careers. I started out working for a large CPA firm and then a local firm. I gained valuable insights into the accounting practices and problems of a wide variety of businesses. Most young women and men would tell you that their experiences working for a CPA firm were invaluable. After an audit is completed many companies offer the CPAs working on the audit well-paid positions in the business. Who knows, you might end up being the author of *Accounting For Dummies,* although I should warn you that my coauthor and son, Tage, has first dibs on continuing this book.

By the way, if you're interested in accounting, you may think about getting a Ph.D. in accounting and becoming an accounting professor. After a few years in public accounting, I went back to school, got my Ph.D., and spent the rest of my career in higher education. These days, the starting salaries for new assistant professors of accounting are well into six digits!

Chapter 2

Financial Statements and Accounting Standards

- -

In This Chapter

▶ Fleshing out the three key financial statements

▶ Noting the difference between profit and cash flow

▶ Finding answers in the financial statements

▶ Knowing the nature of accounting standards

- -

*C*hapter 1 presents a brief introduction to the three primary business financial statements: the *income statement*, the *balance sheet*, and the *statement of cash flows*. In this chapter, you get more interesting tidbits about these three *financials*, as they're sometimes called. Then, in Part II, you really get the goods. Remember when you were learning to ride a bicycle? Chapter 1 is like getting on the bike and learning to keep your balance. In this chapter, you put on your training wheels and start riding. Then, when you're ready, the chapters in Part II explain all 21 gears of the financial statements bicycle, and then some.

In this chapter, I explain that net income, which is the bottom-line profit of a business reported in its income statement, does not produce cash flow of the same amount. Profit-making activities cause many changes in the financial condition of a business — not just in the cash account. Many people assume that making a profit increases a business's cash balance by the same amount, and that's the end of it. Making profit leaves many footprints on the financial condition of a business, which you learn in this chapter.

Also in this chapter, I briefly discuss financial accounting and reporting standards. Businesses should comply with established accounting standards that govern the recording of revenue, income, expenses, and losses; put values on assets and liabilities; and present and disclose information in financial reports. The basic idea is that all businesses should follow uniform methods for measuring and reporting profit performance, and reporting financial condition and cash flows. Consistency in accounting from business to business is the goal. I explain who makes the rules, and I discuss important recent developments: the internationalization of accounting standards, and the increasing divide between financial reporting by public and private companies.

Introducing the Basic Content of Financial Statements

This chapter focuses on the basic *information components* of each financial statement reported by a business. In this first step, I don't address the grouping of these information packets within each financial statement. The first step is to get a good idea of the information content reported in financial statements. The second step is to become familiar with more details about the "architecture," rules of classification, and other features of financial statements, which I explain in Part II of the book.

Realizing that form follows function in financial statements

You need realistic business examples to understand the three primary financial statements. The information content of a business's financial statements depends on whether the business sells products or services. For example, the financial statements of a movie theater chain are different from those of a bank, which are different from those of an airline, which are different from an automobile manufacturer. Here, I use two examples that fit a wide variety of businesses.

The first example is a business that sells *products*. The second example is for a business that sells *services*. Note that the two financial statements differ to some degree — not entirely, but in some important respects. The point is that the form of its financial statements follows the function of the business and how it makes profit — whether the business sells products or services to bring in the needed revenue to cover expenses and to provide enough profit after expenses.

Here are the particulars about the product business example:

- It sells products to other businesses (not on the retail level).
- It sells on credit, and its customers take a month or so before they pay.
- It holds a fairly large stock of products awaiting sale (its *inventory*).
- It owns a wide variety of long-term operating assets that have useful lives from 3 to 30 years or longer (building, machines, tools, computers, office furniture, and so on).
- It has been in business for many years and has made a consistent profit.
- It borrows money for part of the total capital it needs.

- ✓ It's organized as a corporation and pays federal and state income taxes on its annual taxable income.

- ✓ It has never been in bankruptcy and is not facing any immediate financial difficulties.

The product company's annual income statement for the year just ended, its balance sheet at the end of the year, and its statement of cash flows for the year are presented in following the sections.

For comparison, financial statements are also presented for a service company. This company doesn't sell products, and it makes no sales on credit; cash is collected at the time of making sales. These are the two main differences compared with the product company.

Dollar amounts in financial statements are typically rounded off, either by not presenting the last three digits (when rounded off to the nearest thousand) or by not presenting the last six digits (when rounded to the nearest million by large companies). I strike a compromise on this issue — I show the last three digits for each item as 000, which means that I rounded off the amount but still show all digits. Many smaller businesses report their financial statement dollar amounts out to the last dollar, or even the last penny for that matter. Keep in mind that too many digits in a dollar amount are hard to comprehend.

The financial statement examples for the product and service businesses are stepping-stone illustrations that are concerned mainly with the basic information components in each statement. Full-blown, classified financial statements are presented in Part II of the book. (I know you are anxious to get to those chapters.) The financial statements in this chapter do not include all the information you see in actual financial statements. Also, I use descriptive labels for each item rather than the terse and technical titles you see in actual financial statements. And I strip out most subtotals that you see in actual financial statements because they are not necessary at this point. So, with all these caveats in mind, let's get going.

Oops, I forgot to mention a couple of things about financial statements. I should give you a quick heads-up on these points. Financial statements are rather stiff and formal. No slang or street language is allowed, and I've never seen a swear word in one. Financial statements would get a G in the movies rating system. Seldom do you see any graphics or artwork in a financial statement itself, although you do see a fair amount of photos and graphics on other pages in the financial reports of public companies. And, there's virtually no humor in financial reports. Don't look for cartoons like the ones by Rich Tennant in this book. (However, I might mention that in his annual letter to the stockholders of Berkshire Hathaway, Warren Buffett includes some wonderful humor to make his points.)

Income statements

The *income statement* is the all-important financial statement that summarizes the profit-making activities of a business over a period of time. Figure 2-1 shows the basic information content of the external income statement for our product company example. *External* means that the financial statement is released outside the business to those entitled to receive it — primarily its shareowners and lenders. Internal financial statements stay within the business and are used mainly by its managers; they are not circulated outside the business because they contain competitive and confidential information.

Company's Name
Income Statement
For Most Recent Year

Sales revenue		$10,400,000
Cost of goods sold expense		$6,240,000
Gross margin		$4,160,000
Selling, general, and administrative expenses	$3,235,000	
Interest expense	$125,000	
Income tax expense	$280,000	
Total other expenses		$3,640,000
Net income		$520,000

Figure 2-1: Income statement for a business that sells products.

Income statement for a product company

Figure 2-1 presents the major ingredients of the income statement for a product company. As you might expect, it starts with sales revenue on the top line. Then the cost of the products (goods) sold is deducted from sales revenue to report *gross margin* (also called gross profit), which is a preliminary, or "first" line, measure of profit before other expenses are taken into account. Next other types of expenses are listed, and their total is deducted from gross margin to reach the final bottomline, called *net income*. Virtually all income statements disclose at least these four expenses. (A business can report more types of expenses in its external income statement, and many do.)

Cost of goods sold expense and selling, general, and administrative expenses take the biggest bites out of sales revenue. The other two expenses (interest and income tax) are relatively small as a percent of annual sales revenue but important enough in their own right to be reported separately. And though you may not need this reminder, bottom-line profit (net income) is the amount of sales revenue in excess of its total expenses. If either sales revenue or any of the expense amounts are wrong, then profit is wrong. (I will harp on this point throughout the book.)

Income statement for a service company

Figure 2-2 presents the income statement for a company that sells services (instead of products). I keep this example the same dollar size as the product company. Notice that annual sales revenue is $10,400,000 for both companies. And, I keep total expenses the same at $9,880,000. (For the product company its $6,240,000 cost of goods sold expense plus its $3,640,000 of other expenses is $9,880,000.) Therefore, net income for both companies is $520,000.

Company's Name
Income Statement
For Most Recent Year

Sales revenue		$10,400,000
Operating expenses	$6,240,000	
Selling, general, and administrative expenses	$3,235,000	
Interest expense	$125,000	
Income tax expense	$280,000	
Total expenses		$9,880,000
Net income		$520,000

Figure 2-2:
Income statement for a business that sells services.

The service business does not sell a product; therefore, it does not have the cost of goods sold expense, and accordingly does not report a gross margin line in its income statement. In place of cost of goods sold it has other types of expenses. In Figure 2-2 operating expenses are $6,240,000 in place of cost of goods sold expense. Service companies differ on how they report their operating expenses. For example, United Airlines breaks out the cost of aircraft fuel, and landing fees. The largest expense of the insurance company State Farm is payments on claims. The movie chain AMC reports film exhibition costs separate from its other operating expenses.

Income statement pointers

Most product and service businesses breakout one or more expenses instead of disclosing just one very broad category for all selling, general, and administrative expenses. For example, a business could disclose expenses for advertising and sales promotion, depreciation, salaries and wages, research and development, and delivery and shipping — though reporting these expenses varies quite a bit from business to business. Businesses do not disclose the compensation of top management in their external financial reports, although this information can be found in the proxy statements of public companies that are filed with the Securities and Exchange Commission. Details disclosed about operating expenses in externally reported financial reports vary from business to business. Financial reporting standards are rather permissive on this point.

Inside most businesses an income statement is called a *P&L (profit and loss) report*. These internal profit performance reports to the managers of a business include a good deal more detailed information about expenses and about sales revenue also. Reporting just four expenses to managers (as shown in Figures 2-1 and 2-2) would not do. Chapter 9 explains P&L reports to managers.

Sales revenue is from the sales of products or services to customers. You also see the term *income*, which generally refers to amounts earned by a business from sources other than sales; for example, a real estate rental business receives rental income from its tenants. (In the two examples for a product and a service company, the businesses have only sales revenue.)

Net income, being the bottom line of the income statement after deducting all expenses from sales revenue (and income, if any), is called, not surprisingly, the *bottom line*. It is also called *net earnings*. A few companies call it *profit* or *net profit*, but such terminology is not common.

The income statement gets the most attention from business managers, lenders, and investors (not that they ignore the other two financial statements). The much abbreviated versions of income statements that you see in the financial press, such as in *The Wall Street Journal,* report the top line (sales revenue and income) and the bottom line (net income) and not much more. Refer to Chapter 4 for more information on income statements.

Balance sheets

A more accurate name for a balance sheet is statement of financial condition, or statement of financial position. But the term *balance sheet* has caught on, and most people use this term. Keep in mind that the "balance" is not important, but rather the information reported in this financial statement. In brief, a balance sheet summarizes on the one hand the assets of the business and on the other hand the sources of the assets. The sources have claims, or entitlements against the assets of the business. Looking at assets is only half the picture. The other half consists of the liabilities and owner equity claims on the assets. Cash is listed first and other assets are listed in the order of their nearness to cash. Liabilities are listed in order of their due dates (the earliest first, and so on). Liabilities are listed ahead of owners' equity.

Balance sheet for a product company

Figure 2-3 shows the building blocks (basic information components) of a typical balance sheet for a business that sells products on credit. One reason the balance sheet is called by this name is that its two sides balance, or are equal in total amounts. In the example, the $5.2 million total of assets equals the $5.2 million total of liabilities and owners' equity. The balance or equality of total assets on the one side of the scale and the sum of liabilities plus owners' equity on the other side of the scale is expressed in the *account-ing equation,* which I discuss in Chapter 1. *Note:* the balance sheet example shown in Figure 2-3 concentrates on the essential elements in this financial statement. In a financial report the balance sheet includes additional features and frills, which I explain in Chapter 5.

Company's Name
Balance Sheet
At End of Most Recent Year

Assets

Cash	$1,000,000
Receivables from sales made on credit	$800,000
Inventory of unsold products, at cost	$1,560,000
Long-term operating assets, at cost less cumulative amount charged off to depreciation expense	$1,840,000
Total assets	$5,200,000

Liabilities and Owners' Equity

Non-interest bearing liabilities from purchases on credit and for unpaid expenses	$650,000
Interest-bearing debt	$2,080,000
Owners' equity capital invested in business plus profit earned and retained in business	$2,470,000
Total liabilities and owners' equity	$5,200,000

Figure 2-3:
Balance sheet for a company that sells products on credit.

Let's take a quick walk through the balance sheet (Figure 2-3). For a company that sells products on credit, assets are reported in the following order: First is cash; then receivables; then cost of products held for sale; and finally the long-term operating assets of the business. Moving to the other side of the balance sheet, the liabilities section starts with the trade liabilities (from buying on credit) and liabilities for unpaid expenses. Following these oper-ating liabilities is the interest-bearing debt of the business. Owners' equity sources are then reported below liabilities. Each of these information packets is called an *account* — so a balance sheet has a composite of asset accounts, liability accounts, and owners' equity accounts.

Balance sheet for a service company

Figure 2-4 presents the typical balance sheet components for a business that sells services (instead of products). Recall that the service company example does not sell on credit; it collects cash at the point of sale. Notice right away that this service business example does not have two sizable assets that the product company has — receivables from credit sales and inventory of products held for sale. Therefore, the total assets of our service company example are considerably smaller. The product company has $5,200,000 total assets (Figure 2-3), whereas the service company has only $2,840,000 total assets (Figure 2-4).

Company's Name
Balance Sheet
At End of Most Recent Year

Assets

Cash	$1,000,000
Long-term operating assets, at cost less cumulative amount charged off to depreciation expense	$1,840,000
Total assets	$2,840,000

Liabilities and Owners' Equity

Non-interest bearing liabilities from purchases on credit and for unpaid expenses	$650,000
Interest-bearing debt	$1,000,000
Owners' equity capital invested in business plus profit earned and retained in business	$1,190,000
Total liabilities and owners' equity	$2,840,000

Figure 2-4: Balance sheet for a service company.

The smaller amount of total assets of the service business means that the other side of its balance sheet is correspondingly smaller as well. In plain terms, this means that the service company does not need to borrow as much money or raise as much capital from its equity owners compared with the product business. Notice, for example, that the interest-bearing debt of the service company is $1.0 million (Figure 2-4) compared with over $2.0 million for the product company (Figure 2-3). Likewise, the total amount of owners' equity for the service business is much smaller than the product company.

Balance sheet pointers

Businesses need a variety of assets. You have *cash,* of course, which every business needs. When selling on credit, a business records a *receivable* that is collected later (typically 30 days or longer). Businesses that sell products carry an *inventory* of products awaiting sale to customers. Businesses need long-term resources that have the generic name *property, plant, and equipment*; this group includes buildings, vehicles, tools, machines, and other resources needed in their operations. All these, and more, go under the collective name "assets."

As you might suspect, the particular assets reported in the balance sheet depend on which assets the business owns. I include just four basic types of assets in Figure 2-3. These are the hardcore assets that a business selling products on credit would have. It's possible that such a business could lease (or rent) virtually all of its long-term operating assets instead of owning them, in which case the business would report no such assets. In this example, the business owns these so-called *fixed assets.* They are *fixed* because they are held for use in the operations of the business and are not for sale, and their usefulness lasts several years or longer.

So, where does a business get the money to buy its assets? Most businesses borrow money on the basis of interest-bearing notes or other credit instruments for part of the total capital they need for their assets. Also, businesses buy many things on credit and at the balance sheet date, owe money to their suppliers, which will be paid in the future. These operating liabilities are never grouped with interest-bearing debt in the balance sheet. The accountant would be tied to the stake for doing such a thing. Note that liabilities are not intermingled among assets — this is a definite no-no in financial reporting. You cannot subtract certain liabilities from certain assets and only report the net balance. You would be given 20 lashes for doing so.

Could a business's total liabilities be greater than its total assets? Well, not likely — unless the business has been losing money hand over fist. In the vast majority of cases a business has more total assets than total liabilities. Why? For two reasons:

- ✔ Its owners have invested money in the business.

- ✔ The business has earned profit over the years, and some (or all) of the profit has been retained in the business. Making profit increases assets; if not all the profit is distributed to owners, the company's assets rise by the amount of profit retained.

In the product company example (refer to Figure 2-3), owners' equity is about $2.5 million, or $2.47 million to be more exact. Sometimes this amount is referred to as *net worth*, because it equals total assets minus total liabilities. However, net worth can be misleading because it implies that the business is worth the amount recorded in its owners' equity accounts. The market value of a business, when it needs to be known, depends on many factors. The amount of owners' equity reported in a balance sheet, which is called its *book value,* is not irrelevant in setting a market value on the business — but it is usually not the dominant factor. The amount of owners' equity in a balance sheet is based on the history of capital invested in the business by its owners and the history of its profit performance and distributions from profit.

A balance sheet could be whipped up anytime you want, say at the end of every day. In fact, some businesses (such as banks and other financial institutions) need daily balance sheets, but most businesses do not prepare balance sheets that often. Typically, preparing a balance sheet at the end of each month is adequate for general management purpose — although a manager may need to take a look at the business's balance sheet in the middle of the month. In external financial reports (those released outside the business to its lenders and investors), a balance sheet is required at the close of business on the last day of the income statement period. If its annual or quarterly income statement ends, say, September 30; then the business reports its balance sheet at the close of business on September 30.

The profit *for the most recent period* is found in the income statement; periodic profit is not reported in the balance sheet. The profit reported in the income statement is before any distributions from profit to owners. The cumulative amount of profit over the years that has not been distributed to its owners is reported in the owners' equity section of the company's balance sheet.

By the way, notice that the balance sheet in Figure 2-3 is presented in a top and bottom format, instead of a left and right side format. Either the vertical or horizontal mode of display is acceptable. You see both the portrait and the landscape layouts in financial reports.

Statement of cash flows

To survive and thrive, business managers confront three financial imperatives:

- ✔ Make an adequate profit
- ✔ Keep financial condition out of trouble and in good shape
- ✔ Control cash flows

The income statement reports whether the business made a profit. The balance sheet reports the financial condition of the business. The third imperative is reported on in the *statement of cash flows,* which presents a summary of the business's sources and uses of cash during the income statement period.

Smart business managers hardly get the word *net income* (or profit) out of their mouths before mentioning *cash flow.* Successful business managers tell you that they have to manage both profit *and* cash flow; you can't do one and ignore the other. Business managers have to deal with a two-headed dragon in this respect. Ignoring cash flow can pull the rug out from under a successful profit formula. My son, Tage, and I have coauthored *Cash Flow For Dummies* (John Wiley & Sons), which you may want to take a peek at.

In the statement of cash flows, the cash activity of the business during the period is grouped into the three basic types of transactions that I discuss in Chapter 1: *profit-making* transactions, *investing* transactions, and *financing* transactions. Figure 2-5 presents just the net cash effects of each of these three types of transactions for the product company example. These are the basic information components of the statement. The net increase or decrease in cash from the three types of cash activities during the period is added to or subtracted from the beginning cash balance to get the cash balance at the end of the year.

Company's Name
Statement of Cash Flows
For Most Recent Year

Cash effect during period from *operating activities* (collecting cash from sales and paying cash for expenses)	$400,000
Cash effect during period from making investments in long-term operating assets	($450,000)
Cash effect during period from transactions with lenders and owners	$200,000
Cash increase during period	$150,000
Cash balance at start of period	$850,000
Cash balance at end of period	$1,000,000

Figure 2-5: Statement of cash flows.

In the product company example, the business earned $520,000 profit (net income) during the year (see Figure 2-1). The result of its profit-making activities was to increase its cash $400,000, which you see in the first part of the statement of cash flows (see Figure 2-5). This still leaves $120,000 of profit to explain, which I get to in the next section. The actual cash inflows from revenues and outflows for expenses run on a different timetable than when the sales revenue and expenses are recorded for determining profit. I give a more comprehensive explanation of the differences between cash flows and sales revenue and expenses in Chapter 6.

The second part of the statement of cash flows sums up the long-term investments made by the business during the year, such as constructing a new production plant or replacing machinery and equipment. If the business sold any of its long-term assets, it reports the cash inflows from these divestments in this section of the statement of cash flows. The cash flows of other investment activities (if any) are reported in this part of the statement as well. As you can see in part of the statement of cash flows (see Figure 2-5), the business invested $450,000 in new long-term operating assets (trucks, equipment, tools, and computers).

The third part of the statement sums up the dealings between the business and its sources of capital during the period — borrowing money from lenders and raising new capital from its owners. Cash outflows to pay debt are reported in this section, as well as cash distributions from profit paid to the owners of the business. The third part of the statement reports that the result of these transactions was to increase cash $200,000 (see Figure 2-5). By the way, in this product company example, the business did not make cash distributions from profit to its owners. It probably could have, but it didn't — which is an important point that I discuss later in the chapter (see the section "Why no cash distribution from profit?").

As you see in Figure 2-5, the net result of the three types of cash activities was a $150,000 increase during the year. The increase is added to the cash balance at the start of the year to get the cash balance at the end of the year, which is $1.0 million. I should make one point clear: The $150,000 cash increase during the year (in this example) is never referred to as a cash flow *bottom line,* or any such thing. The term *bottom line* is strictly reserved for the last line of the income statement, which reports net income — the final profit after all expenses are deducted.

I could tell you that the statement of cash flows is relatively straightforward and easy to understand, but that would be a lie. The statements of cash flows of most businesses are frustratingly difficult to read. (More about this issue in Chapter 6.) Actual cash flow statements have much more detail than the brief introduction to this financial statement in Figure 2-5.

I do not present the statement of cash flows for the service company example, mainly because it would look virtually the same as for the product company example, except that the cash effect for each type of cash activity would be different amounts. Two factors can cause the cash flow from profit-making (operating) activities of a product company to swing widely from its bottom-line profit: changes in receivables, and changes in inventory. A service company does not have these two assets, so its cash flow from profit holds on a steadier course with profit.

Imagine you have a highlighter pen in your hand, and the three basic financial statements of a business are in front of you. What are the most important numbers to mark? Financial statements do *not* have any numbers highlighted; they do not come with headlines like newspapers. You have to find your own headlines. *Bottom-line profit* (net income) in the income statement is one number you would mark for sure. Another key number is *cash flow from operating activities* in the statement of cash flows.

A note about the statement of changes in shareowners' equity

Many financial reports of businesses include a *fourth* financial statement — or at least it's called a "statement." It's really a summary of the changes in the constitute elements of owners' equity (stockholders' equity of a corporation). The corporation is one basic type of legal structure that businesses use. In Chapter 8 I explain the alternative legal structures available for conducting business operations. I don't present a summary here, or statement of changes in owners' equity. I show an example in Chapter 12, in which I explain the preparation of a financial report for release.

When a business has a complex owner's equity structure, a separate summary of changes in the several different components of owners' equity during the period is useful for the owners, the board of directors, and the top-level managers. On the other hand, in some cases the only changes in owners' equity during the period were earning profit and distributing part of the cash flow from profit to owners. In this situation there is not much need for a summary of changes in owners' equity. The financial statements reader can easily find profit in the income statement and cash distributions from profit (if any) in the statement of cash flows. See the section "Why no cash distribution from profit?" later in this chapter for the product company example.

Contrasting Profit and Cash Flow from Profit

Look again at the income statement in Figure 2-1. The product company in our example earned $520,000 net income for the year. However, its statement of cash flows for the same year in Figure 2-5 reports that its profit-making, or operating, activities increased cash only $400,000 during the year. This gap between profit and cash flow from operating activities is not unusual. So, what happened to the other $120,000 of profit? Where is it? Is there some accounting sleight of hand going on? Did the business really earn $520,000 net income if cash increased only $400,000? These are good questions, and I will try to answer them as directly as I can without hitting you over the head with a lot of technical details at this point.

Here's one scenario that explains the $120,000 difference between profit (net income) and cash flow from profit (operating activities):

- ✔ Suppose the business collected $50,000 less cash from customers during the year than the total sales revenue reported in its income statement. (Remember that the business sells on credit, and its customers take time before actually paying the business.) Therefore, there's a cash inflow lag between booking sales and collecting cash from customers. As a result, the business's cash inflow from customers was $50,000 less than the sales revenue amount used to calculate profit for the year.

- ✔ Also suppose that during the year the business made cash payments connected with its expenses that were $70,000 higher than the total amount of expenses reported in the income statement. For example, a business that sells products buys or makes the products, and then holds the products in inventory for some time before it sells the items to customers. Cash is paid out before the cost of goods sold expense is recorded. This is one example of a difference between cash flow connected with an expense and the amount recorded in the income statement for the expense.

In this scenario, the two factors cause cash flow from profit-making (operating) activities to be $120,000 less than the net income earned for the year. Cash collections from customers were $50,000 less than sales revenue, and cash payments for expenses were $70,000 more than the amount of expenses recorded to the year. In Chapter 6, I explain the several factors that cause cash flow and bottom-line profit to diverge.

At this point the key idea to hold in mind is that the sales revenue reported in the income statement does not equal cash collections from customers during the year, and expenses do not equal cash payments during the year. Cash collections from sales minus cash payments for expenses gives cash flow from a company's profit-making activities; sales revenue minus expenses gives the net income earned for the year. Cash flow almost always is different from net income. Sorry mate, but that's how the cookie crumbles.

Gleaning Key Information from Financial Statements

The whole point of reporting financial statements is to provide important information to people who have a financial interest in the business — mainly its outside investors and lenders. From that information, investors and lenders are able to answer key questions about the financial performance and condition of the business. I discuss a few of these key questions in this section. In Chapters 13 and 16 I discuss a longer list of questions and explain financial statement analysis.

How's profit performance?

Investors use two important measures to judge a company's annual profit performance. Here, I use the data from Figures 2-1 and 2-3 for the product company. Of course you can do the same ratio calculations for the service business example. For convenience the dollar amounts here are expressed in thousands:

> ✔ **Return on sales** = profit as a percent of annual sales revenue:
>
> $520 bottom-line annual profit (net income) ÷ $10,400 annual sales revenue = 5.0%
>
> ✔ **Return on equity** = profit as a percent of owners' equity:
>
> $520 bottom-line annual profit (net income) ÷ $2,470 owners' equity = 21.1%

Profit looks pretty thin compared with annual sales revenue. The company earns only 5 percent return on sales. In other words, 95 cents out of every sales dollar goes for expenses, and the company keeps only 5 cents for profit. (Many businesses earn 10 percent or higher return on sales.) However, when profit is compared with owners' equity, things look a lot better. The business earns more than 21 percent profit on its owners' equity. I'd bet you don't have many investments earning 21 percent per year.

Is there enough cash?

Cash is the lubricant of business activity. Realistically a business can't operate with a zero cash balance. It can't wait to open the morning mail to see how much cash it will have for the day's needs (although some businesses try to operate on a shoestring cash balance). A business should keep enough cash on hand to keep things running smoothly even when there are interruptions in the normal inflows of cash. A business has to meet its payroll on time, for example. Keeping an adequate balance in the checking account serves as a buffer against unforeseen disruptions in normal cash inflows.

At the end of the year, the product company in our example has $1 million cash on hand (refer to Figure 2-3). This cash balance is available for general business purposes. (If there are restrictions on how it can use its cash balance, the business is obligated to disclose the restrictions.) Is $1 million enough? Interestingly, businesses do not have to comment on their cash balance. I've never seen such a comment in a financial report.

The business has $650,000 in operating liabilities that will come due for payment over the next month or so (refer to Figure 2-3). So, it has enough cash to pay these liabilities. But it doesn't have enough cash on hand to pay its operating liabilities and its $2.08 million interest-bearing debt (refer to Figure 2-2 again). Lenders don't expect a business to keep a cash balance more than the amount of debt; this condition would defeat the very purpose of lending money to the business, which is to have the business put the money to good use and be able to pay interest on the debt.

Lenders are more interested in the ability of the business to control its cash flows, so that when the time comes to pay off loans it will be able to do so. They know that the other, non-cash assets of the business will be converted into cash flow. Receivables will be collected, and products held in inventory will be sold and the sales will generate cash flow. So, you shouldn't focus just on cash; you should throw the net wider and look at the other assets as well.

Taking this broader approach, the business has $1 million cash, $800,000 receivables, and $1.56 million inventory, which adds up to $3.36 million of cash and cash potential. Relative to its $2.73 million total liabilities ($650,000 operating liabilities plus $2.08 million debt), the business looks in pretty good shape. On the other hand, if it turns out that the business is not able to collect its receivables and is not able to sell its products, it would end up in deep doo-doo.

One other way to look at a business's cash balance is to express its cash balance in terms of how many days of sales the amount represents. In the example, the business has an ending cash balance equal to 35 days of sales, calculated as follows:

$10,400,000 annual sales revenue ÷ 365 days = $28,493 sales per day

$1,000,000 cash balance ÷ $28,493 sales per day = 35 days

The business's cash balance equals a little more than one month of sales activity, which most lenders and investors would consider adequate.

Can you trust financial statement numbers?

Whether the financial statements are correct or not depends on the answers to two basic questions:

- ✓ Does the business have a reliable accounting system in place and employ competent accountants?
- ✓ Have its managers manipulated the business's accounting methods or deliberately falsified the numbers?

Is making profit ethical?

Many people have the view that making profit is unethical; they think profit is a form of theft — from employees who are not paid enough, from customers who are charged too much, from finding loopholes in the tax laws, and so on. (Profit critics usually don't say anything about the ethical aspects of a loss; they don't address the question of who should absorb the effects of a loss.) I must admit that profit critics are sometimes proved right because some businesses make profit by using illegal or unethical means, such as false advertising, selling unsafe products, paying employees lower wages than they are legally entitled to, deliberately under-funding retirement plans for employees, and other immoral tactics. Of course in making profit, a business should comply with all applicable laws, conduct itself in an ethical manner, and play fair with everyone it deals with. In my experience most businesses strive to behave according to high ethical standards, although under pressure they cut corners and take the low road in certain areas. Keep in mind that businesses provide jobs, pay several kinds of taxes, and are essential cogs in the economic system. Even though they are not perfect angels, where would we be without them?

I'd love to tell you that the answer to the first question is always yes, and the answer to the second question is always no. But you know better, don't you?

What can I tell you? There are a lot of crooks and dishonest persons in the business world who think nothing of manipulating the accounting numbers and cooking the books. Also, organized crime is involved in many businesses. And I have to tell you that in my experience many businesses don't put much effort into keeping their accounting systems up to speed, and they skimp on hiring competent accountants. In short, there is a risk that the financial statements of a business could be incorrect and seriously misleading.

To increase the credibility of their financial statements, many businesses hire independent CPA auditors to examine their accounting systems and records and to express opinions on whether the financial statements conform to established standards. In fact, some business lenders insist on an annual audit by an independent CPA firm as a condition of making the loan. The outside, non-management investors in a privately owned business could vote to have annual CPA audits of the financial statements. Public companies have no choice; under federal securities laws, a public company is required to have annual audits by an independent CPA firm.

Two points: CPA audits are not cheap, and these audits are not always effective in rooting out financial reporting fraud by managers. Unfortunately, there have been many cases of CPA auditors not detecting serious financial fraud that had been going on for years right under their auditing noses. Cleverly concealed fraud is very difficult to uncover unless you stumble over it by accident. CPAs are supposed to apply *professional skepticism* in doing their audits, but this doesn't always lead to discovery of fraud.

Why no cash distribution from profit?

In this product company example the business did not distribute any of its profit for the year to its owners. Distributions from profit by a business corporation are called *dividends*. (The total amount distributed is divided up among the stockholders, hence the term "dividends.") Cash distributions from profit to owners are included in the third section of the statement of cash flows (refer to Figure 2-5). But, in the example, the business did not make any cash distributions from profit — even though it earned $520,000 net income (refer to Figure 2-1). Why not?

The business realized $400,000 cash flow from its profit-making (operating) activities (refer to Figure 2-3). In most cases, this would be the upper limit on how much cash a business would distribute from profit to its owners. So you might very well ask whether the business should have distributed, say, at least half of its cash flow from profit, or $200,000, to its owners. If you owned 20 percent of the ownership shares of the business, you would have received 20 percent, or $40,000, of the distribution. But you got no cash return on your investment in the business. Your shares should be worth more because the profit for the year increased the company's owners' equity. But you did not see any of this increase in your wallet.

Deciding whether to make cash distributions from profit to shareowners is in the hands of the directors of a business corporation. Its shareowners elect the directors, and in theory the directors act in the best interests of the share-owners. So, evidently the directors thought the business had better use for the $400,000 cash flow from profit than distributing some of it to shareowners. Generally the main reason for not making cash distributions from profit is to finance the growth of the business — to use all the cash flow from profit for expanding the assets needed by the business at the higher sales level. Ideally, the directors of the business would explain their decision not to distribute any money from profit to the shareowners. But, generally, no such comments are made in financial reports.

Keeping in Step with Accounting and Financial Reporting Standards

The unimpeded flow of capital is critical in a free market economic system and in the international flow of capital between countries. Investors and lenders put their capital to work where they think they can get the best returns on their investments consistent with the risks they're willing to take. To make these decisions, they need the accounting information provided in financial statements of businesses.

Imagine the confusion that would result if every business were permitted to invent its own accounting methods for measuring profit and for putting values on assets and liabilities. What if every business adopted its own individual accounting terminology and followed its own style for presenting financial statements? Such a state of affairs would be a Tower of Babel.

Recognizing U.S. standards

The authoritative standards and rules that govern financial accounting and reporting by businesses in the United States are called *generally accepted accounting principles (GAAP)*. When you read the financial statements of a business, you're entitled to assume that the business has fully complied with GAAP in reporting its cash flows, profit-making activities, and financial condition — *unless* the business makes very clear that it has prepared its financial statements using some other basis of accounting or has deviated from GAAP in one or more significant respects.

If GAAP are not the basis for preparing its financial statements, a business should make very clear which other basis of accounting is being used and avoid using titles for its financial statements that are associated with GAAP. For example, if a business uses a simple cash receipts and cash disbursements basis of accounting — which falls way short of GAAP — it should not use the terms *income statement* and *balance sheet.* These terms are part and parcel of GAAP, and their use as titles for financial statements implies that the business is using GAAP.

I won't bore you with a lengthy historical discourse on the development of accounting and financial reporting standards in the United States. The general consensus (backed by law) is that businesses should use consistent accounting methods and terminology. General Motors and Microsoft should use the same accounting methods; so should Wells Fargo and Apple. Of course, businesses in different industries have different types of transactions, but the same types of transactions should be accounted for in the same way. That is the goal.

There are upwards of 10,000 public companies in the United States and easily more than a million private-owned businesses. Now, am I telling you that all these businesses should use the same accounting methods, terminology, and presentation styles for their financial statements? Putting it in such a stark manner makes me suck in my breath a little. The ideal answer is that all businesses *should* use the same rulebook of GAAP. However, the rulebook permits alternative accounting methods for some transactions. Furthermore, accountants have to interpret the rules as they apply GAAP in actual situations. The devil is in the details.

Financial accounting and reporting by government and not-for-profit entities

In the grand scheme of things, the world of financial accounting and reporting can be divided into two hemispheres: for-profit business entities and not-for-profit entities. A large body of authoritative rules and standards called *generally accepted accounting principles (GAAP)* have been hammered out over the years to govern accounting methods and financial reporting of business entities in the United States. Accounting and financial reporting standards have also evolved and been established for government and not-for-profit entities. This book centers on business accounting methods and financial reporting. Financial reporting by government and not-for-profit entities is a broad and diverse territory, which is beyond the scope of this book. I'll say just a few words here.

People generally don't demand financial reports from government and not-for-profit organizations. Federal, state, and local government entities issue financial reports that are in the public domain, although few taxpayers are interested in reading them. When you donate money to a charity, school, or church, you don't always get financial reports in return. On the other hand, many private, not-for-profit organizations issue financial reports to their members — credit unions, homeowners' associations, country clubs, mutual insurance companies (owned by their policy holders), pension plans, labor unions, healthcare providers, and so on. The members or participants may have an equity interest or ownership share in the organization and, thus, they need financial reports to apprise them of their financial status with the entity.

Government and other not-for profit entities should comply with the established accounting and financial reporting standards that apply to their type of entity. *Caution:* Many not-for-profit entities use accounting methods different than business GAAP — in some cases very different — and the terminology in their financial reports is somewhat different than in the financial reports of business entities.

In the United States, GAAP constitute the gold standard for preparing financial statements of business entities. The presumption is that any deviations from GAAP would cause misleading financial statements. If a business honestly thinks it should deviate from GAAP — in order to better reflect the economic reality of its transactions or situation — it should make very clear that it has not complied with GAAP in one or more respects. If deviations from GAAP are not disclosed, the business may have legal exposure to those who relied on the information in its financial report and suffered a loss attributable to the misleading nature of the information.

I wish I could tell you at this point that financial reporting and accounting standards in the United States have settled down and that except for normal developments things are in a steady state. However, the mechanisms and processes of issuing and enforcing financial reporting and accounting standards are in a state of flux. The biggest changes in the works have to do with the push to internationalize the standards, and the movements toward setting different standards for private companies and for small and medium sized business entities.

Getting to know the U.S. standard setters

Okay, so everyone reading a financial report is entitled to assume that GAAP have been followed (unless the business clearly discloses that it is using another basis of accounting). The basic idea behind the development of GAAP is to measure profit and to value assets and liabilities *consistently* from business to business — to establish broad-scale uniformity in accounting methods for all businesses. The idea is to make sure that all accountants are singing the same tune from the same hymnal. The authoritative bodies write the tunes that accountants have to sing.

Who are these authoritative bodies? In the United States, the highest-ranking authority in the private (non-government) sector for making pronouncements on GAAP — and for keeping these accounting standards up-to-date — is the Financial Accounting Standards Board (FASB). Also, the federal Securities and Exchange Commission (SEC) has broad powers over accounting and financial reporting standards for companies whose securities (stocks and bonds) are publicly traded. Actually, the SEC outranks the FASB because it derives its authority from federal securities laws that govern the public issuance and trading in securities. The SEC has on occasion overridden the FASB, but not very often.

GAAP also include minimum requirements for *disclosure,* which refers to how information is classified and presented in financial statements and to the types of information that have to be included with the financial statements, mainly in the form of footnotes. The SEC makes the disclosure rules for public companies. Disclosure rules for private companies are controlled by GAAP. Chapter 12 explains the disclosures that are required in addition to the three primary financial statements of a business (the income statement, balance sheet, and statement of cash flows).

Internationalization of accounting standards (maybe, maybe not)

Although it's a bit of an overstatement, today the investment of capital knows no borders. U.S. capital is invested in European and other countries, and capital from other countries is invested in U.S. businesses. In short, the flow of capital has become international. U.S. GAAP does not bind accounting and financial reporting standards in other countries, and in fact there are significant differences that cause problems in comparing the financial statements of U.S. companies with those in Europe and other countries.

Outside the United States, the main authoritative accounting standards setter is the International Accounting Standards Board (IASB), which is based in London. The IASB was founded in 2001. Over 7,000 public companies have their securities listed on the several stock exchanges in the European Union (EU) countries. In many regards, the IASB operates in a manner similar to the Financial Accounting Standards Board (FASB) in the United States, and the two have very similar missions. The IASB has already issued many standards, which are called International Financial Reporting Standards.

For some time the FASB and IASB have been working together toward developing global standards that all businesses would follow, regardless of which country a business is domiciled. Of course political issues and national pride come into play. The term *harmonization* is favored, which sidesteps difficult issues regarding the future roles of the FASB and IASB in the issuance of international accounting standards. However, the SEC recently put out a study that could delay if not kill the efforts toward one set of universal financial reporting and accounting standards. Also, the two rule-making bodies have had fundamental disagreements on certain accounting issues. I have my doubts whether a full-fledged universal set of standards will be agreed upon. Stay tuned; it's hard to predict the final outcome.

Divorcing public and private companies

Traditionally, GAAP and financial reporting standards were viewed as equally applicable to public companies (generally large corporations) and private companies (generally smaller). Today, however, we are witnessing a growing distinction between accounting and financial reporting standards for public versus private companies. Although most accountants don't like to admit it, there's always been a de facto divergence in actual financial reporting practices by private companies compared with the more rigorously enforced standards for public companies. For example, a surprising number of private companies still do not include a statement of cash flows in their financial reports, even though this has been a GAAP requirement since 1975.

Although it's hard to prove one way or the other, my view is that the financial reports of private businesses generally measure up to GAAP standards in all significant respects. At the same time, however, there's little doubt that the financial reports of some private companies fall short. As a matter of fact, in the invitation to comment on the proposal to establish an advisory committee for private company accounting standards, the FASB said "compliance with GAAP standards for many for-profit private companies is a choice rather than a requirement because private companies can often control who receives their financial information." Recently a *Private Company Council (PCC)* was established separate from the FASB, but subject to oversight by the FASB. This arrangement is in the early stages at this point, but I would guess that the PCC will become more autonomous from the FASB over time.

Private companies do not have many of the accounting problems of large, public companies. For example, many public companies deal in complex derivative instruments, issue stock options to managers, provide highly developed defined-benefit retirement and health benefit plans for their employees, enter into complicated inter-company investment and joint venture operations, have complex organizational structures, and so on. Most private companies do not have to deal with these issues.

Finally I should mention in passing that the AICPA, the national association of CPAs, has started a project to develop an *Other Comprehensive Basis of Accounting* for privately held small and medium sized entities. Oh boy! What a confusing time for accounting standards. The upshot seems to be that we are drifting towards separate accounting standards for larger public companies versus smaller private companies. Just how different the two sets of standards will be is open to speculation. As the Chinese proverb says: may you live in interesting times.

Following the rules and bending the rules

An often-repeated story concerns three persons interviewing for an important accounting position. They are asked one key question: "What's 2 plus 2?" The first candidate answers, "It's 4," and is told, "Don't call us, we'll call you." The second candidate answers, "Well, most of the time the answer is 4, but sometimes it's 3 and sometimes it's 5." The third candidate answers: "What do you want the answer to be?" Guess who gets the job. This story exaggerates, of course, but it does have an element of truth.

The point is that interpreting GAAP is not cut-and-dried. Many accounting standards leave a lot of wiggle room for interpretation. *Guidelines* would be a better word to describe many accounting rules. Deciding how to account for certain transactions and situations requires seasoned judgment and careful analysis of the rules. Furthermore, many estimates have to be made. (See the sidebar "Depending on estimates and assumptions.") Deciding on accounting methods requires, above all else, *good faith*.

A business may resort to "creative" accounting to make profit for the period look better, or to make its year-to-year profit less erratic than it really is (which is called *income smoothing*). Like lawyers who know where to find loopholes, accountants can come up with inventive interpretations that stay within the boundaries of GAAP. I warn you about these creative accounting techniques — also called *massaging the numbers* — at various points in this book. Massaging the numbers can get out of hand and become accounting fraud, also called *cooking the books*. Massaging the numbers has some basis in honest differences for interpreting the facts. Cooking the books goes way beyond interpreting facts; this fraud consists of *inventing* facts and good old-fashioned chicanery. I say more on accounting fraud in Chapter 7.

Depending on estimates and assumptions

The importance of estimates and assumptions in financial statement accounting is illustrated in a footnote you see in many annual financial reports such as the following:

"The preparation of financial statements in conformity with generally accepted accounting principles requires management to make estimates and assumptions that affect reported amounts. Examples of the more significant estimates include: accruals and reserves for warranty and product liability losses, post-employment benefits, environmental costs, income taxes, and plant closing costs."

Accounting estimates should be based on the best available information, of course, but most estimates are subjective and arbitrary to some extent. The accountant can choose either pessimistic or optimistic estimates, and thereby record either conservative profit numbers or more aggressive profit numbers. One key prediction made in preparing financial statements is called the *going-concern assumption*. The accountant assumes that the business is not facing imminent shutdown of its operations and the forced liquidations of its assets, and that it will continue as usual for the foreseeable future. This rather important pillar of accounting has received renewed attention in the aftermath of the recession of 2008. If a business is in the middle of bankruptcy proceedings, the accountant changes focus to the liquidation values of its assets.

Chapter 3

Keeping the Books

1 think it's safe to say that most folks are not enthusiastic bookkeepers. You probably balance your checkbook against your bank statement every month and somehow manage to pull together all the records you need for your annual federal income tax return. But if you're like me, you stuff your bills in a drawer and just drag them out once a month when you pay them. And when's the last time you prepared a detailed listing of all your assets and liabilities (even though a listing of assets is a good idea for fire insurance purposes)? Personal computer programs are available to make bookkeeping for individuals more organized, but you still have to enter a lot of data into the program, and in my experience most people don't put forth the effort.

Individuals can get along quite well without much bookkeeping — but the exact opposite is true for a business. First of all, a business needs a good bookkeeping system simply to operate day to day. An army marches on its stomach. A business marches on data and information, without which it literally could not make it through the day.

In addition to facilitating day-to-day operations, a company's bookkeeping system serves as the source of information for preparing its periodic financial statements, tax returns, and reports to managers. The accuracy of these reports is critical to the business's survival. If its accounting records are incomplete or inaccurate, its financial statements, tax returns, and management reports are incomplete or inaccurate. And inaccuracy simply won't do. In fact, inaccurate and incomplete bookkeeping records could be construed as evidence of deliberate fraud (or at least of incompetence).

Obviously, then, business managers have to be sure that their company's bookkeeping and accounting system is dependable and up to snuff. This chapter shows you what bookkeepers and accountants do, mainly so you have a clear idea of what it takes to be sure that the information coming out of the accounting system is complete, timely, and accurate.

Bookkeeping and Beyond

Perhaps you noticed in this chapter's opening remarks that I use the terms *bookkeeping* and *accounting*. It's useful to distinguish between the two because they are not completely interchangeable. *Bookkeeping* refers mainly to the recordkeeping aspects of accounting; it is essentially the process (some would say the drudgery) of recording all the detailed information regarding the transactions and other activities of a business (or other organization, venture, or project). The term *accounting* is much broader, going into the realm of designing the bookkeeping system, establishing controls to make sure the system is working well, and analyzing and verifying the recorded information. Accountants give orders; bookkeepers follow them.

Bookkeepers spend most of their work time keeping the recordkeeping process running smoothly according to the system established by the business — and they also spend a fair amount of time dealing with problems that inevitably arise in recording so much information. Accountants, on the other hand, have a different focus. You can think of accounting as what goes on before and after bookkeeping. Accountants prepare reports based on the information accumulated by the bookkeeping process: financial statements, tax returns, and various confidential reports to managers.

Measuring profit performance is a critical task for accountants — a task that depends on the accuracy and completeness of the information recorded by the bookkeeper. The accountant decides how to measure sales revenue and expenses to determine the profit or loss for the period. The tough questions about profit — how to measure it in our complex and advanced economic environment, and what profit consists of — can't be answered through bookkeeping alone.

Taking a Panoramic View of Bookkeeping and Accounting

Figure 3-1 presents a panoramic view of bookkeeping and accounting for a business (and other entities that carry on business activities). This brief overview can't do justice to all the details of bookkeeping and accounting, of course. But it serves to clarify important differences between bookkeeping and accounting. Bookkeeping has two main jobs: recording the financial effects and other relevant details of the wide variety of transactions and other activities of the entity; and generating a *constant* stream of documents and electronic outputs to keep the business operating every day.

Accounting, on the other hand, focuses on the *periodic* preparation of three main types of output — reports to managers, tax returns (income tax, sales tax, payroll tax, and so on), and financial statements and reports. These outputs are done according to certain schedules. For example, financial statements are usually prepared every quarter (3 months) and at the end of the year (12 months).

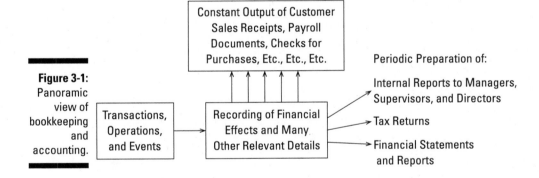

Figure 3-1:
Panoramic
view of
bookkeeping
and
accounting.

Constant Output of Customer
Sales Receipts, Payroll
Documents, Checks for
Purchases, Etc., Etc., Etc.

Transactions,
Operations,
and Events

Recording of Financial
Effects and Many
Other Relevant Details

Periodic Preparation of:

Internal Reports to Managers,
Supervisors, and Directors

Tax Returns

Financial Statements
and Reports

This book is concerned predominately with financial and management accounting. *Financial accounting* refers to the periodic preparation of general-purpose financial statements (see Chapters 4 through 7 as well as Chapter 12). *General purpose* means that the financial statements are prepared according to standards established for financial reporting outside the business, mainly for the lenders and owners of the business. These financial statements are useful to managers as well, but managers need more information than is reported in the external financial statements of a business. Much of this management information is confidential and not for circulation outside the business. *Management accounting* refers to the preparation of internal accounting reports for business managers (see Chapters 8 through 11).

This chapter offers a brief survey of bookkeeping, which you may find helpful before moving on to the financial and management accounting chapters of the book. Or, you may simply skim the rest of the chapter before moving on to later chapters. Or, you could stop right here and move on to the later chapters. I won't be offended.

Pedaling Through the Bookkeeping Cycle

Figure 3-2 presents a condensed overview of the bookkeeping cycle. These are the basic steps in virtually every bookkeeping system. The steps are done in the order presented, although the methods by which the steps are done vary from business to business. For example, entering the details of a sale can be done by scanning bar codes in a grocery store, or could require an in-depth legal interpretation for a complex order from a customer for an expensive piece of equipment. Each basic step is explained briefly as follows. (See also "Double-Entry Accounting for Single-Entry Minded People," later in this chapter, which explains how the books are kept in balance by using debits and credits for recording transactions.)

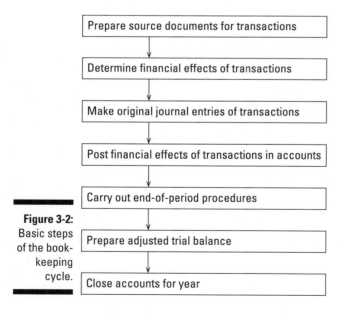

Figure 3-2: Basic steps of the bookkeeping cycle.

- Prepare source documents for transactions
- Determine financial effects of transactions
- Make original journal entries of transactions
- Post financial effects of transactions in accounts
- Carry out end-of-period procedures
- Prepare adjusted trial balance
- Close accounts for year

1. **Prepare *source documents* for all transactions, operations, and other events of the business; source documents are the starting point in the bookkeeping process.**

   When buying products, a business gets a *purchase invoice* from the supplier. When borrowing money from the bank, a business signs a *note payable,* a copy of which the business keeps. When a customer uses a credit card to buy the business's product, the business gets the *credit card slip* as evidence of the transaction. When preparing payroll checks, a business depends on *salary rosters* and *time cards.* All of these key business forms serve as sources of information into the bookkeeping system — in other words, information the bookkeeper uses in recording the financial effects of the activities of the business.

2. **Determine the *financial effects* of the transactions, operations, and other events of the business.**

   The activities of the business have financial effects that must be recorded — the business is better off, worse off, or at least "different off" as the result of its transactions. Examples of typical business transactions include paying employees, making sales to customers, borrowing money from the bank, and buying products that will be sold to customers. The bookkeeping process begins by determining the relevant information about each transaction. The chief accountant of the business establishes the rules and methods for measuring the financial effects of transactions. Of course, the bookkeeper should comply with these rules and methods.

3. **Make *original entries* of financial effects in journals, with appropriate references to source documents.**

   Using the source documents, the bookkeeper makes the first, or original, entry for every transaction into a journal; this information is later posted in accounts (see next step). A *journal* is a chronological record of transactions in the order in which they occur — like a very detailed personal diary.

   Here's a simple example that illustrates recording a transaction in a journal. Expecting a big demand from its customers, a retail bookstore purchases, on credit, 100 copies of *Accounting For Dummies,* 5th Edition, from the publisher, Wiley. The books are received and placed on the shelves. (One hundred copies is a lot to put on the shelves, but my relatives promised to rush down and buy several copies each.) The bookstore now owns the books and also owes Wiley $1,500, which is the cost of the 100 copies. Here we look only at recording the purchase of the books, not recording subsequent sales of the books and paying the bill to Wiley.

The bookstore has established a specific inventory asset account called "Inventory–Trade Paperbacks" for books like mine. And the purchase liability to the publisher should be entered in the account "Accounts Payable–Publishers." Therefore, the original journal entry for this purchase records an increase in the inventory asset account of $1,500 and an increase in the liability accounts payable of $1,500. Notice the balance in the two sides of the transaction: an asset increases $1,500 on the one side and a liability increases $1,500 on the other side. All is well (assuming there are no mistakes.)

In ancient days, bookkeepers had to record journal entries by hand, and even today there's nothing wrong with a good hand-entry (manual) bookkeeping system. But bookkeepers now can use computer programs that take over many of the tedious chores of bookkeeping (see the last section in this chapter, "Using Accounting Software in the Cloud and on the Ground"). Of course, typing has replaced hand cramps with carpal tunnel syndrome, but at least the work gets done more quickly and with fewer errors!

4. *Post* **the financial effects of transactions to accounts, with references to and tie-ins to original journal entries.**

   As Step 3 explains the pair of changes for the bookstore's purchase of 100 copies of my book is first recorded in an original journal entry. Then, sometime later, the financial effects are *posted,* or recorded in the separate accounts — one an asset and the other a liability. Only the official, established chart, or list of accounts, should be used in recording transactions. An *account* is a separate record, or page as it were, for each asset, each liability, and so on. One transaction affects two or more accounts. The journal entry records the whole transaction in one place; then each piece is recorded in the accounts that are affected by the transaction.

   I can't exaggerate the importance of entering transaction data correctly and in a timely manner. The prevalence of data entry errors is one important reason that most retailers use cash registers that read bar-coded information on products, which more accurately captures the necessary information and speeds up the entry of the information.

5. **Perform** *end-of-period procedures* **— the critical steps for getting the accounting records up-to-date and ready for the preparation of management accounting reports, tax returns, and financial statements.**

   A *period* is a stretch of time — from one day (even one hour) to one month to one quarter (three months) to one year — that is determined by the needs of the business. A year is the longest period of time that a business would wait to prepare its financial statements. Most businesses need accounting reports and financial statements at the end of each quarter, and many need monthly financial statements.

Before the accounting reports can be prepared at the end of the period (refer to Figure 3-1), the bookkeeper needs to bring the accounts of the business up-to-date and to complete the bookkeeping process. One such end-of-period requirement, for example, is recording the *depreciation expense* for the period (see Chapter 4 for more on depreciation). Another thing is getting an actual count of the business's inventory so that the inventory records can be adjusted to account for shoplifting, employee theft, and other losses.

The accountant needs to be heavily involved in end-of-period procedures and be sure to check for errors in the business's accounts. Data entry clerks and bookkeepers may not fully understand the unusual nature of some business transactions and may have entered transactions incorrectly. One reason for establishing *internal controls* (discussed in "Enforce strong internal controls," later in this chapter) is to keep errors to an absolute minimum. Ideally, accounts should contain very few errors at the end of the period, but the accountant can't make any assumptions and should make a final check for any errors that may have fallen through the cracks.

6. **Compile the *adjusted trial balance* for the accountant, which is the basis for preparing management reports, tax returns, and financial statements.**

   After all the end-of-period procedures have been completed, the bookkeeper compiles a comprehensive listing of all accounts, which is called the *adjusted trial balance.* Modest-sized businesses maintain hundreds of accounts for their various assets, liabilities, owners' equity, revenue, and expenses. Larger businesses keep thousands of accounts, and very large businesses may keep more than 10,000 accounts. In contrast, external financial statements and tax returns contain a relatively small number of accounts. For example, a typical external balance sheet reports only 25 to 30 accounts (maybe even fewer). Apple, for example, reported only 20 accounts in its June 30, 2012 balance sheet. The annual income tax return (Form 1120) for a business corporation contains a relatively small number of accounts.

   The accountant takes the adjusted trial balance and telescopes similar accounts into one summary amount that is reported in a financial report or tax return. For example, a business may keep hundreds of separate inventory accounts, every one of which is listed in the adjusted trial balance. The accountant collapses all these accounts into one summary inventory account that is presented in the balance sheet of the business. In grouping the accounts, the accountant should comply with established financial reporting standards and income tax requirements.

7. *Close the books* — **bring the bookkeeping for the fiscal year just ended to a close and get things ready to begin the bookkeeping process for the coming fiscal year.**

   Books is the common term for a business's complete set of accounts. (Well, okay, we should also include journal entries in the definition of books but you get the point.) A business's transactions are a constant stream of activities that don't end tidily on the last day of the year, which can make preparing financial statements and tax returns challenging. The business has to draw a clear line of demarcation between activities for the year (the 12-month accounting period) ended and the year yet to come by *closing the books* for one year and starting with fresh books for the next year.

 Most medium-size and larger businesses have an *accounting manual* that spells out in great detail the specific accounts and procedures for recording transactions. A business should regularly review its chart of accounts and accounting rules and policies and make revisions. Companies do not take this task lightly; discontinuities in the accounting system can be major shocks and have to be carefully thought out. Nevertheless, bookkeeping and accounting systems can't remain static for very long. If these systems were never changed, bookkeepers would still be sitting on high stools making entries with quill pens and bottled ink in leather-bound ledgers.

Managing Your Bookkeeping and Accounting System

In my experience, too many business managers and owners ignore their bookkeeping and accounting systems or take them for granted — unless something goes wrong. They assume that if the books are in balance, everything is okay. The section "Double-Entry Accounting for Single-Entry Minded People," later in this chapter, covers exactly what it means to have "books in balance" — it does *not* necessarily mean that everything is okay.

To determine whether your bookkeeping system is up to snuff, check out the following sections, which provide a checklist of the most important elements of a good system.

Categorize your financial information: The chart of accounts

Suppose that you're the accountant for a corporation and you're faced with the daunting task of preparing the annual federal income tax return for the business. For instance, the Internal Revenue Service (IRS) requires that you report the following kinds of expenses (and this list contains just the minimum!):

- Advertising
- Bad debts
- Charitable contributions
- Compensation of officers
- Cost of goods sold
- Depreciation
- Employee benefit programs
- Interest
- Pensions and profit-sharing plans
- Rents
- Repairs and maintenance
- Salaries and wages
- Taxes and licenses

You must provide additional information for some of these expenses. For example, the cost of goods sold expense is determined in a schedule that also requires inventory cost at the beginning of the year, purchases during the year, cost of labor during the year (for manufacturers), other costs, and inventory cost at year-end.

Where do you start? Well, if it's March 1 and the corporate tax return deadline is March 15, you start by panicking — unless you were smart enough to think ahead about the kinds of information your business would need to report. In fact, when your accountant first designs your business's accounting system, he or she should dissect every report to managers, the external financial statements, and the tax returns, breaking down all the information into basic account categories such as those I just listed.

For each category of information that you will need to prepare a report, you need an *account,* a record of the activities in that category. An account is basically a focused history of a particular dimension of a business. Individuals can have accounts, too — for example, your checkbook is an account of the cash inflows and outflows and the balance of your checking account (assuming that you remember to record all activities and reconcile your checkbook against your bank statement). I doubt that you keep a written account of the coin and currency in your wallet, pockets, glove compartment, and sofa cushions, but a business needs to keep track of all its cash no matter where it is. An account serves as the source of information for preparing financial statements, tax returns, and reports to managers.

The term *general ledger* refers to the complete set of accounts established and maintained by a business. The *chart of accounts* is the formal index of these accounts — the complete listing and classification of the accounts used by the business to record its transactions. *General ledger* usually refers to the actual accounts and often to the balances in these accounts at some particular time. The chart of accounts, even for a relatively small business, contains more than 100 accounts. Larger business organizations need thousands of accounts. The larger the number, the more likely that the accounts are given number codes according to some scheme — for example, all assets may be in the 100 to 300 range, all liabilities in the 400 to 500 range, and so on.

As a business manager, you should make sure that the controller (chief accountant), or perhaps an outside CPA consultant, reviews the chart of accounts periodically to determine whether the accounts are up-to-date and adequate for the business's needs. Over time, income tax rules change, the company goes into new lines of business, the company adopts new employee benefit plans, and so on. Most businesses are in constant flux, and the chart of accounts has to keep up with these changes.

Standardize source document forms and processing procedures

Just like we need a constant circulation of blood to live, businesses need a constant flow of paperwork. Even in this modern age of the Internet, electronic communication, and computers a business generates and depends on a lot of paperwork. And, much of this paperwork is used in the accounting process. Placing an order to buy products, selling a product to a customer, determining the earnings of an employee for the month — virtually every business transaction needs paperwork, generally known as *source documents.* Source documents serve as legal evidence of the terms and conditions agreed upon by the business and the other person or organization that it's dealing with. Both parties receive some kind of source document. For example, for a sale at a cash register, the customer gets a sales receipt, and the business keeps a running record of all the transactions in the register, which can be printed out later if need be.

More than you may want to know right now about types of accounts

Accounts fall into two basic types according to which financial statement their balances are reported in:

- **Balance sheet accounts:** Assets, liabilities, and owners' equity accounts

- **Income statement accounts:** Revenue and income accounts, and expense and loss accounts

In other words, the accounts are divided between those that constitute the financial condition of the business (assets, liabilities, and owners' equity accounts) and those that summarize the profit-making activities of the business (revenue and expenses, plus income and loss accounts).

In actual practice a business needs other types of accounts as well. For example, a business keeps so-called *contra* accounts, which are the negative side of certain accounts. Two main examples are these:

- *Accumulated depreciation,* the balance of which is deducted from the original cost balance of long-term operating assets that are being depreciated over time

- *Allowance for doubtful accounts,* the balance of which is deducted from the balance of the accounts receivable asset account in anticipation that some receivables will not be collected

Note: Although a business reports a statement of cash flows, in addition to its balance sheet and income statement, the cash flow amounts that are reported in the cash flow statement are prepared from information already included in the balance sheet and income statement accounts (see Chapter 6). So rest assured that the balance sheet and income statement accounts taken together are all the accounts a business needs.

Clearly, an accounting system needs to standardize the forms and procedures for processing and recording all normal, repetitive transactions and should control the generation and handling of these source documents. From the bookkeeping point of view, these business forms and documents are very important because they provide the input information needed for recording transactions in the business's accounts. Sloppy paperwork leads to sloppy accounting records, and sloppy accounting records just won't do when the time comes to prepare tax returns and financial statements.

If you're the owner of a small business, you may want to check out an office supply store to see the kinds of forms that you can buy right off the shelf. You can find many of the basic forms and documents that you need for executing and recording business transactions. Also, computer accounting software packages today include templates for most business forms and source documents needed by a business.

Hire competent personnel

A business shouldn't be penny-wise and pound-foolish: What good is meticulously collecting source documents if the information on those documents isn't entered into your system correctly? You shouldn't try to save a few bucks by hiring the lowest-paid people you can find. Bookkeepers and accountants, like all other employees in a business, should have the skills and knowledge needed to perform their functions. Here are some guidelines for choosing the right people to enter and control the flow of your business's data and for making sure that those people *remain* the right people:

- **College degree:** Many accountants in business organizations have a college degree with a major in accounting. However, as you move down the accounting department, you find that more and more employees do not have a college degree and perhaps don't even have any courses in accounting — they learned bookkeeping methods and skills through on-the-job training. Although these employees may have good skills and instincts, my experience has been that they tend to do things by the book. So you want to at least look twice at a potential employee who has no college-based accounting background.

- **CPA, CMA, and CGMA:** When hiring higher-level accountants in a business organization, you want to determine whether they should be certified public accountants (CPAs). Larger businesses insist on this credential, along with a specific number of years' experience in public accounting. Until recently the other main professional accounting credential was the CMA, or certified management accountant, sponsored by the Institute of Management Accountants (IMA). The CMA credential is American born and bred. In contrast, the Chartered Global Management Accountant, or CGMA designation, is co-sponsored by the American Institute of CPAs and the British Chartered Institute of Management Accountants. Unlike the CPA license, the CMA and CGMA designations recognize professional achievement and experience but the government does not regulate these credentials. (I discuss the CPA and CGMA in Chapter 1.)

Note: For bookkeepers, the American Institute of Professional Bookkeepers sponsors the Certified Bookkeeper designation. For more information, go to its website: www.AIPB.org.

In my opinion, a business is prudent to require the CPA, CGMA, or CMA credential for its chief accountant (who usually holds the title of *controller*). Alternatively, a business could regularly consult with a CPA in public practice for advice on its accounting system and on accounting problems that come up.

✔ **Continuing education:** Bookkeepers and accountants need continuing education to keep up with changes in the income tax law and financial reporting requirements, as well as changes in how the business operates. Ideally, bookkeepers and accountants should be able to spot needed improvements and implement these changes — to make accounting reports to managers more useful. Fortunately, many short-term courses, online programs, and the like are available at very reasonable costs for keeping up on the latest accounting developments. Many continuing education courses are available on the Internet, but you should be cautious and check out the standards of an Internet course. States require that CPAs in public practice take 30 to 40 hours per year of continuing education to keep their licenses.

✔ **Integrity:** Possibly the most important quality to look for is also the hardest to judge. Bookkeepers and accountants need to be honest people because of the control they have over your business's financial records. Conduct a careful background check when hiring new accounting personnel. After you hire them, periodically (and discreetly) check whether their lifestyles match their salaries, but be careful not to invade their privacy. Small-business owners and managers have closer day-in and day-out contact with their accountants and bookkeepers, which can be a real advantage — they get to know their accountants and bookkeepers on a personal level. Even so, you can find many cases where a trusted bookkeeper has embezzled many thousands of dollars over the years. I could tell you many true stories about long-time, "trusted" bookkeepers that made off with some of the family fortune.

Enforce strong internal controls

Any accounting system worth its salt should establish and vigorously enforce effective *internal controls* — basically, additional forms and procedures over and above what's needed strictly to move operations along. These additional procedures serve to deter and detect errors (honest mistakes) and all forms of dishonesty by employees, customers, suppliers, and even managers themselves. Unfortunately, many businesses pay only lip service to internal controls; they don't put into place good internal controls, or they don't seriously enforce their internal controls (they just go through the motions).

Internal controls are like highway truck weigh stations, which make sure that a truck's load doesn't exceed the limits and that the truck has a valid plate. You're just checking that your staff is playing by the rules. For example, to prevent or minimize shoplifting, most retailers now have video surveillance, as well as tags that set off the alarms if the customer leaves the store with the tag still on the product. Likewise, a business should implement certain procedures and forms to prevent (as much as possible) theft, embezzlement, kickbacks, fraud, and simple mistakes by its own employees and managers.

Internal controls against mistakes and theft

Accounting is characterized by a lot of paperwork — forms and procedures are plentiful. Most business managers and employees have their enthusiasm under control when it comes to the paperwork and procedures that the accounting department requires. One reason for this attitude, in my experience, is that non-accountants fail to appreciate the need for accounting controls.

These *internal controls* are designed to minimize errors in bookkeeping that processes a great deal of detailed information and data. Equally important, controls are necessary to deter employee fraud, embezzlement, and theft, as well as fraud and dishonest behavior against the business from the outside. Every business is a target for fraud and theft, such as customers who shoplift; suppliers who deliberately ship less than the quantities invoiced to a business and hope that the business won't notice the difference (called *short-counts*); and even dishonest managers themselves, who may pad expense accounts or take kickbacks from suppliers or customers.

For these reasons a business should take steps to avoid being an easy target for dishonest behavior by its employees, customers, and suppliers. Every business should institute and enforce certain control measures, many of which are integrated into the accounting process. Following are five common examples of internal control procedures:

✔ Requiring a second signature on cash disbursements over a certain dollar amount

✔ Matching up receiving reports based on actual counts and inspections of incoming shipments with purchase orders before cutting checks for payment to suppliers

✔ Requiring both a sales manager's and another high-level manager's approval for *write-offs* of customers' overdue receivable balances (that is, closing the accounts on the assumption that they won't be collected), including a checklist of collection efforts that were undertaken

✔ Having auditors or employees who do not work in the warehouse take surprise counts of products stored in the company's warehouse and compare the counts with inventory records

✔ Requiring mandatory vacations by every employee, particularly bookkeepers and accountants, during which time someone else does that person's job (because a second person may notice irregularities or deviations from company policies)

The Sarbanes-Oxley Act of 2002 applies to public companies that are subject to the federal Securities and Exchange Commission (SEC) jurisdiction. Congress passed this law mainly in response to Enron and other massive financial reporting fraud disasters. The act, which is implemented through the SEC and the Public Company Accounting Oversight Board (PCAOB), requires that public companies establish and enforce a special module of internal controls over their external financial reporting. Although the law applies only to public companies, some accountants worry that the requirements of the law will have a trickle-down effect on smaller private businesses as well. Personally, I don't see this happening but you never know.

Tage Tracy, my son and coauthor (*Cash Flow For Dummies*, Wiley), has many years of experience working closely with small businesses. He has found that many small-business owners tend to think that they're immune to embezzlement and fraud by their loyal and trusted employees. These are personal friends, after all. Yet, in fact, many small businesses are hit very hard by fraud and usually can least afford the consequences. Most studies of fraud in small businesses have found that the average loss is well into six figures! You know, even in a friendly game of poker with my buddies, we always cut the deck before dealing the cards around the table. Your business, too, should put checks and balances into place to discourage dishonest practices and to uncover any fraud and theft as soon as possible.

Get involved with end-of-period procedures

Suppose that all transactions during the year have been recorded correctly. Therefore, the accounts of the business are ready for preparing its financial statements, aren't they? Not so fast! Certain additional procedures are necessary at the end of the period to make sure that the accounts are correct and complete for preparing financial statements and income tax returns for the year. Two main things have to be done at the end of the period:

- ✔ **Record normal, routine *adjusting entries*:** For example, depreciation expense isn't a transaction as such and therefore isn't included in the flow of transactions recorded in the day-to-day bookkeeping process. (Chapter 4 explains depreciation expense.) Similarly, certain other expenses and income may not have been associated with a specific transaction and, therefore, have not been recorded. In many businesses there is a normal lag in recording certain transactions, such as billing customers for services already provided. These "catch up" entries should be recorded. Year-end adjusting entries are necessary to have correct balances for determining profit for the period. The purpose is to make the revenue, income, expense, and loss accounts up-to-date and correct for the year.

- ✔ ***Make a careful sweep of all matters*** **to check for other developments that may affect the accuracy of the accounts:** For example, the company may have discontinued a product line. The remaining inventory of these products may have to be removed from the inventory asset account, with a corresponding loss recorded in the period. Or the company may have settled a long-standing lawsuit, and the amount of damages needs to be recorded. Layoffs and severance packages are another example of what the chief accountant needs to look for before preparing reports.

Lest you think of accounting as dry and dull, let me tell you that end-of-period accounting procedures can stir up controversy of the heated-debate variety. These procedures require that the accountant make decisions and judgment calls that upper management may not agree with. For example, the accountant may suggest recording major losses that would put a big dent in profit for the year or cause the business to report a loss. The outside CPA auditor (assuming that the business has an independent audit of its financial statements) often gets in the middle of the argument. These kinds of debates are precisely why business managers need to know some accounting: to hold up your end of the argument and participate in the great sport of yelling and name-calling — strictly on a professional basis, of course.

Leave good audit trails

Good accounting systems leave good *audit trails*. An audit trail is a clear-cut, well-marked path of the sequence of events leading up to an entry in the accounts, starting with the source documents and following through to the final posting in the accounts. So an auditor can "re-walk" the path. Even if a business doesn't have an outside CPA do an annual audit, the accountant has frequent occasion to go back to the source documents and either verify certain information in the accounts or reconstruct the information in a different manner. Suppose that a salesperson is claiming some suspicious-looking travel expenses; the accountant would probably want to go through all this person's travel and entertainment reimbursements for the past year.

If the IRS comes in for a field audit of your income tax return, you'd better have good audit trails to substantiate all your expense deductions and sales revenue for the year. The IRS has rules about saving source documents for a reasonable period of time and having a well-defined process for making bookkeeping entries and keeping accounts. Think twice before throwing away source documents too soon. Also, ask your accountant to demonstrate and lay out for your inspection the audit trails for key transactions, such as cash collections, sales, cash disbursements, and inventory purchases. Even computer-based accounting systems recognize the importance of audit trails. Well-designed computer programs provide the ability to backtrack through the sequence of steps in the recording of specific transactions.

Keep alert for unusual events and developments

Business managers should encourage their accountants to stay alert to anything out of the ordinary that may require attention. Suppose that the accounts receivable balance for a customer is rapidly increasing — that is, the customer is buying more and more from your company on credit but isn't paying for these purchases quickly. Maybe the customer has switched more of his company's purchases to your business and is buying more from you only because he is buying less from other businesses. But maybe the customer is planning to stiff your business and take off without paying his debts. Or maybe the customer is planning to go into bankruptcy soon and is stockpiling products before the company's credit rating heads south.

Don't forget internal time bombs: A bookkeeper's reluctance to take a vacation could mean that she doesn't want anyone else looking at the books.

To some extent, accountants have to act as the eyes and ears of the business. Of course, that's one of the main functions of a business manager as well, but the accounting staff can play an important role.

Design truly useful reports for managers

I have to be careful in this section because I have strong opinions on this matter. I have seen too many off-the-mark accounting reports to managers — reports that are difficult to decipher and not very useful or relevant to the manager's decision-making needs and control functions. These bad reports waste the manager's time, one of the most serious offenses in management accounting.

Part of the problem lies with the managers themselves. As a business manager, have you told your accounting staff what you need to know, when you need it, and how to present it in the most efficient manner? When you stepped into your position, you probably didn't hesitate to rearrange your office, and maybe you even insisted on hiring your own support staff. Yet you most likely lay down like a lapdog regarding your accounting reports. Maybe you assume that the reports have been done a certain way and that arguing for change is no use.

On the other hand, accountants bear a good share of the blame for poor management reports. Accountants should proactively study the manager's decision-making responsibilities and provide the information that is most useful, presented in the most easily digestible manner.

In designing the chart of accounts, the accountant should keep in mind the type of information needed for management reports. To exercise control, managers need much more detail than what's reported on tax returns and external financial statements. And as I explain in Chapter 9, expenses should be regrouped into different categories for management decision-making analysis. A good chart of accounts looks to both the external and the internal (management) needs for information.

So what's the answer for a manager who receives poorly formatted reports? Demand a report format that suits your needs! See Chapter 9 for a useful profit report model, and show it to your accountant as well.

Double-Entry Accounting for Single-Entry-Minded People

Businesses and nonprofit entities use *double-entry accounting*. But I've never met an individual who uses double-entry accounting in personal bookkeeping. Instead, individuals use single-entry accounting. For example, when you write a check to make a payment on your credit card balance, you undoubtedly make an entry in your checkbook to decrease your bank balance. And that's it. You make just one entry — to decrease your checking account balance. It wouldn't occur to you to make a second, companion entry to decrease your credit card liability balance. Why? Because you don't keep a liability account for what you owe on your credit card. You depend on the credit card company to make an entry to decrease your balance.

Businesses and nonprofit entities have to keep track of their liabilities as well as their assets. And they have to keep track of *all* sources of their assets. (Some part of their total assets comes from money invested by their owners, for example.) When a business writes a check to pay one of its liabilities, it makes a two-sided (or double) entry — one to decrease its cash balance and the second to decrease the liability. This is double-entry accounting in action. Double-entry does *not* mean a transaction is recorded twice; it means both sides of the transaction are recorded at the same time.

The two-sided nature of business accounting is summarized in the *accounting equation*:

Total assets = Total liabilities + Total owners' equity

The accounting equation reflects that there are claims against the assets, which are the liabilities and owners' equity of the entity. Or, putting it differently, accounting keeps track of the sources of assets (liabilities and owners' equity) as well as the assets.

The accounting equation is a very condensed version of the balance sheet. The balance sheet is the financial statement that summarizes a business's assets on the one side and its liabilities plus its owners' equity on the other side. As I just mentioned liabilities and owners' equity are the sources of its assets. Each source has different types of claims on the assets, which I explain in Chapter 5.

One main function of the bookkeeping/accounting system is to record all transactions of a business — every single last one. If you look at transactions through the lens of the accounting equation, there is a beautiful symmetry in transactions (well, beautiful to accountants at least). All transactions have a natural balance. The sum of financial effects on one side of a transaction equals the sum of financial effects on the other side.

Suppose a business buys a new delivery truck for $65,000 and pays by check. The truck asset account increases by the $65,000 cost of the truck, and cash decreases $65,000. Here's another example: A company borrows $2 million from its bank. Its cash increases $2 million, and the liability for its note payable to the bank increases the same amount.

Just one more example: Suppose a business suffers a loss from a tornado because some of its assets were not insured (dumb!). The assets destroyed by the tornado are written off (decreased to zero balances), and the amount of the loss decreases owners' equity the same amount. The loss works its way through the income statement but ends up as a decrease in owners' equity.

Virtually all business recordkeeping systems use *debits and credits* for making sure that both sides of transactions are recorded and for keeping the two sides of the accounting equation in balance. A change in an account is recorded as either a debit or a credit according to the rules presented in Figure 3-3.

Figure 3-3:
Rules for debits and credits.

	Assets	= Liabilities	+ Owners' Equity
Increase	Debit	Credit	Credit
Decrease	Credit	Debit	Debit

An increase in an asset is tagged as a debit; an increase in a liability or owners' equity account is tagged as a credit. Decreases are just the reverse. Following this scheme, the total of debits must equal the total of credits in recording every transaction. In brief: *Debits have to equal credits.* Isn't that clever? Well, the main point is that the method works. Debits and credits have been used for centuries. (A book published in 1494 described how business traders and merchants of the day used debits and credits in their bookkeeping.)

Note: Sales revenue and expense accounts also follow debit and credit rules. Revenue increases owners' equity (thus is a credit), and an expense decreases owners' equity (thus is a debit).

The *balance* in an account at a point in time equals the increases less the decreases recorded in the account. Following the rules of debits and credits, asset accounts have debit balances, and liabilities and owners' equity accounts have credit balances. (Yes, a balance sheet account can have a wrong-way balance in unusual situations, such as cash having a credit balance because the business has written more checks than it has in its checking account.) The total of accounts with debit balances should equal the total of accounts with credit balances. When the total of debit balance accounts equals the total of credit balance accounts, the *books are in balance.*

Even when the books are in balance, errors are still possible. The bookkeeper may have recorded debits or credits in wrong accounts, or may have entered wrong amounts, or may have missed recording some transactions altogether. Having balanced books simply means that the total of accounts with debit balances equals the total of accounts with credit balances. The important thing is whether the books (the accounts) have *correct* balances, which depends on whether all transactions and other developments have been recorded correctly.

Juggling the Books to Conceal Embezzlement and Fraud

Fraud and illegal practices occur in large corporations and in one-owner/manager-controlled small businesses — and in every size business in between. Some types of fraud are more common in small businesses, including *sales skimming* (not recording all sales revenue, to deflate the taxable income of the business and its owner) and the recording of personal expenses through the business (to make these expenses deductible for income tax). Some kinds of fraud are committed mainly by large businesses, including paying bribes to public officials and entering into illegal conspiracies to fix prices or divide the market. The purchasing managers in any size business can be tempted to accept kickbacks and under-the-table payoffs from vendors and suppliers.

Some years ago we hosted a Russian professor who was a dedicated Communist. I asked him what surprised him the most on his first visit to the United States. Without hesitation he answered, "*The Wall Street Journal.*" I was puzzled. He then explained that he was amazed to read so many stories about business fraud and illegal practices in the most respected financial newspaper in the world. Many financial reporting fraud stories are on the front pages today, as when I wrote the previous editions of this book. And there are a number of stories of companies that agreed to pay large fines for illegal practices (usually without admitting guilt).

I'm fairly sure that none of this is news to you. You know that fraud and illegal practices happen in the business world. My point in bringing up this unpleasant topic is that fraud and illegal practices require manipulation of a business's accounts. For example, if a business pays a bribe it does not record the amount in a bald-faced account called "bribery expense." Rather the business disguises the payment by recording it in a legitimate expense account (such as repairs and maintenance expense, or legal expense). If a business records sales revenue before sales have taken place (a not uncommon type of financial reporting fraud), it does not record the false revenue in a separate account called "fictional sales revenue." The bogus sales are recorded in the regular sales revenue account.

A gray area in financial reporting

In some situations, the same person or the same group of investors controls two or more businesses. Revenue and expenses can be arbitrarily shifted among the different business entities under common control. For one person to have a controlling ownership interest in two or more businesses is perfectly legal, and such an arrangement often makes good business sense. For example, a retail business rents a building from a real estate business, and the same person is the majority owner of both businesses. The problem arises when that person arbitrarily sets the monthly rent to shift profit between the two businesses; a high rent generates more profit for the real estate business and lower profit for the retail business. This kind of maneuver may be legal, but it raises a touchy accounting issue.

Readers of financial statements are entitled to assume that all activities between the business and the other parties it deals with are based on what's called *arm's-length bargaining,* meaning that the business and the other parties have a purely business relationship. When that's not the case, the financial report should — but usually doesn't — use the term *related parties* to describe persons and organizations that are not at arm's length with the business. According to financial reporting standards, a business should disclose any substantial related-party transactions in its external financial statements.

Here's another example of an illegal practice. *Money laundering* involves taking money from illegal sources (such as drug dealing) and passing it through a business to make it look legitimate — to give the money a false identity. This money can hardly be recorded as "revenue from drug sales" in the accounts of the business. If an employee embezzles money from the business, he has to cover his tracks by making false entries in the accounts or by not making entries that should be recorded.

Manipulating accounts to conceal fraud, illegal activities, and embezzlement is generally called *juggling the accounts.* Another term you probably have heard is *cooking the books.* Although this term is sometimes used in the same sense of juggling the accounts, the term cooking the books more often refers to deliberate accounting fraud in which the main purpose is to produce financial statements that tell a better story than are supported by the facts. Now here's an irony: When crooks commit accounting fraud they also need to know the real story, so they keep two sets of books – one for the fraud numbers and one for the real numbers.

When the accounts have been juggled or the books have been cooked, the financial statements of the business are distorted, incorrect, and misleading. Lenders, other creditors, and the owners who have capital invested in the business rely on the company's financial statements. Also, a business's managers and board of directors (the group of people who oversee a business corporation) may be misled — assuming that they're not a party to the fraud, of course — and may also have liability to third-party creditors and investors for their failure to catch the fraud. Creditors and investors who end up suffering losses have legal grounds to sue the managers and directors (and perhaps the independent auditors who did not catch the fraud) for damages suffered.

I think that most persons who engage in fraud also cheat on their federal income taxes; they don't declare the ill-gotten income. Needless to say, the IRS is on constant alert for fraud in federal income tax returns, both business and personal returns. The IRS has the authority to come in and audit the books of the business and also the personal income tax returns of its managers and investors. Conviction for income tax evasion is a felony, I might point out.

Using Accounting Software in the Cloud and on the Ground

It would be possible, though not very likely, that a very small business would keep its books the old-fashioned way — record all transactions and do all the other steps of the bookkeeping cycle with pen and paper and by making handwritten entries. However, even a small business has a relatively large number of transactions that have to be recorded in journals and accounts, to say nothing about the end-of-period steps in the bookkeeping cycle (refer to Figure 3-2).

When mainframe computers were introduced in the 1950s and 1960s, one of their very first uses was for accounting chores. However, only large businesses could afford these electronic behemoths. Smaller businesses didn't use computers for their accounting until some years after personal computers came along in the 1980s. A bewildering array of computer software packages is available today for small- and medium-size businesses. (Larger corporations tend to develop their own computer-based accounting systems; they write their own code.)

Many businesses do their accounting work in-house. They use their own computers and buy the accounting software they need. They may use an outside firm to handle certain accounting chores, such as payroll. Alternatively, a business can do some or most of its accounting in the *cloud* as it is called. The term cloud refers to large-scale offsite computer servers that a business connects with over the Internet. The cloud can be used simply as the backup storage location for the company's accounting records. Cloud servers have the reputation of being very difficult to break into by hackers. Cloud providers offer a wide variety of accounting and business software and services that are too varied to discuss here. In short, a business can do almost all its accounting in the cloud. Of course, it still needs very strong controls over the transmission of accounting information to and from the cloud. More and more businesses seem to be switching to the cloud for doing more and more of their accounting tasks.

There are accounting software packages for every size business, from small (say, $5 million annual sales or less and 20 employees or less) to very large ($500 million annual sales and up and 500 employees or more). Developing and marketing accounting software is a booming business. Today a business can select from a wide array of accounting software packages: QuickBooks, Peachtree, NaVision, GreatPlains, MAS2000, and others. You could go to Google or Yahoo! and type "accounting software" in the search field, but be prepared for many, many references. Except for larger entities that employ their own accounting software and information technology experts, most businesses need the advice and help of outside consultants in choosing, implementing, upgrading, and replacing accounting software.

If I were giving a talk to owners/managers of small to middle-size businesses, I would offer the following words of advice about accounting software:

- ✔ Choose your accounting software very carefully. It's hard to pull up stakes and switch to another software package. Changing even just one module, such as payroll or inventory, in your accounting software can be quite difficult.

- ✔ In evaluating accounting software, you and your accountant should consider three main factors: ease of use; whether it has the particular features and functionality you need; and the likelihood that the vendor will continue in business and be around to update and make improvements in the software.

- ✔ In real estate, the prime concern is "location, location, location." The watchwords in accounting software are "security, security, security." You need very tight controls over all aspects of using the accounting software and who is authorized to make changes in any of the modules of the accounting software.

- ✔ Although accounting software offers the opportunity to exploit your accounting information (mine the data), you have to know exactly what to look for. The software does not do this automatically. You have to ask for the exact type of information you want and insist that it be pulled out of the accounting data.

- ✔ Even when using advanced, sophisticated accounting software, a business has to design the specialized reports it needs for its various managers and make sure that these reports are generated correctly from the accounting database.

- ✔ Never forget the "garbage in, garbage out" rule. Data entry errors can be a serious problem in computer-based accounting systems. You can minimize these input errors, but it is next to impossible to eliminate them altogether. Even barcode readers make mistakes, and the barcode tags themselves may have been tampered with. Strong internal controls for the verification of data entry are extremely important.

✔ Make sure your accounting software leaves good audit trails, which you need for management control, for your CPA when auditing your financial statements, and for the IRS when it decides to audit your income tax returns. The lack of good audit trails looks very suspicious to the IRS.

✔ Online accounting systems that permit remote input and access over the Internet or a local area network with multiple users present special security problems. Think twice before putting any part of your accounting system online (and if you do, institute air tight controls).

Smaller businesses, and even many medium-size businesses, don't have the budget to hire full-time information system and information technology specialists. They use consultants to help them select accounting software packages, install software, and get it up and running. Like other computer software, accounting programs are frequently revised and updated. A consultant can help keep a business's accounting software up-to-date, correct flaws and security weaknesses in the program, and take advantage of its latest features.

Part II
Exploring Financial Statements

The 5th Wave   By Rich Tennant

"I like the numbers on this company. They show a very impressive acquittal to conviction ratio."

In this part . . .

Financially speaking, managers, owners, and lenders want to know three basic things about a business: its profit or loss, its financial condition, and its cash flows. Accountants answer this call for information by regularly preparing three financial statements, which are detailed in this part.

The *income statement* summarizes the profit-making activities of the business and its bottom-line profit or loss for the period. The *balance sheet* reports the financial position of the business at a point in time — especially on the last day of the profit period. The *statement of cash flows* reports the amount of cash generated from profit and other sources of cash during the period, and what the business did with this money. Its financial statements tell the financial story of the business, for good or bad.

One word of caution: The numbers you see in its financial statements depend, to a significant extent, on which accounting methods the business chooses. Businesses have more accounting alternatives than you may think. In painting the financial picture of a business, the accountant can use somber or vivid colors from the palette of acceptable accounting methods.

Chapter 4

Reporting Profit

*I*n this chapter, I lift up the hood and explain how the profit engine runs. Making a profit is the main financial goal of a business. (Not-for-profit organizations and government entities don't aim to make profit, but they should break even and avoid a deficit.) Accountants are the profit scorekeepers in the business world and are tasked with measuring the most important financial number of a business. I should warn you right here that measuring profit is a challenge. Determining the correct amounts for revenue and expenses to record is no walk in the park.

Managers have the demanding tasks of making sales and controlling expenses, and accountants have the tough job of measuring revenue and expenses and preparing financial reports that summarize the profit-making activities. Also, accountants are called on to help business managers analyze profit for decision-making, which I explain in Chapter 9. And accountants prepare profit budgets for managers, which I cover in Chapter 10.

This chapter explains how profit activities are reported in a business's financial reports to its owners and lenders. Revenue and expenses change the financial condition of the business, a fact often overlooked when reading a profit report. I explain these asset and liability changes in the chapter. Business managers, creditors, and owners should understand the vital connections between revenue and expenses and their corresponding assets and liabilities. Recording revenue and expenses (as well as gains and losses) is governed by established accounting standards, which I discuss in Chapter 2. The accountant should follow the standards, of course, but there is a lot of wiggle room for interpretation.

Presenting Typical Income Statements

At the risk of oversimplification, I would say that businesses make profit three basic ways:

✔ Selling *products* (with allied services) and controlling the cost of the products sold and other operating costs

✔ Selling *services* and controlling the cost of providing the services and other operating costs

✔ *Investing* in assets that generate investment income and market value gains and controlling operating costs

Obviously, this list isn't exhaustive, but it captures a large swath of business activity. In this chapter, I concentrate on the first and second ways of making profit: selling products and selling services. Products range from automobiles to computers to food to clothes to jewelry. Services range from transportation to entertainment to consulting. The customers of a business may be the final consumers in the economic chain, or a business may sell to other businesses.

Looking at a product business

Figure 4-1 presents a typical profit report for a *product-oriented* business; this report, called the *income statement,* would be sent to its outside owners and lenders. The report could just as easily be called the *net income statement* because the bottom-line profit term preferred by accountants is *net income,* but the word *net* is dropped off the title and it's most often called the income statement. Alternative titles for the external profit report include *earnings statement, operating statement, statement of operating results,* and *statement of earnings.* (**Note:** Profit reports distributed to managers inside a business are usually called *P&L* [profit and loss] statements, but this moniker is not used in external financial reporting.)

The heading of an income statement identifies the business (which in this example is incorporated — thus the term "Inc." following the name), the financial statement title ("Income Statement"), and the time period summarized by the statement ("Year Ended December 31, 2013"). I explain the legal organization structures of businesses in Chapter 8.

You may be tempted to start reading an income statement at the bottom line. But this financial report is designed for you to read from the top line (sales revenue) and proceed down to the last — the bottom line (net income). Each step down the ladder in an income statement involves the deduction of an expense. In Figure 4-1, four expenses are deducted from the sales revenue amount, and four profit lines are given: gross margin; operating earnings; earnings before income tax; and, finally, net income.

Typical Product Business, Inc.
Income Statement
For Year Ended December 31, 2013

Sales Revenue	$26,000,000
Cost of Goods Sold Expense	14,300,000
Gross Margin	$11,700,000
Selling, General and Administrative Expenses	8,700,000
Operating Earnings	$3,000,000
Interest Expense	400,000
Earnings Before Income Tax	$2,600,000
Income Tax Expense	910,000
Net Income	$1,690,000

Figure 4-1: Typical income statement for a business that sells products.

Looking at a service business

For comparison Figure 4-2 presents a typical income statement for a *service-oriented* business. I keep the sales revenue and operating earnings the same for both businesses, so you can compare the two. If a business sells services and does not sell products, it does not have a cost of goods sold expense; therefore, the company does not show a gross margin line. Notice in Figure 4-2 that the first profit line is *operating earnings*, which is profit before interest and income tax. The business in Figure 4-2 discloses three broad types of expenses. In passing you might notice that the interest expense for the service business is lower than for the product business (see Figure 4-1). Therefore, it has higher earnings before income tax and higher net income.

You find many variations in the reporting of expenses. A business — whether a product or service company — has fairly wide latitude regarding the number of expense lines to disclose in its external income statement. Accounting standards do not dictate that particular expenses must be disclosed. Public companies must disclose certain expenses in their publicly available fillings with the federal Securities and Exchange Commission (SEC). Filing reports to the SEC is one thing; in their reports to shareholders, most businesses are relatively stingy regarding how many expenses are revealed in their income statements.

Typical Service Business, Inc.
Income Statement
For Year Ended December 31, 2013

Sales Revenue	$26,000,000
Marketing and Selling Expenses	4,325,000
Operating and Administrative Expenses	8,700,000
Employee Compensation Expenses	9,975,000
Operating Earnings	$3,000,000
Interest Expense	200,000
Earnings Before Income Tax	$2,800,000
Income Tax Expense	980,000
Net Income	$1,820,000

Figure 4-2:
Typical
income
statement
for a
business
that sells
services.

Taking care of some housekeeping details

I want to point out a few things about income statements that accountants assume everyone knows but, in fact, are not obvious to many people. (Accountants do this a lot: They assume that the people using financial statements know a good deal about the customs and conventions of financial reporting, so they don't make things as clear as they could.) For an accountant, the following facts are second nature:

- **Minus signs are missing.** Expenses are deductions from sales revenue, but hardly ever do you see minus signs in front of expense amounts to indicate that they are deductions. Forget about minus signs in income statements, and in other financial statements as well. Sometimes parentheses are put around a deduction to signal that it's a negative number, but that's the most you can expect to see.

- **Your eye is drawn to the bottom line.** Putting a double underline under the final (bottom-line) profit number for emphasis is common practice but not universal. Instead, net income may be shown in bold type. You generally don't see anything as garish as a fat arrow pointing to the profit number or a big smiley encircling the profit number — but again, tastes vary.

- **Profit isn't usually called *profit*.** As you see in Figures 4-1 and 4-2, bottom-line profit is called *net income*. Businesses use other terms as well, such as *net earnings* or just *earnings*. (Can't accountants agree on anything?) In this book, I use the terms *net income* and *profit* interchangeably.

✔ **You don't get details about sales revenue.** The sales revenue amount in an income statement is the combined total of all sales during the year; you can't tell how many different sales were made, how many different customers the company sold products or services to, or how the sales were distributed over the 12 months of the year. (Public companies are required to release quarterly income statements during the year, and they include a special summary of quarter-by-quarter results in their annual financial reports; private businesses may or may not release quarterly sales data.) Sales revenue does not include sales and excise taxes that the business collects from its customers and remits to the government.

Note: In addition to sales revenue from selling products and/or services, a business may have income from other sources. For instance, a business may have earnings from investments in marketable securities. In its income statement, investment income goes on a separate line and is not commingled with sales revenue. (The businesses featured in Figures 4-1 and 4-2 do not have investment income.)

✔ **Gross margin matters.** The *cost of goods sold* expense is the cost of products sold to customers, the sales revenue of which is reported on the *sales revenue* line. The idea is to match up the sales revenue of goods sold with the cost of goods sold and show the *gross margin* (also called *gross profit),* which is the profit before other expenses are deducted. The other expenses could in total be more than gross margin, in which case the business would have a net loss for the period. (A bottom-line loss usually has parentheses around it to emphasize that it's a negative number.)

Note: Companies that sell services rather than products (such as airlines, movie theaters, and CPA firms) do not have a cost of goods sold expense line in their income statements, as I mention earlier. Nevertheless some service companies report a cost of sales expense, and these businesses may also report corresponding gross margin line of sorts. This is one more example of the variation in financial reporting from business to business.

✔ **Operating costs are lumped together.** The broad category *selling, general, and administrative expenses* (refer to Figure 4-1) consists of a wide variety of costs of operating the business and making sales. Some examples are:

- Labor costs (employee wages and salaries, plus retirement benefits, health insurance, and payroll taxes paid by the business)

- Insurance premiums

- Property taxes on buildings and land

- Cost of gas and electric utilities

- Travel and entertainment costs

- Telephone and Internet charges

- Depreciation of operating assets that are used more than one year (including buildings, land improvements, cars and trucks, computers, office furniture, tools and machinery, and shelving)

- Advertising and sales promotion expenditures

- Legal and audit costs

As with sales revenue, you don't get much detail about operating expenses in a typical income statement.

Your job: Asking questions!

The worst thing you can do when presented with an income statement is to be a passive reader. You should be inquisitive. An income statement is not fulfilling its purpose unless you grab it by its numbers and start asking questions.

For example, you should be curious regarding the size of the business (see the nearby sidebar "How big is a big business, and how small is a small business?"). Another question to ask is: How does profit compare with sales revenue for the year? Profit (net income) equals what's left over from sales revenue after you deduct all expenses. The business featured in Figure 4-1 squeezed $1.69 million profit from its $26 million sales revenue for the year, which equals 6.5 percent. (The service business did a little better; see Figure 4-2.) This ratio of profit to sales revenue means expenses absorbed 93.5 percent of sales revenue. Although it may seem rather thin, a 6.5 percent profit margin on sales is quite acceptable for many businesses. (Some businesses consistently make a bottom-line profit of 10 to 20 percent of sales, and others are satisfied with a 1 or 2 percent profit on sales revenue.) Profit ratios on sales vary widely from industry to industry.

I mention earlier in this chapter (see "Looking at a service business") that accounting standards are relatively silent regarding which expenses have to be disclosed on the face of an income statement or elsewhere in a financial report. For example, the amount a business spends on advertising does not have to be disclosed. (In contrast, the rules for filing financial reports with the Securities and Exchange Commission [SEC] require disclosure of certain expenses, such as repairs and maintenance expenses. Keep in mind that the SEC rules apply only to public businesses.) The newly established Private Company Council (see Chapter 2) may decide to lay down some rules regarding expense disclosure by private businesses — but I doubt whether this will be a high priority as it gets off and running.

How big is a big business, and how small is a small business?

One key measure of the size of a business is the number of employees it has on its payroll. Could the business shown in Figure 4-1 have 500 employees? Probably not. This would mean that the annual sales revenue per employee would be only $52,000 ($26 million annual sales revenue divided by 500 employees). But the annual wage per employee in many industries today is over $35,000 and much higher in some industries. Much more likely, the number of full-time employees in this business is closer to 100. This number of employees yields $260,000 sales revenue per employee, which means that the business could probably afford an average annual wage of $40,000 per employee, or higher. Do the math to check this out.

Public companies generally report their numbers of employees in their annual financial reports, but private businesses generally do not. U.S. accounting standards do not require that the total number and total compensation of employees be reported in the external financial statements of a business, or in the footnotes to the financial statements.

The definition of a "small business" is not uniform. Generally the term refers to a business with less than 100 full-time employees, but in some situations, it refers to businesses with less than 20 employees. Say a business has 20 full-time employees on its payroll who earn an average of $30,000 annual wages (a low amount). This costs $600,000 for its annual payroll before employee benefits (such as Social Security taxes, 401K matching retirement plan, health insurance, and so on) are figured in. Product businesses need to earn annual gross margin equal to two or three times their basic payroll expense.

In the product business example shown in Figure 4-1, expenses such as labor costs and advertising expenditures are buried in the all-inclusive *selling, general, and administrative expenses* line. (If the business manufactures the products it sells instead of buying them from another business, a good part of its annual labor cost is included in its *cost of goods sold* expense.) Some companies disclose specific expenses such as advertising and marketing costs, research and development costs, and other significant expenses. In short, income statement expense disclosure practices vary considerably from business to business.

Another set of questions you should ask in reading an income statement concern the *profit performance* of the business. Refer again to the product company's profit performance report (refer to Figure 4-1). Profit-wise, how did the business do? Underneath this question is the implicit question: relative to what? Generally speaking, three sorts of benchmarks are used for evaluating profit performance:

- Broad, industry-wide performance averages
- Immediate competitors' performances
- The business's own performance in recent years

The P word

I'm sure you won't be surprised to hear that the financial objective of every business is to earn an adequate profit on a sustainable basis. In the pursuit of profit, a business should behave ethically, stay within the law, care for its employees, and be friendly to the environment. I don't mean to preach here. But the blunt truth of the matter is that *profit* is a dirty word to many people, and the profit motive is a favorite target of many critics who blame the push for profit for unsafe working conditions, outsourcing, wages that are below the poverty line, and other ills of the economic system. The profit motive is an easy target for criticism.

You hear a lot about the profit motive of business, but you don't see the *P word* in many external financial reports. The financial press uses the term profit but also alternative terms, in particular *earnings*. For example, *The Wall Street Journal* and *The New York Times* use the term *earnings reports*. If you look in financial statements, the term *net income* is used most often for the bottom-line profit that a business earns. Accountants prefer *net income,* although they also use other names, like *net earnings* and *net operating earnings.*

In short, *profit* is more of a street name; in polite company, you generally say *net income.* However, I must point out one exception. I have followed the financial reports of Caterpillar, Inc., for many years. Caterpillar uses the term *profit* for the bottom line of its income statement; it's one of the few companies that call a spade a spade.

Finding Profit

As I say in the previous section, when reading an income statement your job is asking pertinent questions. Here's an important question: What happened to the product company's financial condition as the result of earning $1.69 million net income for the year (refer to Figure 4-1)? The financial condition of a business consists of its assets on the one side and its liabilities and owners' equity on the other side. (The financial condition of a business at a point in time is reported in its *balance sheet,* which I discuss in detail in Chapter 5.)

To phrase the question a little differently: How did the company's assets, liabilities, and owners' equity change during the year as the result of its revenue and expense transactions that yielded $1.69 million profit? Revenue and expenses are not ephemeral things, like smoke blowing in the wind. These two components of profit cause real changes in assets and liabilities. Figure 4-3 summarizes the effects of recording revenue on the one hand, and expenses on the opposite hand. A business may also record a *gain,* which has the same effect as revenue (that is, an increase in an asset or a decrease in a liability). And a business may record a *loss* in addition to its normal operating expenses. A loss has the same effect as an expense (that is, a decrease in an asset or an increase in a liability).

				Liabilities			Owners' Equity	
	Assets	=	Operating Liabilities	+	Debt	Invested Capital	+	Retained Earnings
Revenue	+		−		n/a	n/a		+
Expenses	−		+		n/a	n/a		−

Figure 4-3:
Financial effects of revenue and expenses.

In Figure 4-3 I expand the accounting equation (Assets = Liabilities + Owners' Equity) by separating two distinct kinds of liabilities and two distinct sources of owners' equity. Certain liabilities emanate naturally out of the normal operating activities of the business, from buying things on credit and delaying payment for expenses. These are called *operating liabilities. Debt* is from borrowing money. Interest is paid on debt; interest is not paid on operating liabilities. Debt can run for many months or years; operating liabilities are generally payable in 30 to 120 days.

Owners' equity comes from two sources. The first source is capital invested in the business by its shareowners at the start of the business, and from time to time thereafter if the business needs more capital from its owners. The second source is profit earned by the business that is not distributed, or paid out to its owners. The retention of profit increases the owners' equity of the business. The second source of owners' equity is called *retained earnings*. (For more information on this term see the sidebar "So, why is it called retained earnings?".)

So, the owners' equity of a business increases for two quite different reasons: The owners invest money in the business, and the business makes a profit. Naturally, a business keeps two types of accounts for owners' equity: one for invested capital and one for retained earnings. In most situations not all of annual profit is distributed to owners but is retained in the business. Unfortunately, the retained earnings account sounds like an asset in the minds of many people. It is not! It is a source-of-assets account, not an asset account. It's on the right-hand side of the accounting equation; assets are on the left side.

One important lesson of Figure 4-3 is that debt and owners' equity-invested capital are *not* involved in recording revenue and expenses. Notice that revenue is recorded by increasing an asset or decreasing a liability. Revenue increases retained earnings (before expenses are considered). Some businesses receive cash from their customers before delivering the product or service, such as newspapers, insurance companies, airlines, and so on. When the money is first received it's recorded in an operating liability account. Later, when the product or service is delivered to the customer, the appropriate amount is recorded as a decrease in the liability.

So why is it called retained earnings?

The ending balance reported in the retained earnings account is the amount after recording increases and decreases in the account during the period, starting with the opening balance at the start of the period, of course. The retained earnings account increases when the business makes a profit and decreases when the business distributes some of the profit to its owners. That is, the total amount of profit paid out to the owners is recorded as a decrease in the retained earnings account. (Exactly how the profit is divided among the owners depends on the ownership structure of the business; see Chapter 8.)

Bonus question: Why doesn't a business pay out all its annual profit to owners? One reason is that the business may not have converted all its profit into cash by the end of the year and may not have enough cash to distribute all the profit to the owners. Or the business may have had the cash but needed it for other purposes, such as growing the company by buying new buildings and equipment or spending the money on research and development of new products. Reinvesting the profit in the business in this way is often referred to as *plowing back* earnings. A business should always make good use of its cash flow instead of letting the cash pile up in the cash account. See Chapter 6 for more on cash flow from profit.

Expenses are the opposite of revenue, as Figure 4-3 shows. In recording an expense an asset is decreased or an operating liability is increased. Expenses also decrease retained earnings of course. Figure 4-4 shows an example where the business recorded $10,000 revenue (or $10,000,000 rounded off if you prefer). We assume that the business does not collect money in advance from its customers, so all the revenue for the period was recorded by increases in assets. If the business had no expenses its retained earnings would have increased $10,000 during the period (see the increase in this owners' equity account Figure 4-4). But, of course, the business did have expenses.

The business recorded $8,500 in expenses during the period, so notice that retained earnings decreases this amount. The $8,500 in expenses had the impact of decreasing assets $8,100 and increasing operating liabilities $400. Don't overlook the fact that expenses impact both assets and operating liabilities.

The bottom line, as we say in the business world, is that the business earned $1,500 profit. Check out the profit line in Figure 4-4. Retained earnings increased $1,500. What's the makeup of this profit? Assets increased $1,900 (good) and operating liabilities increased $400 (bad), for a net positive effect of $1,500, the amount of profit for the period. Whew! Even this simple example takes several steps to understand. But that's the nature of profit.

You can't get around the fact that assets and operating liabilities change in the process of making profit. The next section explores in more detail which particular assets and operating liabilities are involved in recording revenue and expenses. Later in the chapter I discuss gains and losses (in the section "Reporting Extraordinary Gains and Losses").

Figure 4-4: Example of financial effects of making profit through end of year.

| | Assets | = | Liabilities | | | Owners' Equity | | |
			Operating Liabilities	+	Debt	Invested Capital	+	Retained Earnings
Revenue	$10,000				n/a	n/a		$10,000
Expenses	($8,100)		$400		n/a	n/a		($8,500)
Profit	$1,900		$400					$1,500

The product business in the Figure 4-1 example earned $1.69 million profit for the year. Therefore, its retained earnings increased this amount because the bottom-line amount of net income for the period is recorded in this owners' equity account. We know this for sure, but what we can't tell from the income statement is how the assets and operating liabilities of the business were affected by its sale and expense activities during the period.

The financial gyrations in assets and operating liabilities from profit-making activities is especially important for business managers to understand and pay attention to because they have to manage and control the changes. It would be dangerous to simply assume that making a profit has only beneficial effects on assets and liabilities. One of the main purposes of the statement of cash flows, which I discuss in Chapter 6, is to summarize the financial changes caused by the profit activities of the business during the year.

To summarize, the product company's $1.69 million net income resulted in some combination of changes in its assets and operating liabilities, such that its owners' equity (specifically, retained earnings) increased $1.69 million. One such scenario is given in Figure 4-5, which reflects the company's profit-making activities through the end of the year. By year end most of the operating liabilities that were initially recorded for expenses have been paid, which is reflected in the $24,010,000 decrease in assets. Still, operating liabilities did increase $300,000 during the year. Cash has not yet been used to pay these liabilities. I discuss these changes in more detail later in the chapter (see the section "Summing Up the Diverse Financial Effects of Making Profit").

			Liabilities			**Owners' Equity**		
	Assets	**=**	**Operating Liabilities**	**+**	**Debt**	**Invested Captial**	**+**	**Retained Earnings**
Revenue	$26,000,000							$26,000,000
Expenses	($24,010,000)		$300,000					($24,310,000)
Profit	$1,990,000		$300,000		n/a	n/a		$1,690,000

Figure 4-5: Financial changes from its profit-making activities through end of year for product company example.

Getting Particular about Assets and Operating Liabilities

The sales and expense activities of a business involve inflows and outflows of cash, as I'm sure you know. What you may not know, however, is that the profit-making process of a business that sells products on credit also involves four other basic assets and three basic types of operating liabilities. Each of the following sections explains one of these assets and operating liabilities. This gives you a better understanding of what's involved in making profit and how profit-making activities change the financial make up of a business.

Making sales on credit → Accounts receivable asset

Many businesses allow their customers to buy their products or services on credit. They use an asset account called *accounts receivable* to record the total amount owed to the business by its customers who have made purchases "on the cuff" and haven't paid yet. In most cases, a business doesn't collect all its receivables by the end of the year, especially for credit sales that occur in the last weeks of the year. It records the sales revenue and the cost of goods sold expense for these sales as soon as a sale is completed and products are delivered to the customers. This is one feature of the *accrual basis of accounting,* which records revenue when sales are made and records expenses when these costs are incurred.

When sales are made on credit, the accounts receivable asset account is increased; later, when cash is received from the customer, cash is increased and the accounts receivable account is decreased. Collecting the cash is the follow-up transaction trailing along after the sale is recorded. So, there is a two-step process: Make the sale, and Collect cash from the customer. Through the end of the year the amount of cash collections may be less than the total recorded sales revenue, in which case the accounts receivable asset account increases from the start to the end of the period. The amount of the asset increase had not been collected in cash by the end of the year. Cash flow is lower by the amount of the asset increase.

The balance of accounts receivable at the end of the year is the amount of sales revenue that has not yet been converted to cash. Accounts receivable represents cash waiting in the wings to be collected in the near future (assuming that all customers pay their accounts owed to the business on time). Until the money is actually received, the business is without the cash inflow. I explain cash flow in more depth in Chapter 6.

Selling products → Inventory asset

The *cost of goods sold* is one of the primary expenses of businesses that sell products. (In Figure 4-1, notice that this expense is equal to more than half the sales revenue for the year.) This expense is just what its name implies: the cost that a business pays for the products it sells to customers. A business makes profit by setting its sales prices high enough to cover the costs of products sold, the costs of operating the business, interest on borrowed money, and income taxes (assuming that the business pays income tax), with something left over for profit.

When the business acquires a product, the cost of the product goes into an *inventory asset* account (and, of course, the cost is either deducted from the cash account or added to a liability account, depending on whether the business pays with cash or buys on credit). When a customer buys that product, the business transfers the cost of the product from the inventory asset account to the *cost of goods sold* expense account because the product is no longer in the business's inventory; the product has been delivered to the customer.

The first layer in the income statement of a product company is deducting the cost of goods sold expense from the sales revenue for the goods sold. Almost all businesses that sell products report the cost of goods sold as a separate expense in their income statements, as you see in Figure 4-1. Most report this expense as shown in Figure 4-1 so that gross margin is reported. But some product companies simply report cost of goods sold as one expense among many and do not call attention to gross margin. For example, Ford Motor and General Mills (think Cheerios) do not report gross margin.

A business that sells products needs to have a stock of those products on hand to sell to its customers. This stockpile of goods on the shelves (or in storage space in the backroom) waiting to be sold is called *inventory*. When you drive by an auto dealer and see all the cars, SUVs, and pickup trucks waiting to be sold, remember that these products are inventory. The cost of unsold products (goods held in inventory) is not yet an expense; only after the products are actually sold does the cost get listed as an expense. In this way, the cost of goods sold expense is correctly matched against the sales revenue from the goods sold. Correctly matching expenses against sales revenue is the essence of accounting for profit.

So, the cost of goods sold expense involves two steps: the products to be sold are purchased or manufactured; later, the products are sold at which time the expense is recorded. A business may acquire more products than it sells during the year. In this case the inventory asset account increases by the cost of the unsold products. The cost of goods sold expense would have an albatross around its neck, as it were — the increase in inventory of products not yet sold by the end of the period.

Prepaying operating costs → *Prepaid expense asset*

Prepaid expenses are the opposite of unpaid expenses. For example, a business buys fire insurance and general liability insurance (in case a customer who slips on a wet floor or is insulted by a careless salesperson sues the business). Insurance premiums must be paid ahead of time, before coverage starts. The premium cost is allocated to expense in the actual periods benefited. At the end of the year, the business may be only halfway through the insurance coverage period, so it charges off only half the premium cost as an expense. (For a six-month policy, you charge one-sixth of the premium cost to each of the six months covered.) So at the time the premium is paid, the entire amount is recorded in the prepaid expenses asset account, and for each month of coverage, the appropriate fraction of the cost is transferred to the insurance expense account.

Another example of something initially put in the prepaid expenses asset account is when a business pays cash to stock up on office supplies that it may not use for several months. The cost is recorded in the prepaid expenses asset account at the time of purchase; when the supplies are used, the appropriate amount is subtracted from the prepaid expenses asset account and recorded in the office supplies expense account.

Using the prepaid expenses asset account is not so much for the purpose of reporting all the assets of a business, because the balance in the account compared with other assets and total assets is typically small. Rather, using this account is an example of allocating costs to expenses in the period benefited by the costs, which isn't always the same period in which the business pays those costs. The prepayment of these expenses lays the groundwork for continuing operations seamlessly into the next year.

So, for some expenses there is a two-step process: the expenses paid for in advance and the cost of the advance payment is allocated to expense over time. As with inventory, a business may prepay more than is recorded as expense during the period, in which case the prepaid expenses asset account increases.

Fixed assets → Depreciation expense

Long-term operating assets that are not held for sale in the ordinary course of business are called generically *fixed assets*; these include buildings, machinery, office equipment, vehicles, computers and data-processing equipment, shelving and cabinets, and so on. *Depreciation* refers to spreading out the cost of a fixed asset over the years of its useful life to a business, instead of charging the entire cost to expense in the year of purchase. That way, each year of use bears a share of the total cost. For example, autos and light trucks are typically depreciated over five years; the idea is to charge a fraction of the total cost to depreciation expense during each of the five years. (The actual fraction each year depends on which method of depreciation used, which I explain in Chapter 7.)

Of course, depreciation applies only to fixed assets that you buy, not those you rent or lease. If you lease or rent fixed assets, which is quite common, the rent you pay each month is charged to *rent expense.* (I won't go into the current controversy regarding leases and rent expense.) Depreciation is a real expense but not a cash outlay expense in the year it is recorded. The cash outlay occurs when the fixed asset is acquired. See the "Depreciation and cash flow" sidebar for more information.

Take a look back at the product company example in Figure 4-1. From the information supplied in its income statement, we don't know how much depreciation expense the business recorded in 2013. However, the footnotes to its financial statements reveal this amount. In 2013, the business recorded $775,000 depreciation expense. Basically, this expense decreases the book value (the recorded value) of its depreciable assets. Chapter 5 goes into more detail regarding how depreciation expense is recorded.

TECHNICAL STUFF

Depreciation and cash flow

Depreciation is good news for cash flow. This concept gets a little complex, so stay with me here. To start with, fixed assets wear out and lose their economic usefulness over time. Some fixed assets last many years, such as office furniture and buildings. Other fixed assets last just a few years, such as delivery trucks and computers. Accountants argue, quite logically, that the cost of a fixed asset should be spread out or allocated over its predicted useful life to the business. Depreciation methods are rather arbitrary, but any reasonable method is much better than the alternative of charging off the entire cost of a fixed asset in the year it is acquired.

A business has to pass the cost of its fixed assets through to its customers and recover the cost of its fixed assets through sales revenue. A good example to illustrate this critical point is a taxicab driver who owns his cab. He sets his fares high enough to pay for his time; to pay for the insurance, license, gas, and oil; and to recover the cost of the cab. Included in each fare is a tiny fraction of the cost of the cab, which over the course of the year adds up to the depreciation expense that he passed on to his passengers and collected in fares. At the end of the year, he has collected a certain amount of money that pays him back for part of the cost of the cab.

In summary, fixed assets are gradually *liquidated,* or turned back into cash, each year. Part of sales revenue recovers some of the cost of fixed assets, which is why the decrease in the fixed assets account to record depreciation expense has the effect of increasing cash (assuming your sales revenue is collected in cash during the year). What the company does with this cash recovery is another matter. Sooner or later, you need to replace fixed assets to continue in business.

Unpaid expenses → Accounts payable, accrued expenses payable, and income tax payable

A typical business pays many expenses *after* the period in which the expenses are recorded. Following are some common examples:

- ✔ A business hires a law firm that does a lot of legal work during the year, but the company doesn't pay the bill until the following year.

- ✔ A business matches retirement contributions made by its employees but doesn't pay its share until the following year.

- ✔ A business has unpaid bills for telephone service, gas, electricity, and water that it used during the year.

Accountants use three different types of liability accounts to record a business's unpaid expenses:

- ✔ **Accounts payable:** This account is used for items that the business buys on credit and for which it receives an invoice (a bill). For example, your business receives an invoice from its lawyers for legal work done. As soon as you receive the invoice, you record in the accounts payable liability account the amount that you owe. Later, when you pay the invoice, you subtract that amount from the accounts payable account, and your cash goes down by the same amount.

- ✔ **Accrued expenses payable:** A business has to make estimates for several unpaid costs at the end of the year because it hasn't received invoices or other types of bills for them. Examples of accrued expenses include the following:

  - Unused vacation and sick days that employees carry over to the following year, which the business has to pay for in the coming year

  - Unpaid bonuses to salespeople

  - The cost of future repairs and part replacements on products that customers have bought and haven't yet returned for repair

  - The daily accumulation of interest on borrowed money that won't be paid until the end of the loan period

  Without invoices to reference, you have to examine your business operations carefully to determine which liabilities of this sort to record.

- ✔ **Income tax payable:** This account is used for income taxes that a business still owes to the IRS at the end of the year. The income tax expense for the year is the total amount based on the taxable income for the entire year. Your business may not pay 100 percent of its income tax expense during the year; it may owe a small fraction to the IRS at year's end. You record the unpaid amount in the income tax payable account.

  Note: A business may be organized legally as a *pass-through tax entity* for income tax purposes, which means that it doesn't pay income tax itself but instead passes its taxable income on to its owners. Chapter 8 explains these types of business entities. The example I offer here is for a business that is an ordinary corporation that pays income tax.

Summing Up the Diverse Financial Effects of Making Profit

Business managers should understand not only how to make profit, but also the full range of financial effects of making profit. Profit does not simply mean an increase in cash. Sales revenue and expenses affect several assets other than cash and operating liabilities. I realize that I make this point several times in this chapter, so forgive me if I seem to be harping. I simply want to drive home the importance of understanding this fact.

The *profit-making activities* of a business include more than just recording revenue and expenses. Additional transactions are needed, which take place before or after revenue and expenses occur. These before-and-after transactions include the following:

- Collecting cash from customers for credit sales made to them, which takes place after recording the sales revenue

- Purchasing (or manufacturing) products that are put in inventory and held there until the products are sold sometime later, at which time the cost of products sold is charged to expense in order to match up with the revenue from the sale

- Paying certain costs in advance of when they are charged to expense

- Paying for products bought on credit and for other items that are not charged to expense until sometime after the purchase

- Paying for expenses that have been recorded sometime earlier

- Making payments to the government for income tax expense that has already been recorded

To sum up, the profit-making activities of a business include both making sales and incurring expenses as well as the various transactions that take place before and after the occurrence of revenue and expenses. Only revenue and expenses are reported in the income statement; however, the other transactions change assets and liabilities, and they definitely affect cash flow. I explain how the changes in assets and liabilities caused by the allied transactions affect cash flow in Chapter 6.

Figure 4-6 is a summary of the changes in assets and operating liabilities through the end of the year caused by the product company's profit-making activities. Keep in mind that these changes include the sales and expense transactions and the preparatory and follow-through transactions. This sort of summary can be prepared for business managers, but is not presented in external financial reports.

Figure 4-6:
Here's an example of changes in assets and operating liabilities from profit-making activities through end of year for product company (dollar amounts in thousands).

Assets		Operating Liabilities		Retained Earnings
Cash	$1,515	Payables for purchases on credit	$125	
Receivables from credit sales	$450	Accrual of unpaid expenses	$150	
Inventory of unsold products	$725	Income tax payable	$25	
Prepaid expenses	$75			
Depreciable assets	($775)			
Total assets	$1,990 —	Total operating liabilities	$300 =	$1,690 Profit

Notice the differences in Figure 4-6 compared with the earlier accounting equation-based figures. The columns for debt and owners' equity-invested capital are not included because these two are not affected by the profit-making activities of the business. In other words, making profit affects only assets, operating liabilities, and retained earnings. The bottom line in Figure 4-6 shows that the $1,990,000 total increase in assets minus the $300,000 total increase in operating liabilities equals the $1,690,000 profit for the year.

With the summary in Figure 4-6 you can find profit. The summary reveals what profit consists of, or the substance of profit based on the profit-making activities of the business. The $1,515,000 increase in cash is the largest component of profit for the year, and the other changes in assets and operating liabilities fill out the rest of the picture. The business is $1,690,000 better off from earning that much profit. This better offness is distributed over five assets and three liabilities. You can't look only to cash. You have to look at the other changes as well.

Reporting Extraordinary Gains and Losses

I have a small confession to make: The income statement examples shown in Figures 4-1 and 4-2 are sanitized versions when compared with actual income statements in external financial reports. Suppose you took the trouble to read 100 income statements. You'd be surprised at the wide range of things you'd find in these statements. But I do know one thing for certain you would discover.

Many businesses report *unusual, extraordinary gains and losses* in addition to their usual revenue, income, and expenses. Remember that recording a gain increases an asset or decreases a liability. And, recording a loss decreases an asset or increases a liability. When a business has recorded an extraordinary gain or loss during the period, its income statement is divided into two sections:

✔ The first section presents the *ordinary, continuing sales, income, and expense operations* of the business for the year.

✔ The second section presents any *unusual, extraordinary, and nonrecurring gains and losses* that the business recorded in the year.

The road to profit is anything but smooth and straight. Every business experiences an occasional *discontinuity* — a serious disruption that comes out of the blue, doesn't happen regularly or often, and can dramatically affect its bottom-line profit. In other words, a discontinuity is something that disturbs the basic continuity of its operations or the regular flow of profit-making activities.

Here are some examples of discontinuities or out of left field types of impacts:

✔ **Downsizing and restructuring the business:** Layoffs require severance pay or trigger early retirement costs; major segments of the business may be disposed of, causing large losses.

✔ **Abandoning product lines:** When you decide to discontinue selling a line of products, you lose at least some of the money that you paid for obtaining or manufacturing the products, either because you sell the products for less than you paid or because you just dump the products you can't sell.

✔ **Settling lawsuits and other legal actions:** Damages and fines that you pay — as well as awards that you *receive* in a favorable ruling — are obviously nonrecurring extraordinary losses or gains (unless you're in the habit of being taken to court every year).

✔ **Writing down (also called *writing off*) damaged and impaired assets:** If products become damaged and unsellable, or fixed assets need to be replaced unexpectedly, you need to remove these items from the assets accounts. Even when certain assets are in good physical condition, if they lose their ability to generate future sales or other benefits to the business, accounting rules say that the assets have to be taken off the books or at least written down to lower book values.

✔ **Changing accounting methods:** A business may decide to use a different method for recording revenue and expenses than it did in the past, in some cases because the accounting rules (set by the authoritative accounting governing bodies — see Chapter 2) have changed. Often, the new method requires a business to record a one-time cumulative effect caused by the switch in accounting method. These special items can be huge.

> ✔ **Correcting errors from previous financial reports:** If you or your accountant discovers that a past financial report had an accounting error, you make a catch-up correction entry, which means that you record a loss or gain that had nothing to do with your performance this year.

According to financial reporting standards, a business must make these one-time losses and gains very visible in its income statement. So in addition to the main part of the income statement that reports normal profit activities, a business with unusual, extraordinary losses or gains must add a second layer to the income statement to disclose these out-of-the-ordinary happenings.

If a business has no unusual gains or losses in the year, its income statement ends with one bottom line, usually called *net income* (which is the situation shown in Figures 4-1 and 4-2). When an income statement includes a second layer, that line becomes *net income from continuing operations before unusual gains and losses*. Below this line, each significant, nonrecurring gain or loss appears.

Say that a business suffered a relatively minor loss from quitting a product line and a very large loss from a major lawsuit whose final verdict went against the business. The second layer of the business's income statement would look something like the following (in thousands of dollars):

Net income from continuing operations	$267,000
Discontinued operations, net of income taxes	($20,000)
Earnings before effect of legal verdict	$247,000
Loss due to legal verdict, net of income taxes	($456,000)
Net earnings (loss)	($209,000)

The gains and losses reported in the second layer of an external income statement are generally complex and may be quite difficult to follow. So where does that leave you? In assessing the implications of extraordinary gains and losses, use the following questions as guidelines:

> ✔ Were the annual profits reported in prior years overstated?

> ✔ Why wasn't the loss or gain recorded on a more piecemeal and gradual year-by-year basis instead of as a one-time charge?

> ✔ Was the loss or gain really a surprising and sudden event that could not have been anticipated?

> ✔ Will such a loss or gain occur again in the future?

Every company that stays in business for more than a couple of years experiences a discontinuity of one sort or another. But beware of a business that takes advantage of discontinuities in the following ways:

- **Discontinuities become continuities:** This business makes an extraordinary loss or gain a regular feature on its income statement. Every year or so, the business loses a major lawsuit, abandons product lines, or restructures itself. It reports "nonrecurring" gains or losses from the same source on a recurring basis.

- **A discontinuity is used as an opportunity to record all sorts of write-downs and losses:** When recording an unusual loss (such as settling a lawsuit), the business opts to record other losses at the same time, and everything but the kitchen sink (and sometimes that, too) gets written off. This so-called *big-bath* strategy says that you may as well take a big bath now in order to avoid taking little showers in the future.

A business may just have bad (or good) luck regarding extraordinary events that its managers could not have predicted. If a business is facing a major, unavoidable expense this year, cleaning out all its expenses in the same year so it can start off fresh next year can be a clever, legitimate accounting tactic. But where do you draw the line between these accounting manipulations and fraud? All I can advise you to do is stay alert to these potential problems.

Correcting Common Misconceptions About Profit

Many people (perhaps the majority) think that the amount of the bottom-line profit increases cash by the same amount. This is not true, as I show in Figure 4-6 and as I explain in Chapter 6. In almost all situations the assets and operating liabilities used in recording profit had changes during the period that inflate or deflate cash flow from profit. This is not an easy lesson to learn. Sure, it would be simpler if profit equals cash flow, but it doesn't. Sorry, but that's the way it is.

Another broad misconception about profit is that the numbers reported in the income statement are precise and accurate and can be relied on down to the last dollar. Call this the *exactitude* misconception. Virtually every dollar amount you see in an income statement probably would have been different if a different accountant had been in charge. I don't mean that some accountants are dishonest and deceitful. It's just that business transactions can get very complex and require forecasts and estimates. Different accountants would arrive at different interpretations of the "facts" and, therefore, record different amounts of revenue and expenses. Hopefully the accountant keeps consistent over time, so that year-to-year comparisons are valid.

Another serious misconception is that if profit is good, the financial condition of the business is good. At the time of writing this sentence the profit of Apple is very good. But I didn't automatically assume that its financial condition was equally good. I looked in Apple's balance sheet and found that its financial condition is very good indeed. (It had more cash and marketable investments on hand than the economy of many countries.) But, the point is that its bottom line doesn't tell you anything about the financial condition of the business. You find this in the balance sheet.

Closing Comments

The income statement occupies center stage; the bright spotlight is on this financial statement because it reports profit or loss for the period. But remember that a business reports three primary financial statements — the other two being the balance sheet and the statement of cash flows, which I discuss in the next two chapters. The three statements are like a three-ring circus. The income statement may draw the most attention, but you have to watch what's going on in all three places. As important as profit is to the financial success of a business, the income statement is not an island unto itself.

Also, keep in mind that financial statements are supplemented with footnotes and contain other commentary from the business's executives. If the financial statements have been audited, the CPA firm includes a short report stating whether the financial statements have been prepared in conformity with the appropriate accounting standards.

I don't like closing this chapter on a sour note, but I must point out that an income statement you read and rely on — as a business manager, investor, or lender — may not be true and accurate. In most cases (I'll even say in the large majority of cases), businesses prepare their financial statements in good faith, and their profit accounting is honest. They may bend the rules a little, but basically their accounting methods are within the boundaries of GAAP even though the business puts a favorable spin on its profit number.

But some businesses resort to accounting fraud and deliberately distort their profit numbers. In this case, an income statement reports false and misleading sales revenue and/or expenses in order to make the bottom-line profit appear to be better than the facts would support. If the fraud is discovered at a later time, the business puts out revised financial statements. Basically, the business in this situation rewrites its profit history.

By the way, look at Figure 4-6 again. This summary provides a road map of sorts for understanding accounting fraud. The fraudster knows that he has to cover up and conceal his accounting fraud. Suppose the fraudster wants to make reported profit higher. But how? The fraudster has to overstate revenue or understate expenses. *And*, he has to overstate one of the assets or understate one of the operating liabilities you see in Figure 4-6. The crook cannot simply jack up revenue or downsize an expense. To keep things in order the fraudster has to balance the error in the income statement with an error in an asset or operating liability. If revenue is overstated, for example, most likely the ending balance of receivables is overstated the same amount.

I wish I could say that financial reporting fraud doesn't happen very often, but the number of high-profile accounting fraud cases over the recent decade (and longer in fact) has been truly alarming. The CPA auditors of these companies did not catch the accounting fraud, even though this is one purpose of an audit. Investors who relied on the fraudulent income statements ended up suffering large losses.

Anytime I read a financial report, I keep in mind the risk that the financial statements may be "stage managed" to some extent — to make year-to-year reported profit look a little smoother and less erratic, and to make the financial condition of the business appear a little better. Regretfully, financial statements don't always tell it as it is. Rather, the chief executive and chief accountant of the business fiddle with the financial statements to some extent. I say much more about this tweaking of a business's financial statements in later chapters.

Chapter 5

Reporting Financial Condition

This chapter explores one of the three primary financial statements reported by businesses — the *balance sheet*, which is also called the *statement of financial condition* and the *statement of financial position*. This financial statement is a summary at a point in time of the assets of a business on the one hand, and the liabilities and owners' equity sources of the business on the other hand. It's a two-sided financial statement, which is condensed in the *accounting equation*:

Assets = Liabilities + Owners' equity

The balance sheet may seem to stand alone — like an island to itself — because it's presented on a separate page in a financial report. But keep in mind that the assets and liabilities reported in a balance sheet are the results of the activities, or transactions, of the business. *Transactions* are economic exchanges between the business and the parties it deals with: customers, employees, vendors, government agencies, and sources of capital. Transactions are the stepping stones from the start-of-the year to the end-of-the-year financial condition.

In contrast to the *income statement*, which I explain in Chapter 4, the balance sheet does not have a natural bottom line, or one key figure that is the focus of attention. The balance sheet reports various assets, liabilities, and sources of owners' equity. Cash is the most important asset but other assets are important as well. Short-term liabilities are compared against cash and assets that can be converted into cash quickly. The balance sheet, as I explain in this chapter has to be read as a whole — you can't focus only on one or two items in this financial summary of the business.

Presenting the Balance Sheet

Figure 5-1 presents a two-year, comparative balance sheet for the product business example that I introduce in Chapter 4. The balance sheet is at the close of business, December 31, 2012 and 2013. In most cases financial statements are not completed and released until a few weeks after the balance sheet date. Therefore, by the time you read this financial statement it's already somewhat out of date, because the business has continued to engage in transactions since December 31, 2013. When significant changes have occurred in the interim between the closing date of the balance sheet and the date of releasing its financial report, a business should disclose these subsequent developments in the footnotes to the financial statements.

The balance sheet in Figure 5-1 is reported in the vertical, or portrait, layout with assets on top and liabilities and owners' equity on the bottom. Alternatively, a balance sheet may be presented in the horizontal or landscape mode with liabilities and owners' equity on the right side and assets on the left.

If a business does not release its annual financial report within a few weeks after the close of its fiscal year, you should be alarmed. There are reasons for such a delay, and the reasons are all bad. One reason might be that the business's accounting system is not functioning well and the controller (chief accounting officer) has to do a lot of work at year-end to get the accounts up to date and accurate for preparing its financial statements. Another reason is that the business is facing serious problems and can't decide on how to account for the problems. Perhaps a business may be delaying the reporting of bad news. Or the business may have a serious dispute with its independent CPA auditor that has not been resolved.

The balance sheet presented in Figure 5-1 includes a column for *changes* in the assets, liabilities, and owners' equity over the year (from year end 2012 through year end 2013). Including these changes is not required by financial reporting standards, and in fact most businesses do not include the changes. It certainly is acceptable to report balance sheet changes; but because it's not mandated most companies don't. I include the changes for ease of reference in this chapter. Transactions generate changes in assets, liabilities, and owners' equity, which I summarize later in the chapter (see the section "Understanding That Transactions Drive the Balance Sheet").

Typical Product Business, Inc.
Statement of Financial Condition
at December 31, 2012 and 2013
(Dollar amount in thousands)

Assets	2012	2013	Change
Cash	$2,275	$2,165	($110)
Accounts Receivable	$2,150	$2,600	$450
Inventory	$2,725	$3450	$725
Prepaid Expenses	$525	$600	$75
Current Assets	$7,675	$8,815	
Property Plant and Equipment	$11,175	$12,450	$1,275
Accumulated Depreciation	($5,640)	($6,415)	($775)
Net of Depreciation	$5,535	$6,035	
Total Assets	$13,210	$14,850	$1,640

Liabilities and Owners' Equity	2012	2013	Change
Accounts Payable	$640	$765	$125
Accrued Expenses Payable	$750	$900	$150
Income Tax Payable	$90	$115	$25
Short-term Notes Payable	$2,150	$2,250	$100
Current Liabilities	$3,630	$4,030	
Long-term Notes Payable	$3,850	$4,000	$150
Owners' Equity:			
Invested Capital	$3,100	$3,250	$150
Retained Earnings	$2,630	$3,570	$940
Total Owners' Equity	$5,730	$6,820	
Total Liabilities and Owners' Equity	$13,210	$14,850	$1,640

Figure 5-1: Typical comparative balance sheet for a product business at the end of its two most recent years (in vertical, or portrait format).

Doing a preliminary read of the balance sheet

Now suppose you own the business whose balance sheet is shown in Figure 5-1. (More likely you would not own 100 percent of the ownership shares of the business; you would own the majority of shares, which gives you working control of the business.) You've already digested your most recent annual income statement (refer to Figure 4-1), which reports that you earned $1,690,000 net income on annual sales of $26,000,000. What more do you need to know? Well, you need to check your financial condition, which is reported in the balance sheet.

Is your financial condition viable and sustainable to continue your profit making endeavor? The balance sheet helps answer this critical question. Perhaps you are on the edge of going bankrupt even though you are making a profit. Your balance sheet definitely is where to look for telltale information about possible financial troubles.

In reading through a balance sheet such as the one shown in Figure 5-1, you may notice that it doesn't have a punch line like the income statement does. The income statement's punch line is the net income line, which is rarely humorous to the business itself but can cause some snickers among analysts. You can't look at just one item on the balance sheet, murmur an appreciative "ah-ha," and rush home to watch the game. You have to read the whole thing (sigh) and make comparisons among the items. Chapters 13 and 16 offer more information on interpreting financial statements.

On first glance you might be somewhat alarmed that your cash balance decreased $110,000 during the year (refer to Figure 5-1). Didn't you make a tidy profit? Why would your cash balance go down? Well, think about it. Many other transactions affect your cash balance. For example, did you invest in new long-term operating assets (called *property, plant and equipment* in the balance sheet)? Yes you did, as a matter of fact: These fixed assets increased $1,275,000 during the year (again, see Figure 5-1).

Overall your total assets increased $1,640,000 (see Figure 5-1 again). All assets except cash increased during the year. One big reason is the $940,000 increase in your retained earnings owners' equity. I explain in Chapter 4 that earning profit increases retained earnings. Profit was $1,690,000 for the year but retained earnings increased only $940,000. Therefore, part of profit was distributed to the owners, which decreases retained earnings. I discuss these things and other balance sheet interpretations as we move through the chapter. For now, the preliminary read of the balance sheet does not indicate any serious, earth-shaking financial problems facing your business.

The balance sheet of a service business looks pretty much the same as a product business (see Figure 5-1) — except a service business does not report an inventory of products held for sale. If it sells on credit, a service business has an accounts receivable asset, just like a product company that sells on credit. The size of its total assets relative to annual sales revenue for a service business varies greatly from industry to industry, depending on whether the service industry is *capital intensive* or not. Some service businesses, such as airlines, for-profit hospitals, and hotel chains, for example, need to make heavy investments in long-term operating assets. Other service businesses do not.

The balance sheet is unlike the income and cash flow statements, which report flows over a period of time (such as sales revenue that is the cumulative amount of all sales during the period). The balance sheet presents the *balances* (amounts) of a company's assets, liabilities, and owners' equity at an instant in time. Notice the two quite different meanings of the term *balance*. As used in *balance sheet*, the term refers to the equality of the two opposing sides of a business — total assets on the one side and total liabilities and owners' equity on the other side, like a scale with equal weights on both sides. In contrast, the *balance* of an account (asset, liability, owners' equity, revenue, and expense) refers to the amount in the account after recording increases and decreases in the account — the net amount after all additions and subtractions have been entered. Usually, the meaning of the term is clear in context.

An accountant can prepare a balance sheet at any time that a manager wants to know how things stand financially. Some businesses — particularly financial institutions such as banks, mutual funds, and securities brokers — need balance sheets at the end of each day, in order to track their day-to-day financial situation. For most businesses, however, balance sheets are prepared only at the end of each month, quarter, and year. A balance sheet is always prepared at the close of business on the last day of the profit period. In other words, the balance sheet should be in sync with the income statement.

Kicking balance sheets out into the real world

The statement of financial condition, or balance sheet, shown earlier in Figure 5-1 is about as lean and mean as you'll ever read. In the real world many businesses are fat and complex. Also, I should make clear that Figure 5-1 shows the content and format for an *external* balance sheet, which means a balance sheet that is included in a financial report released outside a business to its owners and creditors. Balance sheets that stay within a business can be quite different.

Internal balance sheets

For internal reporting of financial condition to managers, balance sheets include much more detail, either in the body of the financial statement itself or, more likely, in supporting schedules. For example, just one cash account is shown in Figure 5-1, but the chief financial officer of a business needs to know the balances on deposit in each of the business's checking accounts.

As another example, the balance sheet shown in Figure 5-1 includes just one total amount for accounts receivable, but managers need details on which customers owe money and whether any major amounts are past due. Greater detail allows for better control, analysis, and decision-making. Internal balance sheets and their supporting schedules should provide all the detail that managers need to make good business decisions. See Chapter 14 for more detail on how business managers use financial reports.

External balance sheets

Balance sheets presented in external financial reports (which go out to investors and lenders) do not include a whole lot more detail than the balance sheet shown in Figure 5-1. However, external balance sheets must *classify* (or group together) short-term assets and liabilities. These are called *current assets* and *current liabilities*, as you see in Figure 5-1. For this reason, external balance sheets are referred to as *classified* balance sheets.

Let me make clear that the CIA does not vet balance sheets to keep secrets from being disclosed that would harm national security. The term *classified,* when applied to a balance sheet, does not mean restricted or top secret; rather, the term means that assets and liabilities are sorted into basic classes, or groups, for external reporting. Classifying certain assets and liabilities into *current* categories is done mainly to help readers of a balance sheet more easily compare current assets with current liabilities for the purpose of judging the short-term solvency of a business.

Judging Liquidity and Solvency

Solvency refers to the ability of a business to pay its liabilities on time. Delays in paying liabilities on time can cause very serious problems for a business. In extreme cases, a business can be thrown into *involuntary bankruptcy*. Even the threat of bankruptcy can cause serious disruptions in the normal operations of a business, and profit performance is bound to suffer. The *liquidity* of a business is not a well-defined term; it can take on different meanings. However, generally it refers to the ability of a business to keep its cash balance and its cash flows at adequate levels so that operations are not disrupted by cash shortfalls. For more on this important topic check out the book that my son, Tage, and I coauthored, *Cash Flow For Dummies* (Wiley, 2012).

If current liabilities become too high relative to current assets — which constitute the first line of defense for paying current liabilities — managers should move quickly to resolve the problem. A perceived shortage of current assets relative to current liabilities could ring alarm bells in the minds of the company's creditors and owners.

Therefore, notice the following points in Figure 5-1 (dollar amounts refer to year-end 2013):

✔ The first four asset accounts (cash, accounts receivable, inventory, and prepaid expenses) are added to give the $8,815,000 subtotal for *current assets*.

✔ The first four liability accounts (accounts payable, accrued expenses payable, income tax payable, and short-term notes payable) are added to give the $4.03 million subtotal for *current liabilities*.

✔ The total interest-bearing debt of the business is separated between $2.25 million in *short-term* notes payable (those due in one year or sooner) and $4 million in *long-term* notes payable (those due after one year).

The following sections offer more detail about current assets and liabilities.

Current assets and liabilities

Short-term, or *current,* assets include:

✔ Cash

✔ Marketable securities that can be immediately converted into cash

✔ Assets converted into cash within one operating cycle, the main components being accounts receivable and inventory

The *operating cycle* refers to the repetitive process of putting cash into inventory, holding products in inventory until they are sold, selling products on credit (which generates accounts receivable), and collecting the receivables in cash. In other words, the operating cycle is the "from cash — through inventory and accounts receivable — back to cash" sequence. The operating cycles of businesses vary from a few weeks to several months, depending on how long inventory is held before being sold and how long it takes to collect cash from sales made on credit.

Short-term, or *current,* liabilities include non-interest-bearing liabilities that arise from the operating (sales and expense) activities of the business. A typical business keeps many accounts for these liabilities — a separate account for each vendor, for instance. In an external balance sheet you usually find only three or four operating liabilities, and they are not labeled as non-interest-bearing. It is assumed that the reader knows that these operating liabilities don't bear interest (unless the liability is seriously overdue and the creditor has started charging interest because of the delay in paying the liability).

The balance sheet example shown in Figure 5-1 discloses three operating liabilities: accounts payable, accrued expenses payable, and income tax payable. Be warned that the terminology for these short-term operating liabilities varies from business to business.

In addition to operating liabilities, interest-bearing notes payable that have maturity dates one year or less from the balance sheet date are included in the current liabilities section. The current liabilities section may also include certain other liabilities that must be paid in the short run (which are too varied and technical to discuss here).

Current and quick ratios

The sources of cash for paying current liabilities are the company's current assets. That is, current assets are the first source of money to pay current liabilities when these liabilities come due. Remember that current assets consist of cash and assets that will be converted into cash in the short run. To size up current assets against total current liabilities, the *current ratio* is calculated. Using information from the company's balance sheet (refer to Figure 5-1), you compute its year-end 2013 *current ratio* as follows:

$8,815,000 current assets ÷ $4,030,000 current liabilities = 2.2 current ratio

Generally, businesses do not provide their current ratio on the face of their balance sheets or in the footnotes to their financial statements — they leave it to the reader to calculate this number. On the other hand, many businesses present a financial highlights section in their financial report, which often includes the current ratio.

The *quick ratio* is more restrictive. Only cash and assets that can be immediately converted into cash are included, which excludes accounts receivable, inventory, and prepaid expenses. The business in our example does not have any short-term marketable investments that could be sold on a moment's notice. So, only cash is included for the ratio. You compute the quick ratio as follows (refer to Figure 5-1):

$2,165,000 quick assets ÷ $4,030,000 current liabilities = .54 quick ratio

Folklore has it that a company's current ratio should be at least 2.0 and its quick ratio 1.0. However, business managers know that acceptable ratios depend a great deal on general practices in the industry for short-term borrowing. Some businesses do well with current ratios less than 2.0 and quick ratios less than 1.0, so take these benchmarks with a grain of salt. Lower ratios do not necessarily mean that the business won't be able to pay its short-term (current) liabilities on time. Chapters 13 and 16 explain solvency in more detail.

Preparing multiyear statements

The three primary financial statements of a business, including the balance sheet, are generally reported in a two- or three-year comparative format. To give you a sense of comparative financial statements, I present a two-year comparative format for the balance sheet example in Figure 5-1. Two- or three-year comparative financial statements are *de rigueur* in filings with the Securities and Exchange Commission (SEC). Public companies have no choice, but private businesses are not under the SEC's jurisdiction. Accounting standards favor presenting comparative financial statements for two or more years, but I've seen financial reports of private businesses that do not present information for prior years.

The main reason for presenting two- or three-year comparative financial statements is for *trend analysis*. The business's managers, as well as its outside investors and creditors, are extremely interested in the general trend of sales, profit margins, ratio of debt to equity, and many other vital signs of the business. Slippage in the ratio of gross margin to sales from year to year, for example, is a very serious matter.

Understanding That Transactions Drive the Balance Sheet

A balance sheet is a snapshot of the financial condition of a business at an instant in time — the most important moment in time being at the end of the last day of the income statement period. If you read Chapter 4, you noticed that I continue using the same example in this chapter. The *fiscal,* or accounting, year of the business ends on December 31. So its balance sheet is prepared at the close of business at midnight December 31. (A company should end its fiscal year at the close of its natural business year or at the close of a calendar quarter — September 30, for example.) This freeze-frame nature of a balance sheet may make it appear that a balance sheet is static. Nothing is further from the truth. A business does not shut down to prepare its balance sheet. The financial condition of a business is in constant motion because the activities of the business go on nonstop.

Transactions change the makeup of a company's balance sheet — that is, its assets, liabilities, and owners' equity. The transactions of a business fall into three basic types:

 ✔ **Operating activities, which also can be called profit-making activities:** This category refers to making sales and incurring expenses, and also includes accompanying transactions that lead or follow the recording of sales and expenses. For example, a business records sales revenue when sales are made on credit, and then, later, records cash collections from customers. The transaction of collecting cash is the indispensable follow-up to making the sale on credit. For another example, a business purchases products that are placed in its inventory (its stock of products awaiting sale), at which time it records an entry for the purchase. The expense (the cost of goods sold) is not recorded until the products are actually sold to customers. Keep in mind that the term *operating activities* includes the associated transactions that precede or are subsequent to the recording of sales and expense transactions.

✔ **Investing activities:** This term refers to making investments in assets and (eventually) disposing of the assets when the business no longer needs them. The primary examples of investing activities for businesses that sell products and services are *capital expenditures,* which are the amounts spent to modernize, expand, and replace the long-term operating assets of a business. A business may also invest in *financial assets*, such as bonds and stocks or other types of debt and equity instruments. Purchases and sales of financial assets are also included in this category of transactions.

✔ **Financing activities:** These activities include securing money from debt and equity sources of capital, returning capital to these sources, and making distributions from profit to owners. Note that distributing profit to owners is treated as a financing transaction. For instance when a business corporation pays cash dividends to its stockholders the distribution is treated as a financing transaction. The decision whether or not to distribute some of its profit depends on whether the business needs more capital from its owners, to grow the business or to strengthen its solvency. Retaining part or all of profit for the year is one way of increasing the owner's equity in the business. I discuss this topic later in the chapter (see "Financing a Business: Sources of Cash and Capital" later in the chapter).

Figure 5-2 presents a summary of changes in assets, liabilities, and owners' equity during the year for the business example I introduce in Chapter 4. Notice the middle three columns in Figure 5-2, for each of the three basic types of transactions of a business. One column is for changes caused by its revenue and expenses and their connected transactions during the year, which collectively are called *operating activities* (although I prefer to call them *profit-making* activities). The second column is for changes caused by its *investing activities* during the year. The third column is for the changes caused by its *financing activities.*

Note: Figure 5-2 does not include subtotals for current assets and liabilities. (The formal balance sheet for this business is presented in Figure 5-1). Businesses do not report a summary of changes in their assets, liabilities, and owners' equity such as Figure 5-2. (Personally I think that such a summary would be helpful to users of financial reports.) The purpose of Figure 5-2 is to demonstrate how the three major types of transactions during the year change the assets, liabilities, and owner's equity accounts of the business during the year.

The 2013 income statement of the business is shown in Figure 4-1 in Chapter 4. You may want to flip back to this financial statement. On sales revenue of $26 million, the business earned $1.69 million bottom-line profit (net income) for the year. The sales and expense transactions of the business during the year plus the associated transactions connected with sales and expenses cause the changes shown in the operating activities column in Figure 5-2. You can see in Figure 5-2 that the $1.69 million net income has increased the business's owners' equity–retained earnings by the same amount.

The operating activities column in Figure 5-2 is worth lingering over for a few moments because the financial outcomes of making profit are seen in this column. In my experience, most people see a profit number, such as the $1.69 million in this example, and stop thinking any further about the financial outcomes of making the profit. This is like going to a movie because you like its title, but you don't know anything about the plot and characters. You probably noticed that the $1,515,000 increase in cash in this column differs from the $1,690,000 net income figure for the year. The cash effect of making profit (which includes the associated transactions connected with sales and expenses) is almost always different than the net income amount for the year. Chapter 6 on cash flows explains this difference.

Typical Product Business, Inc.
Statement of Changes in Assets, Liabilities, and Owners' Equity
For Year Ended December 31, 2013
(Dollar amount in thousands)

Assets	Beginning Balances	Operating Activities	Investing Activities	Financing Activities	Ending Balances
Cash	$2,275	$1,515	($1,275)	($350)	$2,165
Accounts Receivable	$2,150	$450			$2,600
Inventory	$2,725	$725			$3,450
Prepaid Expenses	$525	$75			$600
Property Plant and Equipment	$11,175		$1,275		$12,450
Accumulated Depreciation	($5,640)	($775)			($6,415)
Totals	$13,210	$1,990	$0	($350)	$14,850

Liabilities and Owners' Equity					
Accounts Payable	$640	$125			$765
Accrued Expenses Payable	$750	$150			$900
Income Tax Payable	$90	$25			$115
Short-term Notes Payable	$2,150			$100	$2,250
Long-term Notes Payable	$3,850			$150	$4,000
Owners' Equity - Invested Capital	$3,100			$150	$3,250
Owners' Equity - Retained Earnings	$2,630	$1,690		($750)	$3,570
Totals	$13,210	$1,990		($350)	$14,850

Figure 5-2: Summary of changes in assets, liabilities, and owners' equity during the year according to basic types of transactions.

The summary of changes presented in Figure 5-2 gives a sense of the balance sheet in motion, or how the business got from the start of the year to the end of the year. It's very important to have a good sense of how transactions propel the balance sheet. A summary of balance sheet changes, such as shown in Figure 5-2, can be helpful to business managers who plan and control changes in the assets and liabilities of the business. They need a clear understanding of how the three basic types of transactions change assets and liabilities. Also, Figure 5-2 provides a useful platform for the statement of cash flows, which I explain in Chapter 6.

Coupling the Income Statement and Balance Sheet

Chapter 4 explains that sales and expense transactions change certain assets and liabilities of a business. (These changes are summarized in Figure 5-2.) Even in the relatively straightforward business example introduced in Chapter 4, we see that cash and four other assets are involved, and three liabilities are involved in the profit-making activities of a business. I explore these key interconnections between revenue and expenses and the assets and liabilities of a business here. It turns out that the profit-making activities of a business shape a large part of its balance sheet.

Figure 5-3 shows the vital links between sales revenue and expenses and the assets and liabilities that are driven by these profit-seeking activities. Note that I do not include cash in Figure 5-3. Sooner or later, sales and expenses flow through cash; cash is the pivotal asset of every business. Chapter 6 examines cash flows and the financial statement that reports the cash flows of a business. Here I focus on the noncash assets of a business, as well as its liabilities and owners' equity accounts that are directly affected by sales and expenses. You may be anxious to examine cash flows, but as we say in Iowa, "Hold your horses." I'll get to cash in Chapter 6.

The income statement in Figure 5-3 continues the same business example I introduce in Chapter 4. It's the same income statement but with one modification. Notice that the depreciation expense for the year is pulled out of *selling, general, and administrative* expenses. We need to see depreciation expense on a separate line.

Figure 5-3 highlights the key connections between particular assets and liabilities and sales revenue and expenses. Business managers need a good understanding of these connections to control assets and liabilities. And outside investors and creditors should understand these connections to interpret the financial statements of a business (see Chapters 13 and 16).

Figure 5-3:
The connections between sales revenue and expenses and the non-cash assets, liabilities, and owners' equity driven by these profit-making activities.

Income Statement		Non-Cash Assets	
Sales Revenue	$26,000,000	Accounts Receivable	$2,600,000
Cost of Goods Sold Expense	14,300,000	Inventory	$3,450,000
Gross Margin	$11,700,000	Prepaid Expenses	$600,000
Depreciation Expense	775,000	Fixed Assets, at Original Cost	$12,450,000
Selling, General and Administrative Expenses	7,925,000	Accumulated Depreciation	($6,415,000)
Operating Expenses	$3,000,000	**Liabilities**	
Interest Expense	400,000	Accounts Payable	$765,000
Earnings Before Income Tax	$2,600,000	Accrued Expenses Payable	$900,000
Income Tax Expense	910,000	Income Tax Payable	$115,000
Net Income	$1,690,000	**Owners' Equity**	
		Retained Earnings	$3,570,000

Turning over assets

Assets should be *turned over,* or put to use, by making sales. The higher the turnover — the more times the assets are used, and then replaced — the better because every sale is a profit-making opportunity. The *asset turnover ratio* compares annual sales revenue with total assets. In our example, the company's asset turnover ratio is computed as follows for the year 2013 (using relevant data from Figures 5-1 and 5-3):

$26,000,000 annual sales revenue ÷ $14,850,000 total assets = 1.75 asset turnover ratio

Some industries are very capital-intensive, which means that they have low asset turnover ratios; they need a lot of assets to support their sales. For example, gas and electric utilities are capital-intensive. Many retailers, on the other hand, do not need a lot of assets to make sales. Their asset turnover ratios are relatively high; their annual sales are three, four, or five times their assets. Our business example that has a 1.75 asset turnover ratio falls in the broad middle range of businesses that sell products.

Sizing up assets and liabilities

Although the business example I use in this chapter is hypothetical, I didn't make up the numbers at random. For the example, I use a medium-sized business that has $26 million in annual sales revenue. The other numbers in its income statement and balance sheet are realistic relative to each other. I assume that the business earns 45 percent gross margin ($11.7 million gross margin ÷ $26 million sales revenue = 45 percent), which means its cost of goods sold expense is 55 percent of sales revenue. The sizes of particular assets and liabilities compared with their relevant income statement numbers vary from industry to industry, and even from business to business in the same industry.

Based on its history and operating policies, the managers of a business can estimate what the size of each asset and liability should be, which provide useful *control benchmarks* against which the actual balances of the assets and liabilities are compared, to spot any serious deviations. In other words, assets (and liabilities, too) can be too high or too low relative to the sales revenue and expenses that drive them, and these deviations can cause problems that managers should try to remedy.

For example, based on the credit terms extended to its customers and the company's actual policies regarding how aggressively it acts in collecting past-due receivables, a manager determines the range for the proper, or within-the-boundaries, balance of accounts receivable. This figure is the control benchmark. If the actual balance is reasonably close to this control benchmark, accounts receivable is under control. If not, the manager should investigate why accounts receivable is smaller or larger than it should be.

The following sections discuss the relative sizes of the assets and liabilities in the balance sheet that result from sales and expenses (for the fiscal year 2013). The sales and expenses are the *drivers,* or causes, of the assets and liabilities. If a business earned profit simply by investing in stocks and bonds, it would not need all the various assets and liabilities explained in this chapter. Such a business — a mutual fund, for example — would have just one income-producing asset: investments in securities. This chapter focuses on businesses that sell products on credit.

Sales revenue and accounts receivable

In Figure 5-3 annual sales revenue for the year 2013 is $26 million. The year-end accounts receivable is one-tenth of this, or $2.6 million. So the average customer's credit period is roughly 36 days: 365 days in the year times the 10 percent ratio of ending accounts receivable balance to annual sales revenue.

Of course, some customers' balances are past 36 days, and some are quite new; you want to focus on the average. The key question is whether a customer credit period averaging 36 days is reasonable.

Suppose that the business offers all customers a 30-day credit period, which is fairly common in business-to-business selling (although not for a retailer selling to individual consumers). The relatively small deviation of about 6 days (36 days average credit period versus 30 days normal credit terms) probably is not a significant cause for concern. But suppose that, at the end of the period, the accounts receivable had been $3.9 million, which is 15 percent of annual sales, or about a 55-day average credit period. Such an abnormally high balance should raise a red flag; the responsible manager should look into the reasons for the abnormally high accounts receivable balance. Perhaps several customers are seriously late in paying and should not be extended new credit until they pay up.

Cost of goods sold expense and inventory

In Figure 5-3 the cost of goods sold expense for the year 2013 is $14.3 million. The year-end inventory is $3.45 million, or about 24 percent. In rough terms, the average product's inventory holding period is 88 days — 365 days in the year times the 24 percent ratio of ending inventory to annual cost of goods sold. Of course, some products may remain in inventory longer than the 88-day average, and some products may sell in a much shorter period than 88 days. You need to focus on the overall average. Is an 88-day average inventory holding period reasonable?

The "correct" average inventory holding period varies from industry to industry. In some industries, especially heavy equipment manufacturing, the inventory holding period is very long — three months or longer. The opposite is true for high-volume retailers, such as retail supermarkets, that depend on getting products off the shelves as quickly as possible. The 88-day average holding period in the example is reasonable for many businesses but would be too high for some businesses.

The managers should know what the company's average inventory holding period should be — they should know what the control benchmark is for the inventory holding period. If inventory is much above this control benchmark, managers should take prompt action to get inventory back in line (which is easier said than done, of course). If inventory is at abnormally low levels, this should be investigated as well. Perhaps some products are out of stock and should be immediately restocked to avoid lost sales.

Fixed assets and depreciation expense

As Chapter 4 explains, depreciation is a relatively unique expense. Depreciation is like other expenses in that all expenses are deducted from sales revenue to determine profit. Other than this, however, depreciation is very different from other expenses. When a business buys or builds a long-term operating asset, the cost of the asset is recorded in a specific fixed asset account. *Fixed* is an overstatement; although the assets may last a long time, eventually they are retired from service. The main point is that the cost of a long-term operating or fixed asset is spread out, or allocated, over its expected useful life to the business. Each year of use bears some portion of the cost of the fixed asset.

The depreciation expense recorded in the period does not require any further cash outlay during the period. (The cash outlay occurred when the fixed asset was acquired, or perhaps later when a loan is secured for part of the total cost.) Rather, depreciation expense for the period is that quota of the total cost of a business's fixed assets that is allocated to the period to record the cost of using the assets during the period. Depreciation depends on which method is used to allocate the cost of fixed assets over their estimated useful lives. I explain different depreciation methods in Chapter 7.

The higher the total cost of its fixed assets (called *property, plant, and equipment* in a formal balance sheet), the higher a business's depreciation expense. However, there is no standard ratio of depreciation expense to the cost of fixed assets. The annual depreciation expense of a business seldom is more than 10 to 15 percent of the original cost of its fixed assets. Either the depreciation expense for the year is reported as a separate expense in the income statement (as in Figure 5-3), or the amount is disclosed in a footnote.

Because depreciation is based on the gradual charging off or writing-down of the cost of a fixed asset, the balance sheet reports not one but two numbers: the original (historical) cost of its fixed assets and the *accumulated depreciation* amount (the total amount of depreciation that has been charged to expense from the time of acquiring the fixed assets to the current balance sheet date). The purpose isn't to confuse you by giving you even more numbers to deal with. Seeing both numbers gives you an idea of how old the fixed assets are and also tells you how much these fixed assets originally cost.

In the example we're working with in this chapter, the business has, over several years, invested $12,450,000 in its fixed assets (that it still owns and uses), and it has recorded total depreciation of $6,415,000 through the end of the most recent fiscal year, December 31, 2013. (Refer to the balance sheet presented in Figure 5-1.) The business recorded $775,000 depreciation expense in its most recent year. (See its income statement in Figure 5-3.)

You can tell that the company's collection of fixed assets includes some old assets because the company has recorded $6,415,000 total depreciation since assets were bought — a fairly sizable percent of original cost (more than half). But many businesses use accelerated depreciation methods that pile up a lot of the depreciation expense in the early years and less in the back years (see Chapter 7 for more details), so it's hard to estimate the average age of the company's assets. A business could discuss the actual ages of its fixed assets in the footnotes to its financial statements, but hardly any businesses disclose this information — although they do identify which depreciation methods they are using.

Operating expenses and their balance sheet accounts

Take another look at Figure 5-3 and notice that sales, general, and administrative (SG&A) expenses connect with three balance sheet accounts: prepaid expenses, accounts payable, and accrued expenses payable. The broad SG&A expense category includes many different types of expenses in making sales and operating the business. (Separate detailed expense accounts are maintained for specific expenses; depending on the size of the business and the needs of its various managers, hundreds or thousands of specific expense accounts are established.)

Many expenses are recorded when paid. For example, wage and salary expenses are recorded on payday. However, this record-as-you-pay method does not work for many expenses. For instance, insurance and office supplies costs are *prepaid,* and then released to expense gradually over time. The cost is initially put in the *prepaid expenses* asset account. (Yes, I know that "prepaid expenses" doesn't sound like an asset account, but it is.) Other expenses are not paid until weeks after the expenses are recorded. The amounts owed for these unpaid expenses are recorded in an *accounts payable* or in an *accrued expenses payable* liability account.

For more detail regarding the use of these accounts in recording expenses you might want to refer to Chapter 4. Remember that the accounting objective is to match expenses with sales revenue for the year, and only in this way can the amount of profit be measured for the year. So expenses recorded for the year should be the correct amounts, regardless of when they're paid.

What about cash?

A business's cash account consists of the money it has in its checking accounts plus the money that it keeps on hand. Cash is the essential lubricant of business activity. Sooner or later, virtually all business transactions pass through the cash account. Every business needs to maintain a working cash balance as a buffer against fluctuations in day-to-day cash receipts and payments. You can't really get by with a zero cash balance, hoping that enough customers will provide enough cash to cover all the cash payments that you need to make that day.

At year-end 2013, the cash balance of the business whose balance sheet is presented in Figure 5-1 is $2,165,000, which equals a little more than four weeks of annual sales revenue. How large a cash balance should a business maintain? This question has no simple answer. A business needs to determine how large a cash safety reserve it's comfortable with to meet unexpected demands on cash while keeping the following points in mind:

✔ Excess cash balances are unproductive and don't earn any profit for the business.

✔ Insufficient cash balances can cause the business to miss taking advantage of opportunities that require quick action — such as snatching up a prized piece of real estate that just came on the market or buying out a competitor.

Intangible assets and amortization expense

Although our business example does not include these kinds of assets, many businesses invest in intangible assets. *Intangible* means without physical existence, in contrast to buildings, vehicles, and computers. For example:

✔ A business may purchase the customer list of another company that is going out of business.

✔ A business may buy patent rights from the inventor of a new product or process.

✔ A business may buy another business lock, stock, and barrel and may pay more than the total of the individual assets of the company being bought are worth — even after adjusting the particular assets to their current values. The extra amount is for *goodwill*, which may consist of a trained and efficient workforce, an established product with a reputation for high quality, or a very valuable location.

Only intangible assets that are purchased are recorded by a business. A business must expend cash, or take on debt, or issue owners' equity shares for an intangible asset in order to record the asset on its books. Building up a good reputation with customers or establishing a well-known brand is not recorded as an intangible asset. You can imagine the value of Coca-Cola's brand name, but this "asset" is not recorded on the company's books. (However, Coca-Cola protects its brand name with all the legal means at its disposal.)

The cost of an intangible asset is recorded in an appropriate asset account, just like the cost of a tangible asset is recorded in a fixed asset account. Whether or when to allocate the cost of an intangible asset to expense has proven to be a very difficult issue in practice, not easily amenable to accounting rules. At one time the cost of most intangible assets were charged off according to some systematic method. The fraction of the total cost charged off in one period is called *amortization expense*. Currently, however, the cost of an intangible asset is not charged to expense unless its value has been impaired. Testing for impairment is a very messy process. I do not go into the technical details here; because our business example doesn't include any intangible assets, there is no amortization expense.

Debt and interest expense

Look back at the balance sheet shown in Figure 5-1. Notice that the sum of this business's short-term (current) and long-term notes payable at year-end 2013 is $6.25 million. From its income statement in Figure 5-3 we see that its interest expense for the year is $400,000. Based on the year-end amount of debt, the annual interest rate is about 6.4 percent. (The business may have had more or less borrowed at certain times during the year, of course, and the actual interest rate depends on the debt levels from month to month.)

For most businesses, a small part of their total annual interest is unpaid at year-end; the unpaid part is recorded to bring interest expense up to the correct total amount for the year. In Figure 5-3, the accrued amount of interest is included in the *accrued expenses payable* liability account. In most balance sheets you don't find accrued interest payable on a separate line; rather, it's included in the accrued expenses payable liability account. However, if unpaid interest at year-end happens to be a rather large amount, or if the business is seriously behind in paying interest on its debt, it should report the accrued interest payable as a separate liability.

Income tax expense and income tax payable

In Figure 5-3, earnings before income tax — after deducting interest and all other expenses from sales revenue — is $2.6 million. The actual taxable income of the business for the year probably is different than this amount because of the many complexities in the income tax law. In the example, I use a realistic 35 percent tax rate, so the income tax expense is $910,000 of the pretax income of $2.6 million.

A large part of the federal and state income tax amounts for the year must be paid before the end of the year. But a small part is usually still owed at the end of the year. The unpaid part is recorded in the *income tax payable* liability account, as you see in Figure 5-3. In the example, the unpaid part is $115,000 of the total $910,000 income tax for the year, but I don't mean to suggest that this ratio is typical. Generally, the unpaid income tax at the end of the year is fairly small, but just how small depends on several technical factors.

Net income and cash dividends (if any)

The business in our example earned $1.69 million net income for the year (see Figure 5-3). Earning profit increases the owners' equity account *retained earnings* by the same amount, which is indicated by the line of connection from net income to retained earnings in Figure 5-3. The $1.69 million profit (here I go again using the term *profit* instead of *net income*) either stays in the business or some of it is paid out and divided among the owners of the business.

During the year the business paid out $750,000 total cash distributions from its annual profit. This is included in Figure 5-2's summary of transactions — look in the financing activities column on the retained earnings line. If you own 10 percent of the shares you would receive one-tenth, or $75,000 cash, as your share of the total distributions. Distributions from profit to owners (shareholders) are not expenses. In other words, bottom-line net income is before any distributions to owners. Despite the importance of distributions from profit you can't tell from the income statement or the balance sheet the amount of cash dividends. You have to look in the statement of cash flows for this information (which I explain in Chapter 6).

Financing a Business: Sources of Cash and Capital

To run a business, you need financial backing, otherwise known as *capital*. In broad overview, a business raises capital needed for its assets by buying things on credit, waiting to pay some expenses, borrowing money, getting owners to invest money in the business, and making profit that is retained in the business. Borrowed money is known as *debt*; capital invested in the business by its owners and retained profits are the two sources of *owners' equity*.

How did the business whose balance sheet is shown in Figure 5-1 finance its assets? Its total assets are $14,850,000 at year-end 2013. The company's profit-making activities generated three liabilities — accounts payable, accrued expenses payable, and income tax payable — and in total these three liabilities provided $1,780,000 of the total assets of the business. Debt provided $6,250,000, and the two sources of owners' equity provided the other $6,820,000. All three sources add up to $14,850,000 million, which equals total assets, of course. Otherwise, its books would be out of balance, which is a definite no-no.

Accounts payable, accrued expenses payable, and income tax payable are short-term, non-interest-bearing liabilities that are sometimes called *spontaneous liabilities* because they arise directly from a business's expense activities — they aren't the result of borrowing money but rather are the result of buying things on credit or delaying payment of certain expenses.

It's hard to avoid these three liabilities in running a business; they are generated naturally in the process of carrying on operations. In contrast, the mix of debt (interest-bearing liabilities) and equity (invested owners' capital and retained earnings) requires careful thought and high-level decisions by a business. There's no natural or automatic answer to the debt-versus-equity question. The business in the example has a large amount of debt relative to its owners' equity, which would make many business owners uncomfortable.

Debt is both good and bad, and in extreme situations it can get very ugly. The advantages of debt are:

- Most businesses can't raise all the capital they need from owners' equity sources, and debt offers another source of capital (though, of course, many lenders are willing to provide only part of the capital that a business needs).

- Interest rates charged by lenders are lower than rates of return expected by owners. Owners expect a higher rate of return because they're taking a greater risk with their money — the business is not required to pay them back the same way that it's required to pay back a lender. For example, a business may pay 6 percent annual interest on its debt and be expected to earn a 12 percent annual rate of return on its owners' equity. (See Chapter 13 for more on earning profit for owners.)

The disadvantages of debt are:

- A business must pay the fixed rate of interest for the period even if it suffers a loss for the period or earns a lower rate of return on its assets.

- A business must be ready to pay back the debt on the specified due date, which can cause some pressure on the business to come up with the money on time. (Of course, a business may be able to *roll over* or renew its debt, meaning that it replaces its old debt with an equivalent amount of new debt, but the lender has the right to demand that the old debt be paid and not rolled over.)

Financial leverage: Taking a chance on debt

The large majority of businesses borrow money to provide part of the total capital needed for their assets. The main reason for debt is to close the gap between how much capital the owners can come up with and the amount the business needs. Lenders are willing to provide the capital because they have a senior claim on the assets of the business. Debt has to be paid back before the owners can get their money out of the business. A business's owners' equity provides a relatively permanent base of capital and gives its lenders a cushion of protection.

The owners use their capital invested in the business as the basis to borrow. For example, for every two bucks the owners have in the business, lenders may be willing to add another dollar (or even more). Using owners' equity as the basis for borrowing is referred to as *financial leverage,* because the equity base of the business can be viewed as the fulcrum, and borrowing is the lever for lifting the total capital of the business.

A business can realize a financial leverage gain by making more EBIT (earnings before interest and income tax) on the amount borrowed than the interest on the debt. On the flip side, using debt may not yield a financial leverage gain, but rather a financial leverage *loss.* Suppose EBIT equals zero for the year. Nevertheless, the business must pay the interest on its debt. So, the business would have a bottom-line loss for the year.

If a business defaults on its debt contract — it doesn't pay the interest on time or doesn't pay back the debt on the due date — it faces some major unpleasantness. In extreme cases, a lender can force it to shut down and liquidate its assets (that is, sell off everything it owns for cash) to pay off the debt and unpaid interest. Just as you can lose your home if you don't pay your home mortgage, a business can be forced into involuntary bankruptcy if it doesn't pay its debts. A lender may allow the business to try to work out its financial crisis through bankruptcy procedures, but bankruptcy is a nasty affair that invariably causes many problems and can really cripple a business.

Recognizing the Hodgepodge of Values Reported in a Balance Sheet

In my experience, the values reported for assets in a balance sheet can be a source of confusion for business managers and investors, who tend to put all dollar amounts on the same value basis. In their minds, a dollar is a dollar, whether it's in accounts receivable, inventory, property, plant and equipment, accounts payable, or retained earnings. But as a matter of fact, some dollars are much older than other dollars.

The dollar amounts reported in a balance sheet are the result of the transactions recorded in the assets, liabilities, and owners' equity accounts. (Hmm, where have you heard this before?) Some transactions from years ago may still have life in the present balances of certain assets. For example, the land owned by the business that is reported in its balance sheet goes back to the transaction for the purchase of the land, which could be 20 or 30 years ago. The balance in the land asset is standing in the same asset column, for example, as the balance in the accounts receivable asset, which likely is only 1 or 2 months old.

Book values are the amounts recorded in the accounting process and reported in financial statements. Do not assume that the book values reported in a balance sheet equal the current *market values.* Generally speaking, the amounts reported for cash, accounts receivable, and liabilities are equal to or are very close to their current market or settlement values. For example, accounts receivable will be turned into cash for the amount recorded on the balance sheet, and liabilities will be paid off at the amounts reported in the balance sheet. It's the book values of fixed assets, as well as any other assets in which the business invested some time ago that are likely lower than their current replacement values.

Also, keep in mind that a business may have "unrecorded" assets. These off balance sheet assets include such things as a well-known reputation for quality products and excellent service, secret formulas (think Coca-Cola here), patents that are the result of its research and development over the years, and a better trained workforce than its competitors. These are intangible assets that the business did not purchase from outside sources, but rather accumulated over the years through its own efforts. These assets, though not reported in the balance sheet, should show up in better than average profit performance in its income statement.

The current replacement values of a company's fixed assets may be quite a bit higher than the recorded costs of these assets, in particular for buildings, land, heavy machinery, and equipment. For example, the aircraft fleet of United Airlines, as reported in its balance sheet, is hundreds of millions of dollars less than the current cost it would have to pay to replace the planes. Complicating matters is the fact that many of its older planes are not being produced any more, and United would replace the older planes with newer models.

Businesses are not permitted to write up the book values of their assets to current market or replacement values. (Well, investments in marketable securities held for sale or available for sale have to be written up, or down, but this is an exception to the general rule.) Although recording current market values may have intuitive appeal, a market-to-market valuation model is not practical or appropriate for businesses that sell products and services. These businesses do not stand ready to sell their assets (other than inventory); they need their assets for operating the business into the future. At the end of their useful lives, assets are sold for their disposable values (or traded in for new assets).

Don't think that the market value of a business is simply equal to its owners' equity reported in its most recent balance sheet. Putting a value on a business depends on several factors in addition to the latest balance sheet of the business. My son, Tage, and I discuss business valuation in our book *Small Business Financial Management Kit For Dummies* (John Wiley & Sons).

Chapter 6

Reporting Cash Flows and Changes in Stockholders' Equity

. . . .

In This Chapter

▶ Presenting the statement of cash flows in two flavors

▶ Earning profit versus generating cash flow from profit

▶ Reading lines and between the lines in the statement of cash flows

▶ Offering advice and observations on cash flow

▶ Summarizing changes in stockholders' equity in a statement

. . . .

*T*his chapter explains the third primary financial statement reported by businesses — the *statement of cash flows*. (The other two are the *income statement* and the *balance sheet*, which I explain in Chapters 4 and 5.) This financial statement explains why cash flow from profit differs from bottom-line profit, and summarizes the investing and financing activities of the business during the period.

It may appear that this is an odd mix to put into one financial statement, but it actually makes sense. Earning profit (net income) generates net cash inflow (at least it should). Making profit is a primary source of cash to a business. The investing and financing transactions of a business hinge on its cash flow from profit. All sources and uses of cash hang together and should be managed in an integrated manner.

The chapter concludes with a brief — and I mean very brief — explanation of the *statement of changes in stockholders' equity*. This is not a "full size" financial statement. In fact, it's not really a financial statement at all. It's a schedule of changes during the period in a company's various stockholders' equity components. When a business has a complicated ownership structure this summary is helpful to sort out what happened to its owners' equity during the period. It pulls together all the changes in one place.

Meeting the Statement of Cash Flows

The income statement (Chapter 4) has a natural structure:

Revenue – Expenses = Profit (Net Income)

So does the balance sheet (Chapter 5):

Assets = Liabilities + Owners' Equity

The statement of cash flows does not have an obvious natural structure. So, the accounting rule-making body had to decide on the basic format for the statement. They settled on the following structure:

± Cash Flow From Operating Activities
± Cash Flow From Investing Activities
± Cash Flow From Financing Activities
= Cash Increase or Decrease During Period
+ Beginning Cash Balance
= Ending Cash Balance

The ± signs mean that the cash flow could be positive or negative. Generally the cash flow from investing activities of product businesses is negative, which means that the business spent more on new investments in long-term assets than cash received from disposals of previous investments. And, generally the cash flow from operating activities (profit-making activities) should be positive, unless the business suffered a big loss for the period that drained cash out of the business.

The three-fold classification of activities (transactions) reported in the statement of cash flows — operating, investing, and financing — are the same ones I introduce in Chapter 5, in which I explain the balance sheet. In Chapter 5, Figure 5-2 summarizes these transactions for the product company example that I continue in this chapter. It would help to read Chapter 5 before this chapter, but this chapter has all the information you need to understand the statement of cash flows.

In the example the business's cash balance decreases $110,000 during the year. You see this decrease in the company's balance sheets for the years ended December 31, 2012 and 2013 (see Figure 5-1). The business started the year with $2,275,000 cash and ended the year with $2,165,000. What does the balance sheet, by itself, tell you about the reasons for the cash decrease? The two-year comparative balance sheet provides some clues about the reasons for the cash decrease. However, answering such a question is not the purpose of a balance sheet.

Presenting the direct method

The statement of cash flows begins with the cash from making profit, or *cash flow from operating activities*, as accountants call it. *Operating activities* is the term that accountants have adopted for sales and expenses, which are the "operations" that a business carries out to earn profit. Furthermore, the term *operating activities* also includes the transactions that are coupled with sales and expenses. For example, making a sale on credit is an operating activity, and so is collecting the cash from the customer that takes place at a later time. Recording sales and expenses can be thought of as primary operating activities because they affect profit. Their associated transactions are secondary operating activities because they don't affect profit. But they affect cash flow, which I explain in this chapter.

Figure 6-1 presents the statement of cash flows for the product business example I introduce in Chapters 4 and 5. What you see in the first section of the statement of cash flows is called the *direct method* for reporting cash flow from operating activities. The dollar amounts are the cash flows connected with sales and expenses. For example, the business collected $25,550,000 from customers during the year, which is the direct result of making sales. The company paid $15,025,000 for the products it sells, some of which was to increase its inventory of products awaiting sale next period.

Note: Because I use the same business example in this chapter that I use in Chapters 4 and 5, you may want to take a moment to review the 2013 income statement in Figure 4-1. And you may want to review Figure 5-2, which summarizes how the three types of activities changed its assets, liabilities, and owners' equity accounts during the year 2013. (Go ahead, I'll wait.)

The basic idea of the direct method is to present the sales revenue and expenses of the business on a *cash basis*, in contrast to the amounts reported in the income statement that are on the *accrual basis* for recording revenue and expenses. Rather than explain again in detail the accrual basis, I'll just remind you that accountants record sales on credit when the sales take place even though cash is not collected from customers until sometime later. And, cash payments for expenses occur before or after the expenses are recorded. (For more information review Chapter 4.)

The cash flows you see in Figure 6-1 for revenue and expenses differ from the amounts you see in the income statement (see Figure 4-1). Herein lies a problem with the direct method. If you, a conscientious reader of the financial statements of a business, compare the revenues and expenses reported in the income statement with the cash flow amounts reported in the statement of cash flows, you might get somewhat confused. Which set of numbers is the correct one? Well, both are. The numbers in the income statement are the "true" numbers for measuring profit for the period. The numbers in the statement of cash flows are additional information for you to ponder.

Typical Product Business, Inc.
Statement of Cash Flows
for Year Ended December 31, 2013
(Dollar amounts in thousands)

Cash Flows From Operating Activities

Collections from sales		$25,550
Payments for products	($15,025)	
Payments for selling, general, and administrative costs	($7,750)	
Payments for interest on debt	($375)	
Payments on income tax	($885)	($24,035)
Cash Flow From Operating Activities		$1,515

Cash Flows From Investing Activities

Expenditures on Property, Plant & Equipment	($1,275)

Cash Flows From Financing Activities

Short-term Debt Increase	$100	
Long-term Debt Increase	$150	
Capital Stock Issue	$150	
Dividends Paid Stockholders	($750)	($350)
Decrease In Cash During Year		($110)
Beginning Cash Balance		$2,275
Ending Cash Balance		$2,165

Figure 6-1:
The statement of cash flows, showing the *direct method* for presenting cash flow from operating activities.

Notice in Figure 6-1 that cash flow from operating activities for the year is $1,515,000, which is less than the company's $1,690,000 net income for the year (refer to Figure 4-1). The accounting rule-making board thought that financial report readers would want some sort of explanation for the difference between these two important financial numbers. Therefore, the board decreed that a statement of cash flows that uses the direct method of reporting cash flow from operating liabilities should also include a reconciliation schedule that explains the difference between cash flow from operating activities and net income. Whoa! This is a lot to read.

Opting for the indirect method

Having to read both the operating activities section of the cash flow statement and a supplemental schedule gets to be rather demanding for financial statement readers. Accordingly, the accounting rule-making body decided to permit an alternative method for reporting cash flow from operating activities. The alternative method starts with net income, and then makes adjustments in order to reconcile cash flow from operating activities with net income. This alternative method is called the *indirect method,* which I show in Figure 6-2. The rest of the cash flow statement is not affected by which method is selected for reporting cash flow from operating activities. Compare the investing and financing activities in Figures 6-1 and 6-2; they are the same.

 By the way, the adjustments to net income in the indirect method for reporting cash flow from operating activities (see Figure 6-2) constitute the supplemental schedule of changes in assets and liabilities that has to be included under the direct method. So, the indirect method kills two birds with one stone as it were: net income is adjusted to the cash flow basis, and the changes in assets and liabilities affecting cash flow are included in the statement. So, it should be no surprise to you that the vast majority of businesses use the indirect method.

Typical Product Business, Inc.
Statement of Cash Flows
for Year Ended December 31, 2013
(Dollar amounts in thousands)

Cash Flows From Operating Activities

Net Income		$1,690
Adjustments to Net Income For Determining Cash Flow:		
Accounts Receivable Increase	($450)	
Inventory Increase	($725)	
Prepaid Expenses Increase	($75)	
Depreciation Expense	$775	
Accounts Payable Increase	$125	
Accrued Expenses Increase	$150	
Income Tax Payable Increase	$25	($175)
Cash Flow From Operating Activities		$1,515

Cash Flows From Investing Activities

Expenditures on Property, Plant & Equipment	($1,275)

Cash Flows From Financing Activities

Short-term Debt Increase	$100	
Long-term Debt Increase	$150	
Capital Stock Issue	$150	
Dividends Paid Stockholders	($750)	($350)
Decrease In Cash During Year		($110)
Beginning Cash Balance		$2,275
Ending Cash Balance		$2,165

Figure 6-2: The statement of cash flows, showing the *indirect method* for presenting cash flow from operating activities.

The indirect method for reporting cash flow from operating activities focuses on the *changes* during the year in the assets and liabilities that are directly associated with sales and expenses. I explain these connections between revenue and expenses and their corresponding assets and liabilities in Chapter 4. (You can trace the amounts of these changes back to Figure 5-1, which includes the start-of-year and end-of-year balances of the balance sheet accounts for the business example.)

Both the direct method and the indirect method report the same cash flow from operating activities for the period. Almost always this important financial metric for a business differs from the amount of its bottom-line profit, or net income for the same period. Why? Read on.

Dissecting the Divergence Between Cash Flow and Net Income

A positive cash flow from operating activities is the amount of cash generated by a business's profit-making operations during the year, and does not include any other sources of cash during the year. Cash flow from operating activities depends on a business's ability to turn profit into available cash — cash in the bank that can be used for the needs of the business. As you see in Figure 6-1 or Figure 6-2 (take your pick), the business in our example generated $1,515,000 cash from its profit-making activities in the year. As they say in New York, "That isn't chopped liver."

The business in our example experienced a strong growth year. Its accounts receivable and inventory increased by relatively large amounts. In fact, all its assets and liabilities intimately connected with sales and expenses increased; their ending balances are larger than their beginning balances (which are the amounts carried forward from the end of the preceding year). Of course, this may not always be the case in a growth situation; one or more assets and liabilities could decrease during the year. For flat, no-growth situations, it's likely that there will be a mix of modest-sized increases and decreases.

The following sections explain how the asset and liability changes affect cash flow from operating activities. As a business manager, you should keep a close watch on the changes in each of your assets and liabilities and understand the cash flow effects caused by these changes. Investors and lenders should focus on the business's ability to generate a healthy cash flow from operating activities, so they should be equally concerned about these changes. In some situations these changes can signal serious problems!

I realize that you may not be too interested in the details that I discuss in the following sections. With this in mind, at the start of each section I present the punch line. If you wish, you can just read this and move on. But the details are fascinating (well, at least to accountants).

Note: Instead of using the full phrase "cash flow from operating activities" every time, I use the shorter term "cash flow" in the following sections. All data for assets and liabilities are found in the two-year comparative balance sheet of the business (see Figure 5-1).

Accounts receivable change

Punch Line: An increase in accounts receivable hurts cash flow; a decrease helps cash flow.

The accounts receivable asset shows how much money customers who bought products on credit still owe the business; this asset is a promise of cash that the business will receive. Basically, accounts receivable is the amount of uncollected sales revenue at the end of the period. Cash does not increase until the business collects money from its customers.

The business started the year with $2.15 million and ended the year with $2.6 million in accounts receivable. The beginning balance was collected during the year, but the ending balance had not been collected at the end of the year. Thus the *net* effect is a shortfall in cash inflow of $450,000. The key point is that you need to keep an eye on the increase or decrease in accounts receivable from the beginning of the period to the end of the period. Here's what to look for:

- ✔ If the amount of credit sales you made during the period is greater than what you collected from customers during the period, your accounts receivable *increased* over the period, and you need to *subtract* from net income that difference between start-of-period accounts receivable and end-of-period accounts receivable. In short, an increase in accounts receivable hurts cash flow by the amount of the increase.

- ✔ If the amount you collected from customers during the period is greater than the credit sales you made during the period, your accounts receivable *decreased* over the period, and you need to *add* to net income that difference between start-of-period accounts receivable and end-of-period accounts receivable. In short, a decrease in accounts receivable helps cash flow by the amount of the decrease.

In our business example, accounts receivable increased $450,000. Cash collections from sales were $450,000 less than sales revenue. Ouch! The business increased its sales substantially over the last period, so its accounts receivable increased. When credit sales increase a company's accounts receivable generally increases about the same percent, as it did in this example. (If the business takes longer to collect its credit sales then its accounts receivable would increase even more than can be attributable to the sales increase.) In this example the higher sales revenue was good for profit but bad for cash flow.

The "lagging behind" effect of cash flow is the price of growth — business managers, lenders, and investors need to understand this point. Increasing sales without increasing accounts receivable is a happy situation for cash flow, but in the real world you usually can't have one increase without the other.

Inventory change

Punch Line: An increase in inventory hurts cash flow; a decrease helps cash flow.

Inventory is usually the largest short-term, or *current,* asset of businesses that sell products. If the inventory account is greater at the end of the period than at the start of the period — because unit costs increased or because the quantity of products increased — the amount the business actually paid out in cash for inventory purchases (or for manufacturing products) is more than what the business recorded in the cost of goods sold expense for the period.

In our business example, inventory increased $725,000 from start-of-year to end-of-year. In other words, to support its higher sales levels in 2013, this business replaced the products that it sold during the year *and* increased its inventory by $725,000. The business had to come up with the cash to pay for this inventory increase. Basically, the business wrote checks amounting to $725,000 more than its cost of goods sold expense for the period. This step-up in its inventory level was necessary to support the higher sales level, which increased profit even though cash flow took a hit.

Prepaid expenses change

Punch Line: An increase in prepaid expenses (an asset account) hurts cash flow; a decrease helps cash flow.

A change in the prepaid expenses asset account works the same way as a change in inventory and accounts receivable, although changes in prepaid expenses are usually much smaller than changes in the other two asset accounts.

The beginning balance of prepaid expenses is charged to expense this year, but the cash of this amount was actually paid out last year. This period (the year 2013 in our example), the business paid cash for next period's prepaid expenses, which affects this period's cash flow but doesn't affect net income until next period. In short, the $75,000 increase in prepaid expenses in this business example has a negative cash flow effect.

As it grows, a business needs to increase its prepaid expenses for such things as fire insurance (premiums have to be paid in advance of the insurance coverage) and its stocks of office and data processing supplies. Increases in accounts receivable, inventory, and prepaid expenses are the cash flow price a business has to pay for growth. Rarely do you find a business that can increase its sales revenue without increasing these assets.

Depreciation: Real, but noncash expense

Punch Line: Recording depreciation expense decreases the book value of long-term operating (fixed) assets. There is no cash outlay when recording depreciation expense. Each year the business converts part of the total cost invested in its fixed assets into cash. It recovers this amount through cash collections from sales. The cash inflow from sales revenue "reimburses" the business for the use of its long-term operating assets as they gradually wear out over time.

The amount of depreciation expense recorded in the period is a portion of the original cost of the business's fixed assets, most of which were bought and paid for years ago. (Chapters 4 and 5 explain more about depreciation.) Because the depreciation expense is not a cash outlay this period, the amount is added to net income to determine cash flow from operating activities (see Figure 6-2).

For measuring profit, depreciation is definitely an expense — no doubt about it. Buildings, machinery, equipment, tools, vehicles, computers, and office furniture are all on an irreversible journey to the junk heap (although buildings usually take a long time to get there). Fixed assets (except for land) have a limited, finite life of usefulness to a business; depreciation is the accounting method that allocates the total cost of fixed assets to each year of their use in helping the business generate sales revenue.

In our example, the business recorded $775,000 depreciation expense for the year. Instead of looking at depreciation as only an expense, consider the investment-recovery cycle of fixed assets. A business invests money in its fixed assets that are then used for several or many years. Over the life of a fixed asset, a business has to recover through sales revenue the cost invested in the fixed asset (ignoring any salvage value at the end of its useful life). In a real sense, a business "sells" some of its fixed assets each period to its customers — it factors the cost of fixed assets into the sales prices that it charges its customers.

For example, when you go to a supermarket, a very small slice of the price you pay for that quart of milk goes toward the cost of the building, the shelves, the refrigeration equipment, and so on. (No wonder they charge so much!) Each period, a business recoups part of the cost invested in its fixed assets. In the example, $775,000 of sales revenue went toward reimbursing the business for the use of its fixed assets during the year.

The business in our example does not own any intangible assets and, thus, does not record any amortization expense. (See Chapter 5 for an explanation of intangible assets and amortization.) If a business does own intangible assets, the amortization expense on these assets for the year is treated the same as depreciation is treated in the statement of cash flows. In other words, the recording of amortization expense does not require cash outlay in the year being charged with the expense. The cash outlay occurred in prior periods when the business invested in intangible assets.

Changes in operating liabilities

Punch Line: An increase in a short-term operating liability helps cash flow; a decrease hurts cash flow.

The business in our example, like almost all businesses, has three basic liabilities inextricably intertwined with its expenses:

- ✔ Accounts payable
- ✔ Accrued expenses payable
- ✔ Income tax payable

When the beginning balance of one of these liability accounts is the same as its ending balance (not too likely, of course), the business breaks even on cash flow for that liability. When the end-of-period balance is higher than the start-of-period balance, the business did not pay out as much money as was recorded as an expense in the year.

In our business example, the business disbursed $640,000 to pay off last year's accounts payable balance. (This $640,000 was the accounts payable balance at December 31, 2012, the end of the previous fiscal year.) Its cash this year decreased $640,000 because of these payments. But this year's ending balance sheet (at December 31, 2013) shows accounts payable of $765,000 that the business will not pay until the following year. This $765,000 amount was recorded to expense in the year 2013. So, the amount of expense was $125,000 more than the cash outlay for the year; or, in reverse, the cash outlay was $125,000 less than the expense. An increase in accounts payable benefits cash flow for the year. In other words, an increase in accounts payable has a positive cash flow effect (until the liability is paid later). An increase in accrued expenses payable or income tax payable works the same way.

In short, liability increases are favorable to cash flow — in a sense, the business ran up more on credit than it paid off. Such an increase means that the business delayed paying cash for certain things until next year. So you need to add the increases in the three liabilities to net income to determine cash flow, as you see in the statement of cash flows (refer to Figure 6-2). The business avoided cash outlays to the extent of the increases in these three liabilities. In some cases, of course, the ending balance of an operating liability may be lower than its beginning balance, which means that the business paid out more cash than the corresponding expenses for the period. In this case, the decrease is a negative cash flow factor.

Putting the cash flow pieces together

Taking into account all the adjustments to net income, the company's cash balance increased $1,515,000 from its operating activities during the course of the year. The operating activities section in the statement of cash flows (refer to Figure 6-2) shows the stepping-stones from net income to the amount of cash flow from operating activities.

Recall that the business experienced sales growth during this period. The downside of sales growth is that assets and liabilities also grow — the business needs more inventory at the higher sales level and also has higher accounts receivable. The business's prepaid expenses and liabilities also increased, although not nearly as much as accounts receivable and inventory. Still, the business had $1,515,000 cash at its disposal. What did the business do with this $1,515,000 of available cash? You have to look to the remainder of the cash flow statement to answer this very important question.

Sailing Through the Rest of the Statement of Cash Flows

After you get past the first section of the statement of cash flows, the remainder is a breeze. Well, to be fair, you *could* encounter some rough seas in the remaining two sections. But generally speaking, the information in these sections is not too difficult to understand. The last two sections of the statement report on the other sources of cash to the business and the uses the business made of its cash during the year.

Investing activities

The second section of the statement of cash flows (see Figure 6-1 or 6-2) reports the investment actions that a business's managers took during the year. Investments are like tea leaves, which serve as indicators regarding what the future may hold for the company. Major new investments are the sure signs of expanding or modernizing the production and distribution facilities and capacity of the business. Major disposals of long-term assets and shedding off a major part of the business could be good news or bad news for the business, depending on many factors. Different investors may interpret this information differently, but all would agree that the information in this section of the cash flow statement is very important.

Certain long-lived operating assets are required for doing business. For example, Federal Express and UPS wouldn't be terribly successful if they didn't have airplanes and trucks for delivering packages and computers for tracking deliveries. When these assets wear out, the business needs to replace them. Also, to remain competitive, a business may need to upgrade its equipment to take advantage of the latest technology or to provide for growth. These investments in long-lived, tangible, productive assets, which are called *fixed assets* for short, are critical to the future of the business. In fact, these cash outlays are called *capital expenditures* to stress that capital is being invested for the long haul.

One of the first claims on cash flow from operating activities is for capital expenditures. Notice that the business spent $1,275,000 on fixed assets, which are referred to more formally as *property, plant, and equipment* in the cash flow statement (to keep the terminology consistent with account titles used in the balance sheet — the term *fixed assets* is rather informal).

A typical statement of cash flows doesn't go into much detail regarding exactly what specific types of fixed assets the business purchased (or constructed): how many additional square feet of space the business acquired, how many new drill presses it bought, and so on. Some businesses do leave a clearer trail of their investments, though. For example, in the footnotes or elsewhere in their financial reports, airlines generally describe how many new aircraft of each kind were purchased to replace old equipment or to expand their fleets.

Usually, a business disposes of some of its fixed assets every year because they reached the end of their useful lives and will no longer be used. These fixed assets are sent to the junkyard, traded in on new fixed assets, or sold for relatively small amounts of money. The value of a fixed asset at the end of its useful life is called its *salvage value*. The disposal proceeds from selling fixed assets are reported as a source of cash in the investing activities section of the statement of cash flows. Usually, these amounts are fairly small. Also, a business may sell off fixed assets because it's downsizing or abandoning a major segment of its business; these cash proceeds can be fairly large.

Financing activities

Note in the annual statement of cash flows for the business example (refer to Figure 6-1 or 6-2) that cash flow from operating activities is a positive $1,515,000 and the negative cash flow from investing activities is $1,275,000. The result to this point, therefore, is a net cash increase of $240,000, which would have increased the company's cash balance this much if the business had no financing activities during the year. However, the business increased its short-term and long-term debt during the year, its owners invested additional money in the business, and it distributed some of its profit to stockholders. The third section of the cash flow statement summarizes these *financing activities* of the business over the period.

The managers did not have to go outside the business for the $1,515,000 cash increase generated from its operating activities for the year. Cash flow from operating activities is an *internal* source of money generated by the business itself, in contrast to *external* money that the business raises from lenders and owners. A business does not have to go hat in hand for external money when its internal cash flow is sufficient to provide for its growth. Making profit is the cash flow spigot that should always be turned on.

I should mention that a business that earns a profit could, nevertheless, have a *negative* cash flow from operating activities — meaning that despite posting a net income for the period, the changes in the company's assets and liabilities cause its cash balance to decrease. In reverse, a business could report a bottom-line *loss* for the year, yet it could have a *positive* cash flow from its operating activities. The cash recovery from depreciation plus the cash benefits from decreases in its accounts receivable and inventory could be more than the amount of loss. More realistically, a loss usually leads to negative cash flow, or very little positive cash flow.

The term *financing* refers to a business raising capital from debt and equity sources — by borrowing money from banks and other sources willing to loan money to the business and by its owners putting additional money in the business. The term also includes the flip side — that is, making payments on debt and returning capital to owners. The term *financing* also includes cash distributions by the business from profit to its owners. By the way, keep in mind that interest on debt is an expense that is reported in the income statement.

Most businesses borrow money for the short term (generally defined as less than one year), as well as for longer terms (generally defined as more than one year). In other words, a typical business has both short-term and long-term debt. (Chapter 5 explains that short-term debt is presented in the current liabilities section of the balance sheet.)

The business in our example has both short-term and long-term debt. Although this is not a hard-and-fast rule, most cash flow statements report just the *net* increase or decrease in short-term debt, not the total amounts borrowed and total payments on short-term debt during the period. In contrast, both the total amounts of borrowing from and repayments on long-term debt during the year are generally reported in the statement of cash flows — the numbers are reported gross, instead of net.

In our example, no long-term debt was paid down during the year, but short-term debt was paid off during the year and replaced with new short-term notes payable. However, only the $100,000 net increase is reported in the cash flow statement. The business also increased its long-term debt $150,000 (refer to Figure 6-1 or 6-2).

The financing section of the cash flow statement also reports the flow of cash between the business and its owners (stockholders of a corporation). Owners can be both a *source* of a business's cash (capital invested by owners) and a *use* of a business's cash (profit distributed to owners). The financing activities section of the cash flow statement reports additional capital raised from its owners, if any, as well as any capital returned to the owners. In the cash flow statement, note that the business issued additional stock shares for $150,000 during the year, and it paid a total of $750,000 cash dividends from profit to its owners.

Be an Active Reader

As a business lender or investor your job is to ask questions (at least in your own mind) when reading a financial statement. You should be an active reader, not a ho-hum passive reader, in reading the statement of cash flows. You should mull over certain questions to get full value out of the statement.

The statement of cash flows reveals what financial decisions the business's managers made during the period. Of course, management decisions are always subject to second-guessing and criticizing, and passing judgment based on reading a financial statement isn't totally fair because it doesn't capture the pressures the managers faced during the period. Maybe they made the best possible decisions in the circumstances. Then again, maybe not.

One issue, in my mind, comes to the forefront when reading the company's statement of cash flows. The business in our example (see Figure 6-1 or 6-2) distributed $750,000 cash from profit to its owners — a 44 percent *payout ratio* (which equals the $750,000 distribution divided by its $1,690,000 net income). In analyzing whether the payout ratio is too high, too low, or just about right, you need to look at the broader context of the business's sources of and needs for cash.

The company's $1,515,000 cash flow from operating activities is enough to cover the business's $1,275,000 capital expenditures during the year and still leave $240,000 available. The business increased its total debt $250,000. Combined, these two cash sources provided $490,000 to the business. The owners also kicked in another $150,000 during the year, for a grand total of $640,000. Its cash balance did not increase this amount because the business paid out $750,000 dividends from profit to its stockholders. So, its cash balance dropped $110,000.

If I were on the board of directors of this business, I certainly would ask the chief executive why cash dividends to shareowners were not limited to $240,000 in order to avoid the increase in debt and to avert having shareowners invest additional money in the business. I would probably ask the chief executive to justify the amount of capital expenditures as well. Being an old auditor, I tend to ask tough questions and raise sensitive issues.

Recognize Shortcomings of the Depreciation Add-back Shortcut

Rather than wading through all the lines in the operating activities section of the cash flow statement (see Figure 6-2 for example), financial report readers may be tempted to take a shortcut. They simply add depreciation (and amortization, if any) to net income and call this cash flow from profit. By adding back depreciation expense to bottom-line profit you get a first cut at determining cash flow from profit. But this shortcut ignores the other factors that affect cash flow from profit, and I don't recommend it. I have to admit, however, that this shortcut is better than nothing. Deprecation is often the largest adjustment to net income to get to cash flow. Nevertheless, the other items (changes in accounts receivable, inventory, and so on) can have major effects on cash flow and should not be overlooked.

Some small and privately owned businesses do not report a statement of cash flows — though according to current financial reporting standards that apply to all businesses they should. I've seen several small privately owned businesses that don't go to the trouble of preparing this financial statement. Perhaps someday accounting standards for private and smaller businesses will waive the requirement for the cash flow statement. (I discuss developments of accounting standards for larger public versus smaller private companies in Chapter 2.) Without a cash flow statement the reader of the financial report could add back depreciation to net income to get a starting point. From there on it gets more challenging to determine cash flow from profit. Adding depreciation to net income is no more than a first step in determining cash flow from profit.

Pinning Down "Free Cash Flow"

A term has emerged in the lexicon of finance: *free cash flow*. This piece of language is not — I repeat, *not* — an officially defined term by any authoritative accounting or financial institution rule-making body. Furthermore, the term does *not* appear in cash flow statements reported by businesses. Rather, *free cash flow* is street language, and the term appears in *The Wall Street Journal* and *The New York Times*. Securities brokers and investment analysts use the term freely (pun intended). Unfortunately, the term *free cash flow* hasn't settled down into one universal meaning, although most usages of the term have something to do with cash flow from operating activities.

The term *free cash flow* has been used to mean the following:

✔ Net income plus depreciation expense, plus any other expense recorded during the period that does not involve the outlay of cash — such as amortization of costs of the intangible assets of a business, and other asset write-downs that don't require cash outlay

✔ Cash flow from operating activities as reported in the statement of cash flows, although the very use of a different term (*free cash flow*) suggests that a different meaning is intended

✔ Cash flow from operating activities minus the amount spent on capital expenditures during the year (purchases or construction of property, plant, and equipment)

✔ Earnings before interest, tax, depreciation, and amortization (EBITDA) — although this definition ignores the cash flow effects of changes in the short-term assets and liabilities directly involved in sales and expenses, and it obviously ignores that interest and income tax expenses in large part are paid in cash during the period

In the strongest possible terms, I advise you to be very clear on which definition of *free cash flow* a speaker or writer is using. Unfortunately, you can't always determine what the term means even in context. Be careful out there.

One definition of free cash flow, in my view, is quite useful: cash flow from operating activities minus capital expenditures for the year. The idea is that a business needs to make capital expenditures in order to stay in business and thrive. And to make capital expenditures, the business needs cash. Only after paying for its capital expenditures does a business have "free" cash flow that it can use as it likes. In the example in this chapter, the free cash flow according to "Tracy's" (that's me!) definition is:

$1,515,000 cash flow from operating activities – $1,275,000
capital expenditures = $240,000 free cash flow

In many cases, cash flow from operating activities falls short of the money needed for capital expenditures. To close the gap a business has to borrow more money, persuade its owners to invest more money in the business, or dip into its cash reserve. Should a business in this situation distribute any of its profit to owners? After all, it has a cash *deficit* after paying for capital expenditures. But, in fact, many businesses make cash distributions from profit to their owners even when they don't have any free cash flow (as I just defined it).

The Cash Flow Statement in the Real World: A Good Idea Gone Awry?

Being an elder statesman in accounting (at least that's how I like to imagine myself), I remember the days before the cash flow statement was required to be included in financial reports of businesses. (Those were the days, but that's another story.) There was constant urging to require a summary of cash flows in financial reports. Finally in 1974 the cash flow statement was made mandatory. Most financial report users, in my view, thought that this new financial statement would be quite useful and should open the door for deeper insights into the business. However, over the years I have seen serious problems develop in the actual reporting of cash flows.

Would you like to hazard a guess regarding the average number of lines in the cash flow statements of publicly owned corporations? Typically, their cash flow statements have 30 to 40 or more lines of information by my reckoning. So it takes quite a while to read the cash flow statement — more time than the average reader probably has available. Each line of information in a financial statement should be a truly useful piece of information. Too many lines baffle the reader rather than clarify the overall cash flows of the business. In reading many statements of cash flows over the years, I have to question why companies overload this financial statement with so much technical information. One could even suspect that many businesses deliberately obscure their statements of cash flows.

Also, I must say that you don't hear a lot of feedback on the cash flow statement from principal external users of financial reports, such as business lenders and investors. I wonder how financial-report users would react if the cash flow statement were accidently omitted from a company's annual financial report. How many would notice the missing financial statement and complain? The SEC and other regulators would take action, of course. But in my view few readers would even notice the omission. In contrast, if a business failed to include an income statement or balance sheet, it would hear from its lenders and owners, that's for sure.

Looking Quickly at the Statement of Changes in Stockholders Equity

Larger businesses generally have more complicated ownership structures than smaller- and medium-size companies. Larger businesses are most often organized as a corporation in contrast to other forms of legal structures. (I discuss the legal organization of business in Chapter 8.) Corporations can issue more than one class of stock shares, and many do. One class may have preferences over the other class, and thus are called *preferred stock*. A corporation may have both voting and non-voting stock shares. Also, business corporations, believe it or not, can engage in cannibalization; they buy their own stock shares, somewhat like eating your own offspring. A corporation may not cancel the shares it has purchased. Shares of itself that are held by the business are called *treasury stock*.

Well, I could go on and on. But the main point is that many businesses, especially larger public companies, engage in a broad range of activities during the year involving changes in their owners' equity components. These owners' equity activities tend to get lost from view in a comparative balance sheet and in the statement of cash flows. Yet the activities can be very important. Therefore, the business prepares a separate statement of changes in stockholders' equity covering the same periods as its income statements.

Here's another point: The statement of changes in stockholders' equity is where you find certain technical gains and losses that increase or decrease owners' equity but that are *not* reported in the income statement. You have to read this summary of changes in the owners' equity accounts to find out whether the business had any such gains or losses. Look in a column headed *comprehensive income* for these gains and losses, which I warn you in advance are very technical.

The general format of the statement of changes in stockholders' equity includes columns for each class of stock, treasury stock, retained earnings, and the comprehensive income element of owners' equity. Professional stock analysts have to pore over these statements. Average financial report readers probably quickly turn the page when they see this statement. But, it's worth a quick glance if nothing else.

I explain more about statement of changes in stockholders' equity in Chapter 12. At this early point in the book I simply want to alert you to the fact that many financial reports include a statement of changes in stockholders' equity in addition to their three primary financial statements. It's not really a full-fledged financial statement. Rather, it serves as a columnar footnote for the various owners' equity accounts in the balance sheet.

Chapter 7

Accounting Alternatives

· ·

· ·

*T*his chapter explains that when recording revenue, expenses, and other transactions of a business, the accountant generally must choose among different methods for capturing the economic reality of the transactions. You might think that accountants are in unified agreement on the exact ways for recording business transactions, but I must tell you that this isn't the case. An old joke is that when two economists get together there are three economic opinions. It's not that different in accounting.

The financial statements reported by a business are just one version of its financial history and performance. A different accountant for the business undoubtedly would have presented a different version. The income statement and balance sheet of a business depend on which particular accounting methods the accountant chooses. Moreover, on orders from management the financial statements could be tweaked to make them look better. I discuss how businesses can (and do!) put spin on their financial statements in Chapter 12.

It's one thing to be generally aware that financial statements depend on the choice of accounting methods used to prepare the statements. It's quite another to see the effects in action. In this chapter I present two opposing versions of the financial statements for a business. I explain the reasons for the differences in its revenue, expenses, assets, liabilities, and owners' equity. And, I explain the main accounting alternatives for two major expenses of businesses that sell products — cost of goods sold and depreciation.

Accounting for the economic activity of a business can be compared to judging a beauty contest. There might be agreement among the judges that all the contestants are goodlooking, but ranking the contestants is sure to vary from judge to judge. Beauty is in the eye of the beholder, as they say.

Setting the Stage

Let me get directly to the point. The dollar amounts reported in the financial statements of a business are not simply "facts" that depend only on good bookkeeping. Here's why different accountants record transactions differently. The accountant:

- ✔ Must make choices among different accounting methods for recording the amounts of revenue and expenses.

- ✔ Can select between pessimistic or optimistic estimates and forecasts when recording certain revenue and expenses.

- ✔ Has some wiggle room in implementing accounting methods, especially regarding the precise timing of when to record sales and expenses.

- ✔ Can carry out certain tactics at year-end to put a more favorable spin on the financial statements, usually under the orders or tacit approval of top management. I discuss these manipulations in Chapter 12 on getting the financial report ready for release.

The popular notion is that accounting is an exact science and that the amounts reported in the financial statements are true and accurate down to the last dollar. When people see an amount reported to the last digit in a financial statement, they naturally get the impression of exactitude and precision. However, in the real world of business the accountant has to make many arbitrary choices between alternative ways for recording revenue and expenses, and for recording changes in their corresponding assets and liabilities. (In Chapter 4 I explain that revenue and expenses are coupled with assets and liabilities.)

I don't discuss accounting errors in this chapter. It's always possible that the accountant doesn't fully understand the transaction being recorded, or relies on misleading information, with the result that the entry for the transaction is wrong. And, bookkeeping processing slip-ups happen. The term *error* generally refers to honest mistakes; there is no intention of manipulating the financial statements. Unfortunately, a business may not detect accounting mistakes, and therefore its financial statements end up being misleading to one degree or another. (I point out in Chapter 3 that a business should institute effective internal controls for preventing accounting errors.)

Taking Financial Statements with a Grain of Salt

Suppose that you have the opportunity and the ready cash to buy a going business. The business I have in mind is the very one I use as the example in the previous three chapters in which I explain the income statement (Chapter 4), the balance sheet (Chapter 5), and the statement of cash flows (Chapter 6). Of course, you should consider many factors in deciding your offering price. The company's most recent financial statements would be your main source of information in reaching a decision — not the *only* source, of course, but the most important source for financial information about the business.

I recommend that you employ an independent CPA who has a professional credential in business valuation. The CPA could also examine the company's recordkeeping and accounting system, to determine whether the accounts of the business are complete, accurate, and in conformity with the applicable accounting standards. The CPA should also test for possible fraud and any accounting shenanigans in the financial statements. As the potential buyer of the business you can't be too careful. You don't want the seller of the business to play you for a sucker.

Only one set of financial statements is included in a business's financial report: one income statement, one balance sheet, and one statement of cash flows. A business does not provide a second, alternative set of financial statements that would have been generated if the business had used different accounting methods and if the business had not tweaked its financial statements. The financial statements would have been different if alternative accounting methods had been used to record sales revenue and expenses and if the business had not engaged in certain end-of-period maneuvers to make its financial statements look better. (My late father-in-law, a successful businessman, called these tricks of the trade "fluffing the pillows.")

Taking an alternative look at the company's financial statements

Everyone that has a financial stake in a business should understand and keep in mind the bias or tilt of the financial statements they're reading. Using a baseball analogy, the version of financial statements in your hands may be in left field, right field, or center field. All versions are in the ballpark of general accounting standards, which define the playing field but don't dictate that every business has to play straight down the middle. In their financial reports, businesses don't comment on whether their financial statements as a whole are liberal, conservative, or somewhere in between. However, a business does have to disclose in the footnotes to its statements its major accounting methods. (See Chapter 12 that discusses getting a financial report ready for release.)

As the potential buyer of a business, you have to decide on what the business is worth. Generally speaking, the two most important factors are the profit performance of the business (reported in its income statement) and the composition of assets, liabilities, and owners' equity of the business (reported in its balance sheet). For instance, how much would you pay for a business that has never made a profit and whose liabilities are more than its assets? There's no simple formula for calculating the market value for a business based on its profit performance and financial condition. But, quite clearly, the profit performance and financial condition of a business are dominant factors in setting its market value.

Figure 7-1 presents a comparison that you never see in real-life financial reporting. The Actual column in Figure 7-1 presents the income statement and balance sheet reported by the business. The Alternative column reveals an income statement for the year and the balance sheet at year-end that the business could have reported (but didn't) if it had used alternative but acceptable accounting methods.

Assuming you read Chapters 4 and 5, the actual account balances in the income statement and balance sheet should be familiar — these are the same numbers from the financial statements I use in those chapters. The dollar amounts in the Alternative column are the amounts that would have been recorded using different accounting methods. We don't particularly need the statement of cash flows here, because cash flow from profit (operating activities) is the same amount under both accounting scenarios and the cash flows from investing and financing activities are the same.

The business in our example adopted accounting methods that maximized its recorded profit, which recognize profit as soon as possible. Some businesses go the opposite direction. They adopt conservative accounting methods for recording profit performance, and they wouldn't think of tinkering with their financial statements at the end of the year, even when their profit performance falls short of expectations and their financial condition has some trouble spots. The Alternative column in Figure 7-1 reports the results of conservative accounting methods that could have been used by the business (but were not). As you see in Figure 7-1 using the alternative accounting methods results in less favorable measures of profit and financial condition.

Typical Product Business, Inc.
(In thousands of dollars)

Two Income Statements for Year Ended December 31, 2013

	Actual	Alternative	Difference
Sales Revenue	$26,000	$25,775	($225)
Cost of Goods Sold Expense	$14,300	$14,580	($280)
Gross Margin	$11,700	$11,195	
Operating Expenses	$8,700	$8,830	($130)
Operating Earnings	$3,000	$2,365	
Interest Expense	$400	$400	$0
Earnings Before Income Tax	$2,600	$1,965	
Income Tax Expense	$910	$615	$295
Net Income	$1,690	$1,350	($340)

Two Balance Sheets at December 31, 2013

Assets	Actual	Alternative	Difference
Cash	$2,165	$2,165	$0
Accounts Receivable	$2,600	$2,255	($345)
Inventory	$3,450	$2,750	($700)
Prepaid Expenses	$600	$550	($50)
Current Assets	$8,815	$7,720	
Property Plant and Equipment	$12,450	$12,225	($225)
Accumulated Depreciation	$6,415	$7,435	($1,020)
Net of depreciation	$6,035	$4,790	
Total Assets	$14,850	$12,510	($2,340)

Liabilities and Owners' Equity			
Accounts Payable	$765	$765	$0
Accrued Expenses Payable	$900	$1,002	$102
Income Tax Payable	$115	$78	($37)
Short-term Notes Payable	$2,250	$2,250	$0
Current Liabilities	$4,030	$4,095	
Long-term Notes Payable	$2,000	$2,000	$0
Owners' Equity:			
Invested Capital	$3,250	$3,250	$0
Retained Earnings	$5,570	$3,165	($2,405)
Total owners' equity	$8,820	$6,415	
Total Liabilities and Owners' Equity	$14,850	$12,510	($2,340)

Figure 7-1:
Actual versus alternative income statement and balance sheet for a company.

Faking the financials

While preparing the alternative financial statements for the business example in this chapter, I was reminded how relatively easy it is to prepare fraudulent, made-to-order financial statements. You would "adjust" the recorded amounts in the revenue and expense accounts, and in the asset, liability, and retained earnings accounts to fit your purpose. Lest you ever think of doing this I must warn you that it's not quite as easy as it looks. Changing a revenue or expense account also involves changing an asset or liability account. You have to know which accounts go with which other accounts.

For example, say you want to make cost of goods sold expense lower. You could arbitrarily decrease the balance in this expense account. And you also have to increase the balance in the inventory account (or possibly some other asset account) and in the retained earnings account in order to keep the books in balance, so that total assets equal the total of liabilities and owners' equity. Being a financial statements fraudster requires some accounting savvy to make the fraud-based numbers plausible.

Now, you may very well ask, "Where in the devil did you get the numbers for the alternative financial statements?" The dollar amounts in the Alternative column are my best estimates of what conservative numbers would be for this business — a company that has been in business for several years, has made a profit most years, and has not gone through bankruptcy. Both the actual and the alternative financial statements are hypothetical but realistic and are not dishonest or deceitful. (See the sidebar "Faking the financials.")

Spotting significant differences

It's a little jarring to see a second set of numbers for the bedrock financial statements, such as the income statement and balance sheet. You're bound to raise your eyebrows when I say that both sets of accounting numbers are true and correct, yet different. Financial report users have been conditioned to accept one version for these two financial statements without thinking about what alternative financial statements would look like. Seeing an alternative scenario takes a little time to get used to, like learning how to drive on the left side of the road in Great Britain. There's always an alternative set of numbers lurking in the shadows, even though you don't get to see them.

The differences in revenue and expenses don't look that big, until you get to the bottom line. Net income is $340,000 lower in the alternative scenario, which is 20 percent smaller. Suppose that in putting a market value on the business, you use the earnings multiple method. (For more information on the valuation of a small business, see *Small Business Financial Management*

Kit For Dummies, which I coauthored with my son, Tage C. Tracy [John Wiley & Sons]). Suppose you are willing to pay six times the most recent annual profit of the business. (I certainly don't mean to suggest that six times earnings is a standard multiple for all small businesses.) Using the actual financial statements, you would offer $10.74 million for the business ($1.69 million net income × 6 = $10.14 million). If the alternative accounting methods was used, you would offer only $8.1 million ($1.35 million net income × 6 = $8.1 million). If the business had used the more conservative accounting methods, you would offer $2.04 million less for the business!

The balance sheet differences look more sizable, and they are. Accounts receivable and inventory are significantly lower in the alternative scenario. And, the book value of its fixed assets (original cost minus accumulated depreciation) is significantly smaller. In both scenarios the actual condition and usability of its fixed assets (space in its buildings, output of its machinery and equipment, future miles of its trucks, and so on) are the same. In the alternative scenario these key assets of the business just have a much lower reported value.

And I'm sure you noticed that the company's retained earnings balance is $2,405,000 lower in the alternative scenario. Its retained earnings balance is 43 percent smaller! This much less profit would have been recorded over the years if the business had used the alternative accounting methods. Keep in mind that it took all the years of its existence to accumulate the $2,405,000 difference. The net income difference for its latest year (2013) is responsible for only $340,000 of the cumulative, total difference in retained earnings.

Explaining the Differences

In the following discussion you need to refer to the Differences column in Figure 7-1. We start by checking the $2,405,000 difference in *retained earnings*. Recall that profit is recorded in this owners' equity account. Because retained earnings is $2,405,000 lower, the cumulative profit of the business would be $2,405,000 lower if it had used the conservative accounting methods.

Remember the following about revenue and expenses:

✔ Recording sales revenue increases an asset (or decreases a liability in some cases).

✔ Recording an expense decreases an asset or increases a liability.

Therefore, assets are lower and/or liabilities are higher having used the alternative accounting methods, and collectively these differences should equal the difference in retained earnings. In Figure 7-1 total assets are $2,340,000 lower in the alternative scenario. And liabilities are $65,000 higher ($102,000 higher Accrued Expenses Payable minus the $37,000 lower amount of Income Tax Payable = $65,000 higher liabilities). Therefore, the difference in retained earnings checks out:

> $2,340,000 smaller amount of assets + $65,000 higher amount of liabilities = $2,405,000 less net income recorded over the years

The following sections briefly explain each of the differences in Figure 7-1, except the retained earnings difference that I explain just above. I keep the explanations relatively brief and to the point. The idea is to give you a basic taste of some of the reasons for the differences.

Accounts receivable and sales revenue

Here are some common reasons why the balance of the accounts receivable asset is lower when conservative accounting methods are adopted:

✔ A business waits a little longer to record sales made on credit, to be more certain that all aspects of delivering products and the acceptance by customers are finalized, and there is little chance of the products being returned by the customers. This delay in recording sales causes its accounts receivable balance to be slightly lower, because at December 31, 2013 credit sales of $345,000 were not yet recorded that were still in the process of final acceptance by the customers. (Of course the cost of goods sold for these sales would not have been recorded either.)

If products are returnable and the deal between the seller and buyer does not satisfy normal conditions for a completed sale, the recording of sales revenue should be postponed until the return privilege no longer exists. For example, some products are sold *on approval,* which means the customer takes the product and tries it out for a few days or longer to see if the customer really wants it.

Businesses should be consistent from year to year regarding when they record sales. For some businesses, the timing of recording sales revenue is a major problem — especially when the final acceptance by the customer depends on performance tests or other conditions that must be satisfied. Some businesses engage in *channel stuffing* by forcing their dealers or customers to take delivery of more products than they wanted to buy. A good rule to follow is to read the company's footnote in its financial statements that explains its revenue recognition method, to see whether there is anything unusual. If the footnote is vague, be careful — be very careful!

✔ A business may be quicker in writing off a customer's past due balance as uncollectible. After it has made a reasonable effort to collect the debt but a customer still hasn't sent a check, a more conservative business writes off the balance as a *bad debts* expense. It decreases the past due accounts receivable balance to zero and records an expense of the same amount. In contrast, a business could wait much longer to write off a customer's past due amount. Both accounting methods end up writing off a customer's debt if it has been outstanding too long — but a company could wait until the last minute to make the write-off entry.

Inventory and cost of goods sold expense

The business in the example sells products mainly to other businesses. A business either manufactures the products its sells or purchases products for resale to customers. (Chapter 11 explains the determination of product costs for manufacturing businesses.) At this point it is not too important whether the business manufactures or purchases the products it sells. The costs of its products have drifted upward over time because of inflation and other factors. The business increased its sales prices to keep up with the product cost increases. When product costs change a business must choose which accounting method it uses for recording cost of goods sold expense.

One accounting method takes product costs out of the inventory asset account and records the costs to cost of goods sold expense in the sequence in which the costs were entered in the asset account. This scheme is called the first-in, first-out (FIFO) method. Instead, a business may choose to use the reverse method in which the latest product costs entered in the inventory asset account are selected for recording cost of goods sold expense, which leaves the oldest product costs in the asset account. This method is called the last-in, first-out (LIFO) method. I explain these two opposing methods in more detail later in the chapter (see *Calculating Cost of Goods Sold Expense and Inventory Cost*). FIFO is being used in the actual scenario and LIFO is what you see in the alternative scenario in Figure 7-1.

When product costs drift upward over time the FIFO method yields a lower cost of goods sold expense and a higher inventory asset balance compared with LIFO. In Figure 7-1 we see that inventory is $700,000 lower in the alternative accounting scenario and that cost of goods sold expense is $280,000 higher. The $700,000 lower inventory balance is the cumulative effect of using LIFO, including the carry forward effects from previous years.

Some of the $700,000 inventory difference and some of the $280,000 cost of goods expense difference for 2013 are due to differences in how rigorously the business applies the *lower of cost or market* (LCM) rule. Before being sold, products may suffer loss in value due to deterioration, damage, theft, lower replacement costs, and diminished sales demand. A business tests regularly for such product losses and records the losses by decreasing its inventory balance and charging cost of goods sold expense. The LCM test can be applied loosely or tightly. It is applied more strictly in the alternative accounting scenario than in the actual scenario, which results in a larger amount of write-down of inventory (and higher expense).

Fixed assets and depreciation expense

All accountants agree that the costs of long-term operating assets that have limited useful lives to a business should be spread out over those predicted useful lives instead of being charged off entirely to expense in the year of acquisition. These long-lived operating assets are labeled *property, plant and equipment* in Figure 7-1, and less formally are called *fixed assets.* (The cost of land owned by a business is not depreciated because land is a property right that has perpetual life.) The allocation of the cost of a fixed asset over its estimated useful economic life to a business is called *depreciation.* The principle of depreciation is beyond criticism, but the devil is in the details.

The original costs of fixed assets should theoretically include certain costs in addition to their purchase or construction costs. However, in actual practice these fringe costs are not always included in the original cost of fixed assets. For example, it is theoretically correct to include installation costs of putting into place and connecting electrical and other power sources of heavy machinery and equipment. It is correct to include the cost of painting logos on the sides of delivery trucks. The cost of an older building just bought by a business should include the preparatory cleanup costs and the safety inspection cost. But in practice a business may not include such additional costs in the original costs of its fixed assets.

In the actual accounting scenario the business does include these additional costs in the original costs of its fixed assets, which means that the cost balances of its fixed assets are $225,000 higher compared with the alternative, conservative scenario (see Figure 7-1). These additional costs are not expensed immediately but are included in the total amount to be depreciated over future years. Also, in the actual scenario the company uses *straight-line depreciation* (discussed later), which spreads out the cost of a fixed asset evenly over the years of its useful life.

In the alternative conservative scenario the business does not include any costs other than purchase or construction costs in its fixed asset accounts, which means the additional costs are charged to expense immediately. Also, and most importantly, the business uses *accelerated depreciation* (discussed later) for allocating the cost of its fixed assets to expense. Higher amounts are allocated to early years and smaller amounts to later years. The result is that the accumulated depreciation amount in the alternative scenario is

$1,020,000 higher, which signals that a lot more depreciation expense has been recorded over the years.

Accrued expenses payable, income tax payable, and expenses

A typical business at the end of the year has liabilities for certain costs that have accumulated but that will not be paid until sometime after the end of the year — costs that are an outgrowth of the current year's operating activities. These delayed-payment expenses should be recorded and matched against the sales revenue for the year. For example, a business should accrue (calculate and record) the amount it owes to its employees for unused vacation and sick pay. A business may not have received its property tax bill yet, but it should estimate the amount of tax to be assessed and record the proper portion of the annual property tax to the current year. The accumulated interest on notes payable that hasn't been paid yet at the end of the year should be recorded.

Here's another example: Most products are sold with expressed or implied warranties and guarantees. Even if good quality controls are in place, some products sold by a business don't perform up to promises, and the customers want the problems fixed. A business should estimate the cost of these future obligations and record this amount as an expense in the same period that the goods are sold (along with the cost of goods sold expense, of course). It should not wait until customers actually return products for repair or replacement because if it waits to record the cost then some of the expense for the guarantee work would not be recorded until the following year. After being in business a few years, a company can forecast with reasonable accuracy the percent of products sold that will be returned for repair or replacement under the guarantees and warranties offered to its customers. On the other hand, brand new products that have no track record may be a serious problem in this regard.

In the actual scenario the business does not make the effort to estimate future product warranty and guaranty costs and certain other costs that should be accrued. It records these costs on a when-paid basis. It waits until it actually incurs these costs to record an expense. The company has decided that although its liabilities are understated, the amount is not material. In the alternative scenario, on the other hand, the business takes the high road and goes to the trouble of estimating future costs that should be matched against sales revenue for the year. Therefore, its accrued expenses payable liability account is $102,000 higher (see Figure 7-1).

In the alternative conservative scenario (see Figure 7-1) I assume that the business uses the same accounting methods for income tax, which gives a lower taxable income and income tax for the year. Accordingly, notice that the income tax expense for the year is $295,000 lower and the year-end balance of income tax payable is lower. A business makes installment payments during the year on its estimated income tax for the year, so only a fraction of the annual income tax is still unpaid at the end of the year. (A business may use different accounting methods for income tax than it does for recording its transactions, which leads to complexities I don't follow here.)

Wrapping things up

In the business example (Figure 7-1) the accounts payable liability is the same in both scenarios. These short-term operating liabilities are definite amounts for definite services or products that have been received by the business. There are no accounting alternatives in recording accounts payable. Also, cash has the same year-end balance in both scenarios because these transactions are recorded when cash is received and paid out. (Well, a business may do a little "window dressing" to bump up its reported cash balance, which I discuss in Chapter 12.) Finally, the accounts not affected by recording revenue and expenses are the same in both accounting scenarios, which are notes payable and owners' invested capital.

To be frank, my numbers for the alternative, conservative scenario are no more than educated guesses. Businesses keep only one set of books. Even a business itself doesn't know how different its financial statements would be if it had used different accounting methods. Financial report readers can read the footnotes to determine whether liberal or conservative accounting methods are being used. Footnotes are not easy to read. It is very difficult, if not impossible, to determine exactly how much profit would have been and how much different balance sheet amounts would be if alternative accounting methods had been used by a business.

If you own or manage a business, I strongly encourage you to get involved in deciding which accounting methods to use for measuring your profit and how these methods are actually implemented. Chapter 15 explains that a manager has to answer questions about his or her financial reports on many occasions, so you should know which accounting methods are used to prepare the financial statements. However, "get involved" should not mean manipulating the amounts of sales revenue and expenses recorded in the year — to make profit look higher, to smooth fluctuations in profit from year to year, or to improve the amounts of assets and liabilities reported in your ending balance sheet. You shouldn't even consider doing these things. (Of course these manipulations go on in the real world. Some people also drive under the influence, but that doesn't mean you should.)

Calculating Cost of Goods Sold Expense and Inventory Cost

Companies that sell products must select which method to use for recording cost of goods sold expense, which is the sum of the costs of the products sold to customers during the period. You deduct cost of goods sold from sales revenue to determine *gross margin* — the first profit line on the income statement (refer to Figure 7-1). Cost of goods sold is a very important figure; if gross margin is wrong, bottom-line profit (net income) is wrong.

A business can choose between two opposite methods for recording its cost of goods sold and the cost balance that remains in its inventory asset account:

   ✔ The first-in, first-out (FIFO) cost sequence
   ✔ The last-in, first-out (LIFO) cost sequence

Other methods are acceptable, but these two are the primary options.

Product costs are entered in the inventory asset account in the order the products are acquired, but they are not necessarily taken out of the inventory asset account in this order. The FIFO and LIFO terms refer to the order in which product costs are *taken out* of the inventory asset account. You may think that only one method is appropriate; however, accounting standards permit these two alternatives.

The choice between the FIFO and LIFO accounting methods does *not* depend on the actual physical flow of products. Generally speaking, products are delivered to customers in the order the business bought or manufactured the products — one reason being that a business does not want to keep products in inventory too long because the products might deteriorate or show their age. So, products generally move out of inventory in a first-in, first-out sequence. Nevertheless, a business may choose the last-in, first-out accounting method. Read on.

FIFO (first-in, first-out)

With the FIFO method, you charge out product costs to cost of goods sold expense in the chronological order in which you acquired the goods. The procedure is that simple. It's like the first people in line to see a movie get in the theater first. The ticket-taker collects the tickets in the order in which they were bought.

Suppose that you acquire four units of a product during a period, one unit at a time, with unit costs as follows (in the order in which you acquire the items): $100, $102, $104, and $106, for a total of $412. By the end of the period, you have sold three of these units. Using FIFO, you calculate the cost of goods sold expense as follows:

$$\$100 + \$102 + \$104 = \$306$$

In short, you use the first three units to calculate cost of goods sold expense.

The cost of the ending inventory asset, then, is $106, which is the cost of the most recent acquisition. The $412 total cost of the four units is divided between $306 cost of goods sold expense for the three units sold and the $106 cost of the one unit in ending inventory. The total cost has been accounted for; nothing has fallen between the cracks.

FIFO has two things going for it:

✔ Products generally move out of inventory in a first-in, first-out sequence: The earlier acquired products are delivered to customers before later acquired products are delivered, so the most recently purchased products are the ones still in ending inventory to be delivered in the future. Using FIFO, the inventory asset reported in the balance sheet at the end of the period reflects recent purchase (or manufacturing) costs, which means the balance in the asset is close to the current *replacement costs* of the products.

✔ When product costs are steadily increasing, many (but not all) businesses follow a first-in, first-out sales price strategy and hold off raising sales prices as long as possible. They delay raising sales prices until they have sold their lower-cost products. Only when they start selling from the next batch of products, acquired at a higher cost, do they raise sales prices. I favor the FIFO cost of goods sold expense method when a business follows this basic sales pricing policy, because both the expense and the sales revenue are better matched for determining gross margin. I realize that sales pricing is complex and may not follow such a simple process, but the main point is that many businesses use a FIFO-based sales pricing approach. If your business is one of them, I urge you to use the FIFO expense method to be consistent with your sales pricing.

LIFO (last-in, first-out)

Remember the movie ticket-taker I mentioned earlier? Think about that ticket-taker going to the *back* of the line of people waiting to get into the next showing and letting them in first. The later you bought your ticket, the sooner you get into the theater. This is what happens in the LIFO method, which stands for *last-in, first-out*. The people in the front of a movie line wouldn't stand for it, of course, but the LIFO method is acceptable for determining the cost of goods sold expense for products sold during the period.

The main feature of the LIFO method is that it selects the *last* item you purchased, and then works backward until you have the total cost for the total number of units sold during the period. What about the ending inventory — the products you haven't sold by the end of the year? Using the LIFO method, the earliest cost remains in the inventory asset account (unless all products are sold and the business has nothing in inventory).

Using the same example from the preceding section, assume that the business uses the LIFO method. The four units, in order of acquisition, had costs of $100, $102, $104, and $106. If you sell three units during the period, the LIFO method calculates the cost of goods sold expense as follows:

$$\$106 + \$104 + \$102 = \$312$$

The ending inventory cost of the one unit not sold is $100, which is the oldest cost. The $412 total cost of the four units acquired less the $312 cost of goods sold expense leaves $100 in the inventory asset account. Determining which units you actually delivered to customers is irrelevant; when you use the LIFO method, you always count backward from the most recent unit you acquired.

The two main arguments in favor of the LIFO method are these:

- ✔ Assigning the most recent costs of products purchased to the cost of goods sold expense makes sense because you have to replace your products to stay in business, and the most recent costs are closest to the amount you will have to pay to replace your products. Ideally, you should base your sales prices not on original cost but on the cost of replacing the units sold.

- ✔ During times of rising costs, the most recent purchase cost maximizes the cost of goods sold expense deduction for determining taxable income, and thus minimizes income tax. In fact, LIFO was invented for income tax purposes. True, the cost of inventory on the ending balance sheet is lower than recent acquisition costs, but the taxable income effect is more important than the balance sheet effect.

But here are the reasons why LIFO is problematic:

- ✔ Unless you are able to base sales prices on the most recent purchase costs or you raise sales prices as soon as replacement costs increase — and most businesses would have trouble doing this — using LIFO depresses your gross margin and, therefore, your bottom-line net income.

✔ The LIFO method can result in an ending inventory cost value that's seriously out of date, especially if the business sells products that have very long lives. For instance, for several years, Caterpillar's LIFO-based inventory has been billions less than what it would have been under the FIFO method.

✔ Unscrupulous managers can use the LIFO method to manipulate their profit figures if business isn't going well. They deliberately let their inventory drop to abnormally low levels, with the result that old, lower product costs are taken out of inventory to record cost of goods sold expense. This gives a one-time boost to gross margin. These "LIFO liquidation gains" — if sizable in amount compared with the normal gross profit margin that would have been recorded using current costs — have to be disclosed in the footnotes to the company's financial statements. (Dipping into old layers of LIFO-based inventory cost is necessary when a business phases out obsolete products; the business has no choice but to reach back into the earliest cost layers for these products. The sales prices of products being phased out usually are set low, to move the products out of inventory, so gross margin is not abnormally high for these products.)

If you sell products that have long lives and for which your product costs rise steadily over the years, using the LIFO method has a serious impact on the ending inventory cost value reported on the balance sheet and can cause the balance sheet to look misleading. Over time, the current cost of replacing products becomes further and further removed from the LIFO-based inventory costs. In our business example (Figure 7-1) the 2013 balance sheet may very well include products with 2003, 1997, or 1980 costs. As a matter of fact, the product costs reported for inventory could go back even further.

Note: A business must disclose in a footnote with its financial statements the difference between its LIFO-based inventory cost value and its inventory cost value according to FIFO. However, not many people outside of stock analysts and professional investment managers read footnotes very closely. Business managers get involved in reviewing footnotes in the final steps of getting annual financial reports ready for release (see Chapter 12). If your business uses FIFO, ending inventory is stated at recent acquisition costs, and you do not have to determine what the LIFO value would have been.

Many products and raw materials have very short lives; they're regularly replaced by new models (you know, with those "New and Improved!" labels) because of the latest technology or marketing wisdom. These products aren't around long enough to develop a wide gap between LIFO and FIFO, so the accounting choice between the two methods doesn't make as much difference as with long-lived products.

Another serious problem with LIFO has emerged recently. I discuss in Chapter 2 that for several years there have been continuing and serious efforts towards developing one unified set of global accounting and financial reporting standards. How this will all turn out is anyone's guess. More problems have arisen that anyone would have predicted. In any case, the international standards group does not approve LIFO. This position does not seem, at this time, open to negotiation. So, LIFO may become obsolete if international accounting standards are adopted.

One last note: FIFO and LIFO are not the only games in town. Businesses use other methods for cost of goods sold and inventory, including average cost methods, retail-price based methods, and so on. We don't have the time here to go into these other methods. FIFO and LIFO dominate.

Recording Depreciation Expense

In theory, depreciation expense accounting is straightforward enough: You divide the cost of a fixed asset (except land) among the number of years that the business expects to use the asset. In other words, instead of having a huge lump-sum expense in the year that you make the purchase, you charge a fraction of the cost to expense for each year of the asset's lifetime. Using this method is much easier on your bottom line in the year of purchase, of course.

Theories are rarely as simple in real life as they are on paper, and this one is no exception. Do you divide the cost *evenly* across the asset's lifetime, or do you charge more to certain years than others? Furthermore, when it eventually comes time to dispose of fixed assets, the assets may have some disposable, or *salvage,* value. In theory, only cost minus the salvage value should be depreciated. But in actual practice most companies ignore salvage value and the total cost of a fixed asset is depreciated. Moreover, how do you estimate how long an asset will last in the first place? Do you consult an accountant psychic hot line?

As it turns out, the IRS runs its own little psychic business on the side, with a crystal ball known as the Internal Revenue Code. Okay, so the IRS can't tell you that your truck is going to conk out in five years, seven months, and two days. The Internal Revenue Code doesn't give you predictions of how long your fixed assets will *last*; it only tells you what kind of time line to use for income tax purposes, as well as how to divide the cost along that time line.

Hundreds of books have been written on depreciation, but the book that really counts is the Internal Revenue Code. Most businesses adopt the useful lives allowed by the income tax law for their financial statement accounting; they don't go to the trouble of keeping a second depreciation schedule for financial reporting. Why complicate things if you don't have to? Why keep one depreciation schedule for income tax and a second for preparing your financial statements?

The IRS rules offer two depreciation methods that can be used for particular classes of assets. Buildings must be depreciated just one way, but for other fixed assets you can take your pick:

- **Straight-line depreciation:** With this method, you divide the cost evenly among the years of the asset's estimated lifetime. Buildings have to be depreciated this way. Assume that a building purchased by a business costs $390,000, and its useful life — according to the tax law — is 39 years. The depreciation expense is $10,000 (1/39 of the cost) for each of the 39 years. You may choose to use the straight-line method for other types of assets. After you start using this method for a particular asset, you can't change your mind and switch to another depreciation method later.

- **Accelerated depreciation:** Actually, this term is a generic catchall for several different kinds of methods. What they all have in common is that they're *front-loading* methods, meaning that you charge a larger amount of depreciation expense in the early years and a smaller amount in the later years. The term *accelerated* also refers to adopting useful lives that are shorter than realistic estimates. (Very few automobiles are useless after five years, for example, but they can be fully depreciated over five years for income tax purposes.)

The *salvage value* of fixed assets (the estimated disposal values when the assets are taken to the junkyard or sold off at the end of their useful lives) is ignored in the calculation of depreciation for income tax. Put another way, if a fixed asset is held to the end of its entire depreciation life, then its original cost will be fully depreciated, and the fixed asset from that time forward will have a zero book value. (Recall that *book value* is equal to original cost minus the balance in the accumulated depreciation account.)

Fully depreciated fixed assets are grouped with all other fixed assets in external balance sheets. All these long-term resources of a business are reported in one asset account called *property, plant and equipment* (instead of the term *fixed assets*). If all its fixed assets were fully depreciated, the balance sheet of a company would look rather peculiar — the cost of its fixed assets would be offset by its accumulated depreciation. Keep in mind that the cost of land (as opposed to the structures on the land) is not depreciated. The original cost of land stays on the books as long as the business owns the property.

The straight-line depreciation method has strong advantages: It's easy to understand, and it stabilizes the depreciation expense from year to year. Nevertheless, many business managers and accountants favor an accelerated depreciation method in order to minimize the size of the checks they have to write to the IRS in the early years of using fixed assets. This lets the business keep the cash, for the time being, instead of paying more income tax. Keep in mind, however, that the depreciation expense in the annual income statement is higher in the early years when you use an accelerated depreciation method, and so bottom-line profit is lower. Many accountants and businesses like accelerated depreciation because it paints a more conservative picture of profit performance in the early years. Fixed assets may lose their economic usefulness to a business sooner than expected. If this happens, using the accelerated depreciation method would look very wise in hindsight.

Except for brand-new enterprises, a business typically has a mix of fixed assets — some in their early years of depreciation, some in their middle years, and some in their later years. There is a balancing-out effect among the different vintages of fixed assets being depreciated. Therefore, the overall depreciation expense for the year using accelerated depreciation may not be too different than what the straight-line depreciation amount would be. A business does *not* have to disclose in its external financial report what its depreciation expense would have been if it had been using an alternative method. Readers of the financial statements cannot tell how much difference the choice of accounting methods would have caused in depreciation expense that year.

Scanning Revenue and Expense Horizons

Recording sales revenue and other income can present some hairy accounting problems. As a matter of fact, the — accounting rule-making authorities — rank revenue recognition as a major problem area. A good part of the reason for putting revenue recognition high on the list of accounting problems is that many high profile financial accounting frauds have involved recording bogus sales revenue that had no economic reality. Sales revenue accounting presents challenging problems in some situations. But in my view, the accounting for many key expenses is equally important. Frankly, it's damn difficult to measure expenses on a year-by-year basis.

I could write a book on expense accounting, which would have at least 20 or 30 major chapters. All I can do here is to call your attention to a few major expense accounting issues.

- ✔ **Asset impairment write-downs:** Inventory shrinkage, bad debts, and depreciation by their very nature are asset write-downs. Other asset write-downs are required when an asset becomes *impaired,* which means that it has lost some or all of its economic utility to the business and has little or no disposable value. An asset write-down reduces the book (recorded) value of an asset (and at the same time records an expense or loss of the same amount).

✔ **Employee-defined benefits pension plans and other post-retirement benefits:** The U.S. accounting rule on this expense is extremely complex. Several key estimates must be made by the business, including, for example, the expected rate of return on the investment portfolio set aside for these future obligations. This and other estimates affect the amount of expense recorded. In some cases, a business uses an unrealistically high rate of return in order to minimize the amount of this expense. Using unrealistically optimistic rates of investment return is a pernicious problem at the present time.

✔ **Certain discretionary operating expenses:** Many operating expenses involve timing problems and/or serious estimation problems. Furthermore, some expenses are discretionary in nature, which means how much to spend during the year depends almost entirely on the discretion of managers. Managers can defer or accelerate these expenses in order to manipulate the amount of expense recorded in the period. For this reason, businesses filing financial reports with the SEC are required to disclose certain of these expenses, such as repairs and maintenance expense, and advertising expense. (To find examples, go to the Securities and Exchange Commission website at www.sec.gov.)

✔ **Income tax expense:** A business can use different accounting methods for some of the expenses reported in its income statement than it uses for calculating its taxable income. Oh, boy! The hypothetical amount of taxable income, as if the accounting methods used in the income statement were used in the tax return, is calculated; then the income tax based on this hypothetical taxable income is figured. This is the income tax expense reported in the income statement. This amount is reconciled with the actual amount of income tax owed based on the accounting methods used for income tax purposes. A reconciliation of the two different income tax amounts is provided in a technical footnote schedule to the financial statements.

✔ **Management stock options:** A *stock option* is a contract between an executive and the business that gives the executive the option to purchase a certain number of the corporation's capital stock shares at a fixed price (called the *exercise* or *strike* price) after certain conditions are satisfied. Usually a stock option does not vest until the executive has been with the business for a certain number of years. The question is whether the granting of stock options should be recorded as an expense. This issue had been simmering for some time. The U.S. rule-making body finally issued a pronouncement that requires a value measure be put on stock options when they are issued and that this amount be recorded as an expense.

You could argue that management stock options are simply an arrangement between the stockholders and the privileged few executives of the business, by which the stockholders allow the executives to buy shares at bargain prices. The granting of stock options does not reduce the assets or increase the liabilities of the business, so you could argue that stock options are not a direct expense of the business; instead, the cost falls on the stockholders. Allowing executives to buy stock shares at below-market prices increases the number of shares over which profit has to be spread, thus decreasing earnings per share. Stockholders have to decide whether they are willing to do this; the granting of management stock options must be put to a vote by the stockholders.

Please don't think that the short list above does justice to all the expense accounting problems of businesses. U.S. businesses — large and small, public and private — operate in a highly developed and very sophisticated economy. One result is that expense accounting has become very complicated and confusing.

Part III

Accounting in Managing a Business

The 5th Wave   By Rich Tennant

"I think I'm finally getting the hang of this accounting system. It's even got a currency conversion function. Want to see how much we lost in rupees?"

In this part . . .

This part of the book, in short, explains how accounting helps managers achieve the financial objectives of the business.

To survive and thrive, a business faces four inescapable financial imperatives: securing enough capital for the business, making adequate profit, turning its profit into cash flow on a timely basis, and keeping its financial condition in good shape. Its managers should understand the financial statements of the business (see Part II). In addition, business managers should take advantage of time-tested accounting tools and techniques to help them achieve the financial goals of the business.

To begin this part, Chapter 8 explains that business founders must decide which legal structure to use from several alternatives. Chapter 9 demonstrates that business managers need a well-thought-out P&L (profit and loss) report for understanding and analyzing profit — one that serves as the touchstone model for making decisions regarding sales prices, costs, marketing and procurement strategies, and so on.

Chapter 10 explains that budgeting, whether done on a big-time or a small-scale basis, is a valuable technique for planning and setting financial goals. Lastly, Chapter 11 examines the costs that managers work with day in and day out. Managers may think they understand the cost figures they work with, but they may not fully appreciate the problems in measuring costs.

Chapter 8

Deciding the Legal Structure for a Business

The obvious reason for investing in a business rather than putting your hard-earned money in a safer type of investment is the potential for greater rewards. Note the word *potential*. As one of the owners of a business, you're entitled to your fair share of the business's profit, as are the other owners of course. At the same time you're subject to the risk that the business could go down the tubes, taking your money with it.

Ignore the risks for a moment and look at just the rosy side of the picture: Suppose the doohickeys that your business sells become the hottest products of the year. Sales are booming, and you start looking at buying a five-bedroom mansion with an ocean view. Don't make that down payment just yet — you may not get as big a piece of the profit pie as you're expecting. There could be claims that rank ahead of you, and you may not see *any* profit after all these claims are satisfied. In any case, the way the profit is divided among owners depends on the business's legal structure.

This chapter shows you how legal structure determines your share of the profit — and how changes beyond your control can make your share less valuable. It also explains how the legal structure determines whether the business as a separate entity pays income taxes. In one type of legal structure, the business pays income taxes *and* its owners pay a second layer of income taxes on the distributions of profit to them by the business. In this case, Uncle Sam gets *two* bites of the profit apple.

Securing Capital: Starting With Owners

Every business needs capital. Capital provides the money for the assets a business needs to make sales and carry on its operations. Common examples of assets are the working cash balance a business needs for day-to-day activities, products held in inventory for sale, and long-life operating assets (buildings, machines, computers, office equipment, and so on). A rough guideline is this: Businesses that sell products need capital equal to one-half of annual sales revenue. Of course, this ratio varies from industry to industry. Many manufactures need a high ratio of capital to sales, so they are referred to as *capital intensive*.

One of the first questions that sources of business capital ask is: How is the business entity organized legally? In other words, which specific form or legal structure is being used by the business? The different types of business legal entities present different risks and offer different rewards to business capital sources.

Where does a business get the capital it needs? Whatever its legal structure, the answer comes down to two basic sources: debt and equity. *Debt* refers to the money borrowed by a business, and *equity* refers to money invested in the business by owners plus profit earned and retained in the business (instead of being distributed to its owners). No matter which type of legal entity form it uses, every business needs a foundation of ownership (equity) capital. Owners' equity is the hard-core capital base of a business.

I might add that in starting a new business from scratch, its founders typically must invest a lot of *sweat equity,* which refers to the grueling effort and long hours to get the business off the ground and up and running. The founders don't get paid for their sweat equity, and it does not show up in the accounting records of the business. You don't find the personal investment of time and effort for sweat equity in a balance sheet.

Contrasting two sources of owners' equity

Every business — regardless of how big it is, whether it's publicly or privately owned, and whether it's just getting started or is a mature enterprise — has owners. No business can get all the capital it needs by borrowing. The owners provide the business with its start-up and its continuing base of capital, which as I just mentioned is generally referred to as *equity*. Without the foundation of equity capital a business would not be able to get credit from its suppliers, and it couldn't borrow money. As they say in politics, the owners must have some skin in the game.

The equity capital in a business always carries the risk of loss to its owners. So, what do the owners expect and want from taking on this risk? Their expectations include the following:

- ✔ They expect the business to earn profit on their equity capital in the business and to share in that profit by receiving cash distributions from profit, and from increases in the value of their ownership shares — with no guarantee of either.

- ✔ They may expect to directly participate in the management of the business, or they may plan to hire someone else to manage the business. In smaller businesses, an owner may be one of the managers and may sit on the board of directors. In very large businesses, however, you are just one of thousands of owners who elect a representative board of directors to oversee the managers of the business and protect the interests of the non-manager owners.

- ✔ Looking down the line to the eventual demise of the business, they expect to receive a proportionate share of the proceeds if the business is sold, or receive a proportionate share of ownership when another business buys or merges with the business, or they may end up with nothing in the event the business goes kaput and there's nothing left after paying off the creditors of the business.

When owners invest money in a business, the accountant records the amount of money as an increase in the company's *cash* account. And, using double-entry accounting, the amount invested in the business is recorded as an increase in an *owners' equity*. (I explain double-entry accounting and debits and credits in Chapter 3.) Owners' equity also increases when a business makes profit. See Chapters 4 and 7 for more on why earning profit increases the amount of assets minus expenses, which is called *net worth*, and that this push-up in net worth from profit is balanced by recording the increase in owners' equity.

So, there are two distinct sources of owners' equity. Also, certain legal requirements often come into play regarding the minimum amount of owners' capital that has to be maintained by a business for the protection of creditors. Therefore, the owners' equity of a business is divided into two separate types of accounts:

- ✔ **Invested capital:** This type of owners' equity account records the amounts of money that owners have invested in the business, which could have been many years ago. Owners may invest additional capital from time to time, but generally speaking they cannot be forced to put additional money in a business (unless the business issues *assessable* ownership shares, which is unusual). Depending on the legal form of the entity and other factors a business may keep two or more accounts for the invested capital from its owners.

✔ **Retained earnings:** The profit earned by a business over the years that has been retained and not distributed to its owners is accumulated in the retained earnings account. If all profit had been distributed every year, retained earnings would have a zero balance. (If a business has never made a profit, its accumulated loss would cause retained earnings to have a negative balance, which generally is called a *deficit*.) If none of the annual profits of a business had been distributed to its owners, the balance in retained earnings would be the cumulative profit earned by the business since it opened its doors (net of any losses along the way).

Whether to retain part or all of annual net income is one of the most important decisions that a business makes; distributions from profit have to be decided at the highest level of a business. A growing business needs additional capital for expanding its assets, and increasing the debt load of the business usually cannot supply all the additional capital. So, the business *plows back* some of its profit for the year rather than giving it out to its owners. In the long run this may be the best course of action because it provides additional capital for growth.

Leveraging equity capital with debt

Suppose a business has $10 million in total assets. (You find assets in the balance sheet of a business — see Chapter 5.) This doesn't mean that it has $10 million of owners' equity. Assuming the business has a good credit rating, it probably has some amount of trade credit, which is recorded in the *accounts payable* liability account (as I explain in Chapter 5.) Also, there are other kinds of operating liabilities. Let's say that its accounts payable and other operating liabilities total $2 million. This leaves $8 million to account for.

It's possible that all $8 million is provided by equity capital (that is, the sum of money invested by its owners plus the accumulated balance of retained earnings). But more than likely, the business would have borrowed money, which is recorded in notes payable and similarly titled liability accounts. The basic idea of borrowing money is to leverage its owners' equity capital. For example, suppose the $8 million in our example is split $3 million debt and $5 million owners' equity. The business has three dollars of debt capital for every five dollars of equity capital. The business is leveraging its equity capital, or using its equity capital to increase the total capital of the business.

Some businesses depend on debt for more than half of their total capital. In contrast, some businesses have virtually no debt at all. You find many examples of both public and private companies that have no borrowed money. But as a general rule, most businesses carry some debt (and therefore, have interest expense).

The debt decision is not really an accounting responsibility as such; although once the decision is made to borrow money the accountant is very involved in recording debt and interest transactions. Deciding on debt is the responsibility of the chief financial officer and chief executive of the business. In medium-sized and smaller businesses, the chief accounting officer (controller) may also serve as the chief financial officer. In larger businesses, two different persons hold the top financial and accounting positions.

The loan contract between a business and its lender may prohibit the business from distributing profit to owners during the period of the loan. Or, the loan agreement may require that the business maintain a minimum cash balance. Generally speaking, the higher the ratio of debt to equity, the more likely a lender will charge higher interest rates and insist on tougher conditions, because the lender has higher risk that the business might default on the loan.

When borrowing money the president or another officer in his or her capacity as an official agent of the business signs a note payable document to the bank or other lender. In addition, the bank or other lender may ask the major investors in a smaller, privately owned business to guarantee the note payable of the business *as individuals,* in their personal capacities — and it may ask their spouses to guarantee the note payable as well. One way of doing this is for the individuals to endorse the note payable. Or, a separate legal instrument of guarantee may be used. In any case, the individuals promise to pay the note if the business can't. You should definitely understand your personal obligations if you are inclined to guarantee a note payable of a business. You take the risk that you may have to pay some part or perhaps the entire amount of the loan from your personal assets.

Recognizing the Legal Roots of Business Entities

One of the most important aspects of our legal system, from the business and economic point of view, is that the law enables *entities* to be created for conducting business activities. These entities are separate and distinct from the individual owners of the business. Business entities have many of the rights of individuals. Business entities can own property and enter into contracts, for example. In starting a business venture, one of the first things the founders have to do is select which type of legal structure to use — which usually requires the services of a lawyer who knows the laws of the state in which the business is organized.

A business may have just one or more owners. A one-owner business may choose to operate as a *sole proprietorship*; a multi-owner business must choose to be a *corporation,* a *partnership,* or a *limited liability company.* The most common type of business is a corporation (although the number of sole proprietorships would be larger if you include part-time, self-employed persons in this category).

No legal structure is inherently better than another; which one is right for a particular business is something that the business's managers and founders need to decide at the time of starting the business. The advice of a lawyer is usually needed. The following discussion focuses on the basic types of legal entities that owners can use for their business. Later in the chapter, I explain how the legal structure determines the income tax paid by the business and its owners, which is always an important consideration.

Incorporating a Business

The law views a *corporation* as a real, live person. Like an adult, a corporation is treated as a distinct and independent individual who has rights and responsibilities. (A corporation can't be sent to jail, but its officers can be put in the slammer if they are convicted of using the corporate entity for carrying out fraud.) A corporation's "birth certificate" is the legal form that is filed with the Secretary of State of the state in which the corporation is created (incorporated). A corporation must also have a legal name, like an individual. Some names cannot be used, such as the State Department of Motor Vehicles; you need to consult a lawyer on this point.

The corporate legal form offers several important advantages. A corporation has *unlimited life*; it stays alive until the shareowners vote to terminate the entity. The ownership interests in a corporation, specifically the shares of stock issued by the corporation, are generally *transferable.* You can sell your shares to another person or bequeath them in your will to your grandchildren. You don't need the approval of the other shareholders to transfer ownership of your shares. Each ownership share has one vote in the election of directors of a business corporation (generally speaking). In turn, the directors hire and fire the key officers of the corporation. This provides a practical way to structure the management of a business.

Just as a child is separate from his or her parents, a corporation is separate from its owners. The corporation is responsible for its own debts. The bank can't come after you if your neighbor defaults on his or her loan, and the bank can't come after you if the corporation you have invested money in goes belly up. If a corporation doesn't pay its debts, its creditors can seize only the corporation's assets, not the assets of the corporation's owners.

This important legal distinction between the obligations of the business entity and its individual owners is known as *limited liability* — that is, the limited liability of the owners. Even if the owners have deep pockets, they have no legal exposure for the unpaid debts of the corporation (unless they've used the corporate shell to defraud creditors). The legal fence between a corporation and its owners is sometimes called the "corporate shield" because it protects the owners from being held responsible for the debts of the corporation. So, when you invest money in a corporation as an owner, you know that the most you can lose is the amount you put in. You may lose every dollar you put in, but the corporation's creditors cannot reach through the corporate entity to grab your assets to pay off the liabilities of the business. (But, to be prudent, you should check with your lawyer on this issue — just to be sure.)

Issuing stock shares

When raising equity capital, a corporation issues ownership shares to persons who invest money in the business. These ownership shares are documented by stock certificates, which state the name of the owner and how many shares are owned. The corporation has to keep a register of how many shares everyone owns, of course. (An owner can be an individual, another corporation, or any other legal entity.) Actually, many public corporations use an independent agency to maintain their ownership records. In some situations stock shares are issued in *book entry form,* which means you get a formal letter (not a fancy engraved stock certificate) attesting to the fact that you own so many shares. Your legal ownership is recorded in the official "books," or stock registry of the business.

The owners of a corporation are called *stockholders* because they own stock shares issued by the corporation. The stock shares are *negotiable,* meaning the owner can sell them at any time to anyone willing to buy them without having to get the approval of the corporation or other stockholders. *Publicly owned corporations* are those whose stock shares are traded in public markets, such as the New York Stock Exchange and NASDAQ. There is a ready market for the buying and selling of the stock shares.

The stockholders of a private business have the right to sell their shares, although they may enter into a binding agreement restricting this right. For example, suppose you own 20,000 of the 100,000 stock shares issued by the business. So, you have 20 percent of the voting power in the business (one share has one vote). You may agree to offer your shares to the other shareowners before offering the shares to someone outside the present group of stockholders. Or, you may agree to offer the business itself the right to buy back the shares. In these ways, the continuing stockholders of the business control who owns the stock shares of the business.

Offering different classes of stock shares

Before you invest in stock shares, you should ascertain whether the corporation has issued just one *class* of stock shares. A class is one group, or type, of stock shares all having identical rights; every share is the same as every other share. A corporation can issue two or more different classes of stock shares. For example, a business may offer Class A and Class B stock shares, where Class A stockholders are given the vote in elections for the board of directors but Class B stockholders do not get a vote.

State laws generally are liberal when it comes to allowing corporations to issue different classes of stock shares. A whimsical example is that holders of one class of stock shares could get the best seats at the annual meetings of the stockholders. But whimsy aside, differences between classes of stock shares are significant and affect the value of the shares of each class of stock.

Two classes of corporate stock shares are fundamentally different: *common stock* and *preferred stock*. Here are two basic differences:

✔ Preferred stockholders are promised a certain amount of cash dividends each year (note I said "promised," not "guaranteed"), but the corporation makes no such promises to its common stockholders. Each year, the board of directors must decide how much, if any, cash dividends to distribute to its common stockholders.

✔ Common stockholders have the most risk. A business that ends up in deep financial trouble is obligated to pay off its liabilities first and then its preferred stockholders. By the time the common stockholders get their turn, the business may have no money left to pay them.

Neither of these points makes common stock seem too attractive. But consider the following points:

✔ Preferred stock shares usually are promised a *fixed* (limited) dividend per year and typically don't have a claim to any profit beyond the stated amount of dividends. (Some corporations issue *participating* preferred stock, which gives the preferred stockholders a contingent right to more than just their basic amount of dividends. This topic is too technical to explore further in this book.)

✔ Preferred stockholders generally don't have voting rights, unless they don't receive dividends for one period or more. In other words, preferred stock shareholders usually do not participate in electing the corporation's board of directors or vote on other critical issues facing the corporation.

The advantages of common stock, therefore, are the ability to vote in corporation elections and the unlimited *upside potential*: After a corporation's obligations to its preferred stock are satisfied, the rest of the profit it has earned accrues to the benefit of its common stock.

Here are some important things to understand about common stock shares:

- ✔ Each stock share is equal to every other stock share in its class. This way, ownership rights are standardized, and the main difference between two stockholders is how many shares each owns.

- ✔ The only time a business must return stockholders' capital to them is when the majority of stockholders vote to liquidate the business (in part or in total). Other than this, the business's managers don't have to worry about the stockholders withdrawing capital.

- ✔ A stockholder can sell his or her shares at any time, without the approval of the other stockholders. However, as I mention earlier, the stockholders of a privately owned business may agree to certain restrictions on this right when they first became stockholders in the business.

- ✔ Stockholders can put themselves in key management positions, or they may delegate the task of selecting top managers and officers to the *board of directors,* which is a small group of persons selected by the stockholders to set the business's policies and represent stockholders' interests.

   Now don't get the impression that if you buy 100 shares of IBM you can get yourself elected to its board of directors. On the other hand, if Warren Buffett bought 100 million shares of IBM, he could very well get himself on the board. The relative size of your ownership interest is key. If you put up more than half the money in a business, you can put yourself on the board and elect yourself president of the business. The stockholders who own 50 percent plus one share constitute the controlling group that decides who goes on the board of directors.

Note: The all-stocks-are-created-equal aspect of corporations is a practical and simple way to divide ownership, but its inflexibility can also be a hindrance. Suppose the stockholders want to delegate to one individual extraordinary power, or to give one person a share of profit out of proportion to his or her stock ownership. The business can make special compensation arrangements for key executives and ask a lawyer for advice on the best way to implement the stockholders' intentions. Nevertheless, state corporation laws require that certain voting matters be settled by a majority vote of stockholders. If enough stockholders oppose a certain arrangement, the other stockholders may have to buy them out to gain a controlling interest in the business. (The limited liability company legal structure permits more flexibility in these matters. I talk about this type of legal structure later in the chapter; see the section "Differentiating Partnerships and Limited Liability Companies.")

Determining the market value of stock shares

If you want to sell your stock shares, how much can you get for them? There's a world of difference between owning shares of a public corporation and owning shares of a private corporation. *Public* means there is an active market in the stock shares of the business; the shares are *liquid*. The shares can be converted into cash in a flash by calling your stockbroker or going online to sell them. You can check a daily financial newspaper — such as *The Wall Street Journal* — for the current market prices of many large publicly owned corporations. Or you can go to one of many Internet websites (such as http://finance.yahoo.com) that provide current market prices. But stock shares in privately owned businesses aren't publicly traded, so how can you determine the value of your shares in such a business?

Well, I don't mean to sidestep the question, but stockholders of a private business don't worry about putting a precise market value on their shares — until they are serious about selling their shares, or when something else happens that demands putting a value on the shares. When you die, the executor of your estate has to put a value on the shares you own (excuse me, the shares you *used to* own) for estate tax purposes. If you divorce your spouse, a value is needed for the stock shares you own, as part of the divorce settlement. When the business itself is put up for sale, a value is put on the business; dividing this value by the number of stock shares issued by the business gives the value per share.

Other than during events like these, which require that a value be put on the stock shares, the shareowners of a private business get along quite well without knowing a definite value for their shares. This doesn't mean they have no idea regarding the value of their business and what their shares are worth. They read the financial statements of their business, so they know its profit performance and financial condition. In the backs of their minds they should have a reasonably good estimate regarding how much a willing buyer might pay for the business and the price they would sell their shares for. So even though they don't know the exact market value of their stock shares, they are not completely in the dark about that value.

My son, Tage, and I discuss the valuation of small businesses in our book *Small Business Financial Management Kit For Dummies* (John Wiley & Sons). Space does not permit an extended discussion of business valuation methods here. Generally speaking, the value of ownership shares in a private business depends heavily on the recent profit performance and the current financial condition of the business, as reported in its latest financial statements. The financial statements may have to be *trued up,* as they say, to bring some of the historical cost values in the balance sheet up to current replacement values.

Business valuation is highly dependent on the specific circumstances of each business. The present owners may be very eager to sell out, and they may be willing to accept a low price instead of taking the time to drive a better bargain. The potential buyers of the business may see opportunities that the present owners don't see or aren't willing to pursue. Even Warren Buffett, who has a well-deserved reputation for knowing how to value a business, admits that he's made some real blunders along the way.

Keeping alert for dilution of share value

Watch out for developments that cause a *dilution effect* on the value of your stock shares — that is, that cause each stock share to drop in value. Keep in mind that sometimes the dilution effect may be the result of a good business decision, so even though your share of the business has decreased in the short term, the long-term profit performance of the business (and, therefore, your investment) may benefit. But you need to watch for these developments closely. The following situations cause a dilution effect:

- A business issues additional stock shares at the going market value but doesn't really need the additional capital — the business is in no better profit-making position than it was before issuing the new stock shares. For example, a business may issue new stock shares in order to let a newly hired chief executive officer buy them. The immediate effect may be a dilution in the value per share. Over the long term, however, the new CEO may turn the business around and lead it to higher levels of profit that increase the stock's value.

- A business issues new stock shares at a discount below its stock shares' current value. For example, the business may issue a new batch of stock shares at a price lower than the current market value to employees who take advantage of an employee stock-purchase plan. Selling stock shares at a discount, by itself, has a dilution effect on the market value of the shares. But in the grand scheme of things, the stock-purchase plan may motivate its employees to achieve higher productivity levels, which can lead to superior profit performance of the business.

Now here's one for you: The main purpose of issuing additional stock shares is to deliberately dilute the market value per share. For example, a publicly owned corporation doubles its number of shares by issuing a two-for-one *stock split.* Each shareholder gets one new share for each share presently owned, without investing any additional money in the business. As you would expect, the market value of the stock drops in half — which is exactly the purpose of the split because the lower stock price is better for stock market trading (according to conventional wisdom).

Recognizing conflicts between stockholders and managers

Stockholders are primarily concerned with the profit performance of the business; the dividends they receive and the value of their stock shares depend on it. Managers' jobs depend on living up to the business's profit goals. But whereas stockholders and managers have the common goal of optimizing profit, they have certain inherent conflict of interests:

- ✔ The more money that managers make in wages and benefits, the less stockholders see in bottom-line net income. Stockholders obviously want the best managers for the job, but they don't want to pay any more than they have to. In many corporations, top-level managers, for all practical purposes, set their own salaries and compensation packages.

Most public business corporations establish a compensation committee consisting of *outside* directors that sets the salaries, incentive bonuses, and other forms of compensation of the top-level executives of the organization. An outside director is one who has no management position in the business and who, therefore, should be more objective and should not be beholden to the chief executive of the business. This is good in theory, but it doesn't work out all that well in practice — mainly because the top-level executive of a large public business typically has the dominant voice in selecting the persons to serve on its board of directors. Being a director of a large public corporation is a prestigious position, to say nothing of the annual fees that are fairly substantial at most corporations.

- ✔ The question of who should control the business — managers who are hired for their competence and are intimately familiar with the business, or stockholders, who may have no experience relevant to running this business but whose money makes the business tick — can be tough to answer.

In ideal situations, the two sides respect each other's contributions to the business and use this tension constructively. Of course, the real world is far from ideal, and in some companies, managers control the board of directors rather than the other way around.

As an investor, be aware of these issues and how they affect the return on your investment in a business. If you don't like the way your business is run, you can sell your shares and invest your money elsewhere. (However, if the business is privately owned, there may not be a ready market for its stock shares, which puts you between a rock and a hard place.)

Where profit goes in a corporation

Suppose that a private business earned $1.32 million net income for the year just ended and has issued 400,000 capital stock shares. Divide net income by the number of shares, and you come up with *earnings per share* of $3.30. Assume that the business paid $400,000 cash dividends during the year, or $1.00 per share. The retained earnings account thus increased $2.30 per share (earnings per share minus dividends per share). Although stockholders don't have the cash to show for it, their investment is better off by $2.30 per share, which shows up in the balance sheet as an increase in the retained earnings account. They can hope that the business will use the cash provided from profit to increase future profit, which should lead to higher cash dividends.

Now, suppose the business is a public company that is 1,000 times larger. It earned $1.32 billion on its 400 million capital stock shares and distributed $400 million in cash dividends. You may think that the market value should increase $2.30 per share, because the business earned this much per share that it retained in the business and did not distribute to its shareholders. Your thinking is quite logical: Profit is an increase in the net assets of a business (assets less liabilities, which is also called *net worth*). The business is $2.30 per share "richer" at the end of the year than it was at the start of the year, due to the profit it earned and retained.

Yet it's entirely possible that the market price of the stock shares actually *decreased* during the year. Market prices are governed by psychological, political, and economic factors that go beyond the information in the financial reports of a business. Financial statements are only one of the information sources that stock investors use in making their buy-and-sell decisions. Chapters 13 and 16 explain how stock investors use the information in financial reports.

Differentiating Partnerships and Limited Liability Companies

Suppose you're starting a new business with one or more other owners, but you don't want it to be a corporation. You can choose to create a *partnership* or a *limited liability company,* which are the main alternatives to the corporate form of business.

A partnership is also called a *firm.* You don't see this term used to refer to a corporation or limited liability company nearly as often as you do to a partnership. The term *firm* connotes an association of a group of individuals working together in a business or professional practice.

Compared with the relatively rigid structure of corporations, the partnership and limited liability company forms of legal entities allow the division of management authority, profit sharing, and ownership rights among the owners to be very flexible. Here are the key features of these two legal structures:

- **Partnerships:** Partnerships avoid the double-taxation feature that corporations are subject to (see "Choosing the Right Legal Structure for Income Tax," later in this chapter for details). Partnerships also differ from corporations with respect to owners' liability. A partnership's owners fall into two categories:

  - **General partners** are subject to *unlimited liability.* If a business can't pay its debts, its creditors can reach into general partners' personal assets. General partners have the authority and responsibility to manage the business. They are roughly equivalent to the president and other high-level managers of a business corporation. The general partners usually divide authority and responsibility among themselves, and often they elect one member of their group as the senior general partner or elect a small executive committee to make major decisions.

  - **Limited partners** escape the unlimited liability that the general partners have hanging around their necks. Limited partners are not responsible, as individuals, for the liabilities of the partnership entity. These junior partners have ownership rights to the business's profit, but they don't generally participate in the high-level management of the business. A partnership must have one or more general partners; not all partners can be limited partners.

  Many large partnerships copy some of the management features of the corporate form — for example, a senior partner who serves as chair of the general partners' executive committee acts in much the same way as the chair of a corporation's board of directors.

In most partnerships an individual partner can't sell his interest to an outsider without the consent of all the other partners. You can't just buy your way into a partnership; the other partners have to approve your joining the partnership. In contrast, you can buy stock shares and thereby become part owner of a corporation without the approval of the other stockholders.

- **Limited liability company (LLC):** The LLC is an alternative type of business entity. An LLC is like a corporation regarding limited liability, and it's like a partnership regarding the flexibility of dividing profit among the owners. An LLC can elect to be treated either like a partnership or as a corporation for federal income tax purposes. Usually a tax expert should be consulted on this choice.

  The key advantage of the LLC legal form is its *flexibility* — especially regarding how profit and management authority are determined. For example, an LLC permits the founders of the business to put up, say, only 10 or 20 percent of the money to start a business venture but to keep all management authority in their hands. The other investors share in profit but not necessarily in proportion to their invested capital.

LLCs have a lot more flexibility than corporations, but this flexibility can have a downside. The owners must enter into a very detailed agreement that spells out the division of profit, the division of management authority and responsibility, their rights to withdraw capital, and their responsibilities to contribute new capital as needed. These schemes can get very complicated and difficult to understand, and they may end up requiring a lawyer to untangle them. If the legal structure of an LLC is too complicated and too far off the beaten path, the business may have difficulty explaining itself to a lender when applying for a loan, and it may have difficulty convincing new shareholders to put capital into the business.

A partnership treats salaries paid to partners (at least to its general partners) as distributions from profit. In other words, profit is determined *before* the deduction of partners' salaries. LLCs are more likely to treat salaries paid to owner-managers as an expense (like a corporation). I should warn you that the accounting for compensation and services provided by the owners in an LLC and the partners in a partnership gets rather technical and is beyond the scope of this book.

The partnership or LLC agreement specifies how to divide profit among the owners. Whereas owners of a corporation receive a share of profit directly proportional to the number of common stock shares they own, a partnership or LLC does not have to divide profit according to how much each owner invested. Invested capital is only one of three factors that generally play into profit allocation in partnerships and LLCs:

- **Treasure:** Owners may be rewarded according to how much of the *treasure* — invested capital — they contributed. So if Jane invested twice as much as Joe did, her cut of the profit may be twice as much as Joe's.

- **Time:** Owners who invest more time in the business may receive more of the profit. Some partners or owners, for example, may generate more billable hours to clients than others, and the profit-sharing plan reflects this disparity. Some partners or owners may work only part-time, so the profit-sharing plan takes this factor into account.

- **Talent:** Regardless of capital and time, some partners bring more to the business than others. Maybe they have better business contacts, or they're better *rainmakers* (they have a knack for making deals happen), or they're celebrities whose names alone are worth a special share of the profit. Whatever it is that they do for the business, they contribute much more to the business's success than their capital or time suggests.

Limiting liability: Professional corporations and LLPs

Professional partnerships — physicians, CPAs, lawyers, and so on — may choose to become *professional corporations (PCs),* which are a special type of legal structure that state laws offer to professionals who otherwise would have to operate under the specter of unlimited partnership liability. States also permit *limited liability partnerships (LLPs)* for qualified professionals (such as doctors, lawyers, CPAs, and dentists), in which all the partners have limited liability.

These types of legal entities were recently created in reaction to large damage awards in malpractice lawsuits against partners. The professionals pleaded for protection from the unlimited liability of the partnership form of organization, which they had traditionally used. Until these new types of professional legal entities came along, the code of professional ethics of the various professions required that practitioners operate as a partnership (or as sole practitioners).

Today, almost all professional associations are organized as PCs or LLPs. They function very much as partnerships do but without the unlimited liability feature — which is like having the best of both worlds.

A partnership needs to maintain a separate capital (ownership) account for each partner. The total profit of the entity is allocated into these capital accounts, as spelled out in the partnership agreement. The agreement also specifies how much money each partner can withdraw from his capital account. For example, partners may be limited to withdrawing no more than 80 percent of their anticipated share of profit for the coming year, or they may be allowed to withdraw only a certain amount until they've built up their capital accounts.

Going It Alone: Sole Proprietorships

A *sole proprietorship* is basically the business arm of an individual who has decided not to carry on his or her business activity as a separate legal entity (as a corporation, partnership, or limited liability company). This is the default when you don't establish a legal entity.

This kind of business is not a separate entity; it's like the front porch of a house — attached to the house but a separate and distinct area. You may be a sole proprietor of a business without knowing it! An individual may do house repair work on a part-time basis or be a full-time barber who operates on his own. Both are sole proprietorships. Anytime you regularly provide services for a fee, sell things at a flea market, or engage in any business activity whose primary purpose is to make profit, you are a sole proprietor. If you carry on business activity to make profit or income, the IRS requires that you file a separate Schedule C "Profit or Loss From Business" with your annual individual income tax return. Schedule C summarizes your income and expenses from your sole proprietorship business.

As the sole owner (proprietor), you have *unlimited liability,* meaning that if your business can't pay all its liabilities, the creditors to whom your business owes money can come after your personal assets. Many part-time entrepreneurs may not know this or may put it out of their minds, but this is a big risk to take. I have friends who are part-time business consultants and they operate their consulting businesses as sole proprietorships. If they are sued for giving bad advice, all their personal assets are at risk — though they may be able to buy malpractice insurance to cover these losses.

Obviously, a sole proprietorship has no other owners to prepare financial statements for, but the proprietor should still prepare these statements to know how his or her business is doing. Banks usually require financial statements from sole proprietors who apply for loans. See the "One More Thing" section in this chapter regarding accounting methods that a small, sole proprietorship business could adopt (instead of generally accepted accounting principles that large public companies must follow).

One other piece of advice for sole proprietors: Although you don't have to separate invested capital from retained earnings like corporations do, you should still keep these two separate accounts for owners' equity — not only for the purpose of tracking the business but for the benefit of any future buyers of the business as well.

Sharing profit with customers: Business cooperatives

A business that shares its profit with its customers? Nobody can be *that* generous. Actually, one type of business entity does just that: A *cooperative* pays its customers *patronage dividends* based on its profit for the year — each customer receives a year-end refund based on his or her purchases from the business over the year. Imagine that.

Oh, did I mention that in a cooperative, the customers are the owners? To shop in the cooperative, a customer must invest a certain amount of money in the business. (You knew there had to be a catch somewhere!) I grew up in Iowa.

You see the silos of grain co-ops (cooperative associations) all over the state. They are owned by the farmers who use the co-ops to store and deliver their crops.

Business cooperatives deduct patronage dividends in determining their taxable income for the year. If the business returns all profit to customers as patronage dividends, taxable income is zero. But the owners have to list their patronage dividends on their individual income tax returns for the year (and the co-op reports these distributions to the IRS).

Choosing the Right Legal Structure for Income Tax

While deciding which type of legal structure is best for securing capital and managing their business, owners should also consider the dreaded income tax factor. They should know the key differences between the two alternative kinds of business entities from the income tax point of view:

✓ **Taxable-entity, C corporations:** These corporations are subject to income tax on their annual taxable income. Plus, their stockholders pay a second income tax on cash dividends that the business distributes to them from profit, making C corporations and their owners subject to double taxation. The owners (stockholders) of a C corporation include in their individual income tax returns the cash distributions from the after-tax profit paid to them by the business.

✓ **Pass-through entities — partnerships, S corporations, and LLCs:** These entities do not pay income tax on their annual taxable income; instead, they pass through their taxable income to their owners, who pick up their shares of the taxable income on their individual tax returns. Pass-through entities still have to file tax returns with the IRS, even though they don't pay income tax on their taxable income. In their tax returns, they inform the IRS how much taxable income is allocated to each owner, and they send each owner a copy of this information to include with his or her individual income tax return.

Most LLCs opt to be treated as pass-through entities for income tax purposes. But an LCC can choose instead to be taxed as a C corporation and pay income tax on its taxable income for the year, with its individual shareholders paying a second tax on cash distributions of profit from the LLC. Why would an LCC choose double taxation? Keep reading.

The following sections illustrate the differences between the two types of tax entities for deciding on the legal structure for a business. In these examples, I assume that the business uses the same accounting methods in preparing its income statement that it uses for determining its taxable income — a generally realistic assumption. (I readily admit, however, that there are many technical exceptions to this general rule.) To keep this discussion simple, I consider just the federal income tax, which is much larger than any state income tax that may apply.

C corporations

A corporation that cannot qualify as an S corporation (which I explain in the next section) or that does not elect this alternative if it does qualify, is referred to as a *C corporation* in the tax law. A C corporation is subject to federal income tax based on its taxable income for the year, keeping in mind that there are a host of special tax credits (offsets) that could reduce or even eliminate the amount of income tax a corporation has to pay. I probably don't need to remind you how complicated the federal income tax is.

Suppose a business is taxed as a C corporation. Its abbreviated income statement for the year just ended is shown in Figure 8-1. (See Chapter 4 for more about income statements.)

Figure 8-1:
Abbreviated annual income statement for a C corporation.

Sales revenue	$26,000,000
Expenses, except income tax	($23,800,000)
Earnings before income tax	$2,200,000
Income tax at 34%	($748,000)
Net income	$1,452,000

Now, at this point I had to make a decision. One alternative was to refer to income tax form numbers and to use the tax rates in effect at the time of writing this chapter. The income tax form numbers have remained the same for many years, but the rest of the tax law keeps changing. For instance, Congress shifts tax rates every so often. Furthermore, tax rates are not flat; they're *progressive,* which means that the rates step up from one taxable income bracket to the next higher bracket — for both businesses and individuals. As I have already alluded to, there are many special deductions to determine taxable income, and there are many special tax credits that offset the normal amount of income tax.

Given the complexity and changing nature of the income tax law, in the following discussion I avoid going into details about income tax form numbers and the income tax rates that I use to determine the income tax amounts in each example. By the time you read this section, the tax rates probably will have changed anyway. Let me assure you, however, that I use realistic income tax numbers in the following discussion. (I didn't just look out the window and make up income tax amounts.)

Refer to the C corporation income statement example again (Figure 8-1). Based on its $2.2 million taxable income for the year, the business owes $748,000 income tax — using the current 34 percent tax rate for this level of corporate taxable income. (Most of the annual income tax should have been paid in installments to the IRS before year-end.) The income tax is a big chunk of the business's hard-earned profit before income tax. Finally, don't forget that net income means bottom-line profit after income tax expense.

Being a C corporation, the business pays $748,000 income tax on its profit before tax, which leaves $1,452,000 net income after income tax. Suppose the business distributes $500,000 of its after-tax profit to its stockholders as their just rewards for investing capital in the business. The stockholders include the cash dividends as income in their individual income tax returns. Assuming that all the individual stockholders have to pay income tax on this additional layer of income, as a group they would pay something in the neighborhood of $75,000 income tax to Uncle Sam (based on the current 15 percent rate on corporate dividends).

A business corporation is not legally required to distribute cash dividends, even when it reports a profit and has good cash flow from its operating activities. But paying zero cash dividends may not go down well with all the stockholders. If you've persuaded your Aunt Hilda and Uncle Harry to invest some of their money in your business, and if the business doesn't pay any cash dividends, they may be very upset. The average large public corporation pays out about 30 percent of its after-tax annual net income as cash dividends to its stockholders. It's difficult to say what privately owned corporations do regarding dividends, since the information is not available to the public.

S corporations

A business that meets the following criteria (and certain other conditions) can elect to be treated as an S corporation:

- ✔ It has issued only one class of stock.
- ✔ It has 100 or fewer people holding its stock shares.
- ✔ It has received approval for becoming an S corporation from all its stockholders.

Suppose that the business example I discuss in the previous section qualifies and elects to be taxed as an S corporation. Its abbreviated income statement for the year is shown in Figure 8-2.

Figure 8-2:
Abbreviated
annual
income
statement
for an S
corporation.

Sales revenue	$26,000,000
Expenses, except income tax	($23,800,000)
Earnings before income tax	$2,200,000
Income tax	$0
Net income	$2,200,000

An S corporation pays no income tax itself, as you see in this abbreviated income statement. But it must allocate its $2.2 million taxable income among its owners (stockholders) in proportion to the number of stock shares each owner holds. If you own one-tenth of the total shares, you include $220,000 of the business's taxable income in your individual income tax return for the year whether or not you receive any cash distribution from the profit of the S corporation. That probably pushes you into a high income tax rate bracket.

When its stockholders read the bottom line of this S corporation's annual income statement, it's a good news/bad news thing. The good news is that the business made $2.2 million net income and does not have to pay any corporate income tax on this profit. The bad news is that the stockholders must include their respective shares of the $2.2 million in their individual income tax returns for the year. I can only speculate on the total amount of individual income tax that would be paid by the stockholders as a group. But I would hazard a guess that the amount would be $300,000 or more. An S corporation could distribute cash dividends to its stockholders, to provide them the money to pay the income tax on their shares of the company's taxable income that is passed through to them.

The main tax question concerns how to minimize the overall income tax burden on the business entity and its stockholders. Should the business be an S corporation (assuming it qualifies) and pass through its taxable income to its stockholders, which generates taxable income to them? Or should the business operate as a C corporation (which always is an option) and have its stockholders pay a second tax on dividends paid to them in addition to the income tax paid by the business? Here's another twist: In some cases, stockholders may prefer that their S corporation *not* distribute any cash dividends. They are willing to finance the growth of the business by paying income tax on the taxable profits of the business, which relieves the business from paying income tax. Many factors come into play in choosing between an S and C corporation. There are no simple answers. I strongly advise you to consult a CPA or other tax professional.

Partnerships and LLCs

The LLC type of business entity borrows some features from the corporate form and some features from the partnership form. The LLC is neither fish nor fowl; it's an unusual blending of features that have worked well for many business ventures. A business organized as an LLC has the option to be a pass-through tax entity instead of paying income tax on its taxable income. A partnership doesn't have an option; it's a pass-through tax entity by virtue of being a partnership.

Following are the key income tax features of partnerships and LLCs:

✔ A partnership is a pass-through tax entity, just like an S corporation.

When two or more owners join together and invest money to start a business and don't incorporate and don't form an LLC, the tax law treats the business as a *de facto* partnership. Most partnerships are based on written agreements among the owners, but even without a formal, written agreement, a partnership exists in the eyes of the income tax law (and in the eyes of the law in general).

✔ An LLC has the choice between being treated as a pass-through tax entity and being treated as a taxable entity (like a C corporation). All you need to do is check off a box in the business's tax return to make the choice. (It's hard to believe that anything related to taxes and the IRS is as simple as that!) Many businesses organize as LLCs because they want to be pass-through tax entities (although the flexible structure of the LLC is also a strong motive for choosing this type of legal organization).

The partners in a partnership and the shareholders of an LLC pick up their shares of the business's taxable income in the same manner as the stockholders of an S corporation. They include their shares of the entity's taxable income in their individual income tax returns for the year. For example, suppose your share of the annual profit as a partner, or as one of the LLC's shareholders, is $150,000. You include this amount in your personal income tax return.

Once more, I must mention that choosing the best legal structure for a business is a complicated affair that goes beyond just the income tax factor. You need to consider many other factors, such as the number of equity investors who will be active managers in the business, state laws regarding business legal entities, ease of transferring ownership shares, and so on. After you select a particular legal structure, changing it later is not easy. Asking the advice of a qualified professional is well worth the money and can prevent costly mistakes.

Sometimes the search for the ideal legal structure that minimizes income tax and maximizes other benefits is like the search for the Holy Grail. Business owners should not expect to find the perfect answer — they have to make compromises and balance the advantages and disadvantages. In its external financial reports, a business has to make clear which type of legal entity it is. The type of entity is a very important factor to the lenders and other creditors of the business, and to its owners of course.

One other thing I think bears mentioning here. In this Internet age, many people form their own entities, whether it be a corporation or an LLC, through the assistance of online software and websites, with the assumption that they now have the limited liability asset protection afforded that entity. However, forming an entity and keeping it legal can be a complex task and every state has different rules. One little misstep can make it easy for the corporate shield to be pierced in the event of a lawsuit. It is prudent to hire a competent business attorney to make sure you are protected. Consider it a form of insurance.

One More Thing

Until recently the size and public-versus-private ownership of a business were not considered germane for the accounting and financial reporting standards that should be used by a business. The business world in the United States was under the dominion of one set of accounting and financial reporting standards, called *generally accepted accounting principles* (GAAP) that applied to all businesses. GAAP were considered the gold standard and good for the rest of the world as well. Then about ten years ago the movement toward adopting international standards gained momentum, which continues to this day (see Chapter 2). U.S. GAAP may or may not be replaced with *international financial reporting standards* (IFRS). Frankly, the future for international standards has become doubtful. In any case, public companies in the United States must follow GAAP or IFRS (as the case may turn out to be).

Recently there have been serious efforts promoting more "easy-to-use" accounting and financial reporting standards for private businesses. The Private Company Council (PCC) was established by the Financial Accounting Foundation, which is the mother organization behind the Financial Accounting Standards Board (FASB). The PCC is tasked with making recommendations to the FASB for modifying and making exceptions to GAAP to alleviate the burden on private companies in complying with complex GAAP standards. The PCC has yet to make any recommendations, and I can't say what will happen in this regard. As if this were not enough, there is also a movement within the AICPA to allow small- and medium-sized owner-managed entities to deviate even further from GAAP under a frame of reference called *Other Comprehensive Basis of Accounting*. Have you got all this sorted out? I'm not sure that I have. I grew up with only one set of standards that were called GAAP. But things are changing, that's for sure. Stay tuned.

Chapter 9

Accounting in Managing Profit

- -

In This Chapter

▶ Facing up to the profit-making function of business managers

▶ Scoping the field of managerial accounting

▶ Centering on profit centers

▶ Making internal P&L reports useful

▶ Analyzing profit for fun and more profit

- -

*A*s a manager, you get paid to make profit happen. That's what separates you from the employees at your business. Of course, you should be a motivator, innovator, consensus builder, lobbyist, and maybe sometimes a babysitter, but the hard-core purpose of your job is to make and improve profit. No matter how much your staff loves you (or do they love those doughnuts you bring in every Monday?), if you don't meet your profit goals, you're facing the unemployment line.

Competition in most industries is fierce, and you can never take profit performance for granted. Changes take place all the time — changes initiated by the business and changes from outside forces. Maybe a new superstore down the street is causing your profit to fall off, and you figure that you'll have a huge sale to draw customers, complete with splashy ads on TV and Dimbo the Clown in the store. Whoa, not so fast. First make sure that you can afford to cut prices and spend money on advertising and still turn a profit. Maybe price cuts and Dimbo's balloon creations would keep your cash register singing, but making sales does not guarantee that you make a profit. Profit is a two-sided challenge: Profit comes from making sales *and* controlling expenses.

This chapter focuses on the fundamental factors that drive profit — the *levers of profit*. Business managers need a sure-handed grip on these profit handles. One of the purposes of accounting is to provide this critical information to the managers. Externally reported income statements don't provide all the information that business managers need for sustainable profit performance. Managers need to thoroughly understand their external income statements and also need to look deeper into the bowels of the business.

Helping Managers: The Fourth Vital Task of Accounting

As previous chapters explain, accounting serves critical functions in a business.

- A business needs a dependable recordkeeping and bookkeeping system for operating in a smooth and efficient manner. Strong internal accounting controls are needed to minimize errors and fraud.

- A business must comply with a myriad tax laws, and it depends on its chief accountant (controller) to make sure that all its tax returns are prepared on time and correctly.

- A business prepares financial statements that should conform with established accounting and financial reporting standards, which are reported on a regular basis to its creditors and external shareowners.

- Accounting should help managers in their decision-making, control, and planning. This branch of accounting is generally called *managerial* or *management accounting*.

This is the first of three chapters devoted to managerial accounting. In this chapter, I pay particular attention to reporting profit to managers and providing the essential information needed for plotting profit strategy and controlling profit performance. I also explain how managers can use accounting information in analyzing how they make profit and why profit changes from one period to the next. Chapter 10 concentrates on financial planning and budgeting, and Chapter 11 examines the methods and problems of determining product costs (generally called *cost accounting*).

Designing and monitoring the accounting recordkeeping system, complying with complex federal and state tax laws, and preparing external financial reports put heavy demands on the time and attention of the accounting department of a business. Even so, managers' special needs for additional accounting information should not be given second-level priority or done by default. The chief accountant (controller) has the responsibility of ensuring that the accounting information needs of managers are served with maximum usefulness. Managers should demand this information from their accountants.

Following the organizational structure

In a small business there often is only one manager in charge of profit. As businesses get larger two or more managers have profit responsibility. The first rule of managerial accounting is to follow the organizational structure: to report relevant information for which each manager is responsible. (This principle is logically referred to as *responsibility accounting.*) If a manager is in charge of a product line, for instance, the controller reports the sales and expenses for that product line to the manager in charge.

Two types of organizational business units are of primary interest to managerial accountants:

- ✔ **Profit centers:** These are separate, identifiable sources of sales revenue and expenses so that a measure of profit can be determined for each. A profit center can be a particular product or a product line, a particular location or territory in which a wide range of products are sold, or a channel of distribution. Rarely is the entire business managed as one conglomerate profit center, with no differentiation of its various sources of sales and profit.

- ✔ **Cost centers:** Some departments and other organizational units do not generate sales, but they have costs that can be identified to their operations. Examples are the accounting department, the headquarters staff of a business, the legal department, and the security department. The managers responsible for these organizational units need accounting reports that keep them informed about the costs of running their departments. The managers should keep their costs under control, of course, and they need informative accounting reports to do this.

Note: The term *center* is simply a convenient word to include a variety of types of organizational sub-groups, such as centers, departments, divisions, territories, and other monikers.

Centering on profit centers

In this chapter, I concentrate on accounting for managers of profit centers. I don't mean to shun cost centers, but, frankly, the type of accounting information needed by the managers of cost centers is relatively straightforward. They need a lot of detailed information, including comparisons with last period and with the budgeted targets for the current period. And, I don't mean to suggest that the design of cost center reports is a trivial matter. Sorting out significant cost variances and highlighting these cost problems for management attention is very important. But the spotlight of this chapter is on profit analysis techniques using accounting information for managers with profit responsibility.

Note: I should mention that large businesses commonly create relatively autonomous units within the organization that, in addition to having responsibility for their profit and cost centers, also have broad authority and control over investing in assets and raising capital for their assets. These organization units are called, quite logically, *investment centers*. Basically, an investment center is a mini business within the larger conglomerate. Discussing investment centers is beyond the scope of this chapter.

From a one-person sole proprietorship to a mammoth business organization like General Electric or IBM, one of the most important tasks of managerial accounting is to identify each source of profit within the business and to accumulate the sales revenue and the expenses for each of these sources of profit. Can you imagine an auto dealership, for example, not separating revenue and expenses between its new car sales and its service department? For that matter an auto dealer may earn more profit from its financing operations (originating loans) than from selling new and used cars.

Even small businesses may have a relatively large number of different sources of profit. In contrast, even a relatively large business may have just a few mainstream sources of profit. There are no sweeping rules for classifying sales revenue and costs for the purpose of segregating sources of profit — in other words, for defining the profit centers of a business. Every business has to sort this out on its own. The controller (chief accountant) can advise top management regarding how to organize the business into profit centers. But the main job of the controller is to identify the profit centers that have been (or should be) established by management and to make sure that the managers of these profit centers get the accounting information they need. Of course managers should know how to use the information.

Internal Profit Reporting

External financial statements, including the profit report (income statement) comply with well-established rules and conventions, which I discuss in Chapter 2. In contrast, the format and content of internal accounting reports to managers is a wide-open field. If you could sneak a peek at the internal financial reports of several businesses, I think you would be surprised at the diversity among the businesses. All businesses include sales revenue and expenses in their internal P&L (profit and loss) reports. Beyond this broad comment, it's very difficult to generalize about the specific format and level of detail included in P&L reports, particularly regarding how operating expenses are reported.

Designing internal profit (P&L) reports

Profit performance reports prepared for a business's managers typically are called a *P&L* (profit and loss). These reports should be prepared as frequently as managers need them, usually monthly or quarterly — perhaps even weekly or daily in some businesses. A P&L report is prepared for the manager in charge of each profit center; these confidential profit reports do not circulate outside the business. The P&L contains sensitive information that competitors would love to get hold of.

Accountants are not in the habit of preparing brief, summary-level profit reports. Accountants tend to err on the side of providing too much detailed data and information. Their mantra is to give managers more information, even if the information is not asked for. My attitude is just the reverse. I'm sure it's not news to you that managers are very busy people, and they don't have spare time to waste, whether in reading long rambling e-mails or on multi-page profit reports with too much detail. My preference is that profit reports should be compact for a quick-read. If a manager wants more back-up detail they can request it as time permits. Ideally, the accountant should prepare a profit *main page* that would fit one computer screen, although this may be a smidgeon too small as a practical matter. In any case, keep it brief.

Businesses that sell products deduct the cost of goods sold expense from sales revenue, and then report *gross margin* (alternatively called *gross profit*) — both in their externally reported income statements and in their internal P&L reports to managers. However, internal P&L reports have a lot more detail about sources of sales and the components of cost of goods sold expense. In this chapter, I use the example of a business that sells products. Businesses that sell products manufactured by other businesses generally fall into one of two types: *retailers* that sell products to final consumers, and *wholesalers* (distributors) that sell to retailers. The following discussion applies to both. Also, this chapter lays the foundation for companies that manufacture products, which I discuss in Chapter 11.

One thing I have learned over the years is that there's a need for short-to-the-point, or quick-and-dirty profit models that managers can use for decision-making analysis and plotting profit strategy. By short, I mean on one page or even smaller than one full page. Like on one computer monitor screen, for instance, with which the manager can interact and test the critical factors that drive profit. For example: If sales price were decreased 5 percent to gain 10 percent more sales volume, what would happen to profit? Managers of profit centers need a tool to quickly answer such questions. Later in the chapter I introduce just such a profit analysis template for managers (see "Presenting a Profit Analysis Template").

Reporting operating expenses

Below the gross margin line in an internal P&L statement, reporting practices vary from company to company. There is no standard pattern. One question looms large: How should the *operating expenses* of a profit center be presented in its P&L report? There's no authoritative answer to this question. Different businesses report their operating expenses differently in their internal P&L statements. One basic choice for reporting operating expenses is between the *object of expenditure basis* and the *cost behavior basis*.

Reporting operating expenses on object of expenditure basis

By far the most common way to present operating expenses in a profit center's P&L report is to list them according to the *object of expenditure basis.* This means that expenses are classified according to what is purchased (the object of the expenditure) — such as salaries and wages, commissions paid to salespersons, rent, depreciation, shipping costs, real estate taxes, advertising, insurance, utilities, office supplies, telephone costs, and so on. To do this, the operating expenses of the business have to be recorded in such a way that these costs can be traced to each of its various profit centers. For example, employee salaries of persons working in a particular profit center are recorded as belonging to that profit center.

The object of expenditure basis for reporting operating costs to managers of profit centers is practical. And this information is useful for management control because, generally speaking, controlling costs focuses on the particular items being bought by the business. For example, a profit center manager analyzes wages and salary expense to decide whether additional or fewer personnel are needed relative to current and forecast sales levels. A manager can examine the fire insurance expense relative to the types of assets being insured and their risks of fire losses. For cost control purposes the object of expenditure basis works well. But, there is a downside. This method for reporting operating costs to profit center managers obscures the all-important factor in making profit: *margin.* Managers absolutely need to know margin, as I explain in the following sections.

Separating operating expenses further on their behavior basis

The first and usually largest *variable* expense of making sales is the cost of goods sold expense (for companies that sell products). In addition to cost of goods sold, an obvious variable expense, businesses also have other expenses that depend either on the volume of sales (quantities sold) or the dollar amount of sales (sales revenue). And virtually all businesses have *fixed* expenses that are not sensitive to sales activity — at least, not in the short run. Therefore, it makes sense to take operating expenses classified according to object of expenditure and further classify each expense into either variable or fixed. There would be a variable or fixed tag on each expense.

The principal advantage of separating operating expenses between variable and fixed is that margin can be reported. *Margin* is the residual amount after all variable expenses of making sales are deducted from sales revenue. In other words, margin equals profit after all variable costs are deducted from sales revenue but before fixed costs are deducted from sales revenue. Margin is compared with total fixed costs for the period. This head-to-head comparison of margin against fixed costs is critical. I come back to this important point in the next section.

Although it's hard to know for sure — because internal profit reporting practices of businesses are not publicized or generally available — my experience is that the large majority of companies do not attempt to classify operating expenses as variable or fixed. If you gave me a dollar for every company you found that classifies its operating expenses on the object of expenditure basis and I gave you a dollar for every business that further separates between variable and fixed behavior, I guarantee you that I would end up with many more dollars than you. Yet, for making profit decisions managers absolutely need to know the variable versus fixed nature of their operating expenses.

Presenting a Profit Analysis Template

Figure 9-1 presents a profit analysis template for a profit center example. After arguing for the separation of fixed and variable expenses, you shouldn't be surprised to see in Figure 9-1 that I divide operating expenses according to how they behave relative to sales activity. There are just four lines for expenses — cost of goods sold (a variable expense), two variable operating expenses, and fixed operating expenses. No further details for sales revenue and expenses are included in this profit model, in order to keep the template as brief (and therefore, as useful) as possible.

	Year Ended December 31, 2013		Year Ended December 31, 2012	
Sales volume	100,000 units		97,500 units	
	Per Unit	Totals	Per Unit	Totals
Sales revenue	$100.00	$10,000,000	$98.00	$9,555,000
Cost of goods sold expense	$60.00	$6,000,000	$61.50	$5,996,250
Gross margin	$40.00	$4,000,000	$36.50	$3,558,750
Revenue-driven operating expenses	8.50%	$850,000	8.00%	$764,400
Volume-driven operating expenses	$6.50	$650,000	$6.00	$585,000
Margin	$25.00	$2,500,000	$22.66	$2,209,350
Fixed operating expenses		$1,000,000		$925,000
Operating earnings		$1,500,000		$1,284,350

Figure 9-1: Profit analysis template for a profit center.

Conceivably, such a template such as shown in Figure 9-1 could be the first, top-level page for the formal P&L reports to managers. The following pages would have more detailed information for each line in the profit template. The additional information for each variable and fixed expense would be presented according to the object of expenditure basis. For example, depreciation on the profit center's fixed assets would be one of many items listed in the *fixed expenses* category. The amount of commissions paid to salespersons would be listed in the *revenue-driven expenses* category.

The example shown in Figure 9-1 is for one year. As I mention earlier, profit reports are prepared as frequently as needed by managers, monthly in most cases. Interim P&L reports may be abbreviated versions of the annual report. Keep in mind that this example is for just one slice of the total business, which has other profit centers each with its own profit profile.

The profit template shown in Figure 9-1 includes *sales volume,* which is the total number of units of product sold during the period. Of course, the accounting system of a business has to be designed to accumulate sales volume information for the P&L report of each profit center. Generally speaking, keeping track of sales volume for products is possible, unless the business sells a huge variety of different products. When a business cannot come up with a meaningful measure of sales volume, it still can classify its operating costs between variable and fixed, although it loses the ability to use per-unit values in analyzing profit and has to rely on other techniques.

Separating variable and fixed expenses

For a manager to analyze a business's profit behavior thoroughly, she needs to know which expenses are *variable* and which are *fixed* — in other words, which expenses change according to the level of sales activity in a given period, and which don't. The title of each expense account often gives a pretty good clue. For example, the cost of goods sold expense is variable because it depends on the number of units of product sold, and sales commissions are variable expenses. On the other hand, real estate property taxes and fire and liability insurance premiums are fixed for a period of time. Managers should always have a good feel for how their operating expenses behave relative to sales activity.

Variable expenses

Virtually every business has *variable expenses,* which move up and down in tight proportion with changes in sales volume or sales revenue, like soldiers obeying orders barked out by their drill sergeant. Here are examples of common variable expenses:

- The cost of goods sold expense, which is the cost of products sold to customers
- Commissions paid to salespeople based on their sales
- Franchise fees based on total sales for the period, which are paid to the franchisor
- Transportation costs of delivering products to customers via FedEx, UPS, and freight haulers (railroads and trucking companies)
- Fees that a retailer pays when a customer uses a credit or debit card

Cost of goods sold is usually (but not always) the largest variable expense of a business that sells products, as you would suspect. Other variable expenses are referred to as *operating* expenses, which are the costs of making sales and running the business. The sizes of variable operating expenses, relative to sales revenue, vary from industry to industry. Delivery costs of Wal-Mart and Costco, for instance, are minimal because their customers take the products they buy with them. (Wal-Mart and Costco employees generally don't even help carry purchases to their customers' vehicles.) Other businesses deliver products to their customers' doorsteps, so that expense is obviously much higher (and dependent on which delivery service the company uses — FedEx or UPS versus the U.S. Postal Service, for example).

Fixed expenses

Fixed operating expenses include many different costs that a business is obligated to pay and cannot decrease over the short run without major surgery on the human resources and physical facilities of the business.

As an example of fixed expenses, consider the typical self-service car wash business — you know, the kind where you drive in, put some coins in a box, and use the water spray to clean your car. Almost all the operating costs of this business are fixed; rent on the land, depreciation of the structure and the equipment, and the annual insurance premium don't depend on the number of cars passing through the car wash. The main variable expenses are the water and the soap, and perhaps the cost of electricity.

Fixed expenses are the costs of doing business that, for all practical purposes, are stuck at a certain amount over the short term. Fixed expenses do not react to changes in the sales level. Here are some more examples of fixed operating expenses:

✔ Gas and electricity costs to heat, cool, and light the premises

✔ Employees' salaries and benefits

✔ Real estate property taxes

✔ Annual audit fee (if the business has its financial statements audited)

✔ General liability and officers' and directors' insurance premiums

If you want to decrease fixed expenses significantly, you need to downsize the business (lay off workers, sell off property, and so on). When looking at the various ways for improving profit, significantly cutting down on fixed expenses is generally the last-resort option. Refer to the section "Know your options for improving profit" later in the chapter. A business should be careful not to overreact to a temporary downturn in sales by making drastic reductions in its fixed costs, which it may regret later if sales pick up again.

Stopping at operating earnings

In Figure 9-1, the profit template terminates at the *operating earnings* line; it does not include interest expense or income tax expense. Interest expense and income tax expense are business-wide types of expenses, which are the responsibility of the financial executive(s) of the business. Generally, interest and income tax expenses are not assigned to profit centers, unless a profit center is a rather large and autonomous organizational division of the business that has responsibility for its own assets, finances, and income tax.

The measure of profit before interest and income tax is commonly called *operating earnings* or *operating profit*. It also goes by the name *earnings before interest and tax,* or EBIT. It is not and should not be called *net income,* because this term is reserved for the final bottom-line profit number of a business, after all expenses (including interest and income tax) are deducted from sales revenue.

Focusing on margin — the catalyst of profit

Figure 9-1 includes a very important line of information: *margin* — both *margin per unit* and *total margin*. Margin is your operating profit before fixed expenses are deducted. Don't confuse this number with *gross margin,* which is profit after the cost of goods sold expense is subtracted from sales revenue but before any other expenses are deducted. (Please refer to the sidebar *Different uses of the term margin.*)

With the information in Figure 9-1 in hand, you can dig into the reasons that margin per unit increased from $22.66 in fiscal year 2012 to $25.00 in fiscal year 2013. Two favorable changes occurred: The sales price per unit increased, and the product cost decreased — no small achievement, to be sure! However, the gain in the gross profit per unit was offset by unfavorable changes in both variable operating expenses. The profit center manager must keep on top of these changes.

As a manager, your attention should be riveted on margin per unit, and you should understand the reasons for changes in this key profit driver from period to period. A small change in unit margin can have a big impact on operating earnings. (See "Don't underestimate the impact of small changes in sales price" later in the chapter.)

Different uses of the term *margin*

Gross margin, also called *gross profit,* equals sales revenue minus the cost of goods sold expense. Gross margin does not reflect other variable operating expenses that are deducted from sales revenue. In contrast, the term *margin* refers to sales revenue less *all* variable expenses. Some people use the term *contribution margin* instead of just *margin* to stress that margin contributes toward the recovery of fixed expenses (and to profit after fixed expenses are covered). However, the prefix *contribution* is not really necessary, and I don't use it. Why use two words when one will do?

As a general rule businesses that sell products report gross margin in their external income statements (although some don't). However, they do not disclose their variable and fixed operating expenses. They report expenses according to an object of expenditure basis, such as "marketing, administrative, and general expenses." The broad expense categories reported in external income statements include both variable and fixed cost components. Therefore, the margin of a business (sales revenue after all variable expenses but before fixed expenses) is not reported in its external income statement. Managers carefully guard information about margins. They don't want competitors to know the margins of their business.

Further complicating the issue, unfortunately, is that newspaper reporters frequently use the term *margin* when referring to operating earnings. Inside the world of accounting, however, the term margin means profit after all variable expenses are deducted from sales revenue but before fixed expenses are deducted. So, be careful when you see the term margin: It may refer to gross margin, to what accountants mean by margin, or to operating earnings (used in the press).

Answering Critical Profit Questions

Suppose you are the manager of a profit center, and you have just received your P&L report for the latest year. The first, or top, page of the report is the same as Figure 9-1. There are many more pages to your annual P&L with a lot more details about sales and expenses, but we concentrate on the first page here. So, refer to Figure 9-1 as we go along. You should immediately ask yourself two questions:

- ✔ How did I make $1.5 million profit (operating earnings before interest and income tax) in 2013?

- ✔ Why did my profit increase $215,650 over last year ($1,500,000 in 2013 − $1,284,350 in 2012 = $215,650 profit increase)?

How did you make profit?

Actually, you can answer this profit question three ways (see Figure 9-1 for data):

✔ **Answer # 1: You earned total margin that is more than fixed expenses.**

You earned $25 profit margin per unit and sold 100,000 units; therefore:

$25 unit margin × 100,000 units sales volume = $2,500,000 margin

Your profit center is charged with $1 million fixed expenses for the year; therefore:

$2,500,000 margin − $1,000,000 fixed operating expenses = $1,500,000 operating profit

✔ **Answer # 2: Your sales volume exceeded your break-even point.**

Your break-even point is the sales volume at which total margin exactly equals total fixed expenses. Your break-even point for 2013 was:

$1,000,000 total fixed expenses for year ÷ $25 margin per unit = 40,000 units sales volume break-even point

Your actual sales volume for the year was 100,000 units, or 60,000 units in excess of your break-even point. Each unit sold in excess of break-even generated $25 "pure" profit because the first 40,000 units sold covered your fixed expenses. Therefore:

60,000 units sold in excess of break-even × $25 margin per unit = $1,500,000 operating profit

✔ **Answer # 3: Your high sales volume diluted fixed expenses per unit to below your margin per unit.**

The average fixed expenses per unit sold for the year is:

$1,000,000 total fixed expenses ÷ 100,000 units sold = $10 fixed expenses per unit sold

Your margin per unit was $25; so operating earnings per unit were $15 ($25 margin per unit − $10 fixed expenses per unit = $15 operating earnings per unit). Therefore:

$15 operating earnings per unit × 100,000 units sales volume = $1,500,000 operating earnings

Each answer is valid. In certain situations, one method of analysis is more useful than another. If you were thinking of making a large increase in fixed operating expenses, for example, you should pay attention to the effect on your break-even point; answer #2 is useful in this situation. If you were thinking of changing sales prices, answer #1, which focuses on margin per unit, is very relevant. (See the later section "Using the Profit Template for Decision-Making Analysis.") Likewise, if you're dealing with changes in product cost or variable operating expenses that affect unit margin, answer #1 is very helpful.

Answer #3 is useful to focus on the *full cost* of a product. In the example, the sales price is $100 per unit (refer to Figure 9-1). The total of variable costs per unit is $75 (which includes product cost and the two variable operating costs per unit). The average fixed cost per unit sold is $10, which added to the $75 variable cost per unit gives $85 full cost per unit. Subtracting the full cost per unit from the $100 sales price gives the $15 profit per unit (before interest and income tax expenses are considered).

How did you increase profit?

In your profit center report (refer to Figure 9-1), note that your total fixed expenses increased from $925,000 last year to $1 million in 2013, a $75,000 increase. Of course, you should investigate the reasons for your fixed expense increases. These fixed costs are your responsibility as manager of the profit center. You definitely should know which of these costs were higher than last year, and the reasons for the increases.

In any case, you were able to increase margin more than enough to cover the fixed costs increases and to boost profit. In fact, your margin increased $290,650 over last year ($2,500,000 margin in 2013 – $2,209,350 margin in 2012 = $290,650 margin increase). How did you do this?

This question can be answered more than one way. In my view, the most practical method is to calculate the effect of changes in *sales volume* and the *margin per unit.* Being the superb manager that you are, to say nothing of your marketing genius, your profit center increased sales volume over last year. Furthermore, you were able to increase margin per unit, which is even more impressive. The profit impact of each change is determined as follows (refer to Figure 9-1 for data):

- **Sales volume change impact on profit:**

  $25 margin per unit × 2,500 units sales volume increase = $62,500 increase in margin

- **Margin per unit change impact on profit:**

  $2.34 increase in margin per unit × 97,500 units sales volume last year = $228,150 increase in margin

Even if your sales volume had stayed the same, the $2.34 increase in your margin per unit (from $22.66 to $25) would have increased margin $228,150. And by selling 2,500 more units than last year, you increased margin $62,500. Quite clearly, the major factor was the significant increase in your margin per unit. You were able to increase this key profit driver by more than 10 percent (10.3 percent to be precise). However, you may not be able to repeat this performance in the coming year; you may have to increase sales volume to boost profit next year.

Taking a Closer Look at the Lines in the Profit Template

As the previous sections should make clear, profit center managers depend heavily on the information in their P&L reports. They need to thoroughly understand these profit reports. Therefore, I want to spend some time walking through each element of the profit template. Flip back to Figure 9-1 as I do so.

Sales volume

Sales volume, the first line in the profit template, is the total number of units sold during the period, net of any returns by customers. Sales volume should include only units that actually brought in revenue to the business. In general, businesses do a good job in keeping track of the sales volumes of their products (and services). These are closely monitored figures in, for example, the automobile and personal computer industries.

Now here's a nagging problem: Some businesses sell a huge variety of products. No single product or product line brings in more than a fraction of the total sales revenue. For instance, McGuckin Hardware, a general hardware store in Boulder, carries more than 100,000 products according to its advertising. The business may keep count of customer traffic or the number of individual sales made over the year, but it probably does not track the quantities sold for each and every product it sells. I explore this issue later in the chapter — see the last section, "Closing with a Boozy Example," for more details.

Sales revenue

Sales revenue is the net amount of money received by the business from the sales of products during the period. Notice the word *net* here. The business in our example, like most, offers its customers many incentives to buy its products and to pay quickly for their purchases. The amount of sales revenue in Figure 9-1 is not simply the list prices of the products sold times the number of units sold. Rather, the sales revenue amount takes into account deductions for rebates, allowances, prompt payment discounts, and any other incentives offered to customers that reduce the amount of revenue received by the business. (The manager can ask that these revenue offsets be included in the supplementary layer of schedules to the main page of the P&L report.)

Cost of goods sold

Cost of goods sold is the cost of the products sold during the period. This expense should be net of discounts, rebates, and allowances the business receives from its vendors and suppliers. The cost of goods sold means different things for different types of businesses:

✔ To determine product costs, manufacturers add together three costs:

- The costs of raw materials

- Labor costs

- Production overhead costs

Accounting for the cost of manufactured products is a major function of *cost accounting,* which I discuss in Chapter 11.

✔ For retailers and distributors, product cost basically is purchase cost. However, refer to Chapter 7, where I explain the differences between the FIFO and LIFO methods for releasing inventory costs to the cost of goods sold expense. The profit center manager should have no doubts about which cost of goods sold expense accounting method is being used. For that matter, the manager should be aware of any other costs that are included in total product cost (such as inbound freight and handling costs in some cases).

Dealing with inventory shrinkage

One common problem is where to put the loss from *inventory shrinkage,* which refers to losses from shoplifting by customers, physical deterioration of products as they sit in inventory, employee theft of products, damage caused in the handling and storage of products, and so on. The amount of inventory shrinkage can be included in the cost of goods sold expense, or it may be included in volume-driven operating expenses. A manager definitely should know which other costs have been placed in the cost of goods sold expense, in addition to the product cost of units sold during the period.

Variable operating expenses

In the profit analysis template (Figure 9-1), variable operating expenses are divided into two types: revenue-driven expenses and volume-driven expenses.

Revenue-driven expenses are those that depend primarily on the dollar amount of sales revenue. This group of variable operating expenses includes commissions paid to salespersons based on the dollar amount of their sales, credit card fees paid by retailers, franchise fees based on sales revenue, and any other cost that depends directly on the amount of sales revenue. Notice in Figure 9-1 that these operating expenses are presented as a *percent* of sales price in the per-unit column. In the example these costs equal 8.5 percent, or $8.50 per $100 of sales revenue in 2013 (versus only 8.0 percent in 2012).

Volume-driven expenses are driven by and depend primarily on the number of units sold, or the total quantity of products sold during the period (as opposed to the dollar value of the sales). These expenses include delivery and transportation costs paid by the business, packaging costs, and any costs that depend primarily on the size and weight of the products sold.

Most businesses have both types of variable operating expenses. However, one or the other may be so minor that it would not be useful to report the cost as a separate item. Only the dominant type of variable operating expense would be presented in the profit analysis template; the one expense would absorb the other type — which is good enough for government work, as they say.

Fixed operating expenses

Managers may view fixed operating expenses as an albatross around the neck of the business. In fact, these costs provide the infrastructure and support for making sales. The main characteristic of fixed operating costs is that they do not decline when sales during the period fall short of expectations. A business commits to many fixed operating costs for the coming period. For all practical purposes these costs cannot be decreased much over the short run. Examples of fixed costs are wages of employees on fixed salaries (from managers to maintenance workers), real estate taxes, depreciation and rent on the buildings and equipment used in making sales, and utility bills.

Certain fixed costs can be matched with a particular profit center. For example, a business may advertise a specific product, and the fixed cost of the advertisement can be matched against revenue from sales of that product. A major product line may have its own employees on fixed salaries or its own delivery trucks on which depreciation is recorded. A business may purchase specific liability insurance covering a particular product it sells.

Dealing with a shortcoming

The profit analysis template I show in Figure 9-1 and the techniques for analyzing profit I explain in the section "Answering Critical Profit Questions" hinge on the separation of variable and fixed operating costs. The classification between variable and fixed operating expenses is not needed for external financial statements and income tax returns. Operating expenses are reported on the object of expenditure basis in external financial reports and tax returns, so the accounting systems of many businesses do not tag operating expense accounts as fixed or variable. As a result, variable versus fixed information for operating expenses is not readily available from the accounting system. What's a manager to do?

Well, here's a practical solution: As the profit center manager, you can tell your accountant whether an operating expense is variable or fixed. Give your classification of the operating expenses in your profit center to the accountant, and stress that you want this classification in the profit template for your profit center. This may be extra work for your accountant, but the variable versus fixed classification of operating expense is of great value for your management decision-making, control, and planning.

In contrast, you cannot directly couple company-wide fixed operating expenses to particular products, product lines, or other types of profit units in the organizational structure of a business. General administrative expenses (such as the CEO's annual salary and corporate legal expenses) are incurred on an entity-as-a-whole basis and cannot be connected directly with any particular profit center. A business may, therefore, allocate these fixed costs among its different profit centers. The fixed costs that are handed down from headquarters, if any, are included in *fixed operating expenses* in Figure 9-1.

Using the Profit Template for Decision-Making Analysis

The profit template (refer to Figure 9-1) is very useful for decision-making analysis. To demonstrate, suppose that you're under intense competitive pressure to lower the sales price of one product you sell. This product is one "slice" of the total activity reported in Figure 9-1. Suppose that during the year (2013) you sold 1,000 units of the product at a $100 sales price, and the unit costs of this product are the same as in Figure 9-1.

Your competitors are undercutting your sales price, so you're thinking of cutting the sales price 10 percent next year, or $10 per unit. You predict that the price reduction will boost sales volume 25 percent and increase your market share. Seems like a good idea — or does it? You should run some numbers before making a final decision, just to be sure. Answer #1 in the earlier section *How did you make profit?* is the best method for this analysis. For the year just ended, this product generated $25,000 margin:

$25 margin per unit × 1,000 units sold = $25,000.00 margin

Assuming your prediction about sales volume at the lower price is correct and sales volume increases to 1,250 units, and assuming that the variable costs for the product remain the same, next year you would earn $19,812.50 margin:

$15.85 margin per unit × 1,250 units sold = $19,812.50 margin

Cutting the sales price $10 reduces the margin per unit $9.15. (The revenue-driven operating expense would drop $.85 per unit with the $10.00 sales price decrease.) Therefore, the new margin per unit would be $15.85 per unit. That's a 37 percent drop in margin per unit. A 25 percent gain in sales volume cannot make up for the 37 percent plunge in margin per unit. You'd need a much larger sales volume increase just to keep margin the same as in 2013, and even more sales to increase margin next year. You'd better think twice about dropping the sales price.

You may gain a larger market share, but your margin would drop from $25,000.00 to $19,812.50 on this product if you go ahead with the sales price cut. Is the larger market share worth this much sacrifice of margin? That's why you get paid the big bucks: to make decisions like this. As your controller I can only help you do the analysis and calculate the impact on profit before you make a final decision.

Another factor to consider is this: Fixed expenses (people, warehouse space, distribution channels, and so on) provide the *capacity* to make sales and carry on operations. A small increase in sales volume, such as selling 250 more units of the product in question, should not push up the total fixed expenses of your profit center (unless you are already bursting at the seams). On the other hand, a major sales volume increase across the board would require additional capacity, and your fixed expenses would have to be increased.

This sales price reduction decision is just one example of the many decisions business managers have to deal with day in and day out. The profit analysis template is a useful — indeed an invaluable — analysis framework for many decisions facing business managers.

Tucking Away Some Valuable Lessons

The profit analysis template shown in Figure 9-1 offers managers several important lessons. Like most tools, the more you use it the more you learn. In the following sections I summarize some important lessons from the template.

Recognize the leverage effect caused by fixed operating expenses

Suppose sales volume had been 10 percent higher or lower in 2013, holding other profit factors the same. Would profit have been correspondingly 10 percent higher or lower? The intuitive, knee-jerk reaction answer is yes, profit would have been 10 percent higher or lower. Wouldn't it? Not necessarily. *Margin* would have been 10 percent higher or lower — $250,000 higher or lower ($25 margin per unit × 10,000 units = $250,000).

The $250,000 change in margin would carry down to operating earnings *unless* fixed expenses would have been higher or lower at the different sales volume. The very nature of fixed expenses is that these costs do not change with relatively small changes in sales volume. In all likelihood, fixed expenses would have been virtually the same at a 10 percent higher or lower sales level.

Therefore, operating earnings would have been $250,000 higher or lower. On the base profit of $1.5 million, the $250,000 swing equals a 17 percent shift in profit. Thus, a 10 percent swing in sales volume causes a 17 percent swing in profit. This wider swing in profit is called the *operating leverage* effect. The idea is that a business makes better use of its fixed expenses when sales go up; its fixed expenses don't increase with the sales volume increase. Of course, the downside is that fixed expenses don't decrease when sales volume drops.

Don't underestimate the impact of small changes in sales price

Recall that in the example the sales price is $100, and revenue-driven variable expenses are 8.5 percent of sales revenue (refer to Figure 9-1). Suppose the business had sold the product for $4 more or less than it did, which is only a 4 percent change — pretty small it would seem. This different sales price would have changed its margin per unit $3.66 net of the corresponding change in the revenue-driven variable expenses per unit. ($4 sales price change × 8.5 percent = $.34 per unit, which netted against the $4 sales price change = $3.66 change in margin per unit.)

Therefore, the business would have earned total margin $366,000 higher or lower than it did at the $100 sales price. ($3.66 change in margin per unit × 100,000 units sales volume = $366,000 shift in margin.) Fixed expenses are not sensitive to sales price changes and would have been the same, so the $366,000 shift in margin would carry down to profit.

The $366,000 swing in profit, compared with the $1.5 million baseline profit in the example, equals a 24 percent swing in profit. A 4 percent change in sales price causes a 24 percent change in profit. Recall that a 10 percent change in sales volume causes just a 17 percent change in profit. When it comes to profit impact, sales price changes dominate sales volume changes.

The moral of the story is to protect margin per unit above all else. Every dollar of margin per unit that's lost — due to decreased sales prices, increased product cost, or increases in other variable costs — has a tremendously negative impact on profit. Conversely, if you can increase the margin per unit without hurting sales volume, you reap very large profit benefits.

Know your options for improving profit

Improving profit boils down to three critical factors, listed in order from the most effective to the least effective:

✔ Increasing margin per unit

✔ Increasing sales volume

✔ Reducing fixed expenses

Say you want to improve your profit from the $1.5 million you earned in 2013 to $1.8 million next year, which is a $300,000 or 20 percent increase. Okay, so how are you going to increase profit $300,000? Here are your basic options:

✔ Increase your margin per unit $3, which would raise total margin $300,000 based on the 100,000 units sales volume.

✔ Sell 12,000 additional units at the present margin per unit of $25, which would raise your total margin by $300,000. (12,000 additional units × $25 = $300,000 additional margin.)

✔ Use a combination of these two strategies: Increase both the margin per unit and sales volume such that the combined effect is to improve total margin $300,000.

✔ Reduce fixed expenses $300,000.

The last alternative may not be very realistic. Reducing your direct fixed expenses $300,000, on a base of $1,000,000, would be drastic and probably would reduce your capacity to make sales and carry out the operations in your part of the business. Perhaps you could do a little belt-tightening in your fixed expenses area, but in all likelihood you would have to turn to the other alternatives for increasing your profit.

The second approach is obvious — you just need to set a sales goal of increasing the number of products sold by 12,000 units. (How you motivate your already overworked sales staff to accomplish that sales volume goal is up to you.) But how do you go about the first approach, increasing the margin per unit by $3?

The simplest way to increase margin per unit by $3 would be to decrease your product cost per unit $3. Or you could attempt to reduce sales commissions from $8.50 per $100 of sales to $5.50 per $100 — which may hurt the motivation of your sales force, of course. Or you could raise the sales price about $3.38 (remember that 8.5 percent comes off the top for sales commission, so only $3 would remain to improve the unit margin). Or you could combine two or more such changes so that your unit margin next year would increase $3.

Closing with a Boozy Example

Some years ago, several people I knew pooled their capital and opened a liquor store in a rapidly growing area. In their estimation, the business had a lot of promise. If they had asked me for advice, I would have told them one thing to do during their planning stage — in addition to location analysis and competition analysis, of course. I would have recommended that they run some critical numbers through a basic profit model like Figure 9-1 in order to estimate the annual sales revenue they would need to break even. Of course, they want to do better than break even, but the break-even sales level is a key point of reference.

Starting up any business involves making commitments to a lot of fixed expenses. Leases are signed, equipment is purchased, people are hired, and so on. All this puts a heavy fixed cost burden on a new business. The business needs to make sales and generate margin from the sales that is enough to cover its fixed expenses before it can break into the profit column. So, the first step I would have suggested is that they estimate their fixed expenses for the first year. Next, they should have estimated their profit margin on sales. Here there is a slight problem, but one that is not difficult to deal with.

During their open house for the new store, I noticed the large number of different beers, wines, and spirits available for sale — to say nothing of the different sizes and types of containers many products come in. Quite literally, the business sells thousands of distinct products. The store also sells many products like soft drinks, ice, corkscrews, and so on. Therefore, the business does not have an easy-to-define sales volume factor (the number of units sold) for analyzing profit. The business example I discuss in this chapter uses a sales volume factor, which is the number of units sold during the period. In the liquor store example, this won't work. So, a modification is made. *Total sales revenue* is used for the measure of sales volume, not the number of units (bottles) sold.

The next step, then, is to determine the *average margin as a percent of sales revenue.* I'd estimate that a liquor store's average gross margin (sales revenue less cost of goods sold) is about 25 percent. The other variable operating expenses of the liquor store probably run about 5 percent of sales. (I could be off on this estimate, of course.) So, the average margin would be 20 percent of sales (25 percent gross margin less 5 percent variable operating expenses). Suppose the total fixed operating expenses of the liquor store were $100,000 per month (for rent, salaries, electricity, and so on), which is $1.2 million per year. So, the store needs $6 million in annual sales to break even:

$1,200,000 annual fixed expenses ÷ 20% average margin = $6,000,000 annual sales revenue to break even

Selling $6 million of product a year means moving a lot of booze. The business needs to sell another $1 million to provide $200,000 of operating earnings (at the 20 percent average margin) — to pay interest expense and income tax and leave enough net income for the owners who invested capital in the business and who expect a decent return on their investment.

I'm not privy to the financial statements of the liquor store. It appears that they have been quite successful. Business seems to be booming, even without my advice. Perhaps they did exactly the sort of profit model analysis that I would have recommended.

Chapter 10

Budgeting

- -

In This Chapter

▶ Defining the benefits of budgeting

▶ Budgeting profit and cash flow

▶ Determining whether budgeting is worth it

▶ Keeping budgeting in perspective

▶ Staying flexible with budgets

- -

A business can't open its doors each day without having a pretty good idea of what to expect. And it can't close its doors at the end of the day not knowing what happened. Recall the Boy Scouts' motto: "Be prepared." A business should follow that dictum: It should plan and be prepared for its future, and it should control its actual performance to reach its financial goals.

Business managers can wait for results to be reported to them on a "look back" basis, and then wing it from there. Or, they can look ahead and carefully plan profit, cash flows, and financial condition of the business, to chart its course into the future. The plan provides invaluable benchmarks; actual results can be compared against the plan to detect when things go off course.

Planning the financial future of a business and comparing actual performance against the plan are the essences of *business budgeting*. Budgeting is not an end to itself but rather a means or tool of financial planning and control.

But keep in mind that budgeting costs time and money. The business manager should put budgeting to the classic technique: the cost versus benefit test. Frankly, budgeting may not earn its keep and could actually cause serious problems that contradict the very reasons for doing it.

Budgeting offers important benefits, but a business may decide not to go to the effort of full-scale budgeting. I can't argue with a minimal budgeting strategy for some businesses. However, a business should not throw out the budgeting baby with the bath water. Certain techniques used in budgeting are very useful even when a business doesn't do formal budgeting.

Exploring the Reasons for Budgeting

The financial statements included in the financial reports of a business are prepared *after the fact*; they're based on transactions that have already taken place. (I explain business financial statements in Chapters 4, 5, and 6.) Budgeted financial statements, on the other hand, are prepared *before the fact* and reflect future transactions that are expected to take place based on the business's strategy and financial goals. Budgeted financial statements are not shared outside the business; they are strictly for internal management use.

Business budgeting requires setting specific goals and developing the detailed plans necessary to achieve them. Business budgeting should be built on realistic forecasts for the coming period. *Realistic* means attainable and probable. (In larger organizations managers may set their budget objectives too low and easy, in order to achieve them.) A business budget is an integrated plan of action — not simply a few trend lines on a financial chart. Budgeting is much more than slap-dashing together a few figures. A budget is an integrated financial plan put down on paper — or, more likely these days, entered in computer spreadsheets. (There are several good budgeting software programs on the market today; your CPA or other consultant can advise you on which ones are best for your business.)

Business managers don't (or shouldn't) just look out the window and come up with budget numbers. Budgeting is not pie-in-the-sky wishful thinking. Business budgeting — to have practical value — must start with a broad-based critical analysis of the most recent actual performance and position of the business by the managers who are responsible for the results. Then the managers decide on specific and concrete goals for the coming year. (Budgets can be done for more than one year, but the first stepping stone into the future is the budget for the coming year — see the sidebar "Taking it one game at a time.")

Taking it one game at a time

A company generally prepares one-year budgets, although many businesses also develop budgets for two, three, and five years out. Whenever you reach out beyond a year, what you're doing becomes more tentative and iffy. Making forecasts and estimates for the next 12 months is tough enough. A one-year budget is more definite and detailed in comparison to longer-term budgets. As they say in the sports world, a business should take it one game (or year) at a time. Looking down the road beyond one year is a good idea, to set long-term goals and to develop long-term strategy. But long-term planning is different than short-term budgeting.

In short, budgeting demands a fair amount of managers' time and energy. Budgets should be worth this time and effort. So why should a business go to the trouble of budgeting? Business managers budget and prepare budgeted financial statements for three main reasons: modeling, planning, and control.

Modeling reasons for budgeting

Business managers should make detailed analyses to determine how to improve the financial performance and condition of their business. The status quo is usually not good enough; business managers are paid to improve things — not to simply rest on their past accomplishments. For this reason managers should develop good *models* of profit, cash flow, and financial condition for their business. Models are blueprints or schematics of how things work. A financial model is like a roadmap that clearly marks the pathways to profit, cash flow, and financial condition.

Don't be intimidated by the term *model.* Simply put, a model consists of variables and how they interact. A variable is a critical factor that, in conjunction with other factors, determines results. A model is analytical, but not all models are mathematical. In fact, none of the financial models in this book is the least bit mathematical — but you do have to look at each factor of the model and how it interacts with one or more other factors. Here's an example of an accounting model, which is called the *accounting equation*:

Assets = Liabilities + Owners' equity

This is a very condensed model of the balance sheet. The accounting equation is not detailed enough for budgeting, however. More detail about assets and liabilities is needed for budgeting purposes.

Chapter 9 presents a profit template for managers (see Figure 9-1). This template is, at its core, a model. It includes the critical variables that drive profit: sales volume, sales price, product cost, and so on. A profit model, such as the one in Figure 9-1, provides the framework for understanding and analyzing profit performance. A good profit model also serves as the platform and the point of departure for mapping out profit strategies for the coming period.

Likewise, business managers need a model, or blueprint, in planning cash flow from operating activities. (I explain this vital source of cash flow in Chapter 6.) Managers should definitely forecast the amount of cash they will generate during the coming year from making profit. They need a reliable estimate of this source of cash flow in order to plan for other sources of cash flow they will need during the coming year — to provide the money for replacing and expanding the long-term operating (fixed) assets of the business and to make cash distributions from profit to owners. Managers need a model, or map if you prefer that provides a clear trail of how the sales and expenses of the business drive its assets and liabilities, which in turn drive the cash flow from operating activities.

Most business managers see the advantages of budgeting profit for the coming year; you don't have to twist their arms to convince them. At the same time, many business mangers do not carry through and do not budget changes in assets and liabilities during the coming year, which means they can't budget cash flow from operating activities. All their budget effort is focused on profit, and they leave cash flows and financial condition unattended. This is a dangerous strategy when the business is in a tight cash position. The business should not simply assume that its cash flow from operating activities would be adequate to its needs during the coming year.

Generally, a business should prepare all three budgeted financial statements:

- **Budgeted income statement (profit report):** A profit analysis model, such as the one shown in Figure 9-1, highlights the critical variables that drive profit. Remember that this model separates *variable* and *fixed* expenses and focuses on *sales volume*, *margin per unit*, and other factors that determine profit performance. These are the key factors that must be improved to enhance profit performance in the coming period. The highly condensed basic profit model provides a useful frame of reference for preparing the much more detailed, comprehensive profit budget.

- **Budgeted balance sheet:** The key connections and ratios between sales revenue and expenses and their corresponding assets and liabilities are the elements in the model for the budgeted balance sheet. These vital connections are explained throughout Chapters 4 and 5. The budgeted changes in operating assets and liabilities provide the information needed for budgeting cash flows during the coming year.

- **Budgeted statement of cash flows:** The budgeted changes during the coming year in the assets and liabilities used in making profit (conducting operating activities) determine *cash flow from operating activities* for the coming year (see Chapter 6). In contrast, the cash flows of *investing* and *financing* activities depend on the managers' strategic decisions regarding capital expenditures that will be made during the coming year, how much new capital will be raised from debt and from owners' sources of capital, and the business's policy regarding cash distributions from profit.

In short, budgeting requires good working models of making profit, financial condition (assets and liabilities), and cash flow. Budgeting provides a strong incentive for business managers to develop financial models that help them make strategic decisions, exercise control, and do better planning.

Planning reasons for budgeting

One purpose of budgeting is to force managers to create a definite and detailed financial plan for the coming period. To construct a budget, managers have to establish explicit financial objectives for the coming year and identify exactly what has to be done to accomplish these financial objectives. Budgeted financial statements and their supporting schedules provide clear destination points — the financial flight plan for a business.

The process of putting together a budget directs attention to the specific things that you must do to achieve your profit objectives and optimize your assets and capital. Basically, budgets are a form of planning that push managers to answer the question, "How are we going to get there from here?"

Budgeting can also yield other important planning-related benefits:

- **Budgeting encourages a business to articulate its vision, strategy, and goals.** A business needs a clearly stated strategy guided by an overarching vision, and it should have definite and explicit goals. It is not enough for business managers to have strategies and goals in their heads. Developing budgeted financial statements forces managers to be explicit and definite about the objectives of the business, as well as to formulate realistic plans for achieving the business objectives.

- **Budgeting imposes discipline and deadlines on the planning process.** Busy managers have trouble finding enough time for lunch, let alone planning for the upcoming financial period. Budgeting pushes managers to set aside time to prepare a detailed plan that serves as a road map for the business. Good planning results in a concrete course of action that details how a company plans to achieve its financial objectives.

Control reasons for budgeting

I deliberately put this reason last, after the modeling and planning reasons for budgeting. Many people have the mistaken notion that the purpose of budgeting is to rein in managers and employees, who otherwise would spend money like drunken sailors. Budgeting should not put the business's managers in a financial strait jacket. Tying the hands of managers is not the purpose of budgeting. Having said this, however, it's true that budgets serve a management control function. *Management control,* first and foremost, means achieving the financial goals and objectives of the business, which requires comparing actual performance against some sort of benchmarks and holding individual managers responsible for keeping the business on schedule in reaching its financial objectives.

The board of directors of a corporation focuses its attention on the *master budget* for the whole business: the budgeted income statement, balance sheet, and cash flow statement for the business for the coming year. The chief executive officer (CEO) of the business focuses on the master budget as well, but the CEO must also look at how each manager in the organization is doing on his or her part of the master budget. As you move down the organization chart of a business, managers have narrower responsibilities — say, for the business's northeastern territory or for one major product line. A master budget consists of different segments that follow the business's organizational structure. In other words, the master budget is put together from many pieces, one for each separate organizational unit of the business. For example, the manager of one of the company's far-flung warehouses has a separate budget for expenses and inventory levels for his or her bailiwick.

By using budget targets as benchmarks against which actual performance is compared, managers can closely monitor progress toward (or deviations from) the budget goals and timetable. You use a budget plan like a navigation chart to keep your business on course. Significant variations from the budget raise red flags, in which case you can determine that performance is off course or that the budget needs to be revised because of unexpected developments.

For management control, a budgeted profit report is divided into months or quarters for the coming year. The budgeted balance sheet and budgeted cash flow statement may also be put on a monthly or quarterly basis. The business should not wait too long to compare budgeted sales revenue and expenses against actual performance (or to compare actual cash flows and asset levels against the budget). You need to take prompt action when problems arise, such as a divergence between budgeted expenses and actual expenses.

Profit is the main thing to pay attention to, but accounts receivable and inventory can also get out of control (become too high relative to actual sales revenue and cost of goods sold expense), causing cash flow problems. (Chapter 6 explains how increases in accounts receivable and inventory are negative factors on cash flow.) A business cannot afford to ignore its balance sheet and cash flow numbers until the end of the year.

Additional Benefits of Budgeting

Budgeting has advantages and ramifications that go beyond the financial dimension and have more to do with business management in general. Consider the following:

✔ **Budgeting forces managers to do better forecasting.** Managers should be constantly scanning the business environment to spot changes that will impact the business. Vague generalizations about what the future may hold for the business are not good enough for assembling a budget. Managers are forced to put their predictions into definite and concrete forecasts. For example, a recent issue of a business newsletter listed the following costs that a business has to (or should) forecast (Barbara Weltman *Big Ideas for Small Businesses*, October 1, 2012):

- Wages and salaries

- Insurance (health, business owner policies, workers' compensation)

- Energy costs

- Postage and shipping costs

- Interest rates

- Travel and entertainment

- Technology (software, hardware, and consultants)

- Legal fees, rents, and audits

✔ **Budgeting motivates managers and employees by providing useful yardsticks for evaluating performance.** The budgeting process can have a good motivational impact by involving managers in the budgeting process (especially in setting goals and objectives) and by providing incentives to managers to strive for and achieve the business's goals and objectives. Budgets provide useful information for superiors to evaluate the performance of managers and can be used to reward good results. Employees may be equally motivated by budgets. For example, budgets supply baseline financial information for incentive compensation plans. And the profit plan (budget) for the year can be used to award year-end bonuses according to whether designated goals were achieved.

✔ **Budgeting can assist in the communication between different levels of management.** Putting plans and expectations in black and white in budgeted financial statements — including definite numbers for forecasts and goals — minimizes confusion and creates a kind of common language. As you know, the "failure to communicate" lament is common in many business organizations. Well-crafted budgets can definitely help the communication process.

✔ **Budgeting is essential in writing a business plan.** New and emerging businesses need to present a convincing business plan when raising capital. Because these businesses may have little or no history, the managers and owners must demonstrate convincingly that the company has a clear strategy and a realistic plan to make profit. A coherent, realistic budget forecast is an essential component of a business plan. Venture capital sources definitely want to see the budgeted financial statements of a business.

In larger businesses, budgets are typically used to hold managers accountable for their areas of responsibility in the organization; actual results are compared against budgeted goals and timetables, and variances are highlighted. Managers do not mind taking credit for *favorable* variances, when actual comes in better than budget. But beating the budget for the period does not always indicate outstanding performance. A favorable variance could be the result of gaming the budget in the first place, so that the budgeted benchmarks can be easily achieved.

Likewise, *unfavorable* variances have to be interpreted carefully. If a manager's budgeted goals and targets are fair and reasonable, the manager should be held responsible. The manager should carefully analyze what went wrong and what needs to be improved. Stern action may be called for, but the higher ups should recognize that the budget benchmarks may not be entirely fair; in particular, they should make allowances for unexpected developments that occur after the budget goals and targets are established (such as a hurricane or tornado, or the bankruptcy of a major customer). When managers perceive the budgeted goals and targets to be arbitrarily imposed by superiors and not realistic, serious motivational problems can arise.

Is Budgeting Worth Its Costs?

As you have undoubtedly heard, there's no such thing as a free lunch. Budgeting has its costs, which managers should take into account before rushing into (or continuing with) a full-scale budgeting process. Whether or not to engage in budgeting is a prime example of how managers make tough decisions: comparing costs versus benefits. Budgeting has many benefits, but managers have to weigh these against the costs of budgeting. And by costs, I don't mean just the monetary out-of-pocket costs. The costs of budgeting are in several different dimensions.

Budgeting is not without several serious problems on the practical level. Budgeting looks good in theory, but in actual practice things are not so rosy. Here are some concerns to consider:

- Budgeting takes time, and the one thing all business managers will tell you is that they never have enough time for all the things they should do. The question always is: What else could managers do with their time if budgeting were eliminated or scaled down?

- Budgeting done from the top down (from headquarters down to the lower levels of managers) can stifle innovation and discourage managers from taking the initiative when they should.

✔ Unrealistic budget goals can demotivate managers rather than motivate them.

✔ Managers may *game* the budget, which means they play the budget as a game in which they worry first and foremost about how they will be affected by the budget rather than what's best for the business.

✔ There have been cases in which managers resorted to accounting fraud to make their budget numbers.

There has always been grumbling about budgeting. A well-known adage in the advertising profession is that half of a company's advertising cost is wasted; the problem is that managers don't know which half. Likewise, you could argue that half the cost of budgeting is wasted; although it's difficult to pinpoint which particular aspects of budgeting are not cost effective.

A recent article makes a strongly worded case against budgeting. See *Freed from the Budget*, by Russ Banham, which was posted on the www.CFO.com website and taken from the September 1, 2012 issue of *CFO* magazine. This polemic offers several reasons for not budgeting, including the following:

✔ Budgeting prevents rapid response to unpredictable events

✔ Budgeting stifles initiative and innovations

✔ Budgeting protects non value-adding costs

✔ Budgeting demotivates people

The article makes a good case against budgeting, but in my mind it doesn't provide a very convincing answer to the question: If not budgeting, then what? Quite clearly business managers must plan and control. The trick is how to carry out these tasks in the most effective and efficient manner.

Realizing That Not Everyone Budgets

Most of what I've said so far in this chapter can be likened to a commercial for budgeting — emphasizing the reasons for and advantages of budgeting by a business. So every business does budgeting, right? Nope. Smaller businesses generally do little or no budgeting — and even many larger businesses avoid budgeting, at least in a formal and comprehensive manner. The reasons are many, and mostly practical in nature.

Avoiding budgeting

Some businesses are in relatively mature stages of their life cycle or operate in a mature and stable industry. These companies do not have to plan for any major changes or discontinuities. Next year will be a great deal like last year. The benefits of going through a formal budgeting process do not seem worth the time and cost.

At the other extreme, a business may be in an uncertain environment, where attempting to predict the future seems pointless. A business may lack the expertise and experience to prepare budgeted financial statements, and it may not be willing to pay the cost for a CPA or outside consultant to help.

But what if your business applies for a loan? The lender will demand to see a well-thought-out budget in your business plan, right? Not necessarily. I served on a local bank's board of directors for several years, and I reviewed many loan requests. Our bank did not expect a business to include a set of budgeted financial statements in the loan request package. Of course, we did demand to see the latest financial statements of the business. Very few of our smaller business clients prepared budgeted financial statements.

Relying on internal accounting reports

Although many businesses do not prepare budgets, they still establish fairly specific goals and performance objectives that serve as good benchmarks for management control. Every business — whether it does budgeting or not — should design internal accounting reports that provide the information managers need in running a business. Obviously, managers should keep close tabs on what's going on throughout the business. Some years ago, in one of my classes, I asked students for a short definition of management control. One student answered that management control means "watching everything." That's not bad.

Even in a business that doesn't do budgeting, managers depend on regular profit reports, balance sheets, and cash flow statements. These key internal financial statements should provide detailed management control information. These feedback reports are also used for looking ahead and thinking about the future. Other specialized accounting reports may be needed as well.

Making reports useful for management control

Most business managers, in my experience, would tell you that the accounting reports they get are reasonably good for management control. Their accounting reports provide the detailed information they need for keeping a close watch on the 1,001 details of the business (or their particular sphere of responsibility in the business organization).

What are the criticisms I hear most often about internal accounting reports?

> ✔ They contain too much information.
>
> ✔ All the information is flat, as if each piece of information is equally relevant.

Managers are busy people and have only so much time to read the accounting reports coming to them. Managers have a valid beef on this score, I think. Ideally, significant deviations and problems should be highlighted in the accounting reports they receive — but separating the important from the not-so-important is easier said than done.

Making reports useful for decision making

If you were to ask a cross-section of business managers how useful their accounting reports are for *making decisions,* you would get a different answer than how good the accounting reports are for management control. To improvise on the tag line of the airline I recently flew on: Management decision-making is a whole different animal than management control.

Business managers make many decisions affecting profit: setting sales prices, buying products, determining wages and salaries, hiring independent contractors, and purchasing fixed assets, for example. Managers should carefully analyze how their actions would impact profit before reaching final decisions. Managers need internal profit reports that serve as good profit models — that make clear the critical variables that affect profit. (Figure 10-1 in the next section presents an example). Well-designed management profit reports are absolutely essential for helping managers make good decisions.

Keep in mind that almost all business decisions involve non-financial and non-quantifiable factors that go beyond the information included in accounting reports. For example, the accounting department of a business can calculate the cost savings of a wage cut, or the elimination of overtime hours by employees, or a change in the retirement plan for employees — and the manager would certainly look at this data. But such decisions must consider many other factors, such as effects on employee morale and productivity, the possibility of the union going on strike, legal issues, and so on. In short, accounting reports provide only part of the information needed for business decisions, though an essential part for sure.

Making reports clear and straightforward

Needless to say, the internal accounting reports to managers should be clear and straightforward. The manner of presentation and means of communication should get the manager's attention, and a manager should not have to call the accounting department for explanations.

Designing useful management accounting reports is a challenging task. Within one business organization, an accounting report may have to be somewhat different from one profit center to the next. Standardizing accounting reports may seem like a good idea but may not be in the best interests of the various managers throughout the business — who have different responsibilities and different problems to deal with.

Many of the management accounting reports that I've seen could be improved — substantially! Accounting systems pay so much attention to the demands of preparing external financial statements and tax returns that managers' needs for good internal reports are often overlooked or ignored. The accounting reports in many businesses do not speak to the managers receiving them; the reports are voluminous and technical and are not focused on the most urgent and important problems facing the managers. Designing good internal accounting reports for managers is a challenging task, to be sure. But every business should take a hard look at its internal management accounting reports and identify what should be improved.

Watching Budgeting in Action

Suppose you're the general manager of one of a large company's several divisions, which is a major profit center of the business. (I discuss profit centers in Chapter 9.) You have broad authority to run this division, as well as the responsibility for meeting the financial expectations for your division. To be more specific, your profit responsibility is to produce a satisfactory annual operating profit, which is the amount of earnings before interest and income tax (EBIT). (Interest and income tax expenses are handled at the headquarters level in the organization.)

The CEO has made clear to you that she expects your division to increase EBIT during the coming year by 10 percent, or $256,000 to be exact. In fact, she has asked you to prepare a budgeted profit report showing your plan of action for increasing your division's EBIT by this target amount. She also has asked you to prepare a summary for the budgeted cash flow from operating activities based on your profit plan for the coming year.

Figure 10-1 presents the P&L report of your division for the year just ended. The format of this accounting report follows the profit report template explained in Chapter 9, which is designed for understanding profit behavior and how to increase profit. Note that fixed operating expenses are separated from the two variable operating expenses. (Your actual reports may include more detailed information about sales and expenses.) To keep number crunching to a minimum, I assume that you sell only one product in this example. Most businesses sell a range of products, not just one. So, they have to apply profit analysis to each product, department, product line, or other grouping of the company's sources of profit. See the sidebar "Keeping an eye on sales mix."

Keeping an eye on sales mix

Most businesses, or the major divisions of a large business, sell a mix of several different products. General Motors, for example, sells many makes and models of autos and light trucks, to say nothing about its other products. The next time you visit your local hardware store, take the time to look at the number of products on the shelves. The assortment of products sold by a business and the quantities sold of each that make up its total sales revenue is referred to as its *sales mix*. As a general rule, certain products have higher profit margins than others. Some products may have extremely low profit margins, so they are called *loss leaders*.

The marketing strategy for loss leaders is to use them as magnets, so customers buy your higher profit margin products along with the loss leaders. Shifting the sales mix to a higher proportion of higher profit margin products has the effect of increasing the average profit margin on all products sold. (A shift to lower profit margin products would have the opposite effect, of course.) Budgeting sales revenue and expenses for the coming year must include any planned shifts in the company's sales mix.

	Year Just Ended	
Sales volume	260,000 units	
	Per Unit	Totals
Sales revenue	$100.00	$26,000,000
Cost of goods sold	$55.00	$14,300,000
Gross margin	$45.00	$11,700,000
Revenue-driven expenses	$8.00	$2,080,000
Volume-driven expenses	$5.00	$1,300,000
Margin	$32.00	$8,320,000
Fixed expenses		$5,720,000
Operating profit		$2,600,000

Figure 10-1: P&L report for the year just ended.

Developing your profit improvement strategy and profit budget

Being an experienced manager, you know the importance of protecting your unit margins. Your division sold 260,000 units in the year just ended (see Figure 10-1). Your margin per unit was $32. If all your costs were to remain the same next year (you wish!), you could sell 8,000 more units to reach your $256,000 profit improvement goal:

> $256,000 additional margin needed ÷ $32 margin per unit = 8,000 additional units

The relatively small increase in your sales volume (8,000 additional units ÷ 260,000 units = 3.1 percent) should not increase your fixed expenses — unless you're already operating at full capacity and would have to increase warehouse space and delivery capacity to take on even a small increase in sales volume. But realistically, some or most of your costs will probably increase next year.

Let's take this one step at a time. First, we look at your *fixed expenses* for the coming year. You and your managers, with the assistance of your trusty accounting staff, have analyzed your fixed expenses line by line for the coming year. Some of these fixed expenses will actually be reduced or eliminated next year. But the large majority of these costs will continue next year, and most are subject to inflation. Based on careful studies and estimates, you and your staff forecast total fixed operating expenses for next year will be $6,006,000, which is $286,000 more than the year just ended.

Fortunately, you think that your volume-driven variable expenses should not increase next year. These are mainly transportation costs, and the shipping industry is in a very competitive, hold-the-price-down mode of operations that should last through the coming year. The cost per unit shipped should not increase.

You have decided to hold the revenue-driven operating expenses at 8 percent of sales revenue during the coming year, the same as for the year just ended. These are sales commissions, and you have already announced to your sales staff that their sales commission percentage will remain the same during the coming year. On the other hand, your purchasing manager has told you to plan on a 4 percent product cost increase next year — from $55 per unit to $57.20 per unit, or an increase of $2.20 per unit.

Summing up to this point, your total fixed expenses will increase $286,000 next year, and the $2.20 forecast product cost will drop your margin per unit from $32.00 to $29.80 if your sales price does not increase. One way to achieve your profit goal next year would be to load all the needed increase on sales volume and keep sales price the same. (I'm not suggesting that this strategy is a good one, but it serves as a good point of departure.)

So, what would your sales volume have to be next year? Remember: You want to increase profit $256,000 (orders from on high), and your fixed expenses will increase $286,000 next year. So, your margin goal for next year is determined as follows:

> $8,320,000 margin for year just ended + $286,000 fixed expenses increase + $256,000 profit improvement goal = $8,862,000 margin goal

Without bumping sales price, your margin would be only $29.80 per unit next year. At this margin per unit you will have to sell over 297,000 units:

$8,862,000 total margin goal ÷ $29.80 margin per unit = 297,383 units sales volume

Compared with the 260,000 units sales volume in the year just ended, you would have to increase sales by more than 37,000 units, or more than 14 percent.

You and your sales manager conclude that sales volume cannot be increased 14 percent. You'll have to raise the sales price to compensate for the increase in product cost and to help cover the fixed cost increases. After much discussion, you and your sales manager decide to increase the sales price 3 percent, from $100 to $103. Based on the 3 percent sales price increase and the forecast product cost increase, your unit margin next year would be as follows:

Budgeted Unit Margin Next Year

Sales price	$103.00
Product cost	(57.20)
Revenue-driven operating expenses (@ 8.0%)	(8.24)
Volume-driven operating expenses per unit	(5.00)
Equals: Margin per unit	$32.56

At the budgeted $32.56 margin per unit, you determine the sales volume needed next year to reach your profit goal as follows:

$8,862,000 total margin goal next year ÷ $32.56 margin per unit = 272,174 units sales volume

This sales volume is about 5 percent higher than last year (12,174 additional units over the 260,000 sales volume last year = about a 5 percent increase).

You decide to go with the 3 percent sales price increase combined with the 5 percent sales volume growth as your official budget plan. Accordingly, you forward your budgeted profit report for the coming year to the CEO. Figure 10-2 summarizes this profit budget for the coming year, with comparative figures for the year just ended.

The main page of your budgeted profit report is supplemented with appropriate schedules to provide additional detail about sales by types of customers and other relevant information. Also, your budgeted profit plan is broken down into quarters (perhaps months) to provide benchmarks for comparing actual performance during the year against your budgeted targets and timetable.

	Actual for Year Just Ended		Budgeted for Coming Year	
Sales volume	260,000 units		272,170 units	
	Per Unit	Totals	Per Unit	Totals
Sales revenue	$100.00	$26,000,000	$103.00	$28,033,968
Cost of goods sold	$55.00	$14,300,000	$57.20	$15,568,378
Gross margin	$45.00	$11,700,000	$45.80	$12,465,590
Revenue-driven expenses	$8.00	$2,080,000	$8.24	$2,242,718
Volume-driven expenses	$5.00	$1,300,000	$5.00	$1,360,872
Margin	$32.00	$8,320,000	$32.56	$8,862,000
Fixed expenses		$5,720,000		$6,006,000
Operating profit		$2,600,000		$2,856,000

Figure 10-2: Budgeted profit report for coming year.

Budgeting cash flow for the coming year

The budgeted profit plan (refer to Figure 10-2) is the main focus of attention, but the CEO also requests that all divisions present a *budgeted cash flow from operating activities* for the coming year. **Remember:** The profit you're responsible for as general manager of the division is the amount of operating earnings before interest and income tax (EBIT).

Chapter 6 explains that increases in accounts receivable, inventory, and prepaid expenses *hurt* cash flow from operating activities and that increases in accounts payable and accrued liabilities *help* cash flow. In reading the budgeted profit report for the coming year (refer to Figure 10-2), you see that virtually every budgeted figure for the coming year is higher than the figure for the year just ended. Therefore, your operating assets and liabilities will increase at the higher sales revenue and expense levels next year — unless you can implement changes to prevent the increases.

For example, sales revenue increases from $26,000,000 to the budgeted $28,033,968 next year (refer to Figure 10-2) — an increase of $2,033,968. Your accounts receivable balance was five weeks of annual sales last year. Do you plan to tighten up the credit terms offered to customers next year —a year in which you will raise the sales price and also plan to increase sales volume? I doubt it. More likely, you will attempt to keep your accounts receivable balance at five weeks of annual sales.

Assume that you decide to offer your customers the same credit terms next year. Thus, the increase in sales revenue will cause accounts receivable to increase by $195,574:

5/52 × $2,033,968 sales revenue increase = $195,574 accounts receivable increase

Last year, inventory was 13 weeks of annual cost of goods sold expense. You may be in the process of implementing inventory reduction techniques. If you really expect to reduce the average time inventory will be held in stock before being sold, you should inform your accounting staff so that they can include this key change in the balance sheet and cash flow models. Otherwise, they will assume that the past ratios for these vital connections will continue next year.

Assuming your inventory holding period remains the same, your inventory balance will increase more than $317,000:

13/52 × $1,268,378 cost of goods sold expense increase = $317,055 inventory increase

Figure 10-3 presents a brief summary of your budgeted cash flow from operating activities based on the information given for this example and using your historical ratios for short-term assets and liabilities driven by sales and expenses. *Note:* Increases in accrued interest payable and income tax payable are not included in your budgeted cash flow. Your profit responsibility ends at the operating profit line, or earnings before interest and income tax expenses.

Budgeted Profit (See Figure 10-2)	$2,856,000
Accounts Receivable Increase	(195,574)
Inventory Increase	(317,095)
Prepaid Expenses Increase	(26,226)
Depreciation Expense	835,000
Accounts Payable Increase	34,968
Accrued Expenses Payable Increase	52,453
Budgeted Cash Flow From Operating Activities	$3,239,526

Figure 10-3: Budgeted cash flow from operating activities for the coming year.

You submit this budgeted cash flow from operating activities (see Figure 10-3) to headquarters. Top management expects you to control the increases in your operating assets and liabilities so that the actual cash flow generated by your division next year comes in on target. The cash flow of your division (perhaps minus a small amount needed to increase the working cash balance held by your division) will be transferred to the central treasury of the business. Headquarters will be planning on you generating about $3.2 million cash flow during the coming year.

Considering Capital Expenditures and Other Cash Needs

This chapter focuses on profit budgeting for the coming year and budgeting the cash flow from that profit. These are the two hardcore components of business budgeting, but not the whole story. Another key element of the budgeting process is to prepare a *capital expenditures budget* for your division that goes to top management for review and approval. A business has to take a hard look at its long-term operating assets — in particular, the capacity, condition, and efficiency of these resources — and decide whether it needs to expand and modernize its property, plant, and equipment.

In most cases, a business needs to invest substantial sums of money in purchasing new fixed assets or retrofitting and upgrading its old fixed assets. These long-term investments require major cash outlays. So, each division of a business prepares a formal list of the fixed assets to be purchased, constructed, and upgraded. The money for these major outlays comes from the central treasury of the business. Accordingly, the overall capital expenditures budget goes to the highest levels in the organization for review and final approval. The chief financial officer, the CEO, and the board of directors of the business go over a capital expenditure budget request with a fine-toothed comb (or at least they *should*).

A major factor in analyzing capital expenditures is the *cost of capital*, or the return on investment (ROI) that a business must earn. Cost of capital refers to the time value of money, and is measured based on interest rates and return on equity (ROE) expectations. (See Chapter 13 for more on ROE.) A company's cost of capital depends on its mix of debt and equity and the respective costs of these two capital determinants. The cost of capital is used in *capital budgeting* analysis (another term for capital expenditures analysis), which is beyond the scope of this book. It involves calculating the internal rate of return (IRR) and present value (PV) of the future cash flows from an investment of capital.

At the company-wide level, the financial officers merge the profit and cash flow budgets of all profit centers and cost centers of the business. (A *cost center* is an organizational unit that does not generate revenue, such as the legal and accounting departments.) The budgets submitted by one or more of the divisions may be returned for revision before final approval is given. One concern is whether the collective cash flow total from all the units provides enough money for the capital expenditures that will be made during the coming year — and to meet the other demands for cash, such as for cash distributions from profit. The business may have to raise more capital from debt or equity sources during the coming year to close the gap between cash flow from operating activities and its needs for cash. This is a central topic in the field of business finance and beyond the coverage of this book.

Business budgeting versus government budgeting: Only the name is the same

Business and government budgeting are more different than alike. Government budgeting is preoccupied with allocating scarce resources among many competing demands. From federal agencies down to local school districts, government entities have only so much revenue available. They have to make difficult choices regarding how to spend their limited tax revenue.

Formal budgeting is legally required for almost all government entities. First, a budget request is submitted. After money is appropriated, the budget document becomes legally binding on the government agency. Government budgets are legal strait jackets; the government entity has to stay within the amounts appropriated for each expenditure category. Any changes from the established budgets need formal approval and are difficult to get through the system.

A business is not legally required to use budgeting. A business can implement and use its budget as it pleases, and it can even abandon its budget in midstream. Unlike the government, the revenue of a business is not constrained; a business can do many things to increase sales revenue. A business can pass its costs to its customers in the sales prices it charges. In contrast, government has to raise taxes to spend more (except for federal deficit spending, of course).

Chapter 11

Cost Accounting

· ·

In This Chapter

▶ Measuring costs: The second-most important thing accountants do

▶ Recognizing the different needs for cost information

▶ Determining the right costs for different purposes

▶ Assembling the product cost of manufacturers

▶ Padding profit by producing too many products

· ·

*M*easuring costs is the second most important thing accountants do, right after measuring profit. (Well, the Internal Revenue Service might think that measuring taxable income is the most important.) But really, can measuring a cost be very complicated? You just take numbers off a purchase invoice and call it a day, right? Not if your business manufactures the products you sell — that's for sure! In this chapter, I demonstrate that a cost, any cost, is not as obvious and clear-cut as you may think. Yet, obviously, costs are extremely important to businesses and other organizations.

Consider an example close to home: Suppose you just returned from the grocery store with several items in the bag. What's the cost of the loaf of bread you bought? Should you include the sales tax? Should you include the cost of gas you used driving to the store? Should you include some amount of depreciation expense on your car? Suppose you returned some aluminum cans for recycling while you were at the grocery store, and you were paid a small amount for the cans. Should you subtract this amount against the total cost of your purchases? Or should you subtract the amount directly against the cost of only the sodas in aluminum cans that you bought? And, is cost the *before-tax* cost? In other words, is your cost equal to the amount of income you had to earn before income tax so that you had enough after-tax income to buy the items? And, what about the time you spent shopping? Your time could have been used for other endeavors. I could raise many other such questions, but you get the point.

These questions about the cost of your groceries are interesting (well, to me at least). But you don't really have to come up with definite answers for such questions in managing your personal financial affairs. Individuals don't have to keep cost records of their personal expenditures, other than what's needed for their annual income tax returns. In contrast, businesses must carefully record all their costs correctly so that profit can be determined each period, and so that managers have the information they need to make decisions and to make a profit.

Looking down the Road to the Destination of Costs

All businesses that sell products must know their *product costs* — in other words, the costs of each and every item they sell. Companies that manufacture the products they sell — as opposed to distributors and retailers of products — have many problems in figuring out their product costs. Two examples of manufactured products are a new Cadillac just rolling off the assembly line at General Motors and a copy of my book, *Accounting For Dummies,* 5th Edition, hot off the printing presses.

Most production (manufacturing) processes are fairly complex, so product cost accounting for manufacturers is fairly complex; every step in the production process has to be tracked carefully from start to finish. Many manufacturing costs cannot be directly matched with particular products; these are called *indirect costs.* To arrive at the *full cost* of each product manufactured, accountants devise methods for allocating indirect production costs to specific products. Surprisingly, established accounting standards in the United States, called *generally accepted accounting principles* (GAAP), provide little authoritative guidance for measuring product cost. Therefore, manufacturing businesses have more than a little leeway regarding how to determine their product costs. Even businesses in the same industry — Ford versus General Motors, for example — may use different product cost accounting methods.

Accountants determine many other costs, in addition to product costs:

- ✔ The costs of departments, regional distribution centers, cost centers, and other organizational units of the business
- ✔ The cost of the retirement plan for the company's employees
- ✔ The cost of marketing programs and advertising campaigns
- ✔ The cost of restructuring the business or the cost of a major recall of products sold by the business, when necessary

A common refrain among accountants is "different costs for different purposes." True enough, but at its core, cost accounting serves two broad purposes: measuring profit and providing relevant information to managers for planning, control, and decision-making.

In my experience, people are inclined to take cost numbers for granted, as if they were handed down on stone tablets. The phrase *actual cost* often gets tossed around without a clear definition. An actual cost depends entirely on the particular methods used to measure the cost. I can assure you that these cost measurement methods have more in common with the scores from judges in an ice skating competition than the times clocked in a Formula One auto race. Many arbitrary choices are behind every cost number you see. There's no one-size-fits-all definition of cost, and there's no one correct and best-in-all-circumstances method of measuring cost.

The conundrum is that, in spite of the inherent ambiguity in determining costs, we need exact amounts for costs. In order to understand the income statement and balance sheet that managers use in making their decisions, they should understand the choices an accountant has to make in measuring costs. Some cost accounting methods result in conservative profit numbers; other methods boost profit, at least in the short run. Chapter 7 discusses the choices among different accounting methods that produce financial statements with a conservative or liberal hue.

This chapter covers cost concepts and cost measurement methods that apply to all businesses, as well as basic product cost accounting of manufacturers. I discuss how a manufacturer could be fooling around with its production output to manipulate product cost for the purpose of artificially boosting its profit figure. (Service businesses encounter their own problems in allocating their operating costs for assessing the profitability of their separate sales revenue sources.)

Are Costs Really That Important?

Without good cost information, a business operates in the dark. Cost data is needed for the following purposes:

✔ **Setting sales prices:** The common method for setting sales prices (known as *cost-plus* or *markup on cost*) starts with cost and then adds a certain percentage. If you don't know exactly how much a product costs, you can't be as shrewd and competitive in your pricing as you need to be. Even if sales prices are dictated by other forces and not set by managers, managers need to compare sales prices against product costs and other costs that should be matched against each sales revenue source.

✔ **Formulating a legal defense against charges of predatory pricing practices:** Many states have laws prohibiting businesses from selling below cost except in certain circumstances. And a business can be sued under federal law for charging artificially low prices intended to drive its competitors out of business. Be prepared to prove that your lower pricing is based on lower costs and not on some illegitimate purpose.

✔ **Measuring gross margin:** Investors and managers judge business performance by the bottom-line profit figure. This profit figure depends on the *gross margin* figure you get when you subtract your cost of goods sold expense from your sales revenue. Gross margin (also called *gross profit*) is the first profit line in the income statement (for examples see Figures 4-1 and 9-1, as well as Figure 11-1 later in this chapter). If gross margin is wrong, bottom-line net income is wrong — no two ways about it. The cost of goods sold expense depends on having correct product costs (see "Assembling the Product Cost of Manufacturers" later in this chapter).

✔ **Valuing assets:** The balance sheet reports cost values for many (though not all) assets. To understand the balance sheet you should understand the cost basis of its inventory and certain other assets. See Chapter 5 for more about assets and how asset values are reported in the balance sheet (also called the *statement of financial condition*).

✔ **Making optimal choices:** You often must choose one alternative over others in making business decisions. The best alternative depends heavily on cost factors, and you have to be careful to distinguish *relevant* costs from *irrelevant* costs, as I describe in the section "Relevant versus irrelevant costs," later in this chapter.

In most situations, the historic book value recorded for a fixed asset is an *irrelevant* cost. Say book value is $35,000 for a machine used in the manufacturing operations of the business. This is the amount of original cost that has not yet been charged to depreciation expense since it was acquired, and it may seem quite relevant. However, in deciding between keeping the old machine or replacing it with a newer, more efficient machine, the *disposable value* of the old machine is the relevant amount, not the undepreciated cost balance of the asset.

Suppose the old machine has an estimated $20,000 salvage value at this time; this is the relevant cost for the alternative of keeping it for use in the future — not the $35,000 book value that hasn't been depreciated yet. To keep using it, the business forgoes the $20,000 it could get by selling the asset, and this $20,000 is the relevant cost in this decision situation. Making decisions involves looking forward at the future cash flows of each alternative — not looking backward at historical-based cost values.

Accounting versus economic costs

Accountants focus mainly on *actual costs* (though they disagree regarding how exactly to measure these costs). Actual costs are rooted in the actual, or historical, transactions and operations of a business. Accountants also determine *budgeted costs* for businesses that prepare budgets (see Chapter 10), and they develop *standard costs* that serve as yardsticks to compare with the actual costs of a business.

Other concepts of cost are found in economic theory. You encounter a variety of economic cost terms when reading *The Wall Street Journal,* as well as in many business discussions and deliberations. Don't reveal your ignorance of the following cost terms:

✔ **Opportunity cost:** The amount of income (or other measurable benefit) given up when you follow a better course of action. For example, say that you quit your $50,000 job, invest $200,000 you saved up, and started a new business. You earn $80,000 profit in your new business for the year. Suppose also that you would have earned 5 percent on the $200,000 (a total of $10,000) if you'd kept the money in whatever investment you took it from. So you gave up a $50,000 salary and $10,000 in investment income with your course of action; your opportunity cost is $60,000. Subtract that figure from what your actual course of action netted you — $80,000 — and you end up with a "real" economic profit of $20,000. Your income is $20,000 better by starting your new business according to economic theory.

✔ **Marginal cost:** The *incremental,* out-of-pocket outlay required for taking a particular course of action. Generally speaking, it's the same thing as a *variable* cost (see "Fixed versus variable costs," later in this chapter). Marginal costs are important, but in actual practice managers must recover fixed (or nonmarginal) costs as well as marginal costs through sales revenue in order

to remain in business for any extent of time. Marginal costs are most relevant for analyzing one-time ventures, which don't last over the long term.

✔ **Replacement cost:** The estimated amount it would take today to purchase an asset that the business already owns. The longer ago an asset was acquired, the more likely its current replacement cost is higher than its original cost. Economists are of the opinion that current replacement costs are relevant in making rational economic decisions. For insuring assets against fire, theft, and natural catastrophes, the current replacement costs of the assets are clearly relevant. Other than for insurance, however, replacement costs are not on the front burners of decision making — except in situations in which one alternative being seriously considered actually involves replacing assets.

✔ **Imputed cost:** An ideal, or hypothetical, cost number that is used as a benchmark against which actual costs are compared. Two examples are *standard costs* and the *cost of capital.* Standard costs are set in advance for the manufacture of products during the coming period, and then actual costs are compared against standard costs to identify significant variances. The cost of capital is the weighted average of the interest rate on debt capital and a target rate of return that should be earned on equity capital. The *economic value added* (EVA) method compares a business's cost of capital against its actual return on capital, to determine whether the business did better or worse than the benchmark.

For the most part, these types of cost aren't reflected in financial reports. I've included them here to familiarize you with terms you're likely to see in the financial press and hear on financial talk shows. Business managers toss these terms around a lot.

Becoming More Familiar with Costs

The following sections explain important cost distinctions that managers should understand in making decisions and exercising control. Also, these cost distinctions help managers better appreciate the cost figures that accountants attach to products that are manufactured or purchased by the business.

Retailers (such as Wal-Mart or Costco) purchase products in a condition ready for sale to their customers — although the products have to be removed from shipping containers, and a retailer does a little work making the products presentable for sale and putting the products on display. Manufacturers don't have it so easy; their product costs have to be "manufactured" in the sense that the accountants have to accumulate various production costs and compute the cost per unit for every product manufactured. I focus on the special cost concerns of manufacturers in the upcoming section, "Assembling the Product Cost of Manufacturers."

I cannot exaggerate the importance of correct product costs (for businesses that sell products, of course). The total cost of goods (products) sold is the first, and usually the largest, expense deducted from sales revenue in measuring profit. The bottom-line profit amount reported in a business's income statement depends heavily on whether its product costs have been measured properly during that period. Also, keep in mind that product cost is the value for the inventory asset reported in the balance sheet of a business. (For a balance sheet example see Figure 5-1.)

Direct versus indirect costs

You might say that the starting point for any sort of cost analysis, and particularly for accounting for the product costs of manufacturers, is to clearly distinguish between *direct* and *indirect* costs. Direct costs are easy to match with a process or product, whereas indirect costs are more distant and have to be allocated to a process or product. Here are more details:

 ✔ **Direct costs:** Can be clearly attributed to one product or product line, or one source of sales revenue, or one organizational unit of the business, or one specific operation in a process. An example of a direct cost in the book publishing industry is the cost of the paper that a book is printed on; this cost can be squarely attached to one particular step or operation in the book production process.

✔ **Indirect costs:** Are far removed from and cannot be naturally attached to specific products, organizational units, or activities. A book publisher's telephone and Internet bills are costs of doing business but can't be tied down to just one step in the book editorial and production process. The salary of the purchasing officer who selects the paper for all the books is another example of a cost that is indirect to the production of particular books.

Each business must determine methods of allocating indirect costs to different products, sources of sales revenue, revenue and cost centers, and other organizational units. Most allocation methods are far from perfect and, in the final analysis, end up being arbitrary to one degree or another. Business managers should always keep an eye on the allocation methods used for indirect costs and take the cost figures produced by these methods with a grain of salt. If I were called in as an expert witness in a court trial involving costs, the first thing I'd do is critically analyze the allocation methods used by the business for its indirect costs. If I were on the side of the defendant, I'd do my best to defend the allocation methods. If I were on the side of the plaintiff, I'd do my best to discredit the allocation methods — there are always grounds for criticism.

The cost of filling the gas tank as I drive from Denver to San Diego and back to work with my coauthor and son, Tage, about the book we wrote together, *Cash Flow For Dummies* (John Wiley & Sons), is a direct cost of making the trip. The annual auto license plate fee that I pay to the state of Colorado is an indirect cost of the trip, although it is a direct cost of having the car available during the year.

Fixed versus variable costs

If your business sells 100 more units of a certain item, some of your costs increase accordingly, but others don't budge one bit. This distinction between *variable* and *fixed* costs is crucial:

✔ **Variable costs:** Increase and decrease in proportion to changes in sales or production level. Variable costs generally remain the same per unit of product, or per unit of activity. Additional units manufactured or sold cause variable costs to increase in concert. Fewer units manufactured or sold result in variable costs going down in concert.

✔ **Fixed costs:** Remain the same over a relatively broad range of sales volume or production output. Fixed costs are like a dead weight on the business. Its total fixed costs for the period are a hurdle it must overcome by selling enough units at high enough margins per unit in order to avoid a loss and move into the profit zone. (Chapter 9 explains the *break-even point*, which is the level of sales needed to cover fixed costs for the period.)

Note: The distinction between variable and fixed costs is at the heart of understanding, analyzing, and budgeting profit, which I explain in Chapters 9 and 10. You might want to quickly review Figures 9-1 and 10-1 with these costs in mind.

Relevant versus irrelevant costs

Not every cost is important to every decision a manager needs to make; hence, the distinction between relevant and irrelevant costs:

- **Relevant costs:** Costs that should be considered and included in your analysis when deciding on a future course of action. Relevant costs are *future* costs — costs that you would incur, or bring upon yourself, depending on which course of action you take. For example, say that you want to increase the number of books that your business produces next year in order to increase your sales revenue, but the cost of paper has just shot up. Should you take the cost of paper into consideration? Absolutely — that cost will affect your bottom-line profit and may negate any increase in sales volume that you experience (unless you increase the sales price). The cost of paper is a relevant cost.

- **Irrelevant (or sunk) costs:** Costs that should be disregarded when deciding on a future course of action; if brought into the analysis, these costs could cause you to make the wrong decision. An irrelevant cost is a vestige of the past — that money is gone. For this reason, irrelevant costs are also called *sunk costs*. For example, suppose that your supervisor tells you to expect a slew of new hires next week. All your staff members use computers now, but you have a bunch of typewriters gathering dust in the supply room. Should you consider the cost paid for those typewriters in your decision to buy computers for all the new hires? Absolutely not — that cost should have been written off and is no match for the cost you'd pay in productivity (and morale) for new employees who are forced to use typewriters.

 Generally speaking, most variable costs are relevant because they depend on which alternative is selected. Fixed costs are irrelevant assuming that the decision at hand does not involve doing anything that would change these stationary costs. However, a decision alternative being considered might involve a change in fixed costs, such as moving out of the present building used by the business, downsizing the number of employees on fixed salaries, spending less on advertising (generally a fixed cost), and so on. Any cost, fixed or variable that would be different for a particular course of action being analyzed is relevant for that alternative.

Furthermore, keep in mind that fixed costs can provide a useful gauge of a business's *capacity* — how much building space it has, how many machine-hours are available for use, how many hours of labor can be worked, and so on. Managers have to figure out the best way to utilize these capacities. For example, suppose your retail business pays an annual building rent of $200,000, which is a fixed cost (unless the rental contract with the landlord also has a rent escalation clause based on your sales revenue). The rent, which gives the business the legal right to occupy the building, provides 15,000 square feet of retail and storage space. You should figure out which sales mix of products will generate the highest total *margin* — equal to total sales revenue less total variable costs of making the sales, including the costs of the goods sold and all variable costs driven by sales revenue and sales volume.

Actual, budgeted, and standard costs

The actual costs a business incurs may differ (though we hope not too unfavorably) from its budgeted and standard costs:

- ✔ **Actual costs:** Costs based on actual transactions and operations during the period just ended, or going back to earlier periods. Financial statement accounting is mainly (though not entirely) based on a business's actual transactions and operations; the basic approach to determining annual profit is to record the financial effects of actual transactions and allocate the historical costs to the periods benefited by the costs. But keep in mind that accountants can use more than one method for recording actual costs. Your actual cost may be a little (or a lot) different than my actual cost.

- ✔ **Budgeted costs:** Future costs, for transactions and operations expected to take place over the coming period, based on forecasts and established goals. Fixed costs are budgeted differently than variable costs. For example, if sales volume is forecast to increase by 10 percent, variable costs will definitely increase accordingly, but fixed costs may or may not need to be increased to accommodate the volume increase. In Chapter 10, I explain the budgeting process and budgeted financial statements.

- ✔ **Standard costs:** Costs, primarily in the area of manufacturing, that are carefully engineered based on detailed analysis of operations and forecast costs for each component or step in an operation. Developing standard costs for variable production costs is relatively straightforward because most are direct costs. In contrast, most fixed costs are indirect, and standard costs for fixed costs are necessarily based on more arbitrary methods (see "Direct versus indirect costs," earlier in this chapter). *Note:* Some variable costs are indirect and have to be allocated to specific products in order to come up with a full (total) standard cost of the product.

Product versus period costs

Some costs are linked to particular products, and others are not:

- ✔ **Product costs:** Costs attached directly or allocated to particular products. The cost is recorded in the inventory asset account and stays in that asset account until the product is sold, at which time the cost goes into the cost of goods sold expense account. (See Chapters 4 and 5 for more about these accounts; also, see Chapter 7 for alternative methods for selecting which product costs are first charged to the cost of goods sold expense.)

  For example, the cost of a new Ford Taurus sitting on a car dealer's showroom floor is a product cost. The dealer keeps the cost in the inventory asset account until you buy the car, at which point the dealer charges the cost to the cost of goods sold expense.

- ✔ **Period costs:** Costs that are *not* attached to particular products. These costs do not spend time in the "waiting room" of inventory. Period costs are recorded as expenses immediately; unlike product costs, period costs don't pass through the inventory account first. Advertising costs, for example, are accounted for as period costs and recorded immediately in an expense account. Also, research and development costs are treated as period costs (with some exceptions).

Separating product costs and period costs is particularly important for manufacturing businesses, as you find out in the following section.

Assembling the Product Cost of Manufacturers

Businesses that manufacture products have several cost problems to deal with that retailers and distributors don't have. I use the term *manufacture* in the broadest sense: Automobile makers assemble cars; beer companies brew beer; automobile gasoline companies refine oil; DuPont makes products through chemical synthesis; and so on. Retailers (also called *merchandisers*) and distributors, on the other hand, buy products in a condition ready for resale to the end consumer. For example, Levi Strauss manufactures clothing, and several retailers buy from Levi Strauss and sell the clothes to the public. The following sections describe costs unique to manufacturers.

Minding manufacturing costs

Manufacturing costs consist of four basic types:

- **Raw materials (also called *direct* materials):** What a manufacturer buys from other companies to use in the production of its own products. For example, General Motors buys tires from Goodyear (or other tire manufacturers) that then become part of GM's cars.

- **Direct labor:** Those employees who work on the production line.

- **Variable overhead:** Indirect production costs that increase or decrease as the quantity produced increases or decreases. An example is the cost of electricity that runs the production equipment: Generally you pay for the electricity for the whole plant, not machine by machine, so you can't attach this cost to one particular part of the process. When you increase or decrease the use of those machines, the electricity cost increases or decreases accordingly. (In contrast, the monthly utility bill for a company's office and sales space probably is fixed for all practical purposes.)

- **Fixed overhead:** Indirect production costs that do *not* increase or decrease as the quantity produced increases or decreases. These fixed costs remain the same over a fairly broad range of production output levels (see "Fixed versus variable costs," earlier in this chapter). Three significant examples of fixed manufacturing costs are:

  - Salaries for certain production employees who don't work directly on the production line, such as vice presidents, safety inspectors, security guards, accountants, and shipping and receiving workers.

  - Depreciation of production buildings, equipment, and other manufacturing fixed assets.

  - Occupancy costs, such as building insurance, property taxes, and heating and lighting charges.

Figure 11-1 presents an example for a manufacturer, including the top part of its annual income statement (down to the gross margin line), annual sales volume (generally not disclosed in external financial reports), the summary of manufacturing costs and production output for the year, and the cost components making up the $760 product cost, which equals the total manufacturing costs *per unit*. A business may manufacture 100 or 1,000 different products, or even more, and it must compile a summary of manufacturing costs and production output and determine the product cost of every product. To keep the example easy to follow (but still realistic), Figure 11-1 presents a scenario for a one-product manufacturer. The multiproduct manufacturer has additional accounting problems, but I can't provide that level of detail here. This example exposes the fundamental accounting problems and methods of all manufacturers.

In Figure 11-1 notice in particular that the company's cost of goods sold expense is based on the $760 product cost (or total manufacturing costs per unit). This product cost is determined from the company's manufacturing costs and production output for the period. Product cost includes both the variable costs of manufacture and a calculated amount based on total fixed manufacturing costs for the period divided by total production output for the period.

The information in the manufacturing costs summary (see Figure 11-1) is highly confidential and for management eyes only. Competitors would love to know this information. A company may enjoy a significant cost advantage over its competitors and definitely does not want its cost data to get into their hands.

Income Statement For Year (to Gross Margin Line)

Sales Volume   110,000   Units

	Per Unit	Totals
Sales Revenue	$1,400	$154,000,000
Cost of Goods Sold Expense	($760)	($83,600,000)
Gross Margin	$640	$70,400,000

Manufacturing Costs Summary For Year

Production Capacity   150,000   Units
Actual Output   120,000   Units

Production Cost Components	Per Unit	Totals
Raw Materials	$215	$25,800,000
Direct Labor	$125	$15,000,000
Variable Manufacturing Overhead Costs	$70	$8,400,000
Total Variable Manufacturing Costs	$410	$49,200,000
Fixed Manufacturing Overhead Costs	$350	$42,000,000
Total Manufacturing Costs	$760	$91,200,000
To 10,000 Units Inventory Increase		($7,600,000)
To 110,000 Units Sold (see above)		$83,600,000

Figure 11-1: Manufacturing costs example.

Allocating indirect costs is as simple as ABC — not!

Accountants for manufacturers have developed many methods for allocating indirect overhead costs, most of which are based on a common denominator of production activity, such as direct labor hours or machine hours. A different method has received a lot of press recently: *activity-based costing* (ABC).

With the ABC method, you identify each supporting activity in the production process and collect costs into a separate pool for each identified activity. Then you develop a *measure* for each activity — for example, the measure for the engineering department may be hours, and the measure for the maintenance department may be square feet. You use the activity measures as *cost drivers* to allocate costs to products.

The idea is that the engineering department doesn't come cheap; including the cost of their slide rules and pocket protectors, as well as their salaries and benefits, the total cost per hour for those engineers could be $200 or more. The logic of the ABC cost-allocation method is that the engineering cost per hour should be allocated on the basis of the number of hours (the immediate cause, or driver of the cost) that is required by each product. So if Product A needs 200 hours of the engineering department's time and Product B is a simple product that needs only 20 hours of engineering, you allocate ten times as much of the engineering cost to Product A. In similar fashion, suppose the cost of the maintenance department is $20 per square foot per year. If Product C uses twice as much floor space as Product D, it would be charged with twice as much maintenance cost.

The ABC method has received much praise for being better than traditional allocation methods, especially for management decision making. But keep in mind that this method still requires rather arbitrary definitions of cost drivers, and having too many different cost drivers, each with its own pool of costs, is not practical.

Cost allocation always involves arbitrary methods. Managers should be aware of which methods are being used and should challenge a method if they think that it's misleading and should be replaced with a better (though still somewhat arbitrary) method. I don't mean to put too fine a point on this, but cost allocation essentially boils down to a "my arbitrary method is better than your arbitrary method" argument.

Classifying costs properly

Two vexing issues rear their ugly heads in determining product cost for a manufacturer:

- ✔ **Drawing a bright line between manufacturing costs and non-manufacturing operating costs:** The key difference here is that manufacturing costs are categorized as product costs, whereas non-manufacturing operating costs are categorized as period costs (refer to "Product versus period costs," earlier in this chapter). In calculating product costs, you include only manufacturing costs and not other costs. Remember that period costs are recorded right away as expenses. Here are some examples of each type of cost:

- Wages paid to production line workers are a clear-cut example of a manufacturing cost.

- Salaries paid to salespeople are a marketing cost and are not part of product cost; marketing costs are treated as period costs, which means they are recorded immediately to expense of the period.

- Depreciation on production equipment is a manufacturing cost, but depreciation on the warehouse in which products are stored after being manufactured is a period cost.

- Moving the raw materials and partially-completed products through the production process is a manufacturing cost, but transporting the finished products from the warehouse to customers is a period cost.

The accumulation of direct and indirect production costs starts at the beginning of the manufacturing process and stops at the end of the production line. In other words, product cost stops at the end of the production line — every cost up to that point should be included as a manufacturing cost.

If you misclassify some manufacturing costs as operating costs (non-manufacturing expenses), your product cost calculation will be too low (see the following section, "Calculating product cost"). Also, the Internal Revenue Service may come knocking at your door if it suspects that you deliberately (or even innocently) misclassified manufacturing costs as non-manufacturing costs in order to minimize your taxable income.

✔ **Allocating indirect costs among different products:** Indirect manufacturing costs must be allocated among the products produced during the period. The full product cost includes both direct and indirect manufacturing costs. Creating a completely satisfactory allocation method is difficult; the process ends up being somewhat arbitrary, but it must be done to determine product cost. Managers should understand how indirect manufacturing costs are allocated among products (and, for that matter, how indirect non-manufacturing costs are allocated among organizational units and profit centers). Managers should also keep in mind that every allocation method is arbitrary and that a different allocation method may be just as convincing. (See the sidebar "Allocating indirect costs is as simple as ABC — not!")

Calculating product cost

The basic equation for calculating product cost is as follows (using the example of the manufacturer in Figure 11-1):

$91,200,000 total manufacturing costs ÷ 120,000 units production output = $760 product cost per unit

Looks pretty straightforward, doesn't it? Well, the equation itself may be simple, but the accuracy of the results depends directly on the accuracy of your manufacturing cost numbers. The business example we're using in this chapter manufactures just one product. Even so, a single manufacturing process can be fairly complex, with hundreds or thousands of steps and operations. In the real world, where businesses produce multiple products, your accounting systems must be very complex and extraordinarily detailed to keep accurate track of all direct and indirect (allocated) manufacturing costs.

In our example, the business manufactured 120,000 units and sold 110,000 units during the year, and its product cost per unit is $760. The 110,000 total units sold during the year is multiplied by the $760 product cost to compute the $83.6 million cost of goods sold expense, which is deducted against the company's revenue from selling 110,000 units during the year. The company's total manufacturing costs for the year were $91.2 million, which is $7.6 million more than the cost of goods sold expense. The remainder of the total annual manufacturing costs is recorded as an increase in the company's inventory asset account, to recognize that 10,000 units manufactured this year are awaiting sale in the future. In Figure 11-1, note that the $760 product cost per unit is applied both to the 110,000 units sold and to the 10,000 units added to inventory.

Note: The product cost per unit for our example business is determined for the entire year. In actual practice, manufacturers calculate their product costs monthly or quarterly. The computation process is the same, but the frequency of doing the computation varies from business to business. Product costs likely will vary each successive period the costs are determined. Because the product costs vary from period to period, the business must choose which cost of goods sold and inventory cost method to use. (If product cost happened to remain absolutely flat and constant period to period, the different methods would yield the same results.) Chapter 7 explains the alternative accounting methods for determining cost of goods sold expense and inventory cost value.

Examining fixed manufacturing costs and production capacity

Product cost consists of two distinct components: *variable* manufacturing costs and *fixed* manufacturing costs. In Figure 11-1, note that the company's variable manufacturing costs are $410 per unit and its fixed manufacturing costs are $350 per unit. Now, what if the business had manufactured ten more units? Its total variable manufacturing costs would have been $4,100 higher. The actual number of units produced drives variable costs, so even one more unit would have caused the variable costs to increase. But the company's total fixed costs would have been the same if it had produced ten more units, or 10,000 more units for that matter. Variable manufacturing costs are bought on a per-unit basis, as it were, whereas fixed manufacturing costs are bought in bulk for the whole period.

Fixed manufacturing costs are needed to provide *production capacity* — the people and physical resources needed to manufacture products — for the period. After the business has the production plant and people in place for the year, its fixed manufacturing costs cannot be easily scaled down. The business is stuck with these costs over the short run. It has to make the best use it can from its production capacity.

Production capacity is a critical concept for business managers to stay focused on. You need to plan your production capacity well ahead of time because you need plenty of lead-time to assemble the right people, equipment, land, and buildings. When you have the necessary production capacity in place, you want to make sure that you're making optimal use of that capacity. The fixed costs of production capacity remain the same even as production output increases or decreases, so you may as well make optimal use of the capacity provided by those fixed costs. For example, you're recording the same depreciation amount on your machinery regardless of how you actually use those machines, so you should be sure to optimize the use of those machines (within limits, of course — overworking the machines to the point where they break down won't do you much good).

The burden rate

The fixed cost component of product cost is called the *burden rate*. In our manufacturing example, the burden rate is computed as follows (see Figure 11-1 for data):

> $42,000,000 fixed manufacturing costs for period ÷ 120,000 units production output for period = $350 burden rate

Note that the burden rate depends on the number divided into total fixed manufacturing costs for the period — that is, the production output for the period.

Now, here's an important twist on my example: Suppose the company had manufactured only 110,000 units during the period — equal exactly to the quantity sold during the year. Its variable manufacturing cost per unit would have been the same, or $410 per unit. But its burden rate would have been $381.82 per unit (computed by dividing the $42 million total fixed manufacturing costs by the 110,000 units production output). Each unit sold, therefore, would have cost $31.82 more than in the Figure 11-1 example simply because the company produced fewer units. It would have fewer units of output over which to spread its fixed manufacturing costs. The burden rate is $381.82 at the 110,000 output level but only $350 at the 120,000 output level, or $31.82 higher.

If only 110,000 units were produced, the company's product cost would have been $791.82 ($410 variable costs, plus the $381.82 burden rate). The company's cost of goods sold, therefore, would have been $3.5 million higher for the year ($31.82 higher product cost × 110,000 units sold). This rather significant increase in its cost of goods sold expense is caused by the company producing fewer units, even though it produced all the units that it needed for sales during the year. The same total amount of fixed manufacturing costs is spread over fewer units of production output.

Idle capacity

The production capacity of the business example in Figure 11-1 is 150,000 units for the year. However, this business produced only 120,000 units during the year, which is 30,000 units fewer than it could have. In other words, it operated at 80 percent of production capacity, which results in 20 percent *idle capacity*:

> 120,000 units output ÷ 150,000 units capacity = 80% utilization, or 20% idle capacity

This rate of idle capacity isn't unusual — the average U.S. manufacturing plant normally operates at 80 to 85 percent of its production capacity.

The effects of increasing inventory

Looking back at the numbers shown in Figure 11-1, the company's cost of goods sold benefited from the fact that it produced 10,000 more units than it sold during the year. These 10,000 units absorbed $3.5 million of its total fixed manufacturing costs for the year, and until the units are sold this $3.5 million stays in the inventory asset account (along with the variable manufacturing costs, of course). It's entirely possible that the higher production level was justified — to have more units on hand for sales growth next year. But production output can get out of hand, as I discuss in the following section, "Puffing Profit by Excessive Production."

Managers (and investors as well) should understand the inventory increase effects caused by manufacturing more units than are sold during the year. In the example shown in Figure 11-1, the cost of goods sold expense escaped $3.5 million of fixed manufacturing costs because the company produced 10,000 more units than it sold during the year, thus pushing down the burden rate. The company's cost of goods sold expense would have been $3.5 million higher if it had produced just the number of units it sold during the year. The lower output level would have increased cost of goods sold expense and would have caused a $3.5 million drop in gross margin.

The actual costs/actual output method and when not to use it

The product cost calculation for the business example shown in Figure 11-1 is based on the *actual cost/actual output method,* in which you take your actual costs — which may have been higher or lower than the budgeted costs for the year — and divide by the actual output for the year.

The actual costs/actual output method is appropriate in most situations. However, this method is not appropriate and would have to be modified in two extreme situations:

✔ **Manufacturing costs are grossly excessive or wasteful due to inefficient production operations:** For example, suppose that the business represented in Figure 11-1 had to throw away $1.2 million of raw materials during the year. The $1.2 million should be removed from the calculation of the raw material cost per unit. Instead, you treat it as a period cost — meaning that you record it directly into expense.

Then the cost of goods sold expense would be based on $750 per unit instead of $760, which lowers this expense by $1.1 million (based on the 110,000 units sold). But you still have to record the $1.2 million expense for wasted raw materials, so EBIT would be $100,000 lower.

✔ **Production output is significantly less than normal capacity utilization:** Suppose that the Figure 11-1 business produced only 75,000 units during the year but still sold 110,000 units because it was working off a large inventory carryover from the year before. Then its production output would be 50 percent instead of 80 percent of capacity. In a sense, the business wasted half of its production capacity, and you can argue that half of its fixed manufacturing costs should be charged directly to expense on the income statement and not included in the calculation of product cost.

Puffing Profit by Excessive Production

Whenever production output is higher than sales volume, be on guard. Excessive production can puff up the profit figure. How? Until a product is sold, the product cost goes in the inventory asset account rather than in the cost of goods sold expense account, meaning that the product cost is counted as a *positive* number (an asset) rather than a *negative* number (an expense). Fixed manufacturing overhead cost is included in product cost, which means that this cost component goes into inventory and is held there until the products are sold later. In short, when you overproduce, more of your total of fixed manufacturing costs for the period is moved to the inventory asset account and less is moved into cost of goods sold expense for the year.

You need to judge whether an inventory increase is justified. Be aware that an unjustified increase may be evidence of profit manipulation or just good old-fashioned management bungling. Either way, the day of reckoning will come when the products are sold and the cost of inventory becomes cost of goods sold expense — at which point the cost impacts the bottom line.

Shifting fixed manufacturing costs to the future

The business represented in Figure 11-1 manufactured 10,000 more units than it sold during the year. With variable manufacturing costs at $410 per unit, the business expended $4.1 million more in variable manufacturing costs than it would have if it had produced only the 110,000 units needed for its sales volume. In other words, if the business had produced 10,000 fewer units, its variable manufacturing costs would have been $4.1 million less — that's the nature of variable costs. In contrast, if the company had manufactured 10,000 fewer units, its *fixed* manufacturing costs would not have been any less — that's the nature of fixed costs.

Of its $42 million total fixed manufacturing costs for the year, only $38.5 million ended up in the cost of goods sold expense for the year ($350 burden rate × 110,000 units sold). The other $3.5 million ended up in the inventory asset account ($350 burden rate × 10,000 units inventory increase). The $3.5 million of fixed manufacturing costs that are absorbed by inventory is shifted to the future. This amount will not be expensed (charged to cost of goods sold expense) until the products are sold sometime in the future.

Shifting part of the fixed manufacturing cost for the year to the future may seem to be accounting slight of hand. It has been argued that the entire amount of fixed manufacturing costs should be expensed in the year that these costs are recorded. (Only variable manufacturing costs would be included in product cost for units going into the increase in inventory.) Established accounting standards require that *full* product cost (variable plus fixed manufacturing costs) be used for recording an increase in inventory. This is referred to as *absorption accounting* because fixed manufacturing costs are absorbed, or included in product cost.

In the example shown in Figure 11-1, the 10,000 units increase of inventory includes $3,500,000 of the company's total fixed manufacturing costs for the year:

> $350 burden rate × 10,000 units inventory increase = $3,500,000 fixed manufacturing costs included in inventory increase

Are you comfortable with this effect? The $3,500,000 escapes being charged to cost of goods expense for the time being. It sits in inventory until the products are sold in a later period. This results from using the full cost (absorption) accounting method for fixed manufacturing overhead costs. Now, it may occur to you that an unscrupulous manager could take advantage of this effect to manipulate gross profit for the period.

Let me be very clear here: I'm not suggesting any hanky-panky in the example shown in Figure 11-1. Producing 10,000 more units than sales volume during the year looks — on the face of it — to be reasonable and not out of the ordinary. Yet at the same time, it is naïve to ignore that the business did help its pretax profit to the amount of $3.5 million by producing 10,000 more units than it sold. If the business had produced only 110,000 units, equal to its sales volume for the year, all its fixed manufacturing costs for the year would have gone into cost of goods sold expense. The expense would have been $3.5 million higher, and operating earnings would have been that much lower.

Cranking up production output

Now let's consider a more suspicious example. Suppose that the business manufactured 150,000 units during the year and increased its inventory by 40,000 units. It may be a legitimate move if the business is anticipating a big jump in sales next year. On the other hand, an inventory increase of 40,000 units in a year in which only 110,000 units were sold may be the result of a serious overproduction mistake, and the larger inventory may not be needed next year.

Figure 11-2 shows what happens to production costs and — more importantly — what happens to the profit at the higher production output level. The additional 30,000 units (over and above the 120,000 units manufactured by the business in the original example) cost $410 per unit. (The precise cost may be a little higher than $410 per unit because as you start crowding production capacity, some variable costs per unit may increase a little.) The business would need $12.3 million more for the additional 30,000 units of production output:

> $410 variable manufacturing cost per unit × 30,000 additional units produced = $12,300,000 additional variable manufacturing costs invested in inventory

Again, its fixed manufacturing costs would not have increased, given the nature of fixed costs. Fixed costs stay put until capacity is hit. Sales volume, in this scenario, also remains the same.

Income Statement For Year (to Gross Margin Line)

Sales Volume   110,000   Units

	Per Unit	Totals
Sales Revenue	$1,400	$154,000,000
Cost of Goods Sold Expense	($690)	($75,900,000)
Gross Margin	$710	$78,100,000

Manufacturing Costs Summary For Year

Production Capacity   150,000   Units
Actual Output   150,000   Units

Production Cost Components	Per Unit	Totals
Raw Materials	$215	$32,250,000
Direct Labor	$125	$18,750,000
Variable Manufacturing Overhead Costs	$70	$10,500,000
Total Variable Manufacturing Costs	$410	$61,500,000
Fixed Manufacturing Overhead Costs	$280	$42,000,000
Total Manufacturing Costs	$690	$103,500,000
To 40,000 Units Inventory Increase		($27,600,000)
To 110,000 Units Sold (see above)		$75,900,000

Figure 11-2: Example of when production output greatly exceeds sales volume.

But check out the business's gross margin in Figure 11-2: $78.1 million, compared with $70.4 million in Figure 11-1 — a $7.7 million higher amount, even though sales volume and sales prices remain the same. Whoa! What's going on here? How can cost of goods sold expense be less? The business sells 110,000 units in both scenarios. And variable manufacturing costs are $410 per unit in both cases.

The culprit is the burden rate component of product cost. In the original Figure 11-1 example, total fixed manufacturing costs are spread over 120,000 units of output, giving a $350 burden rate per unit. In the Figure 11-2 example, total fixed manufacturing costs are spread over 150,000 units of output, giving a much lower $280 burden rate, or $70 per unit less. The $70 lower burden rate multiplied by the 110,000 units sold results in a $7.7 million lower cost of goods sold expense for the period, a higher pretax profit of the same amount, and a much improved bottom-line net income.

Being careful when production output is out of kilter with sales volume

In the highly suspect example shown in Figure 11-2, the business produced 150,000 units (full capacity). As a result, its inventory asset includes an additional $7.7 million of the company's fixed manufacturing costs for the year as compared with the original example in Figure 11-1. Its cost of goods sold expense for the year escaped this cost (for the time being). But get this: Its inventory increased 40,000 units, which is quite a large increase compared with the annual sales of 110,000 during the year just ended. Who was responsible for the decision to go full blast and produce up to production capacity? Do the managers really expect sales to jump up enough next year to justify the much larger inventory level? If they prove to be right, they'll look brilliant. But if the output level was a mistake and sales do not go up next year . . . they'll have you-know-what to pay next year, even though profit looks good this year. An experienced business manager knows to be on guard when inventory takes such a big jump.

Summing up, the cost of goods sold expense of a manufacturer, and thus its operating profit, is sensitive to a difference between its sales volume and production output during the year. Manufacturing businesses do not generally discuss or explain in their external financial reports to creditors and owners why production output is different than sales volume for the year. Financial report readers are pretty much on their own in interpreting the reasons for and the effects of under- or over-producing products relative to actual sales volume for the year. All I can tell you is to keep alert and keep in mind the profit impact caused by a major disparity between a manufacturer's production output and sale levels for the year.

Part IV

Preparing and Using Financial Reports

The 5th Wave   By Rich Tennant

"My wife and I handle our own finances. I'm an accountant and she's a grief counselor."

In this part . . .

Financial reports are like newspaper articles. A lot of activity goes on behind the scenes that you may not be aware of. In reading a financial report, you see only the finished product. Chapter 12 gives the inside story of how financial reports are put together. It's not as bad as making sausage, but there are several messy details.

Outside investors in a business — the owners who are not on the inside managing the business — depend on its financial reports as their main source of financial information about the business. Chapter 13 explains financial statement analysis techniques and ratios that investors use for interpreting profit performance and financial condition. Serious investors must know these ratios.

The financial report is the end of the line for the outside investors and lenders of a business. They can't call the business and ask for more information. But the financial statements are just the starting point for the managers of the business. Chapter 14 explains the more detailed and highly confidential accounting information they need for identifying problems and opportunities — in short, running the business.

Chapter 12

Getting a Financial Report Ready

*I*n Chapters 4, 5, and 6, I explain fundamentals of the three primary financial statements of a business. To review briefly:

✓ **Income statement:** Summarizes sales revenue and other income (if any) and expenses and losses (if any) for the period. It ends with the bottom-line profit for the period, which most commonly is called *net income* or *net earnings.* (Inside a business a profit performance statement is commonly called the *Profit & Loss,* or *P&L* report.)

✓ **Balance sheet:** Summarizes financial condition consisting of amounts for assets, liabilities, and owners' equity at the closing date of the income statement period, and at other times as needed by managers. (Its formal name is the *statement of financial condition*, or *statement of financial position.*)

✓ **Statement of cash flows:** Reports the net cash increase or decrease during the period from the profit-making activities reported in the income statement and the reasons why this key figure is different than bottom-line net income for the period. It also summarizes sources and uses of cash during the period from investing and financing activities.

These three statements, plus footnotes to the financials and other content, are packaged into an annual financial report that is distributed to the company's investors and lenders, so they can keep tabs on the business's financial health and performance. Abbreviated versions of their annual reports are distributed quarterly by public companies, as required by federal securities laws. Private companies do not have to provide interim financial reports, though many do. In this chapter, I shine a light on the process of preparing the annual financial report so you can recognize key decisions that must be made before a financial report hits the streets.

Recognizing Top Management's Role

The annual financial report of a business consists of:

- ✔ The three basic financial statements: *income statement*, *balance sheet*, and *statement of cash flows*. This troika of financial statements constitutes the hard core of a financial report (see Chapters 4, 5, and 6 for more on these financial statements). Every financial report should include these three financial statements (well, unless and until different rules are adopted for private companies and owner/managed small businesses).

- ✔ Maybe a *statement of changes in stockholders' (owners') equity*. This statement is not needed when the only changes in the owner's equity during the year are earning profit and paying distributions from profit to owners (these two important items of information are disclosed in the income statement and the statement of cash flows). If there are additional happenings during the year affecting owners' equity, a statement of changes in owners' equity is prepared. I briefly introduce this statement at the end of Chapter 6. In this chapter I probe deeper into this supplement to the three primary financial statements of a business. (See "Statement of Changes in Owners' Equity" at the end of the chapter.)

- ✔ Additional content, such as photographs of executives, vision statements, highlights of key financial performance measures, letters to stockholders from top management, and more. Public companies provide considerably more additional content than private companies. Much of the additional content falls outside the realm of generally accepted accounting principles and to a large extent is at the discretion of the business.

The business's CEO assisted by his or her top lieutenants play an essential role in the preparation of the financial reports of the company — which they (and outside investors and lenders) should understand. The CEO does (or should) perform certain critical steps before a financial report of the company is released to the outside world:

1. **Confers with the company's chief financial officer and controller (chief accountant) to make sure that the latest accounting and financial reporting standards and requirements have been applied in its financial report.** (A smaller business may consult with a CPA on these matters.) In recent years, we've seen a high degree of flux in accounting

and financial reporting standards and requirements. The U.S. and international rule-making bodies as well as the U.S. federal regulatory agency, the Securities and Exchange Commission (SEC), have been busy to say the least. The movement toward international standards has faced strong headwinds but still is pushing ahead. Furthermore, the initiatives for establishing separate standards for private companies and for small owner-managed businesses have gotten off the ground. I don't recall a time when there has been such a flurry of activity concerning financial reporting standards.

A business and its independent CPA auditors cannot simply assume that the accounting methods and financial reporting practices that have been used for many years are still correct and adequate. A business *must* check carefully whether it is in full compliance with current accounting standards and financial reporting requirements.

 2. **Carefully reviews the disclosures to be made in the financial report.** The CEO and financial officers of the business should make sure that the *disclosures* — all information other than the financial statements — are adequate according to financial reporting standards, and that all the disclosure elements are truthful but at the same time, not unnecessarily damaging to the business. Ideally, the disclosures should be written in clear language. I mention this because many disclosures seem purposely difficult to read (excuse me for getting on the soapbox here).

This disclosure review can be compared with the concept of *due diligence,* which is done to make certain that all relevant information is collected, that the information is accurate and reliable, and that all relevant requirements and regulations are being complied with. This step is especially important for public corporations whose securities (stock shares and debt instruments) are traded on securities exchanges. Public businesses fall under the jurisdiction of federal securities laws, which require technical and detailed filings with the SEC.

 3. **Considers whether the financial statement numbers need *touching up.*** The idea here is to smooth the jagged edges of the company's year-to-year profit gyrations or to improve the business's short-term solvency picture. Although this can be described as putting your thumb on the scale, you can also argue that sometimes the scale is a little out of balance to begin with, and the CEO should approve adjusting the numbers in the financial statements in order to make them jibe better with the normal circumstances of the business.

When I discuss the third step later in this chapter, I'm venturing into a gray area that accountants don't much like to talk about. These topics are rather delicate. Nevertheless, in the "real world" of business, top-level managers have to strike a balance between the interests of their business on the one hand and the interests of its owners (investors) and creditors on the other. For a rough comparison, think of the advertising done by a business. Advertising should be truthful, but, as I'm sure you know, businesses have a lot of leeway regarding how to advertise their products, and much advertising uses a lot of hyperbole. Managers exercise the same freedoms in putting together their financial reports. Financial reports may have some hype, and managers may put as much positive spin on bad news as possible without making deceitful and deliberately misleading comments.

Reviewing the Purposes of Financial Reporting

Business managers, creditors, and investors read financial reports because these reports provide information regarding how the business is doing and where it stands financially. If you read financial information on websites, such as Yahoo! Finance, for instance, keep in mind that the information comes from the financial reports issued by the business. The top-level managers of a business, in reviewing the annual financial report before releasing it outside the business, should keep in mind that a financial report is designed to answer certain basic financial questions:

- ✓ Is the business making a profit or suffering a loss, and how much?
- ✓ How do assets stack up against liabilities?
- ✓ Where did the business get its capital, and is it making good use of the money?
- ✓ What is the cash flow from the profit or loss for the period?
- ✓ Did the business reinvest all its profit or distribute some of the profit to owners?
- ✓ Does the business have enough capital for future growth?

People should read a financial report like a road map — to point the way and check how the trip is going. Managing and putting money in a business is a financial journey. A manager is like the driver and must pay attention to all the road signs; investors and lenders are like the passengers who watch the same road signs. Some of the most important road signs are the ratios between sales revenue and expenses and their related assets and liabilities in the balance sheet.

In short, the purpose of financial reporting is to deliver important information to the lenders and shareowners of the business that they need and are entitled to receive. Financial reporting is part of the essential contract between a business and its lenders and investors. Although lawyers may not like this, the contract can be stated in a few words:

Give us your money, and we'll give you the information you need to know regarding how we're doing with your money.

Financial reporting is governed by statutory and common law, and it should abide by ethical standards. Unfortunately, financial reporting sometimes falls short of both legal and ethical standards.

Businesses assume that the readers of the financial statements and other information in their financial reports are knowledgeable about business and finance in general, and understand basic accounting terminology and measurement methods. Financial reporting practices, in other words, take a lot for granted about readers of financial reports. Don't expect to find friendly hand holding and helpful explanations in financial reports. I don't mean to put you off, but reading financial reports is not for the feint of heart. You need to sit down with a cup of coffee (or something stronger) and be ready for serious concentration.

Keeping Current with Accounting and Financial Reporting Standards

Standards and regulatory requirements for accounting and financial reporting don't stand still. For many years, changes in accounting and financial reporting standards moved like glaciers — slowly and not too far. But just like the climate, the activity of the accounting and financial reporting authorities has warmed up. In fact, as I suggest earlier, it's hard to keep up with the changes.

Without a doubt, the rash of accounting and financial reporting scandals over the period 1980-2000 (and continuing to a lesser degree) was one reason for the step-up in activity by the standard setters. The Enron accounting fraud brought down a major international CPA firm (Arthur Andersen) and led to passage of the Sarbanes-Oxley Act of 2002, and its demanding requirements on public companies for establishing and reporting on internal controls to prevent financial reporting fraud. Furthermore, CPA auditors have come under increasing pressure to do better audits, especially by the Public Company Accounting Oversight Board, which is an arm of the Securities and Exchange Commission (SEC).

The other reason for the heightened pace of activity by the standard setters is the increasing complexity of doing business. When you look at how business is being conducted these days, you find more and more complexity — for example, the use of financial derivative contracts and instruments. It's difficult to put definite gain and loss values on these financial devices before the final day of reckoning (when the contracts terminate). The legal exposure of businesses has expanded, especially in respect to environmental laws and regulations.

In my view, the standard setters should be given a lot of credit for their attempts to deal with the problems that have emerged in recent decades and for trying to prevent repetition of the accounting scandals of the past. But the price of doing so has been a rather steep increase in the range and rapidity of changes in accounting and financial reporting standards and requirements. Top-level managers of businesses have to make sure that the financial and accounting officers of the business are keeping up with these changes and make sure that their financial reports follow all current rules and regulations. Managers lean heavily on their chief financial officers and controllers for keeping in full compliance with accounting and financial reporting standards.

It's too early to tell what will happen regarding financial reporting and accounting standards for private companies and for owner-managed small and medium size businesses. The recent establishment of the Private Companies Council (PCC) to recommend standards for private companies has just gotten off the ground at the time of revising this book. No formal recommendations have been made yet to the Financial Accounting Standards Board (FASB). I think that the PCC will zero in on the more complex accounting standards and make some headway in persuading the FASB to relax these standards for private companies. I simply have no idea what will happen regarding permitting smaller owner-managed companies to use an alternative basis of accounting and a simpler framework for financial reporting. It's very possible that down the road we'll end up with three levels of accounting and financial reporting standards: for large public companies, for private companies of all sizes, and for smaller owner-managed businesses. Stay tuned.

Making Sure Disclosure Is Adequate

The financial statements are the backbone of a financial report. In fact, a financial report is not deserving of the name if financial statements are not included. But a financial report is much more than just the financial statements; a financial report needs *disclosures*. Of course, the financial statements themselves provide disclosure of important financial information about the business. The term disclosures, however, usually refers to *additional* information provided in a financial report.

The CEO of a public corporation, the president of a private corporation, or the managing partner of a partnership has the primary responsibility to make sure that the financial statements have been prepared according to applicable accounting and reporting standards and that the financial report provides adequate disclosure. He or she works with the chief financial officer and controller of the business to make sure that the financial report meets the standard of adequate disclosure. (Many smaller businesses hire an independent CPA to advise them on their financial reports.)

For a quick survey of disclosures in financial reports, the following distinctions are helpful:

- ✔ **Footnotes** provide additional information about the figures included in the financial statements. Virtually all financial statements need footnotes to provide additional information for several of the items included in the three financial statements.

- ✔ **Supplementary financial schedules and tables** to the financial statements provide more details than can be included in the body of financial statements.

- ✔ A wide variety of **other information** is presented, some of which is required if the business is a public corporation subject to federal regulations regarding financial reporting to its stockholders. Other information is voluntary and not strictly required legally or by financial reporting standards that apply to the business.

Footnotes: Nettlesome but needed

Footnotes are attached to the three primary financial statements, and are usually placed at the end of the financial statements. Within the financial statements, you see references to particular footnotes. And at the bottom of each financial statement, you find the following sentence (or words to this effect): "The footnotes are integral to the financial statements." You should read all footnotes for a full understanding of the financial statements, although I should mention that some footnotes are dense and technical. For one exercise, try reading a footnote that explains how a public corporation puts the value on its management stock options in order to record the expense for this component of management compensation. Then take two aspirin to get rid of your headache.

Footnotes come in two types:

- ✔ One or more footnotes are included to identify the **major accounting policies and methods** that the business uses. (Chapter 7 explains that a business must choose among alternative accounting methods for recording revenue and expenses, and for their corresponding assets and liabilities.) The business must reveal which accounting methods it uses for booking its revenue and expenses. In particular, the business must identify its cost of goods sold and depreciation expense methods. Some businesses have unusual problems regarding the timing for recording sales revenue, and a footnote should clarify their revenue recognition method. Other accounting methods that have a material impact on the financial statements are disclosed in footnotes as well.

✔ Other footnotes provide **additional information and details** for many assets and liabilities. For example, a business may owe money on many short-term and longer-term debt issues; a footnote presents a schedule of maturity dates and interest rates of the debt issues. Details about stock option plans for executives are the main type of footnote for the capital stock account in the stockholders' equity section of the balance sheet of corporations.

Some footnotes are always required; a financial report would be naked without them. Deciding whether a footnote is needed (after you get beyond the obvious ones disclosing the business's accounting methods) and how to write the footnote is largely a matter of judgment and opinion. The general benchmark is whether footnote information is relevant or not to the investors and creditors of the business. But, how relevant? This is the key question. For public companies, keep in mind that the SEC lays down very specific requirements regarding disclosures in the quarterly and annual filings with it.

One problem that most investors face when reading footnotes — and, for that matter, many managers who should understand their own footnotes but find them a little dense — is that footnotes often deal with complex issues (such as lawsuits) and rather technical accounting matters. Let me cite just one footnote that highlights the latter point. The footnote in the 2011 10-K annual report of Caterpillar, Inc. filed with the SEC describing its post-employment benefit plans runs 11 pages (Pages A42-A52). If you are snowbound some evening and have a computer hookup to the Internet you might read your way through this footnote. Actually, it's not that technical, I suppose, but keeping all the pieces together in your head is very challenging. Caterpillar's post-employment benefit plans footnote is just one of its many footnotes.

Let's look at another footnote in Caterpillar's annual report. For your reading pleasure, here's footnote D in its 2011 annual 10-K report filed with the SEC (page A-12):

> **D. Inventories:** *Inventories are stated at the lower of cost or market. Cost is principally determined using the last-in, first-out (LIFO) method. The value of inventories on the LIFO basis represented about 65% of total inventories at December 31, 2011, and about 70% of total inventories at December 31, 2010 and 2009.*
>
> *If the FIFO (first-in, first-out) method had been in use, inventories would have been $2,422 million, $2,575 million and $3,022 million higher than reported at December 31, 2011, 2010, and 2009 respectively.*

Yes, these dollar amounts are in *millions* of dollars. Caterpillar's inventory cost value for its inventories at the end of 2011 would have been $2,422 billion higher if the FIFO accounting method had been used. Of course, it helps to have to have a basic understanding of the difference between the two accounting methods — LIFO and FIFO — to make sense of this note (see Chapter 7).

You may wonder how different Caterpillar's annual profits would have been if the FIFO cost of goods sold expense accounting method had been in use. A business's managers can ask its accounting department to do this analysis. But, as an outside investor, you would have to compute these amounts yourself (assuming you had all the necessary information). Businesses disclose their accounting methods, but they do not disclose how different annual profits would have been if alternative methods had been used.

Other disclosures in financial reports

The following discussion includes a fairly comprehensive list of the various types of disclosures (in addition to footnotes) found in annual financial reports of publicly owned businesses. A few caveats are in order. First, not every public corporation includes every one of the following items, although the disclosures are fairly common. Second, the level of disclosure by private businesses — after you get beyond the financial statements and footnotes — is generally much less than in public corporations. Third, tracking the actual disclosure practices of private businesses is difficult because their annual financial reports are circulated only to their owners and lenders. (A private business keeps its financial report as private as possible, in other words.) A private business may include one or more of the following disclosures, but by and large it is not required to do so (and, in my experience, few do).

Warren Buffett's annual letter to Berkshire Hathaway shareholders

I'd like to call your attention to one notable exception to the generally self-serving and slanted letter from a business's chief executive officer to its stockholders, which you find in most annual financial reports. Warren Buffett is the Chairman of the Board of Berkshire Hathaway, Inc. He has become very well known and is called the "Oracle of Omaha." Mr. Buffett's letters are the epitome of telling it like it is; they are frank, sometimes with brutal honesty, and quite humorous in places. You can go the website of the company (www.berk shirehathaway.com) and download his most recent letter (and earlier ones if you like). You'll learn a lot about his investing philosophy, and the letters are a delight to read even though they're relatively long (20+ pages usually).

In addition to the three financial statements and footnotes to the financials, public corporations typically include the following disclosures in their annual financial reports to their stockholders:

- **Cover (or transmittal) letter:** A letter from the chief executive of the business to the stockholders, which usually takes credit for good news and blames bad news on big government, unfavorable world political developments, a poor economy, or something else beyond management's control. (See the sidebar "Warren Buffett's annual letter to Berkshire Hathaway shareholders" for a refreshing alternative.)

- **Management's report on internal control over financial reporting:** An assertion by the chief executive officer and chief financial officer regarding their satisfaction with the effectiveness of the internal controls of the business, which are designed to ensure the reliability of its financial reports and to prevent financial and accounting fraud.

- **Highlights table:** A table that presents key figures from the financial statements, such as sales revenue, total assets, profit, total debt, owners' equity, number of employees, and number of units sold (such as the number of vehicles sold by an automobile manufacturer, or the number of "revenue seat miles" flown by an airline, meaning one airplane seat occupied by a paying customer for one mile). The idea is to give the stockholder a financial thumbnail sketch of the business.

- **Management discussion and analysis (MD&A):** Deals with the major developments and changes during the year that affected the financial performance and situation of the business. The SEC requires this disclosure to be included in the annual financial reports of publicly owned corporations.

- **Segment information:** A report of the sales revenue and operating profits (before interest and income tax, and perhaps before certain costs that cannot be allocated among different segments) for the major divisions of the organization, or for its different markets (international versus domestic, for example).

- **Historical summaries:** A financial history that extends back three years of longer that includes information from past financial statements.

- **Graphics:** Bar charts, trend charts, and pie charts representing financial conditions; photos of key people and products.

- **Promotional material:** Information about the company, its products, its employees, and its managers, often stressing an overarching theme for the year. Most companies use their annual financial report as an advertising or PR (public relations) opportunity.

✔ **Profiles:** Information about members of top management and the board of directors. Of course, everyone appears to be well qualified for his or her position. Negative information (such as prior brushes with the law) is not reported. One interesting development in recent years has been that several high level executives have lied about their academic degrees.

✔ **Quarterly summaries of profit performance and stock share prices:** Shows financial performance for all four quarters in the year and stock price ranges for each quarter (required by the SEC for public companies).

✔ **Management's responsibility statement:** A short statement indicating that management has primary responsibility for the accounting methods used to prepare the financial statements, for writing the footnotes to the statements, and for providing the other disclosures in the financial report. Usually, this statement appears near the independent CPA auditor's report.

✔ **Independent auditor's report:** The report from the CPA firm that performed the audit, expressing an opinion on the fairness of the financial statements and accompanying disclosures. Public corporations are required to have audits; private businesses may or may not have their annual financial reports audited. Unfortunately, the wording of audit reports has become more and more difficult to understand. The standards that govern CPA audit reports have mimicked the trend of accounting and financial reporting standards. Audit reports used to be three paragraphs that you could understand with careful reading. Even I can't be sure about some audit reports I read these days.

✔ **Company contact information:** Information on how to contact the company, the website address of the company, how to get copies of the reports filed with the SEC, the stock transfer agent and registrar of the company, and other information. Actually, you can take a short cut: Use a web browser such as Google, Safari, or Yahoo!, and simply type in a brief search name for the company you want to find. Your browser calls up the websites for the company.

✔ **No humor allowed:** Finally, I should mention that annual financial reports have virtually no humor — no cartoons, no one-liners, and no jokes. (Well, the CEO's letter to shareowners may have some humorous comments, even when the CEO doesn't mean to be funny.) I mention this point to emphasize that financial reports are written in a somber and serious vein. Many times in reading an annual financial report I have the reaction that the company should lighten up a little. The tone of most annual financial reports is that the fate of the Western world depends on the financial performance of the company. Gimme a break!

Managers of public corporations rely on lawyers, CPA auditors, and their financial and accounting officers to make sure that everything that should be disclosed in the business's annual financial reports is included, and that the exact wording of the disclosures is not misleading, inaccurate, or incomplete. This is a tall order.

Both federal and state laws, as well as authoritative accounting standards, have to be observed in financial report disclosures. Inadequate disclosure is just as serious as using wrong accounting methods for measuring profit and for determining values for assets, liabilities, and owners' equity. A financial report can be misleading because of improper accounting methods or because of inadequate or misleading disclosure. Both types of deficiencies can lead to nasty lawsuits against the business and its managers.

Putting a Spin on the Numbers (Short of Cooking the Books)

This section discusses two accounting tricks that involve manipulating, or "massaging," the accounting numbers. I don't endorse either technique, but you should be aware of both. In some situations, the financial statement numbers don't come out exactly the way the business prefers. With the connivance of top management, accountants can use certain tricks of the trade — some would say sleight of hand, or shenanigans — to move the numbers closer to what the business prefers. One trick improves the appearance of the *short-term solvency* of the business and the cash balance reported in its balance sheet at the end of the year. The other device shifts some profit from one year to the next to report a smoother trend of net income from year to year.

I don't mean to suggest that all businesses engage in these accounting machinations — but many do. The extent of use of these unholy schemes is hard to pin down because no business would openly admit to using them. The evidence is convincing, however, that many businesses massage their numbers to some degree. I'm sure you've heard the term *loopholes* applied to income tax. Well, some loopholes exist in financial statement accounting as well.

Window dressing for fluffing up the cash balance and cash flow

Suppose you manage a business and your controller has just submitted for your review the *preliminary,* or first draft, of the year-end balance sheet. (Chapter 5 explains the balance sheet, and Figure 5-1 shows a balance sheet for a business.) Figure 12-1 shows the current assets and current liabilities sections of the balance sheet draft, which is all we need here.

Wait a minute: a zero cash balance? How can that be? Maybe your business has been having some cash flow problems and you've intended to increase your short-term borrowing and speed up collection of accounts receivable to help the cash balance. Folks generally don't like to see a zero cash balance — it makes them kind of nervous, to put it mildly, no matter how you try to cushion it. So what do you do to avoid setting off alarm bells?

Your controller is probably aware of a technique called *window dressing,* a very simple method for making the cash balance look better. Suppose your fiscal year-end is October 31. Your controller takes the cash collections from customers paying their accounts receivable that are actually received on November 1, 2, 3, and 4 and records these four days of cash receipts as if these cash collections had been received on October 31. After all, the argument can be made that the customers' checks were in the mail — that money is yours, as far as the customers are concerned.

Window dressing reduces the amount in accounts receivable and increases the amount in cash the same amount — it has no effect on your profit figure for the period. It makes your cash balance look a touch better. Window dressing can also be used to improve other accounts' balances, which I don't go into here. All of these techniques involve holding the books open — to record certain events that take place after the end of the fiscal year (the ending balance sheet date) to make things look better than they actually were at the close of business on the last day of the year.

Figure 12-1:
Current assets and current liabilities of a business, before window dressing.

Cash	$0	Accounts payable		$235,000
Accounts receivable	$486,000	Accrued expenses payable		$187,000
Inventory	$844,000	Income tax payable		$58,000
Prepaid expenses	$72,000	Short-term notes payable		$200,000
Current assets	$1,402,000	Current liabilities		$680,000

Sounds like everybody wins, doesn't it? You look like you've done a better job as manager, and your lenders and investors don't panic. Right? Wrong! Window dressing is deceptive to your creditors and investors, who have every right to expect that the end of your fiscal year as stated on your financial reports is truly the end of your fiscal year. I should mention, however, that when I was in auditing I encountered situations in which a major lender of the business was fully aware that it had engaged in window dressing. The lender did not object because it wanted the business to fluff the pillows to make its balance sheet look better. The loan officer wanted to make the loan to the business look better. Essentially, the lender was complicit in the accounting manipulation.

Window dressing can be a dangerous game to play. Window dressing could be the first step on a slippery slope. A little window dressing today, and tomorrow, who knows — maybe giving the numbers a nudge now will lead to more serious accounting deceptions, or even out-and-out accounting fraud. Moreover, when a business commits some accounting hanky-panky, should the chief executive of the business brief its directors on the accounting manipulation? Things get messy, to say the least!

Also, be aware that window dressing improves cash flow from operating activities, which is an important number in the statement of cash flows that creditors and investors closely watch. (I discuss the statement of cash flows and cash flow from operating activities in Chapter 6.) Suppose, for example, that a business holds open its cash receipts journal for several days after the close of its fiscal year. The result is that its ending cash balance is reported $3.25 million higher than the business actually had in its checking accounts on the balance sheet date. Also, its accounts receivable balance is reported $3.25 million lower than was true at the end of its fiscal year. This makes cash flow from profit (operating activities) $3.25 million higher, which could be the reason in the decision to do some window dressing.

Sanding the rough edges off the year-to-year profit numbers

You should not be surprised when I tell you that business managers are under tremendous pressure to make profit every year and to keep profit on the up escalator year after year. Managers strive to make their numbers and to hit the milestone markers set for the business. Reporting a loss for the year, or even a dip below the profit trend line, is a red flag that stock analysts and investors view with alarm. Everyone likes to see a steady upward trend line for profit; no one likes to see a profit curve that looks like a roller coaster. Most investors want a smooth journey and don't like putting on their investment life preservers.

Managers can do certain things to deflate or inflate profit (net income) recorded in the year, which are referred to as *profit smoothing* techniques. Other names for these techniques are *income smoothing* and *earnings management*. Profit smoothing is like a white lie told for the good of the business and perhaps for the good of managers as well. Managers know that there is always some noise in the accounting system. Profit smoothing muffles the noise.

The general view in the financial community is that profit smoothing is not nearly as serious as *cooking the books,* or *juggling the books.* These terms refer to deliberate, fraudulent accounting practices such as recording sales revenue that has not happened or not recording expenses that have happened. Nevertheless, profit smoothing is still serious and if carried too far could be interpreted as accounting fraud. Managers have gone to jail for fraudulent financial statements.

Theoretically, having an audit by a CPA firm should root out any significant accounting fraud when the business is knowingly perpetrating the fraud or when it is an innocent victim of fraud against the business. But, in fact, there continue to be many embarrassing cases in which the CPA auditor failed to discover major fraud by or against the business. I could write a whole book on accounting fraud and not worry about running out of material. Several books have been published on this topic, which you can find by using the search words "accounting fraud" or "cooking the books" in your search engine. Being a Dummies author I would recommend *Forensic Accounting For Dummies* (John Wiley & Sons*)* by Kass-Shraibman and Sampath.

The pressure on public companies

Managers of publicly owned corporations whose stock shares are actively traded are under intense pressure to keep profits steadily rising. Security analysts who follow a particular company make profit forecasts for the business, and their buy-hold-sell recommendations are based largely on these earnings forecasts. If a business fails to meet its own profit forecast or falls short of stock analysts' forecasts, the market price of its stock shares usually takes a hit. Stock option and bonus incentive compensation plans are also strong motivations for achieving the profit goals set for the business.

The evidence is fairly strong that publicly owned businesses engage in some degree of profit smoothing. Frankly, it's much harder to know whether private businesses do so. Private businesses don't face the public scrutiny and expectations that public corporations do. On the other hand, key managers in a private business may have bonus arrangements that depend on recorded profit. In any case, business investors and managers should know about profit smoothing and how it's done.

Compensatory effects

Most profit smoothing involves pushing some amount of revenue and/ or expenses into years other than those in which they would normally be recorded. For example, if the president of a business wants to report more profit for the year, he or she can instruct the chief accountant to accelerate the recording of some sales revenue that normally wouldn't be recorded until next year, or to delay the recording of some expenses until next year that normally would be recorded this year.

Chapter 7 explains that managers choose among alternative accounting methods for several important expenses (and for revenue as well). After making these key choices, the managers should let the accountants do their jobs and let the chips fall where they may. If bottom-line profit for the year turns out to be a little short of the forecast or target for the period, so be it. This hands-off approach to profit accounting is the ideal way. However, managers often use a hands-on approach — they intercede (one could say interfere) and override the normal methods for recording sales revenue or expenses.

Both managers who do profit smoothing and investors who rely on financial statements in which profit smoothing has been done must understand one thing: These techniques have robbing-Peter-to-pay-Paul effects. Accountants refer to these as *compensatory effects.* The effects next year offset and cancel out the effects this year. Less expense this year is counterbalanced by more expense next year. Sales revenue recorded this year means less sales revenue recorded next year. Of course, the compensatory effects work the other way as well: If a business depresses its current year's recorded profit, its profit next year benefits. In short, a certain amount of profit can be brought forward into the current year or delayed until the following year.

Two profit histories

Figure 12-2 shows, side by side, the annual profit histories of two businesses over six years. Steady Flow, Inc. shows a nice smooth upward trend of profit. Bumpy Ride, Inc., in contrast, shows a zigzag ride over the six years. Both businesses earned the same total profit for the six years combined — in this case, $1,050,449. Their total six-year profit performance is the same, down to the last dollar. Which company would you be more willing to risk your money in? I suspect that you'd prefer Steady Flow, Inc. because of the nice and steady upward slope of its profit history.

I have a secret to share with you: Figure 12-2 is not really for two different companies — actually, the two different profit figures for each year are for the same company. The year-by-year profits shown for Steady Flow, Inc. are the company's *smoothed* profit amounts for each year, and the annual profits for Bumpy Ride, Inc. are the *actual* profits of the same business — the annual profits that were recorded before smoothing techniques were applied.

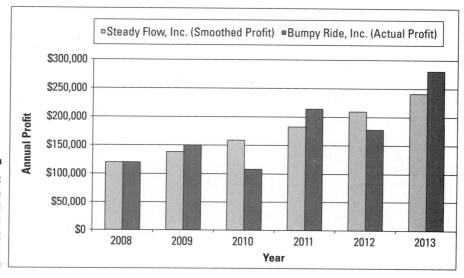

For the first year in the series, 2008, no profit smoothing occurred. The two profit numbers are the same; there was no need for smoothing. For each of the next five years, the two profit numbers differ. The difference between actual profit and smoothed profit for the year is the amount that revenue and/or expenses had to be manipulated for the year. For example, in 2009 actual profit would have been a little too high, so the company accelerated the recording of some expenses that should not have been recorded until the following year (2010); it booked those expenses in 2009. In contrast, in 2012, actual profit was running below the target net income for the year, so the business put off recording some expenses until 2013 to make 2012's profit look better. Does all this make you a little uncomfortable? It should.

Case study in massaging the numbers

When I was in public accounting, one of our clients was a contractor that used the *completed contract method* for recording its sales revenue. Not until the job was totally complete did the company book the sales revenue and deduct all costs to determine the gross margin from the job (in other words, from the contract). In most cases, the company had to return a few weeks after a job was finished for final touch-up work or to satisfy customer complaints. In the past, the company waited for this final visit before calling a job complete. But the year I was on the audit, the company was falling short of its profit goals. So the president decided to move up the point at which a job was called complete. The company decided not to wait for the final visit, which rarely involved more than a few minor expenses. Thus more jobs were completed during the year, more sales revenue and higher gross margin were recorded in the year, and the company met its profit goals.

A business can go only so far in smoothing profit. If a business has a particularly bad year, all the profit-smoothing tricks in the world won't close the gap. And if managers are used to profit smoothing, they may be tempted in this situation to resort to accounting fraud, or cooking the books.

Management discretion in the timing of revenue and expenses

Several smoothing techniques are available for filling the potholes and straightening the curves on the profit highway. Most profit-smoothing techniques require one essential ingredient: management discretion in deciding *when* to record expenses or *when* to record sales. See the following sidebar, "Case study in massaging the numbers."

A common technique for profit smoothing is to delay normal maintenance and repairs, which is referred to as *deferred maintenance.* Many routine and recurring maintenance costs required for autos, trucks, machines, equipment, and buildings can be put off, or deferred, until later. These costs are not recorded to expense until the actual maintenance is done, so putting off the work means recording the expense is delayed.

Here are a few other techniques used:

- A business that spends a fair amount of money for employee training and development may delay these programs until next year so the expense this year is lower.

- A company can cut back on its current year's outlays for market research and product development (though this could have serious long-term effects).

- A business can ease up on its rules regarding when slow-paying customers are written off to expense as *bad debts* (uncollectible accounts receivable). The business can, therefore, put off recording some of its bad debts expense until next year.

- A fixed asset out of active use may have very little or no future value to a business. But instead of writing off the undepreciated cost of the *impaired asset* as a loss this year, the business may delay the write-off until next year.

Keep in mind that most of these costs will be recorded next year, so the effect is to rob Peter (make next year absorb the cost) to pay Paul (let this year escape the cost).

Clearly, managers have a fair amount of discretion over the timing of some expenses, so certain expenses can be accelerated into this year or deferred to next year in order to make for a smoother year-to-year profit trend. But a business does not divulge in its external financial report the extent to which it has engaged in profit smoothing. Nor does the independent auditor comment on the use of profit-smoothing techniques by the business — unless the auditor thinks that the company has gone too far in massaging the numbers and that its financial statements are downright misleading.

Financial reporting on the Internet

Most public companies put their financial reports on their websites. For example, you can go to www.cat.com and navigate to Caterpillar's investors' section, where you can locate its SEC filings and its annual report to stockholders. Each company's website is a little different, but usually you can figure out fairly easily how to download its annual and quarterly financial reports.

Alternatively, you can go to the Securities and Exchange Commission website at www.sec.gov. Most public companies make many filings with the SEC so you have to know which one(s) you want to see. (The annual financial report is form 10-K.) Most company websites take you to their SEC filings with a quick click.

Going Public or Keeping Things Private

Suppose you had the inclination (and the time!) to compare 100 annual financial reports of publicly owned corporations with 100 annual reports of privately owned businesses (assuming you could assemble 100 private company financial reports). You'd see many differences. Public companies are generally much larger (in terms of annual sales and total assets) than private companies, as you would expect. Furthermore, public companies generally are more complex — concerning employee compensation, financing instruments, multinational operations, federal laws that impact big business, legal exposure, and so on.

At the time of revising this book private and public businesses are bound by the same accounting rules for measuring profit and for valuing assets, liabilities, and owners' equity, and for disclosures in their financial reports. (To be more precise, private companies are exempt from a couple of accounting rules but let's not go there.) Many of the accounting and financial reporting standards that have been issued over the last three decades are directed mainly to issues that have come up with public companies; by and large private companies do not have these accounting issues. As I discuss in Chapter 2, the accounting profession has taken initiatives with the goal of recognizing the different information needs from private companies and the different characteristics of the constituents of private companies. In my view, the main purpose is to lighten the accounting and financial reporting burden on private companies, which generally don't have the time or the accounting expertise to comply with the large number of complex standards on the books.

Reports from publicly owned companies

Around 10,000 corporations in the United States are publicly owned, and their stock shares are traded on the New York Stock Exchange, NASDAQ, or other electronic stock markets. Publicly owned companies must file annual financial reports with the SEC — the federal agency that makes and enforces the rules for trading in securities (stocks and bonds). These filings are available to the public on the SEC's huge database (see the sidebar "Financial reporting on the Internet").

The annual financial reports of publicly owned corporations include most of the disclosure items I list earlier in the chapter (see the section "Making Sure Disclosure Is Adequate"). As a result, annual reports published by large publicly owned corporations run 30, 40, or 50 pages (or more). As I've mentioned before the large majority of public companies make their annual reports available on their websites. Many public companies also present condensed versions of their financial reports — see the section "Recognizing condensed versions" later in this chapter.

Annual reports from public companies generally are very well done — the quality of the editorial work and graphics is excellent; the color scheme, layout, and design have good eye appeal. But be warned that the volume of detail in their financial reports is overwhelming. (See the next section for advice on dealing with the information overload in annual financial reports.)

Publicly owned businesses live in a fish bowl. When a company goes public with an *IPO* (initial public offering of stock shares), it gives up a lot of the privacy that a closely held business enjoys. A public company is required to have its annual financial report audited by an independent CPA firm. In doing an audit, the CPA passes judgment on the company's accounting methods and adequacy of disclosure. The CPA auditor has a heavy responsibility to evaluate the client's internal controls to prevent financial reporting fraud.

Reports from private businesses

Compared with their public brothers and sisters, private businesses generally issue less impressive annual financial reports. Their primary financial statements with the accompanying footnotes are pretty much it for most small private businesses. Often, their financial reports may be printed on plain paper and stapled together. A privately held company may have few stockholders, and typically one or more of the stockholders are active managers of the business, who already know a great deal about the business. I suppose that a private company could e-mail its annual financial report to its lenders and shareowners, although I haven't seen this.

Investors in private businesses have one potential advantage compared with public companies. They can request confidential information from managers at the annual stockholders' meetings (which is not practical for a stockholder in a large public corporation). The annual stockholders meeting of a private business is not open to the public, so information can be kept private. Also, major lenders to a private business can demand that certain items of information be disclosed to them on a confidential basis as a condition of the loan.

Up to the present time we have had one set of accounting and financial reporting standards for all businesses, large and small, public and private. However, the blunt truth of the matter is that smaller private companies do not comply fully with all the disclosure requirements that public companies have to comply with. The business and financial communities at large have accepted the "sub par" financial reporting practices of smaller private businesses. Perhaps the recently established Private Company Council (see Chapter 2) will recommend adopting less demanding disclosure rules by private companies. Or, they might leave well enough alone.

A private business may have its financial statements audited by a CPA firm but generally is not required by law to do so. Frankly, CPA auditors cut private businesses a lot of slack regarding disclosure. I don't entirely disagree with enforcing a lower standard of disclosure for private companies. The stock share market prices of public corporations are extremely important, and full disclosure of information should be made publicly available so that market prices are fairly determined. On the other hand, you could argue that the ownership shares of privately owned businesses are not traded, so there's no urgent need for a complete package of information.

Dealing with Information Overload

As a general rule, the larger a business, the longer its annual financial report. I've seen annual financial reports of small, privately owned businesses that you could read in 30 minutes to an hour. In contrast, the annual reports of large, publicly owned business corporations are typically 30, 40, or 50 pages (or more). You would need two hours to do a quick read of the entire annual financial report, without trying to digest its details. My comments in this section refer to the typical annual financial report of a large public company.

If you did try to digest all the details of an annual financial report of a public company, which is a long, dense document not unlike a lengthy legal contract, you would need many hours (perhaps the whole day) to do so. (Also, to get the complete picture, you should read the company's filings with the SEC in conjunction with its annual financial report. Tack on a few more hours for that!) For one thing, there are many, many numbers in an annual financial report. I've never taken the time to count the number of distinct numbers in an average annual financial report, but I can guarantee there are hundreds, and reports for large, diversified, global, conglomerate businesses must have over a thousand.

Browsing based on your interests

How do investors in a business deal with the information overload of annual financial reports? Very few persons take the time to plow through every sentence, every word, every detail, and every number on every page — except for those professional accountants, lawyers, and auditors directly involved in the preparation and review of the financial report. It's hard to say how most managers, investors, creditors, and others interested in annual financial reports go about dealing with the massive amount of information — very little research has been done on this subject. But I have some observations to share with you.

An annual financial report is like the Sunday edition of a large city newspaper, such as *The New York Times* or the *Los Angeles Times.* Hardly anyone reads every sentence on every page of these Sunday papers, much less every word in the advertisements — most people pick and choose what they want to read. They browse their way through the paper, stopping to read only the particular articles or topics they're interested in. Some people just skim through the paper. Some glance at the headlines. I think most investors read annual financial reports like they read Sunday newspapers. The complete information is there if you really want to read it, but most readers pick and choose which information they have time to read in depth.

Annual financial reports are designed for *archival purposes,* not for a quick read. Instead of addressing the needs of investors and others who want to know about the profit performance and financial condition of the business — but have only a limited amount of time available — accountants produce an annual financial report that is a voluminous financial history of the business. Accountants leave it to the users of annual reports to extract the main points. Financial statement readers use certain key ratios and other tests to get a feel for the financial performance and position of the business. (Chapters 13 and 16 explain how readers of financial reports get a fix on the financial performance and position of a business.)

Recognizing condensed versions

Here's a well-kept secret: Many public businesses and nonprofit organizations don't send a complete annual financial report to their stockholders or members. They know that few persons have the time or the technical background to read thoroughly the full-scale financial statements, footnotes, and other disclosures in their comprehensive financial reports. So, they present relatively brief summaries that are boiled-down versions of their complete financial reports. For example, my retirement fund manager, TIAA-CREF, puts out only financial summaries to its participants and retirees. Also, AARP issues condensed financial reports to its members.

Typically, these summaries — called *condensed financial statements* — do not provide footnotes or the other disclosures that are included in the complete and comprehensive annual financial reports. If you really want to see the official financial report of the organization, you can ask its headquarters to send you a copy (or, for public corporations, you can go to the SEC database — see the sidebar "Financial reporting on the Internet").

Using other sources of business information

Keep in mind that annual financial reports are only one of several sources of information to owners, creditors, and others who have a financial interest in the business. Annual financial reports, of course, come out only once a year — usually two months or so after the end of the company's fiscal (accounting) year. You should keep abreast of developments during the year by reading the quarterly reports of the business. Also, you are advised to follow the businesses you invest in by reading the financial press and watching TV programs. And, it's a good idea to keep up with blogs about the companies on the Internet, subscribe to newsletters, and soon. Financial reports present the sanitized version of events; they don't divulge scandals about the business. You have to find out the negative news about a business by the means I just mentioned.

Not everything you may like to know as an investor is included in the annual financial report. For example, information about salaries and incentive compensation arrangements with the top-level managers of the business are disclosed in the *proxy statement,* not in the annual financial report. A proxy statement is the means by which the corporation solicits the vote of stockholders on issues that require stockholder approval — one of which is compensation packages of top-level managers. Proxy statements are filed with the SEC and are available on its database.

Statement of Changes in Owners' Equity

In preparing its financial report, a business needs to decide whether it should include a fourth financial statement in addition to its three primary financial statements (income statement, balance sheet, and statement of cash flows). This additional schedule is called the *statement of changes in owners' equity.* As the name implies, this statement summarizes the activities affecting the business's owners' equity accounts during the period. The balance sheet reports the ending balances of the company's owners' equity accounts but not the activities during the year that caused changes in these accounts.

You find this statement in the financial reports of almost all public companies. Many (most?) smaller private companies, on the other hand, do not need to report this statement because the only changes in their owners' equity accounts are from earning profit (the bottom line in the income statement) and cash distributions from profit (in the financing activities section of the statement of cash flows). So, the following discussion applies mainly to larger public companies.

Owners' equity comes from capital invested in the business by the owners, and profit earned by and retained in the business. The great majority of public businesses are organized legally as corporations, and their owners are called stockholders. A corporation issues ownership shares called *capital stock.* So, *statement of changes in stockholders' equity* is the title used by corporations. (Chapter 8 explains the corporation and other legal types of business entities.)

Many publicly traded corporations have complex ownership structures often consisting of two or more classes of capital stock shares; they usually buy some of their own capital stock shares that are held and not cancelled (called *treasury stock*); and they have certain types of gains or losses during the year that are recorded directly in their stockholders' equity accounts instead of going through the income statement. This is a rather sneaky way of bypassing the income statement. In this way the gains or losses do not affect the bottom-line profit of a business that is reported in its income statement.

In short, public corporations prepare a statement of changes in stockholders' equity to collect together in one place all the various changes in their owners' equity accounts during the year. In particular, you have to read this financial summary to find out whether the business had any gains or losses that are not reported in its income statement. These special gains and losses are grouped into an owners' equity account called *accumulated other comprehensive income.* Hey, I didn't pick this title. It's really a doozy, isn't it?

The special types of gains and losses reported in the statement of stockholders' equity (instead of the income statement; see Figure 12-3) have to do with foreign currency translations, unrealized gains and losses from certain types of securities investments by the business, and changes in liabilities for unfunded pension fund obligations of the business. Being so technical in nature, these gains and losses fall into a twilight zone, as it were. The gains and losses can be tacked on at the bottom of the income statement, or they can be put in the separate statement of changes in owners' equity — it's up to the business to make the choice. Most companies opt for the statement of changes in stockholders' equity on the grounds that their income statements are crowded with a lot of information already.

The Procter & Gamble Company
Consolidated Statements of Shareholders' Equity

Dollars in millions/Shares in thousands	Common Shares Outstanding	Common Stock	Preferred Stock	Additional Paid-In-Capital	Reserve for ESOP Debt Retirement	Accumulated Other Comprehensive Income/(loss)	Treasury Stock	Retained Earnings	Non-controlling Interest	Total
BALANCE JUNE 30, 2009	$2,917,035	$4,007	$1,324	$61,118	$(1,340)	$(3,358)	$(55,961)	$57,309	$283	$63,382
Net earnings								12,736	110	12,846
Other comprehensive income:										
Financial statement translation						(4,194)				(4,194)
Hedges and investment securities, net of $520 tax						867				867
Defined benefit retirement plans, net of $465 tax						(1,137)				(1,137)
Total comprehensive income										$8,382
Dividends to shareholders:										
Common								(5,239)		(5,239)
Preferred, net of tax benefits								(219)		(219)
Treasury purchases	(96,759)						(6,004)			(6,004)
Employee plan issuances	17,616	1		574			616			1,191
Preferred stock conversions	5,579		(47)	7			40			—
ESOP debt impacts					(10)			27		17
Noncontrolling interest, net				(2)					(69)	(71)
BALANCE JUNE 30, 2010	2,843,471	4,008	1,277	61,697	(1,350)	(7,822)	(61,309)	64,614	324	61,439
Net earnings								11,797	130	11,927
Other comprehensive income:										
Financial statement translation						6,493				6,493
Hedges and investment securities, net of $711 tax						(1,178)				(1,178)
Defined benefit retirement plans, net of $302 tax						453				453
Total comprehensive income										$17,695
Dividends to shareholders:										
Common								(5,534)		(5,534)
Preferred, net of tax benefits								(233)		(233)
Treasury purchases	(112,729)						(7,039)			(7,039)
Employee plan issuances	29,729			702			1,033			1,735
Preferred stock conversions	5,266		(43)	6			37			—
ESOP debt impacts					(7)			38		31
Noncontrolling interest, net									(93)	(93)
BALANCE JUNE 30, 2011	2,765,737	4,008	1,234	62,405	(1,357)	(2,054)	(67,278)	70,682	361	68,001
Net earnings								10,756	148	10,904
Other comprehensive income:										
Financial statement translation						(5,990)				(5,990)
Hedges and investment securities, net of $438 tax						721				721
Defined benefit retirement plans, net of $993 tax						(2,010)				(2,010)
Total comprehensive income										$3,625
Dividends to shareholders:										
Common								(5,883)		(5,883)
Preferred, net of tax benefits								(256)		(256)
Treasury purchases	(61,826)						(4,024)			(4,024)
Employee plan issuances	39,546			550			1,665			2,215
Preferred stock conversions	4,576		(39)	6			33			—
ESOP debt impacts					220			50		50
Noncontrolling interest, net									87	307
BALANCE JUNE 30, 2012	$2,748,033	$4,008	$1,195	$63,181	$(1,357)	$(9,333)	$(69,604)	$75,349	$596	$64,035

Figure 12-3:
Example of statement of changes in stockholders' equity.

I selected The Proctor & Gamble Company for an example of the statement of changes in stockholders' equity. This comprehensive example includes everything but the kitchen sink. I don't have space here to explain everything reported in this statement. But I wanted to show you a real-world illustration. Figure 12-3 is a typical example of this financial statement, which suggests an important question: Can the average reader of financial reports understand what's presented in this statement?

Reading a statement of changes in stockholders' equity in an annual financial report can be heavy lifting. The professionals — stock analysts, money and investment managers, and so on — carefully read through and dissect this statement, or at least they should. The average, nonprofessional investor faces an uphill climb in reading this statement. Hopefully you can understand the major items. Good luck.

Chapter 13

How Lenders and Investors Read a Financial Report

· ·

In This Chapter

▶ Looking after your investments

▶ Checking out the auditor's report

▶ Using ratios to interpret profit performance

▶ Using ratios to interpret financial condition

▶ Scanning footnotes and sorting out important ones

· ·

Some years ago, a private business needed additional capital to continue its growth. Its stockholders could not come up with all the additional capital the business needed. So they decided to solicit several people to invest money in the company, including me. (In Chapter 8, I explain corporations and the stock shares they issue when owners invest capital in the business.) I studied the business's most recent financial report. I had an advantage that you can have too if you read this chapter: I know how to read a financial report and what to look for.

After studying the financial report, I concluded that the profit prospects of this business looked promising and that I probably would receive reasonable cash dividends on my investment. I also thought the business might be bought out by a bigger business someday, and I would make a capital gain. That proved to be correct: The business was bought out a few years later, and I doubled my money (plus I earned dividends along the way).

Not all investment stories have a happy ending, of course. As you know, stock share market prices go up *and* down. A business may go bankrupt, causing its lenders and shareowners large losses. This chapter isn't about guiding you toward or away from making specific types of investments. My purpose is to explain basic tools lenders and investors use for getting the most information value out of a business's financial reports — to help you become a more intelligent lender and investor.

This chapter focuses on the *external* financial report that a business sends to its lenders and shareowners. External financial reports are designed for the *non-manager* stakeholders in the business. The business's managers should definitely understand how to read and analyze its external financial statements, but managers should do additional financial analysis, which I discuss in Chapter 14. This additional financial analysis by managers uses confidential accounting information that is not circulated outside the business.

You could argue that this chapter goes beyond the domain of accounting. Yes, this chapter ventures into the field of financial statement analysis. Some argue that this is in the realm of finance and investments, not accounting. Well, my answer is this: I assume one of your reasons for reading this book is to understand and learn how to read financial statements. From this perspective this chapter definitely should be included whether or not the topics fit into a strict definition of accounting.

Knowing the Rules of the Game

When you invest money in a business venture or lend money to a business, you receive regular financial reports from the business. The basic premise of financial reporting is *accountability* — to inform the sources of a business's ownership and debt capital about the financial performance and condition of the business. Abbreviated financial reports are sent to owners and lenders every three months. A full and comprehensive financial report is sent annually. The ratios and techniques of analysis I explain in the chapter are used for both quarterly and annual financial reports.

There are written rules for financial reports, and there are unwritten rules. The written rules in the United States are called *generally accepted accounting principles* (GAAP) and have been called this for many years. At the present time the movement toward adopting international accounting standards is still active. So, the nomenclature and rules of the game are subject to change, as least for public companies. The unwritten rules don't have a name. For instance, there is no explicit rule prohibiting the use of swear words and vulgar expressions in financial reports. Yet, quite clearly, there is a strict unwritten rule against improper language in financial reports. There's one unwritten rule in particular that you should understand: A financial report isn't a confessional. A business doesn't have to lay bare all of its problems in its financial reports. A business doesn't comment on all of its difficulties in reporting its financial affairs to the outside world.

Checking Out the Auditor's Report

There are two types of businesses: those that have audits by independent CPAs and those that don't. All public companies are required by federal securities laws to have annual audits. Private companies are not covered by these laws and generally don't have regular audits. For one thing, audits by CPAs are expensive, and smaller businesses simply can't afford them. On the other hand, many privately owned businesses have audits done because they know that an audit report adds credibility to their financial report, even though the audit is expensive.

If a private business's financial report doesn't include an audit report, you have to trust that the business has prepared accurate financial statements according to authoritative accounting and financial reporting standards and that the footnotes to the financial statements cover all important points and issues. One thing you could do is to find out the qualifications of the company's chief accountant. Is the accountant a CPA? Does the accountant have a college degree with a major in accounting? Does the financial report omit a statement of cash flows or have any other obvious deficiencies?

Many books have been written about financial statement analysis. (That's an understatement!) It's amazing to me that few of these books mention the auditor's report on the financial statements that you're reading. In my thinking the first step in analyzing a financial report should be to read the auditor's opinion (assuming the financial statements have been audited of course). How can you be sure that its accounting methods conform to established standards? How do you know whether the business makes adequate disclosure in its financial reports? Is the business playing by the rules in measuring its profit and in releasing financial information? Well in business, as in politics, the answer is: *Trust, but verify.*

Considering the trustworthiness of financial reports

As I explain in Chapter 12, the top managers with their finance and accounting officers prepare the financial statements of the business and write the footnotes. These executives have a vested interest in the profit performance and financial condition of the business; their yearly bonuses usually depend on recorded profit, for instance. This situation is somewhat like the batter in a baseball game calling the strikes and balls. Where's the umpire? Independent CPA auditors are like umpires in the financial reporting game. The CPA comes in, does an audit of the business's accounting system and methods, and gives a report that is attached to the company's financial statements.

I hope I'm not the first person to point this out to you, but the business world is not like Sunday school. Not everything is honest and straight. A financial report can be wrong and misleading because of innocent, unintentional *errors,* or because of deliberate cold-blooded *fraud.* Errors can happen because of incompetence and carelessness. Audits are one means of keeping misleading financial reporting to a minimum. The CPA auditor should definitely catch all major errors. The auditor's responsibility for discovering fraud is not as clear-cut. You may think catching fraud is the purpose of an audit, but I'm sorry to tell you it's not as simple as that.

The auditor judges whether the business's accounting methods are in accordance with appropriate accounting and financial reporting standards — generally accepted accounting principles (GAAP) for businesses in the United States at this time. In most cases, the auditor's report confirms that everything is hunky-dory, and you can rely on the financial report. However, sometimes an auditor backs away from giving a full-fledged approval of the financial statements, which I discuss in the following sections.

Auditors don't always catch everything, and they sometimes fail to discover major accounting fraud. Also, the implementation of accounting methods is fairly flexible, leaving room for interpretation and creativity that's just short of *cooking the books* (deliberately defrauding and misleading readers of the financial report). Some massaging of the numbers is tolerated by auditors, which may mean that what you see on the financial report isn't exactly an untarnished picture of the business. I explain *window dressing* and *profit smoothing* — two common examples of massaging the numbers — in Chapter 12.

What's in an auditor's report

The large majority of financial statement audit reports give the business a clean bill of health, or what's called a *clean opinion.* (The technical term for this opinion is an *unqualified opinion,* which means that the auditor does not qualify or restrict his opinion regarding any significant matter.) At the other end of the spectrum, the auditor may state that the financial statements are misleading and should not be relied upon. This negative, disapproving audit report is called an *adverse opinion.* That's the big stick that auditors carry: They have the power to give a company's financial statements an adverse opinion, and no business wants that.

The threat of an adverse opinion almost always motivates a business to give way to the auditor and change its accounting or disclosure in order to avoid getting the kiss of death of an adverse opinion. An adverse audit opinion says that the financial statements of the business are misleading. The Securities and Exchange Commission (SEC) does not tolerate adverse opinions by auditors of public businesses; it would suspend trading in a company's securities if the company received an adverse opinion from its CPA auditor.

The clean (unqualified) opinion

If the auditor finds no serious problems, the CPA firm gives the business's financial statements an *unqualified* or *clean* opinion. However, I should warn you that the standard audit report has enough defensive, legalistic language to make even a seasoned accountant blush. If you have any doubts, go to the website of any public corporation, and look at its most recent financial statements, in particular the auditor's report.

The following summary cuts through the jargon and explains what the audit report really says:

Standard Audit Report (Unqualified or Clean Opinion)

1st paragraph	We did an audit, but the financial statements are the responsibility of management; we just express an opinion of them.
2nd paragraph	We carried out audit procedures that provide us a reasonable basis for expressing our opinion, but we don't necessarily catch everything.
3rd paragraph	The company's financial statements conform to accounting and financial reporting standards and are not misleading.

For public companies, the auditor's report must contain a paragraph explaining that the CPA evaluated the company's internal controls over financial reporting, which expresses an opinion on the effectiveness of these controls. This extension of the auditor's report concerning internal controls is the outgrowth of the financial reporting fraud scandals over the last three decades. Top management of the business must also include a statement in the annual financial report giving their opinion on the company's financial reporting internal controls.

Other kinds of audit opinions

An audit report that does *not* give a clean opinion may look similar to a clean-opinion audit report to the untrained eye. Some investors see the name of a CPA firm next to the financial statements and assume that everything is okay — after all, if the auditor had seen a problem, the Feds would have pounced on the business and put everyone in jail, right? Well, not exactly. How do you know when an auditor's report may be something other than a straightforward, no-reservations clean opinion? *Look for more language than just the standard three paragraphs* — that's the key.

It's important to look for additional language in an audit report — it's seldom good news. For example, the auditor's report may point out a flaw in the company's financial statements but not a fatal flaw that would require an adverse opinion. In this situation, the CPA issues a *qualified opinion.* The auditor includes a short explanation of the reasons for the qualification. You don't see qualified audit opinions that often, but you should read the auditor's report to be sure.

One type of an auditor's report is very serious — when the CPA expresses substantial doubts about the capability of the business to continue as a going concern. A *going concern* is a business that has sufficient financial wherewithal and momentum to continue its normal operations into the foreseeable future and would be able to absorb a bad turn of events without having to default on its liabilities. A going concern does not face an imminent financial crisis or any pressing financial emergency. A business could be under some financial distress but overall still be judged a going concern. Unless there is evidence to the contrary, the CPA auditor assumes that the business is a going concern.

But in some situations, the auditor may see unmistakable signs that a business is in deep financial waters and may not be able to convince its creditors and lenders to give it time to work itself out of its present financial difficulties. The creditors and lenders may force the business into involuntary bankruptcy, or the business may make a preemptive move and take itself into voluntary bankruptcy. The equity owners (stockholders of a corporation) may end up holding an empty bag after the bankruptcy proceedings have concluded. (This is one of the risks that stockholders take.) If an auditor has serious concerns about whether the business is a going concern, these doubts are spelled out in the auditor's report.

Massaging the numbers and auditors

In many audits the CPA becomes aware of heavy-handed accounting manipulation (also called *massaging the numbers*) for purposes such as smoothing year-to-year profit, boosting profit for the year, or making the business appear more solvent than it really is. Generally, managers have some ground to stand on; there is some rationale for their accounting machinations. Both the managers and the CPA auditor know what's going on: The financial statements are being tweaked, perhaps to the point of distortion.

What's an auditor to do? The auditor is under pressure to go along with management, even though he may strongly disagree with the accounting manipulations. He knows that better accounting should be used or that disclosure should be more adequate. Too often, instead of holding his ground, the CPA capitulates and does not force management to change. He allows the financial statements to be manipulated. This is a harsh comment, and I don't make it lightly. If you could get frank answers from practicing CPA auditors on this issue, I think you'd find that most agree with me.

Here's my take on the situation: CPA auditors go along with management massaging of the numbers (and "massaging" disclosure) if they think that the financial statements are not seriously misleading. The CPA's rationale is this: Yes, the financial statements could be more correct and could provide better disclosure, but all in all the financial statements are not seriously misleading.

I must acknowledge that in many situations, CPA auditors do stand their ground: They persuade the business not to manipulate its accounting numbers and to provide better disclosure. However, the CPA cannot brag about this in the audit report, saying "We talked management out of manipulating the accounting numbers." CPA auditors deserve a lot of credit for working behind the scenes to enforce accounting and financial reporting standards. At the same time, many auditors could — and should — be tougher.

Discovering fraud, or not

Auditors have trouble discovering fraud for several reasons. The most important reason, in my view, is that those managers who are willing to commit fraud understand that they must do a good job of concealing it. Managers bent on fraud are clever in devising schemes that look legitimate, and they are good at generating false evidence to hide the fraud. These managers think nothing of lying to their auditors. Also, they are aware of the standard audit procedures used by CPAs and design their fraud schemes to avoid audit scrutiny as much as possible.

Over the years, the auditing profession has taken somewhat of a wishy-washy position on the issue of whether auditors are responsible for discovering accounting and financial reporting fraud. The general public is confused because CPAs seem to want to have it both ways. CPAs don't mind giving the impression to the general public that they catch fraud, or at least catch fraud in most situations. However, when a CPA firm is sued because it didn't catch fraud, the CPA pleads that an audit conducted according to generally accepted auditing standards does not necessarily discover fraud in all cases.

In the court of public opinion, it is clear that people think that auditors should discover material accounting fraud — and, for that matter, auditors should discover any other fraud against the business by its managers, employees, vendors, or customers. CPAs refer to the difference between their responsibility for fraud detection (as they define it) and the responsibility of auditors perceived by the general public as the *expectations gap*. CPAs want to close the gap — not by taking on more responsibility for fraud detection, but by lowering the expectations of the public regarding their responsibility.

You'd have to be a lawyer to understand in detail the case law on auditors' legal liability for fraud detection, and I'm not a lawyer. But quite clearly, CPAs are liable for gross negligence in the conduct of an audit. If the judge or jury concludes that gross negligence was the reason the CPA failed to discover fraud, the CPA is held liable. (CPA firms have paid millions and millions of dollars in malpractice lawsuit damages.)

In a nutshell, standard audit procedures do not always uncover fraud, except when the perpetrators of the fraud are particularly inept at covering their tracks. Using tough-minded forensic audit procedures would put auditors in adversarial relationships with their clients, and CPA auditors want to maintain working relationships with clients that are cooperative and friendly. A friendly auditor, some would argue, is an oxymoron. Also, there is the cost factor. Audit costs are already expensive. The CPA audit team spends many hours carrying out many different audit procedures. An audit would cost a lot more if extensive fraud detection procedures were used in addition to normal audit procedures. To minimize their audit costs businesses assume the risk of not discovering fraud. They adopt internal controls (see Chapter 3) that are designed to minimize the incidence of fraud. But, they know that clever fraudsters can circumvent the controls. They view fraud as a cost of doing business (as long as it doesn't get out of hand).

One last point: In many accounting fraud cases that have been reported in the financial press, the auditor knew about the accounting methods of the client but did not object to the misleading accounting — you may call this an *audit judgment failure*. In these cases, the auditor was overly tolerant of questionable accounting methods used by the client. Perhaps the auditor may have had serious objections to the accounting methods, but the client persuaded the CPA to go along with the methods. In many respects, the failure to object to bad accounting is more serious than the failure to discover accounting fraud, because it strikes at the integrity and backbone of the auditor. CPA ethical standards demand that a CPA resign from an audit if the CPA judges that the accounting or financial reporting by the client is seriously misleading. The CPA may have a tough time collecting a fee from the client for the hours worked up to the point of resigning. But the CPA must resign according to professional audit standards.

Becoming a More Savvy Investor

An investment opportunity in a private business won't show up on your doorstep every day. However, if you make it known that you have money to invest as an equity shareholder, you may be surprised at how many offers come your way. Alternatively, you can invest in publicly traded *securities,* those stocks and bonds traded every day in major securities markets. Your stockbroker would be delighted to execute a buy order for 100 shares of, say, Caterpillar for you. Keep in mind that your money does not go to Caterpillar; the company is not raising additional money. Your money goes to the seller of the 100 shares. You're investing in the *secondary capital market* — the trading in stocks by buyers and sellers after the shares were originally issued some time ago. In contrast, I invested in the *primary capital market,* which means that my money went directly to the business.

You may choose not to manage your securities investments yourself. Instead, you can put your money in any of the thousands of mutual funds available today, or in an exchange-traded fund (ETF). You'll have to read other books to gain an understanding of the choices you have for investing your money and managing your investments. Be very careful about books that promise spectacular investment results with no risk and little effort. One book that is practical, well written, and levelheaded is *Investing For Dummies*, by Eric Tyson (John Wiley & Sons).

Investors in a private business have just one main pipeline of financial information about the business they've put their hard-earned money in: its financial reports. Of course, investors should carefully read these reports. By "carefully," I mean they should look for the vital signs of progress and problems. The financial statement ratios that I explain later in this chapter point the way — like signposts on the financial information highway.

Investors in securities of public businesses have many sources of information at their disposal. Of course, they can read the financial reports of the businesses they have invested in and those they are thinking of investing in. Instead of thoroughly reading these financial reports, they may rely on stockbrokers, the financial press, and other sources of information. Many individual investors turn to their stockbrokers for investment advice. Brokerage firms put out all sorts of analyses and publications, and they participate in the placement of new stock and bond securities issued by public businesses. A broker will be glad to provide you information from companies' latest financial reports. So, why should you bother reading this chapter if you can rely on other sources of investment information?

The more you know about interpreting a financial report, the better prepared you are to evaluate the commentary and advice of stock analysts and other investment experts. If you can at least nod intelligently while your stockbroker talks about a business's P/E and EPS, you'll look like a savvy investor — and you may get more favorable treatment. (P/E and EPS, by the way, are two of the key ratios explained later in the chapter.) You may regularly watch financial news on television or listen to one of today's popular radio financial talk shows. The ratios explained in this chapter are frequently mentioned in the media.

This chapter covers financial statement ratios that you should understand, as well as warning signs to look for in audit reports. (Part II of this book explains the three primary financial statements that are the core of every financial report: the income statement, the balance sheet, and the statement of cash flows.) I also suggest how to sort through the footnotes that are an integral part of every financial report to identify those that have the most importance to you.

Looking beyond financial reports

Investors don't rely solely on financial reports when making investment decisions. Analyzing a business's financial reports is just one part of the process. You should consider these additional factors, depending on the business you're thinking about investing in:

- ✔ Industry trends and problems

- ✔ National economic and political developments

- ✔ Threatened action by regulatory agencies against the business

- ✔ Possible mergers, friendly acquisitions, and hostile takeovers

- ✔ Turnover of key executives

- ✔ Labor problems

- ✔ International markets and currency exchange ratios

- ✔ Supply shortages

- ✔ Product surpluses

Whew! This kind of stuff goes way beyond accounting, obviously, and is just as significant as financial statement analysis when you're picking stocks and managing investment portfolios.

Once Again: Contrasting Financial Reports of Private and Public Businesses

Public companies make their financial reports available to the public at large; they don't limit distribution only to their present shareowners and lenders. I don't happen to own any stock shares of Caterpillar. So, how did I get its annual financial report? I simply went to Cat's website. In contrast, private companies generally keep their financial reports private — they distribute their financial reports only to their shareowners and lenders. Even if you were a close friend of the president of a private business, I doubt that the president would let you see a copy of its latest financial report. You may as well ask to see the president's latest individual income tax return. (You're not going to see it, either.)

As I explain in Chapters 2 and 12, the accounting profession is presently considering whether private companies should be relieved of the onerous burdens imposed by certain accounting and financial reporting standards. The almost exclusive focus of the standard setters over the last four decades has been on the accounting and financial reporting problems of large public companies. There seems to be a general feeling that many of these complex standards are not relevant to smaller, private businesses — and that the users of their financial reports are not well served by the standards. In any case, at this time generally accepted accounting principles (GAAP) are the standards that should be used by all businesses, public and private.

Although accountants are loath to talk about it, the blunt fact is that many (perhaps most) private companies simply ignore some authoritative standards in preparing their financial reports. This doesn't mean that their financial reports are misleading — perhaps substandard, but not seriously misleading. In any case, a private business's annual financial report is generally bare bones. It includes the three primary financial statements (balance sheet, income statement, and statement of cash flows), plus some footnotes — and that's about it. I've seen private company financial reports that don't even have a letter from the president. In fact, I've seen financial reports of private businesses (mostly very small companies) that don't include a statement of cash flows, even though this financial statement is required according to GAAP.

Public businesses are saddled with the additional layer of requirements issued by the Securities and Exchange Commission. (This federal agency has no jurisdiction over private businesses.) The financial reports and other forms filed with the SEC are available to the public at www.sec.gov. The anchor of these forms is the annual 10-K, which includes the business's financial statements in prescribed formats, with many supporting schedules and detailed disclosures that the SEC requires.

Most publicly owned businesses present very different annual financial reports to their stockholders compared with their filings with the SEC. A large number of public companies include only *condensed* financial information in their annual stockholder reports (not their full-blown and complete financial statements). They refer the reader to their more detailed SEC financial report for more specifics. The financial information in the two documents can't differ in any material way. In essence, a stock investor can choose from two levels of information — one quite condensed and the other very technical.

A typical annual financial report by a public company to its stockholders is a glossy booklet with excellent art and graphic design, including high-quality photographs. The company's products are promoted, and its people are featured in glowing terms that describe teamwork, creativity, and innovation — I'm sure you get the picture. In contrast, the reports to the SEC look like legal briefs — there's nothing fancy in these filings. The SEC filings contain information about certain expenses and require disclosure about the history of the business, its main markets and competitors, its principal officers, any major changes on the horizon, the major risks facing the business, and so on. Professional investors and investment managers definitely should read the SEC filings. By the way, if you want information on the compensation of the top-level officers of the business, you have to go to its *proxy statement* (see the sidebar "Studying the proxy statement").

Studying the proxy statement

Public corporations solicit their stockholders' votes in the annual election of persons to sit on the board of directors and on other matters that must be put to a vote at the annual stockholders' meeting. The communication for soliciting votes from stockholders is called a *proxy statement* — the reason being that the stockholders give their votes to a *proxy,* or designated person, who actually casts the votes at the annual meeting according to the instructions of the stockholders. The SEC requires many disclosures in proxy statements that are not found in annual financial reports issued to stockholders or in the business's annual 10-K. For example, compensation paid to the top-level officers of the business must be disclosed, as well as their stock holdings. If you own stock in a public corporation, take the time to read through the annual proxy statement you receive.

"Reading" Financial Statements with Ratios

Financial statements have lots of numbers in them. (Duh!) All these numbers can seem overwhelming when you're trying to see the big picture and make general conclusions about the financial performance and condition of the business. Instead of actually reading your way through the financial statements — that is, carefully digesting every line reported in all the financial statements — one approach is to compute certain *ratios* to extract the main messages from the financial statements. You "read" financial statements by computing a relatively few ratios instead of a line-by-line probing of the financial statements. Many financial report readers go directly to ratios and don't bother reading all the lines in the financial statements. In fact, five to ten ratios can tell you a lot about a business.

Financial statement ratios are also useful because they enable you to compare a business's current performance with its past performance or with another business's performance, regardless of whether sales revenue or net income was bigger or smaller for the other years or the other business. In other words, using ratios cancels out size differences. (I bet you knew that, didn't you?)

Surprisingly, you don't find too many ratios in financial reports. Publicly owned businesses are required to report just one ratio (earnings per share, or EPS), and privately owned businesses generally don't report any ratios. Generally accepted accounting principles (GAAP) don't demand that any ratios be reported (except EPS for publicly owned companies). However, you still see and hear about ratios all the time, especially from stockbrokers and other financial professionals, so you should know what the ratios mean, even if you never go to the trouble of computing them yourself.

Ratios do not provide final answers — they're helpful indicators, and that's it. For example, if you're in the market for a house, you may consider cost per square foot (the total cost divided by total square feet) as a way of comparing the prices of the houses you're looking at. But you have to put that ratio in context: Maybe one neighborhood is closer to public transportation than another, and maybe one house needs more repairs than another. In short, the ratio isn't the only factor in your decision.

Figures 13-1 and 13-2 present an income statement and balance sheet for a business that serves as the example for the rest of the chapter. I don't include a statement of cash flows — because no ratios are calculated from data in this financial statement. Well, I should say that no cash flow ratios have yet become household names. But a recent guide put out by the sponsors of the Chartered Global Management Accountant designation includes several cash flow ratios (*CGMA Tools*, 2012). I don't present the footnotes to the company's financial statements, but I discuss reading footnotes in the upcoming section "Frolicking Through the Footnotes." In short, the following discussion focuses on ratios from the income statement and balance sheet.

(Dollar amounts in thousands, except per share amounts)

Income Statement For Year	
Sales Revenue	$ 457,000
Cost of Goods Sold Expense	298,750
Gross Margin	$ 158,250
Sales, Administration, and General Expenses	102,680
Earnings Before Interest and Income Tax	$ 55,570
Interest Expense	6,250
Earnings Before Income Tax	$ 49,320
Income Tax Expense	16,850
Net Income	$ 32,470
Basic Earnings Per Share	$3.82
Diluted Earnings Per Share	$3.61

Figure 13-1: Income statement example.

(Dollar amounts in thousands)

Balance Sheet at End of Year

Assets

Cash	$ 14,850	
Accounts Receivable	42,500	
Inventory	75,200	
Prepaid Expenses	4,100	
Current Assets		$ 136,650
Fixed Assets	$ 246,750	
Accumulated Depreciation	(46,825)	199,925
Total Assets		$ 336,575

Liabilities

Accounts Payable	$ 8,145	
Accrued Expenses Payable	9,765	
Income Tax Payable	945	
Short-term Notes Payable	40,000	
Current Liabilities		$ 58,855
Long-term Notes Payable		60,000

Owners' Equity

Capital Stock (8,500,000 shares)	$ 85,000	
Retained Earnings	132,720	217,720
Total Liabilities and Owners' Equity		$ 336,575

Figure 13-2:
Balance sheet example.

Gross margin ratio

As I explain in Chapters 4 and 9, making bottom-line profit begins with making sales and earning sufficient *gross margin* from those sales. By sufficient, I mean that your gross margin must cover the expenses of making sales and operating the business, as well as paying interest and income tax expenses, so that there is still an adequate amount left over for profit. You calculate the gross margin ratio as follows:

Gross margin ÷ Sales revenue = Gross margin ratio

So a business with a $158.25 million gross margin and $457 million in sales revenue (refer to Figure 13-1) earns a 34.6 percent gross margin ratio. Now, suppose the business had been able to reduce its cost of goods sold expense and had earned a 35.6 percent gross margin. That one additional point (one point equals 1 percent) would have increased gross margin $4.57 million (1 percent × $457 million sales revenue) — which would have trickled down to earnings before income tax, assuming other expenses below the gross margin line had been the same (except income tax). Earnings before income tax would have been 9.3 percent higher:

> $4,570,000 bump in gross margin ÷ $49,320,000 earnings before income tax = 9.3% increase

Never underestimate the impact of even a small improvement in the gross margin ratio!

Investors can track the gross margin ratios for the two or three years whose income statements are included in the annual financial report, but they really can't get behind gross margin numbers for the "inside story." In their financial reports, public companies include a *management discussion and analysis* (MD&A) section that should comment on any significant change in the gross margin ratio. But corporate managers have wide latitude in deciding what exactly to discuss and how much detail to go into. You definitely should read the MD&A section, but it may not provide all the answers you're looking for. You have to search further in stockbroker releases, in articles in the financial press, or at the next professional business meeting you attend.

As I explain in Chapter 9, business managers pay close attention to *margin per unit* and *total margin* in making and improving profit. *Margin* does not mean *gross margin,* but rather it refers to sales revenue minus product cost and all other variable operating expenses of a business. In other words, *margin* is profit before the company's total fixed operating expenses (and before interest and income tax). Margin is an extremely important factor in the profit performance of a business. Profit hinges directly on margin.

In an external financial report the income statement discloses gross margin and operating profit, or earnings before interest and income tax expenses (see Figure 13-1 for instance). However, the expenses between these two profit lines in the income statement are not classified into variable and fixed. Therefore, businesses do not disclose margin information in their external financial reports — they wouldn't even think of doing so. This information is considered to be proprietary in nature; it is kept confidential and out of the hands of competitors. In short, investors do not have access to information about a business's margin or its fixed expenses. Neither GAAP nor the SEC requires that such information be disclosed — and it isn't!

Profit ratio

Business is motivated by profit, so the profit ratio is very important, to say the least. The bottom line is not called *the bottom line* without good reason. The profit ratio indicates how much net income was earned on each $100 of sales revenue:

Net income ÷ Sales revenue = Profit ratio

The business in Figure 13-1 earned $32.47 million net income from its $457 million sales revenue, so its profit ratio equals 7.1 percent, meaning that the business earned $7.10 net income for each $100 of sales revenue. (Thus, its expenses were $92.90 per $100 of sales revenue.) Profit ratios vary widely from industry to industry. A 5 to 10 percent profit ratio is common in many industries, although some high-volume retailers, such as supermarkets, are satisfied with profit ratios around 1 or 2 percent.

You can turn any ratio upside down and come up with a new way of looking at the same information. If you flip the profit ratio over to be sales revenue divided by net income, the result is the amount of sales revenue needed to make $1 profit. Using the same example, $457 million sales revenue ÷ $32.47 million net income = 14.08, which means that the business needs $14.08 in sales to make $1.00 profit. So you can say that net income is 7.1 percent of sales revenue, or you can say that sales revenue is 14.08 times net income.

Earnings per share (EPS), basic and diluted

Publicly owned businesses, according to generally accepted accounting principles (GAAP), must report earnings per share (EPS) below the net income line in their income statements — giving EPS a certain distinction among ratios. Why is EPS considered so important? Because it gives investors a means of determining the amount the business earned on their stock share investments: EPS tells you how much net income the business earned for each stock share you own. The essential equation for EPS is as follows:

Net income ÷ Total number of capital stock shares = EPS

For the example in Figures 13-1 and 13-2, the company's $32.47 million net income is divided by the 8.5 million shares of stock the business has issued to compute its $3.82 EPS.

Note: EPS is extraordinarily important to the stockholders of businesses whose stock shares are publicly traded. These stockholders pay close attention to market price per share. They want the net income of the business to be communicated to them on a per share basis so that they can easily compare it with the market price of their stock shares. The stock shares of privately owned corporations are not actively traded, so there is no readily available market value for the stock shares. Private businesses do not have to report EPS. The thinking behind this exemption is that their stockholders do not focus on per share values and are more interested in the business's total net income.

The business in the example could be listed on the New York Stock Exchange (NYSE). Assume that its capital stock is being traded at $70 per share. The Big Board (as it is called) requires that the *market cap* (total value of the shares issued and outstanding) be at least $100 million and that it have at least 1.1 million shares available for trading. With 8.5 million shares trading at $70 per share, the company's market cap is $595 million, well above the NYSE's minimum. At the end of the year, this corporation has 8.5 million stock shares *outstanding*, which refers to the number of shares that have been issued and are owned by its stockholders. Thus, its EPS is $3.82, as just computed.

But here's a complication: The business is committed to issuing additional capital stock shares in the future for stock options that the company has granted to its executives, and it has borrowed money on the basis of debt instruments that give the lenders the right to convert the debt into its capital stock. Under terms of its management stock options and its convertible debt, the business may have to issue 500,000 additional capital stock shares in the future. Dividing net income by the number of shares outstanding plus the number of shares that could be issued in the future gives the following computation of EPS:

$32,470,000 net income ÷ 9,000,000 capital stock shares issued and potentially issuable = $3.61 EPS

This second computation, based on the higher number of stock shares, is called the *diluted* earnings per share. (*Diluted* means thinned out or spread over a larger number of shares.) The first computation, based on the number of stock shares actually issued and outstanding, is called *basic* earnings per share. Both are reported at the bottom of the income statement — see Figure 13-1.

So, publicly owned businesses report two EPS figures — unless they have a *simple capital structure* that does not require the business to issue additional stock shares in the future. Generally, publicly owned corporations have *complex capital structures* and have to report two EPS figures, as you see in Figure 13-1. Sometimes it's not clear which of the two EPS figures is being used in press releases and in articles in the financial press. You have to be careful to determine which EPS ratio is being used — and which is being used in the calculation of the price/earnings (P/E) ratio (explained in the next section).

The more conservative approach is to use diluted EPS, although this calculation includes a hypothetical number of shares that may or may not be actually issued in the future.

Calculating basic and diluted EPS isn't always as simple as my example may suggest. Here are just two examples of complicating factors that require the accountant to adjust the EPS formula. During the year a company may:

- ✔ **Issue additional stock shares and buy back some of its stock shares.** (Shares of its stock owned by the business itself that are not formally cancelled are called *treasury stock*.) The weighted average number of outstanding stock shares is used in these situations.

- ✔ **Issue more than one class of stock, causing net income to be divided into two or more pools — one pool for each class of stock.** EPS refers to the *common* stock, or the most junior of the classes of stock issued by a business. (Let's not get into *tracking stocks* here, when a business divides itself into two or more sub-businesses and you have an EPS for each sub-part of the business, because few public companies do this.)

Price/earnings (P/E) ratio

The price/earnings (P/E) ratio is another ratio that's of particular interest to investors in public businesses. The P/E ratio gives you an idea of how much you're paying in the current price for stock shares for each dollar of earnings (the net income being earned by the business). Remember that earnings prop up the market value of stock shares.

The P/E ratio is, in one sense, a reality check on just how high the current market price is in relation to the underlying profit that the business is earning. Extraordinarily high P/E ratios are justified when investors think that the company's EPS has a lot of upside potential in the future.

The P/E ratio is calculated as follows:

Current market price of stock ÷ Most recent trailing 12 months diluted EPS* = P/E ratio

* If the business has a simple capital structure and does not report a diluted EPS, its basic EPS is used for calculating its P/E ratio (see the previous section).

The capital stock shares of the business in our example are trading at $70, and its diluted EPS for the latest year is $3.61. **Note:** For the remainder of this section, I will use the term EPS; I assume you understand that it refers to diluted EPS for businesses with complex capital structures, or to basic EPS for businesses with simple capital structures.

Stock share prices of public companies bounce around day to day and are subject to big changes on short notice. To illustrate the P/E ratio, I use the $70 price, which is the closing price on the latest trading day in the stock market. This market price means that investors trading in the stock think that the shares are worth about 19 times EPS ($70 market price ÷ $3.61 EPS = 19). This P/E ratio should be compared with the average stock market P/E to gauge whether the business is selling above or below the market average.

Over the last century, average P/E ratios have fluctuated more than you might think. I remember when the average P/E ratio was less than 10, and a time when it was more than 20. Also, P/E ratios vary from business to business, industry to industry, and year to year. One dollar of EPS may command only a $12 market value for a mature business in a no-growth industry, whereas a dollar of EPS for dynamic businesses in high-growth industries may be rewarded with a $35 market value per dollar of earnings (net income).

Dividend yield

The dividend yield ratio tells investors how much *cash income* they're receiving on their stock investment in a business. Suppose that our business example paid $1.50 cash dividends per share over the last year, which is less than half of its EPS. (I should mention that the ratio of annual dividends per share divided by annual EPS is called the *payout ratio.*) You calculate the dividend yield ratio for this business as follows:

> $1.50 annual cash dividend per share ÷ $70 current market price of stock = 2.1% dividend yield

You can compare the dividend yields of different companies. However, the company that pays the highest dividend yield is not necessarily the best investment. The best investment depends on many factors, including forecasts of earnings and EPS in particular.

Traditionally, the interest rates on high-grade debt securities (U.S. Treasury bonds and Treasury notes being the safest) were higher than the average dividend yield on public corporations. In theory, market price appreciation of the stock shares made up for this gap. Of course, stockholders take the risk that the market value will not increase enough to make their total return on investment rate higher than a benchmark interest rate. Recently, however, the yields on U.S. debt securities have fallen below the dividend yields on many corporate stocks.

Book value, market value, and book value per share

The amount reported in a business's balance sheet for owners' equity is called its *book value*. In the Figure 13-2 example, the book value of owners' equity is $217.72 million at the end of the year. This amount is the sum of the accounts that are kept for owners' equity, which fall into two basic types: *capital accounts* (for money invested by owners minus money returned to them), and *retained earnings* (profit earned and not distributed to the owners). Just like accounts for assets and liabilities, the entries in owners' equity accounts are for the actual, historical transactions of the business.

If you remember only one thing, make sure it's this: Book value is *not* market value. The book value of owners' equity is not directly tied to the market value of a business. You could say that there is a disconnect between book value and market value, although this goes a little too far. Book value may be considered heavily in putting a market value on a business and its ownership shares. Or, it may play only a minor role. Other factors come into play in setting the market value of a business and its ownership shares. Market value may be quite a bit more than book value, or considerably less than book value. In any case, market value is *not* reported in the balance sheet of a business. For example, you do not see the market value of Apple reported in its latest balance sheet or elsewhere in its annual financial report (although public companies include the market price ranges of their capital stock shares for each quarter of the year).

Public companies have one advantage: You can easily determine the current market value of their ownership shares and the market cap for the business as a whole (equal to the number of shares × the market value per share.) The market values of capital stock shares of public companies are easy to find. Stock market prices of the largest public companies are reported every trading day in many newspapers and are available on the Internet.

Private companies have one disadvantage: There is no active trading in their ownership shares to provide market value information. The shareowners of a private business probably have some idea of the price per share that they would be willing to sell their shares for, but until an actual buyer for their shares or for the business as a whole comes down the pike, market value is not known. Even so, in some situations there is a need to put a market value on the business and/or its ownership shares. For example, when a shareholder dies or gets a divorce there is need for a current market value estimate of the owner's shares (for estate tax or divorce settlement purposes). When making an offer to buy a private business, the buyer puts a value on the business, of course. The valuation of a private business is beyond the scope of this book. You can find more on this topic in the book my son, Tage, and I coauthored *Small Business Financial Management Kit For Dummies* (Wiley).

In addition to, or in place of market value per share you can calculate *book value per share*. Generally, the actual number of capital stock shares issued is used for this ratio, not the higher number of shares used in calculating diluted EPS (see the earlier section "Earnings per share (EPS), basic and diluted"). The formula for book value per share is:

> Owners' equity ÷ Actual number of stock shares outstanding = Book value per share

The business shown in Figure 13-2 has issued 8.5 million capital stock shares, which are outstanding (in the hands of stockholders). The book value of its $217.72 million owners' equity divided by this number of stock shares gives a book value per share of $25.61. If the business sold off its assets exactly for their book values and paid all its liabilities, it would end up with $217.72 million left for the stockholders, and it could therefore distribute $25.61 per share to them. But, of course, the company doesn't plan to go out of business, liquidate its assets, and pay off its liabilities anytime soon.

Is book value the major determinant of market value? No, generally speaking book value is not the dominant factor that drives the market price of stock shares or for the business as a whole — not for a public company whose stock shares are traded every day, nor for a private business when a value is being put on the business. EPS is much more important than book value per share for public companies. However, let's not throw out the baby with the bath water — book value per share is not entirely irrelevant. Book value per share is the measure of the recorded value of the company's assets less its liabilities — the net assets backing up the business's stock shares.

Book value per share is important for *value investors*, who pay as much attention to the balance sheet factors of a business as to its income statement factors. They search out companies with stock market prices that are not much higher, or even lower, than book value per share. Part of their theory is that such a business has more assets to back up the current market price of its stock shares, compared with businesses that have relatively high market prices relative to their book value per share. In the example, the business's stock is selling for about 2.8 times its book value per share ($70 market price per share ÷ $25.61 book value per share = 2.8 times). This may be too high for some investors and would certainly give value investors pause before deciding to buy stock shares of the business.

Book value per share can be calculated for a private business, of course. But its capital stock shares are not publicly traded, so there is no market price to compare the book value per share with. Suppose I own 1,000 shares of stock of a private business, and I offer to sell 100 of my shares to you. The book value per share might play some role in our negotiations. However, a more critical factor would be the amount of dividends per share the business will pay in the future, which depends on its earnings prospects. Your main income would be dividends, at least until you had an opportunity to liquidate the shares (which is uncertain for a private business).

Return on equity (ROE) ratio

The return on equity (ROE) ratio tells you how much profit a business earned in comparison to the book value of its owners' equity. This ratio is especially useful for privately owned businesses, which have no easy way of determining the market value of owners' equity. ROE is also calculated for public corporations, but just like book value per share, it generally plays a secondary role and is not the dominant factor driving market prices. Here's how you calculate this ratio:

Net income ÷ Owners' equity = ROE

The business whose income statement and balance sheet are shown in Figures 13-1 and 13-2 earned $32.47 million net income for the year just ended and has $217.72 million owners' equity at the end of the year. Therefore, its ROE is 14.9 percent:

$32,470,000 net income ÷ $217,720,000 owners' equity = 14.9% ROE

Net income increases owners' equity, so it makes sense to express net income as the percentage of improvement in the owners' equity. In fact, this is exactly how Warren Buffett does it in his annual letter to the stockholders of Berkshire Hathaway. Over the 47 years ending in 2011, Berkshire Hathaway's average annual ROE was 19.8 percent, which is truly extraordinary. See the sidebar "If you had invested $1,000 in Berkshire Hathaway in 1965."

If you had invested $1,000 in Berkshire Hathaway in 1965

You probably have heard about **Berkshire Hathaway** and its CEO, Warren Buffett, who usually is in the top few of *Forbes* magazine's annual listing of the 400 richest people in America. Suppose you had invested $1,000 in Berkshire Hathaway in 1965 and held on to your shares for 47 years, to the end of 2011. At that time, the book value of your shares was over $5 million. The market value of Berkshire Hathaway shares was usually higher than their book value over this time period.

This Berkshire Hathaway investment example demonstrates the power of compounding at a high earnings rate over a long stretch of time. Under Mr. Buffett's time as CEO starting in 1965 through the end of 2011, the company earned an average 19.8 percent annual ROE. The actual annual ROE rates for Berkshire Hathaway fluctuated over the 47 years. In fact, ROE was lower than this average in 24 of the 47 years; ROE was negative in 2 of these years. (Data is from Warren Buffett's 2011 annual letter to Berkshire Hathaway's stockholders, which is part of its 2011 annual financial report.)

Current ratio

The current ratio is a test of a business's *short-term solvency* — its capability to pay its liabilities that come due in the near future (up to one year). The ratio is a rough indicator of whether cash on hand plus the cash to be collected from accounts receivable and from selling inventory will be enough to pay off the liabilities that will come due in the next period.

As you can imagine, lenders are particularly keen on punching in the numbers to calculate the current ratio. Here's how they do it:

Current assets ÷ Current liabilities = Current ratio

Note: Unlike most other financial ratios, you don't multiply the result of this equation by 100 and represent it as a percentage.

Businesses are generally expected to maintain a minimum 2 to 1 current ratio, which means its current assets should be twice its current liabilities. In fact, a business may be legally required to stay above a minimum current ratio as stipulated in its contracts with lenders. The business in Figure 13-2 has $136,650,000 in current assets and $58,855,000 in current liabilities, so its current ratio is 2.3. The business shouldn't have to worry about lenders coming by in the middle of the night to break its legs. Chapter 5 discusses current assets and current liabilities and how they are reported in the balance sheet.

Acid-test (quick) ratio

Most serious investors and lenders don't stop with the current ratio for testing the business's short-term solvency (its capability to pay the liabilities that will come due in the short term). Investors, and especially lenders, calculate the *acid-test ratio* — also known as the *quick ratio* or less frequently as the *pounce ratio* — which is a more severe test of a business's solvency than the current ratio. The acid-test ratio excludes inventory and prepaid expenses, which the current ratio includes, and it limits assets to cash and items that the business can quickly convert to cash. This limited category of assets is known as *quick* or *liquid* assets.

You calculate the acid-test ratio as follows:

Liquid assets ÷ Current liabilities = Acid-test ratio

Note: Like the current ratio, you don't multiply the result of this equation by 100 and represent it as a percentage.

The business example in Figure 13-2 has two "quick" assets: $14.85 million cash and $42.5 million accounts receivable, for a total of $57.35 million. (If it had any short-term marketable securities, this asset would be included in its total quick assets.) Total quick assets are divided by current liabilities to determine the company's acid-test ratio, as follows:

$57,350,000 quick assets ÷ $58,855,000 current liabilities = .97 acid-test ratio

The .97 to 1.00 acid-test ratio means that the business would be just about able to pay off its short-term liabilities from its cash on hand plus collection of its accounts receivable. The general rule is that the acid-test ratio should be at least 1.0, which means that liquid (quick) assets should equal current liabilities. Of course, falling below 1.0 doesn't mean that the business is on the verge of bankruptcy, but if the ratio falls as low as 0.5, that may be cause for alarm.

This ratio is also called the *pounce ratio* to emphasize that you're calculating for a worst-case scenario, where a pack of wolves (known as *creditors*) could pounce on the business and demand quick payment of the business's liabilities. But don't panic. Short-term creditors do not have the right to demand immediate payment, except under unusual circumstances. This ratio is a conservative way to look at a business's capability to pay its short-term liabilities — too conservative in most cases.

Return on assets (ROA) ratio and financial leverage gain

As I discuss in Chapter 5, one factor affecting the bottom-line profit of a business is whether it uses debt to its advantage. For the year, a business may realize a *financial leverage gain,* meaning it earns more profit on the money it has borrowed than the interest paid for the use of that borrowed money. In fact, a good part of a business's net income for the year could be due to financial leverage.

The first step in determining financial leverage gain is to calculate a business's return on assets (ROA) ratio, which is the ratio of EBIT (earnings before interest and income tax) to the total capital invested in operating assets. Here's how to calculate ROA:

EBIT ÷ Net operating assets = ROA

Note: This equation uses *net operating assets,* which equals total assets less the non-interest-bearing operating liabilities of the business. Actually, many stock analysts and investors use the total assets figure because deducting all the non-interest-bearing operating liabilities from total assets to determine net operating assets is, quite frankly, a nuisance. But I strongly recommend using net operating assets because that's the total amount of capital raised from debt and equity.

Compare ROA with the interest rate: If a business's ROA is, say, 14 percent and the interest rate on its debt is, say, 6 percent, the business's net gain on its debt capital is 8 percent more than what it's paying in interest. There's a favorable spread of 8 points (one point = 1 percent), which can be multiplied times the total debt of the business to determine how much of its earnings before income tax is traceable to financial leverage gain.

In Figure 13-2, notice that the business has $100 million total interest-bearing debt: $40 million short-term plus $60 million long-term. Its total owners' equity is $217.72 million. So its net operating assets total is $317.72 million (which excludes the three short-term non-interest-bearing operating liabilities). The company's ROA, therefore, is:

$$\$55,570,000 \text{ EBIT} \div \$317,720,000 \text{ net operating assets} = 17.5\% \text{ ROA}$$

The business earned $17.5 million (rounded) on its total debt — 17.5 percent ROA times $100 million total debt. The business paid only $6.25 million interest on its debt. So the business had $11.25 million financial leverage gain before income tax ($17.5 million less $6.25 million).

ROA is a useful ratio for interpreting profit performance, aside from determining financial gain (or loss). ROA is a *capital utilization* test — how much profit before interest and income tax was earned on the total capital employed by the business. The basic idea is that it takes money (assets) to make money (profit); the final test is how much profit was made on the assets. If, for example, a business earns $1 million EBIT on $25 million assets, its ROA is only 4 percent. Such a low ROA signals that the business is making poor use of its assets and will have to improve its ROA or face serious problems in the future.

More ratios?

The previous list of ratios is the bare-bones minimum. You could certainly calculate many more ratios from the financial statements. Examples of other ratios include the inventory turnover ratio and the debt-to-equity ratio, for instance. (Chapter 14 explains additional ratios managers of a business use based on internal information that's not revealed in its external financial statements.) How many different ratios to calculate is a matter of judgment and is limited by the time you have available for reading a financial report.

The ratios explained earlier are the hard-core, everyday tools for interpreting financial statements. Computer-based databases are at our disposal these days. It's relatively easy to find many other financial statement ratios. Which of these additional ratios provide valuable insight? This is the key question. Be careful of wasting time on ratios that don't really add anything to the picture you get from the basic ratios explained in this chapter. Almost any financial statement ratio is interesting, I suppose. For instance, you could calculate the ratio of inventory divided by retained earnings, to see what percent of retained earnings is "tied up" in the inventory asset. (This ratio is not generally computed in financial statement analysis.) I would advise you to limit your attention to the handful of ratios that play a central role in looking after your investments.

Frolicking Through the Footnotes

Reading the footnotes in annual financial reports is no walk in the park. The investment pros read them because in providing consultation to their clients they are required to comply with due diligence standards — or because of their legal duties and responsibilities of managing other peoples' money. When I was an accounting professor, I had to stay on top of financial reporting; every year I read a sample of annual financial reports to keep up with current practices. But beyond the group of people who get paid to read financial reports, does anyone read footnotes?

For a company you've invested in (or are considering investing in), I suggest that you do a quick read-through of the footnotes and identify the ones that seem to have the most significance. Generally, the most important footnotes are those dealing with the following matters:

- ✔ **Stock options awarded by the business to its executives:** The additional stock shares issued under stock options *dilute* (thin out) the earnings per share of the business, which in turn puts downside pressure on the market value of its stock shares, assuming everything else remains the same.

- ✔ **Pending lawsuits, litigation, and investigations by government agencies:** These intrusions into the normal affairs of the business can have enormous consequences.

- ✔ **Employee retirement and other post-retirement benefit plans:** Your concerns here should be whether these future obligations of the business are seriously underfunded. I have to warn you that this particular footnote is one of the most complex pieces of communication you'll ever encounter. Good luck.

✔ **Debt problems:** It's not unusual for companies to get into problems with their debt. Debt contracts with lenders can be very complex and are financial straitjackets in some ways. A business may fall behind in making interest and principal payments on one or more of its debts, which triggers provisions in the debt contracts that give its lenders various options to protect their rights. Some debt problems are normal, but in certain cases lenders can threaten drastic action against a business, which should be discussed in its footnotes.

✔ **Segment information for the business:** Public businesses have to report information for the major segments of the organization — sales and operating profit by territories or product lines. This gives a better glimpse of the different parts making up the whole business. (Segment information may be reported elsewhere in an annual financial report than in the footnotes, or you may have to go to the SEC filings of the business to find this information.)

These are a few of the important pieces of information you should look for in footnotes. But you have to stay alert for other critical matters that a business may disclose in its footnotes, so I suggest scanning each and every footnote for potentially important information. Finding a footnote that discusses a major lawsuit against the business, for example, may make the stock too risky for your stock portfolio.

Chapter 14

Filling Out the Financial Statements for Business Managers

In This Chapter

▶ Recognizing the managerial limits of external financial statements

▶ Examining the additional information needed for managing assets and liabilities

▶ Identifying the in-depth information required for managing profit

▶ Providing additional information for managing operating cash flow

*I*f you're a business manager, I strongly suggest that you read Chapter 13 before continuing with this one. Chapter 13 discusses how a business's lenders and investors read their external financial reports. These stakeholders are entitled to regular financial reports so they can determine whether the business is making good use of their money. The chapter explains key ratios that the external stakeholders can use for interpreting the financial condition and profit performance of a business — which are equally relevant for the managers of the business.

Business managers should understand the financial statement ratios in Chapter 13. Every ratio does double duty; it's useful to business lenders and investors *and* equally useful to business managers. For example, the profit ratio and return on assets ratio are extraordinarily important to both the external stakeholders and the managers of a business — the first measures the profit yield from sales revenue, and the second measures profit on the assets employed by the business.

But as important as they are, the external financial statements do not provide all the accounting information that managers need to plan and control the financial affairs of a business. *Managers need additional information.* Managers who look no further than the external financial statements are being very shortsighted — they don't have all the information they need to do their jobs. The accounts reported in external financial statements are like the table of contents of a book; each account is like a chapter title. Managers need to do more than skim chapter titles. They need to read the chapters.

This chapter looks behind the accounts reported in the external financial statements. I explain the types of additional accounting information that managers need in order to control financial condition and performance, and to plan the financial future of their business.

Building on the Foundation of the External Financial Statements

Managers are problem solvers. Every business has problems, perhaps even some serious ones. However, external financial statements are not designed to expose those problems. Except in extreme cases — in which the business is obviously in dire financial straits — you'd never learn about its problems just from reading its external financial statements. To borrow lyrics from an old Bing Crosby song, external financial statements are designed to "accentuate the positive, eliminate the negative . . . [and] don't mess with Mister In-Between."

Seeking out problems and opportunities

Business managers need more accounting information than what's disclosed in external financial statements for two basic purposes:

- ✔ To alert them to *problems* that exist or may be emerging that threaten the profit performance, cash flow, and financial condition of the business

- ✔ To suggest *opportunities* for improving the financial performance and health of the business

A popular expression these days is "mining the data." The accounting system of a business is a rich mother lode of management information, but you have to dig that information out of the accounting database. Working with the controller (chief accountant), a manager should decide what information she needs beyond what is reported in the external financial statements.

Avoiding information overload

Business managers are very busy people. Nothing is more frustrating than getting reams of information that you have no use for. For that reason, the controller should guard carefully against information overload. While some types of accounting information should stream to business managers on a regular basis, other types should be provided only on an as-needed basis.

Ideally, the controller reads the mind of every manager and provides exactly the accounting information that each manager needs. In practice, that can't always happen, of course. A manager may not be certain about which information she needs and which she doesn't. The flow of information has to be worked out over time.

Furthermore, *how* to communicate the information is open to debate and individual preferences. Some of the additional management information can be put in the main body of an accounting report, but most is communicated in supplemental schedules, graphs, and commentary. The information may be delivered to the manager's computer, or the manager may be given the option to call up selected information from the accounting database of the business.

My point is simply this: Managers and controllers must communicate — early and often — to make sure managers get the information nuggets they need without being swamped with unnecessary data. No one wants to waste precious time compiling reports that are never read. So before a controller begins the process of compiling accounting information for managers' eyes only, be sure there's ample communication about what each manager needs.

Gathering Financial Condition Information

The balance sheet — one of three primary financial statements included in a financial report — summarizes the financial condition of the business. Figure 14-1 lists the basic accounts in a balance sheet, without dollar amounts for the accounts and without subtotals and totals. Just 12 accounts are given in Figure 14-1: five assets (counting fixed assets and accumulated depreciation as only one account), five liabilities, and two owners' equity accounts. A business may report more than just these 12 accounts. For instance, a business may invest in marketable securities, or have receivables from loans made to officers of the business. A business may own intangible assets. A business corporation may issue more than one class of capital stock and would report a separate account for each class. And so on. The idea of Figure 14-1 is to focus on the core assets and liabilities of a typical business.

Assets	Liabilities
Cash	Accounts Payable
Accounts Receivable	Accrued Expenses Payable
Inventory	Income Tax Payable
Prepaid Expenses	Short-term Notes Payable
Fixed Assets	Long-term Notes Payable
Less: Accumulated Depreciation	
	Owners' Equity
	Invested Capital
	Retained Earnings

Figure 14-1:
Hardcore accounts reported in a balance sheet.

Cash

The external balance sheet reports just one cash account. But many businesses keep several bank checking and deposit accounts, and some (such as gambling casinos and food supermarkets) keep a fair amount of currency on hand. A business may have foreign bank deposits in euros, English pounds, or other currencies. Most businesses set up separate checking accounts for payroll; only payroll checks are written against these accounts.

Managers should monitor the balances in every cash account in order to control and optimize the deployment of their cash resources. Therefore, information about each bank account should be reported to the manager.

Managers should ask these questions regarding cash:

- ✔ Is the ending balance of cash the actual amount at the balance sheet date, or did the business engage in *window dressing* in order to inflate its ending cash balance? Window dressing refers to holding the books open after the ending balance sheet date in order to record additional cash inflow as if the cash was received on the last day of the period. Window dressing is not uncommon. (For more details, see Chapter 12.) If window dressing has gone on, the manager should know the true, actual ending cash balance of the business.

- ✔ Were there any *cash out days* during the year? In other words, did the company's cash balance actually fall to zero (or near zero) during the year? How often did this happen? Is there a seasonal fluctuation in cash flow that causes "low tide" for cash, or are the cash out days due to running the business with too little cash?

✔ Are there any limitations on the uses of cash imposed by loan covenants by the company's lenders? Do any of the loans require compensatory balances that require that the business keep a minimum balance relative to the loan balance? In this situation the cash balance is not fully available for general operating purposes.

✔ Are there any out-of-the-ordinary demands on cash? For example, a business may have entered into buyout agreements with a key shareholder or with a vendor to escape the terms of an unfavorable contract. Any looming demands on cash should be reported to managers.

Accounts receivable

A business that makes sales on credit has the accounts receivable asset — unless it has collected all its customers' receivables by the end of the period, which is not very likely. To be more correct, the business has hundreds or thousands of individual accounts receivable from its credit customers. In its external balance sheet, a business reports just one summary amount for all its accounts receivable. However, this total amount is not nearly enough information for the business manager.

Here are some key questions a manager should ask about accounts receivable:

✔ Of the total amount of accounts receivable, how much is current (within the normal credit terms offered to customers), slightly past due, and seriously past due? A past due receivable causes a delay in cash flow and increases the risk of it becoming a *bad debt* (a receivable that ends up being partially or wholly uncollectible).

✔ Has an adequate amount been recorded for bad debts? Is the company's method for determining its bad debts expense consistent year to year? Was the estimate of bad debts this period tweaked in order to boost or dampen profit for the period? Has the IRS raised any questions about the company's method for writing off bad debts? (Chapter 7 discusses bad debts expense.)

✔ Who owes the most money to the business? (The manager should receive a schedule of customers that shows this information.) Which customers are the slowest payers? Do the sales prices to these customers take into account that they typically do not pay on time?

It's also useful to know which customers pay quickly to take advantage of prompt payment discounts. In short, the payment profiles of credit customers are important information for managers.

✔ Are there "stray" receivables buried in the accounts receivable total? A business may loan money to its managers and employees or to other businesses. There may be good business reasons for such loans. In any case, these receivables should not be included with accounts receivable, which should be reserved for receivables from credit sales to customers. Other receivables should be listed in a separate schedule.

Inventory

For businesses that sell products, inventory is typically a major asset. It's also typically the most problematic asset from both the management and accounting points of view. First off, the manager should understand the accounting method being used to determine the cost of inventory and the cost of goods sold expense. (You may want to quickly review the section in Chapter 7 that covers this topic.) In particular, the manager should have a good feel regarding whether the accounting method results in conservative or liberal profit measures.

Managers should ask these questions regarding inventory:

✔ How long, on average, do products remain in storage before they are sold? The manager should receive a *turnover analysis* of inventory that clearly exposes the holding periods of products. Slow-moving products cause nothing but problems. The manager should ferret out products that have been held in inventory too long. The cost of these sluggish products may have to be written down or written off, and the manager has to authorize these accounting entries. The manager should review the sales demand for slow-moving products, of course.

✔ If the business uses the LIFO method (last-in, first-out), was there a *LIFO liquidation gain* during the period that caused an artificial and one-time boost in profit for the year? (I explain this aspect of the LIFO method in Chapter 7.)

The manager should also request these reports:

✔ Inventory reports that include side-by-side comparison of the costs and the sales prices of products (or at least the major products sold by the business). It's helpful to include the mark-up percent for each product, which allows the manager to focus on mark-up percent differences from product to product.

✔ Regular reports summarizing major product cost changes during the period, and forecasts of near-term changes. It may be useful to report the current replacement cost of inventory assuming it's feasible to determine this amount.

Prepaid expenses

Generally, the business manager doesn't need much additional information on this asset. However, there may be a major decrease or increase in this asset from a year ago that is not consistent with the growth or decline in sales from year to year. The manager should pay attention to an abnormal change in the asset. Perhaps a new type of cost has to be prepaid now, such as insurance coverage for employee safety triggered by an OSHA audit of the employee working conditions in the business. A brief schedule of the major types of prepaid expenses is useful.

Fixed assets less accumulated depreciation

Fixed assets is the all-inclusive term for the wide range of long-term operating assets used by a business — from buildings and heavy machinery to office furniture. Except for the cost of land, the cost of a fixed asset is spread over its estimated useful life to the business; the amount allocated to each period is called *depreciation expense.* The manager should know the company's accounting policy regarding which fixed assets are *capitalized* (the cost is recorded in a fixed asset account) and which are *expensed* immediately (the cost is recorded entirely to expense at the time of purchase).

Most businesses adopt a cost limit below which minor fixed assets (a screw-driver, stapler, or wastebasket, for example) are recorded to expense instead of being depreciated over some number of years. The controller should alert the manager if an unusually high amount of these small cost fixed assets were charged off to expense during the year, which could have a significant impact on the bottom line.

The manager should be aware of the general accounting policies of the business regarding estimating useful lives of fixed assets and whether the straight-line or accelerated methods of allocation are used. Indeed, the manager should have a major voice in deciding these policies, and not simply defer to the controller. In Chapter 7, I explain these accounting issues.

Using accelerated depreciation methods may result in certain fixed assets that are fully depreciated but are still in active use. These assets should be reported to the manager — even though they have a zero book value — so the manager is aware that these fixed assets are still being used but no depreciation expense is being recorded for their use.

Generally, the manager does not need to know the current replacement costs of *all* fixed assets — just those that will be replaced in the near future. At the same time, it is useful for the manager to get a status report on the company's fixed assets, which takes more of an engineering approach than an accounting approach. The status report includes information on the capacity, operating efficiency, and projected remaining life of each major fixed asset. The status report should include leased assets that are not owned by the business and which, therefore, are not included in the fixed asset account.

The manager needs an *insurance summary report* for all fixed assets that are (or should be) insured for fire and other casualty losses, which lists the types of coverage on each major fixed asset, deductibles, claims during the year, and so on. Also, the manager needs a list of the various liability risks of owning and using the fixed assets. The manager has to decide whether the risks should be insured.

Accounts payable

As you know, individuals have credit scores that affect their ability to borrow money and the interest rates they have to pay. Likewise, businesses have credit scores. If a business has a really bad credit rating, it may not be able to buy on credit and may have to pay exorbitant interest rates. I don't have space here to go into the details of how credit rankings are developed for businesses. Suffice it to say that a business should pay its bills on time. If a business consistently pays its accounts payable late, this behavior gets reported to a credit rating agency (such as Dun & Bradstreet).

The manager needs a schedule of accounts payable that are *past due* (beyond the credit terms given by the vendors and suppliers). Of course, the manager should know the reasons that the accounts have become overdue. The manager may have to personally contact these creditors and convince them to continue offering credit to the business.

Frankly, some businesses operate on the principle of paying late. Their standard operating procedure is to pay their accounts payable two, three, or more weeks after the due dates. This could be due to not having adequate cash balances or wanting to hang on to their cash as long as possible. In the past, IBM was notorious for paying late, but because its credit rating was unimpeachable, it got away with this policy.

Accrued expenses payable

The controller should prepare a schedule for the manager that lists the major items making up the balance of the accrued expenses payable liability account. Many operating liabilities accumulate or, as accountants prefer to say, *accrue* during the course of the year that are not paid until sometime later. One main example is employee vacation and sick pay; an employee may work for almost a year before being entitled to take two weeks vacation with pay. The accountant records an expense each payroll period for this employee benefit, and it accumulates in the liability account until the liability is paid (the employee takes his vacation). Another payroll-based expense that accrues is the cost of federal and state unemployment taxes on the employer.

Accrued expenses payable can be a tricky liability from the accounting point of view. There's a lot of room for management discretion (or manipulation, depending on how you look at it) regarding which particular operating liabilities to record as expense during the year, and which not to record as expense until they are paid. The basic choice is whether to expense as you go or expense later. If you decide to record the expense as you go through the year, the accountant has to make estimates and assumptions, which are subject to error. Then there's the question of expediency. Employee vacation and sick pay may seem to be obvious expenses to accrue, but in fact many businesses do not accrue the expense on the grounds that it's simply too time consuming and, furthermore, that some employees quit and forfeit the rights to their vacations.

Many businesses guarantee the products they sell for a certain period of time, such as 90 days or one year. The customer has the right to return the product for repair (or replacement) during the guarantee period. For example, when I returned my iPad for repair, Apple should have already recorded in a liability account the estimated cost of repairing iPads that are returned after the point of sale. Businesses have more "creeping" liabilities than you might imagine. With a little work, I could list 20 or 30 of them, but I'll spare you the details. My point is that the manager should know what's in the accrued expenses payable liability account, and what's not. Also, the manager should have a good fix on when these liabilities will be paid.

Income tax payable

It takes an income tax professional to comply with federal and state income tax laws on a business. The manager should make certain that the accountant responsible for its tax returns is qualified and up-to-date.

The controller should explain to the manager the reasons for a relatively large balance in this liability account at the end of the year. In a normal situation, a business should have paid 90 percent or more of its annual income tax by the end of the year. However, there are legitimate reasons that the ending balance of the income tax liability could be relatively large compared with the annual income tax expense — say 20 or 30 percent of the annual expense. It behooves the manager to know the reasons for a large ending balance in the income tax liability. The controller should report these reasons to the chief financial officer and perhaps the treasurer of the business.

The manager should also know how the business stands with the IRS, and whether the IRS has raised objections to the business's tax returns. The business may be in the middle of legal proceedings with the IRS, which the manager should be briefed on, of course. The CEO (and perhaps other top-level managers) should be given a frank appraisal of how things may turn out and whether the business is facing any additional tax payments and penalties. Needless to say, this is very sensitive information, and the controller may prefer that none of it be documented in a written report.

Finally, the chief executive officer working closely with the controller should decide how aggressive to be on income tax issues and alternatives. Keep in mind that tax avoidance is legal, but tax evasion is illegal. As you probably know, the income tax law is exceedingly complex, but ignorance of the law is no excuse. The controller should make abundantly clear to the manager whether the business is walking on thin ice in its income tax returns.

Interest-bearing debt

In Figure 14-1, the balance sheet reports two interest-bearing liabilities: one for short-term debts (those due in one year or less) and one for long-term debt. The reason is that financial reporting standards require that external balance sheets report the amount of *current liabilities* so the reader can compare this amount of short-term liabilities against the total of *current assets* (cash and assets that will be converted into cash in the short term). Interest-bearing debt that is due in one year or less is included in the current liabilities section of the balance sheet. (See Chapter 5 for more details.)

The ending balances of short-term and long-term debt that are reported in the external balance sheet are not nearly enough information for the manager. The best practice is to lay out in one comprehensive schedule for the manager *all* the interest-bearing obligations of the business. The obligations should be organized according to their due (maturity) dates, and the schedule should include other relevant information such as the lender, the interest rate on each debt, the plans to rollover the debt (or not), the collateral, and the main covenants and restrictions on the business imposed by the lender.

Recall that debt is one of the two sources of capital to a business (the other being owners' equity, which I get to next). The sustainability of a business depends on the sustainability of its sources of capital. The more a business depends on debt capital, the more important it is to manage its debt well and maintain excellent relations with its lenders.

Raising and using debt and equity capital, referred to as *financial management* or *corporate finance,* is a broad subject that extends beyond the scope of this book. For more information, look at *Small Business Financial Management Kit For Dummies* (Wiley) — coauthored by my son, Tage, and me, which explains the financial management function in more detail.

Owners' equity

External balance sheets report two kinds of ownership accounts: one for *capital invested* by the owners in the business and one for *retained earnings* (profit that has not been distributed to shareowners). In Figure 14-1, just one invested capital account is shown in the owners' equity section, as if the business has only one class of owners' equity. In fact, business corporations, limited liability companies, partnerships, and other types of business legal entities can have complex ownership structures. The owners' equity sections in their balance sheets may report several invested capital accounts — one for each class of ownership interest in the business.

Broadly speaking, the manager faces three basic issues regarding the owners' equity of the business:

- ✔ Is more capital needed from the owners?
- ✔ Should some capital be returned to the owners?
- ✔ Can and should the business make a cash distribution from profit to the owners and, if so, how much?

These questions belong in the field of financial management and extend beyond the scope of this book. However, I should mention that the external financial statements are very useful in deciding these key financial management issues. For example, the manager needs to know how much total capital is needed to support the sales level of the business. For every $100 of sales revenue, how much total assets does the business need? The *asset turnover ratio* equals annual sales revenue divided by total assets. This ratio provides a good touchstone for the amount of capital being used for sales.

The external financial report of a business does not disclose the individual shareowners of the business and the number of shares each person or institution owns. The manager may want to know this information. Any major change in the ownership of the business usually is important information to the manager.

Culling Profit Information

The sales revenue (and other income if any) and expenses (and losses if any) of a business over a period of time are summarized in a financial statement called the *income statement*. Profit (sales revenue minus expenses) is the bottom line of the income statement. Chapter 4 explains the externally reported income statement, as well as how sales revenue and expenses are interconnected with the operating assets and liabilities of the business. The income statement fits hand in glove with the balance sheet.

Chapter 9 explains internal profit reports to managers, which are called P&L (profit and loss) reports. P&L reports should be designed to help managers in their profit analysis and decision making. Chapter 9 is the logical take-off point for this section, in which I discuss the types of profit information managers need.

Now here's a question that might strike you as rather odd: What is the specific profit motive of the business? For large public companies, it's abundantly clear that their main profit attention is on earnings per share (EPS). (I explain EPS in Chapter 13.) Of course, the company has to earn enough total net income and control the total number of its stock shares in order to hit their EPS targets. The profit objective of public businesses centers on EPS, because EPS plays such a dominant role in determining the market value of its stock shares.

In contrast, the specific profit focus of a private business is not EPS but . . . well, but what? The main objective could be simply the bottom line, which is total net income. A private business may also put heavy importance on its *return on equity* (ROE), which is the measure of profit compared with the equity capital being used to earn that profit. (I introduce ROE in Chapter 13.)

Digging deeper into the return on equity (ROE) measure of profit

Return on equity (ROE) is computed as follows:

Profit/Owners' Equity = ROE

Profit is the bottom-line net income and all components (invested capital and retained earnings) are included in owners' equity. The calculation of ROE is expanded in the DuPont model, which has its origins years ago in the company of the same name. The DuPont model computes return on equity (ROE) in three parts, as follows:

ROE = Profit Ratio × Asset Turnover Ratio × Leverage Ratio

The three ratios in this equation are defined as follows:

ROE = Profit/Sales × Sales/Assets × Assets/Equity

Suppose, for example, that a business earns $50 profit on $1,000 sales, has $500 assets, and $250 owners' equity (meaning that it has $250 liabilities, the other source of total assets). Its ROE is computed as follows using the DuPont model:

ROE = $50/$1,000 × $1,000/$500 × $500/$250

20% ROE = 5% profit ratio × 2.0 asset turnover ratio × 2.0 leverage ratio

In other words, the company earned 5 percent on its sales revenue, turned its assets twice (its sales were two times its assets), and liabilities supply half its total assets so the business has a leverage factor of 2 times the owners' equity capital invested in the business. This is a rough-and-ready model, which has to be refined in the actual context of a business. But it does provide a good overview of the three key factors that determine ROE.

Margin: The catalyst of profit

A business makes profit by earning total margin that exceeds its total fixed expenses for the period. Margin equals sales revenue minus all variable expenses of generating the sales revenue. Cost of goods sold is the main variable expense for companies that sell products. Most businesses have other significant variable expenses, which depend either on sales volume (the quantity of products or services sold) or the dollar amount of sales revenue. Ideally, P&L reports to managers should separate variable from fixed operating expenses, in order to measure margin.

Figure 14-2 presents a skeleton of the P&L report. No dollar amounts are given because I focus on the *kinds* of information that managers need in order to analyze and control profit. Note that operating expenses below the gross margin line are classified between variable and fixed. Therefore, the P&L report includes margin (profit before fixed operating expenses). Income statements in external financial reports do not classify the behavior of operating expenses.

The P&L report stops at the operating profit line, or earnings before interest and income tax expenses. (Interest is in the hands of the chief financial officer of the business, and income tax is best left to tax professionals.)

Start with	**Sales Revenue**
Deduct	**Cost of Goods Sold Expense**
Equals	**Gross Margin**
Deduct	**Variable Operating Expenses**
Equals	**Margin**
Deduct	**Fixed Operating Expenses**
Equals	**Operating Profit***

Figure 14-2: Skeleton of a P&L (profit and loss) report.

* Also called operating earnings, and earnings before interest and taxes (EBIT)

Most businesses sell a wide variety of products and have many sources of sales revenue. The margins per unit on each source of sales vary. It's quite unusual to find a business that earns the same margin ratio on all its sales. The manager needs information on sales revenue and margin for each mainstream source of sales. But the term "mainstream source of sales" has very different meanings for each business. In analyzing profit, one of the main challenges facing business managers is deciding how to organize, categorize, and aggregate the huge volume of data on sales and expenses.

For example, consider a hardware store in Boulder, Colorado that sells more than 100,000 different products (including different sizes of the same products). Suppose it has ten key managers with sales and profit responsibility. This means that each manager would be responsible for 10,000 different sources of sales. It would be possible to report every specific sale to the manager, but this would be absurd! The same is true for a high-volume retailer like Target or Costco. For a Honda or Toyota auto dealer, on the other hand, reporting each new car sale to the manager would be practical.

Regardless of how sales are reported to the manager, *all* variable expenses of each sales source should be matched against the sales revenue in order to determine margin for that source. The alternative is to match only the cost of goods sold expense with sales revenue, which means that the manager knows only gross margin instead of final margin (after variable operating expenses are also deducted from sales revenue).

Sales revenue and expenses

In this section, I offer examples of sales revenue and expense information that managers need that is not reported in the external income statement of a business. Given the very broad range of different businesses and different circumstances, I can't offer much detail.

Here's a sampling of the kinds of accounting information that business managers need either in their P&L reports or in supplementary schedules and analyses:

- **Sales volumes** (quantities sold) for all sources of sales revenue.

- **List sales prices** and **discounts, allowances, and rebates** against list sales prices. For many businesses sales pricing is a two-sided affair that starts with list prices (such as manufacturer's suggested retail price) and includes deductions of all sorts from the list prices.

- **Sales returns** — products that were bought but later returned by customers.

✔ **Special incentives** offer by suppliers that effectively reduce the purchase cost of products.

✔ Abnormal charges for **embezzlement and pilfer age losses.**

✔ Significant **variations in discretionary expenses** from year to year, such as repair and maintenance, employee training costs, and advertising.

✔ **Illegal payments** to secure business, including bribes, kickbacks, and other under-the-table payments. Keep in mind that businesses are not willing to admit to making such payments, much less report them in internal communications. Therefore, the manager should know how these payments are disguised in the accounts of the business.

✔ Sales revenue and margin for **new products.**

✔ Significant **changes in fixed costs** and reasons for the changes.

✔ **Expenses that surged** much more than increases in sales volume or sales revenue.

✔ **New expenses** that show up for the first time.

✔ **Accounting changes** (if any) regarding when sales revenue and expenses are recorded.

The bulleted-list items don't constitute an exhaustive list. But the list covers many important types of information that managers need in order to interpret their P&L reports and to plan profit improvements in the future. Analyzing profit is a very open-ended process. There are many ways to slice and dice sales and expense data. Managers have only so much time at their disposal, but they should take the time to understand and analyze the main factors that drive profit.

Digging into Cash Flow Information

Chapter 6 explains the statement of cash flows included in a business's external financial report. Cash flows fall into three types:

✔ Cash flows from **operating activities** ("operating" refers to making sales and incurring expenses in the process of earning profit)

✔ Cash flows from **investing activities** (outlays for new long-term assets and proceeds from disposals of these assets)

✔ Cash flows from **financing activities** (borrowing and repaying debt; raising capital from and returning capital to owners; and cash distributions from profit to owners)

Distinguishing investing and financing cash flows from operating cash flows

Investing and financing decisions are the heart of business financial management. Every business must secure and invest capital. No capital, no business — it's as simple as that. Inadequate capital clamps limits on the growth potential of a business. In larger businesses, the financing and investing activities are the domain of the chief financial officer (CFO), who works with other high-level executives in setting the financial strategies and policies of the business.

The field of financial management — raising capital for a business and deploying its capital — is beyond the scope of this book. For more information, you can refer to the book I coauthored with my son, Tage, *Small Business Financial Management Kit For Dummies* (John Wiley & Sons).

This section concentrates on cash flow from operating activities. These cash flows are affected by managers with operating responsibilities — managers who have responsibilities for sales and the expenses that are directly connected with making sales. These managers should understand the cash flow impacts of their sales and expenses. (See the sidebar "Cash flow characteristics of sales and expenses.") Their sales and expense decisions drive the operating activity cash flows of the business.

Cash flow characteristics of sales and expenses

In reading their P&L reports, managers should keep in mind that the accountant records sales revenue when sales are made — regardless of when cash is received from customers. Also, the accountant records expenses to match expenses with sales revenue and to put expenses in the period where they belong — regardless of when cash is paid for the expenses. The manager should not assume that sales revenue equals cash inflow, and that expenses equal cash outflow.

The cash flow characteristics of sales and expenses are summarized as follows:

✔ Cash sales generate immediate cash inflow. Keep in mind that sales returns and sales price adjustments after the point of sale reduce cash flow.

✔ Credit sales do not generate immediate cash inflow. There's no cash flow until the customers' receivables are actually collected. There's a cash flow lag from credit sales.

✔ Many operating costs are not paid until several weeks (or months) after they are recorded as expense; and a few operating costs are paid before the costs are charged to expense.

✔ Depreciation expense is recorded by reducing the book value of an asset and does not involve cash outlay in the period when it is recorded. The business paid out cash when the asset was acquired. (Amortization expense on intangible assets is the same.)

Managing operating cash flows

In a small, one-owner/one-manager business, one person has to manage both profit and cash flow from profit. In larger businesses, managers who have profit responsibility may or may not have cash flow responsibility. The profit manager may ignore the cash flow aspects of his sales and expense activities. The responsibility for controlling cash flow falls on some other manager. Of course, someone should manage the cash flows of sales and expenses. The following comments speak to this person in particular.

The net cash flow during the period from carrying on profit-making operations depends on the changes in the operating assets and liabilities directly connected with sales revenue and expenses. Figure 14-3 highlights these assets and liabilities, and also retained earnings. Changes in these accounts during the year determine the cash flow from operating activities. In other words, changes in these accounts boost or crimp cash flow.

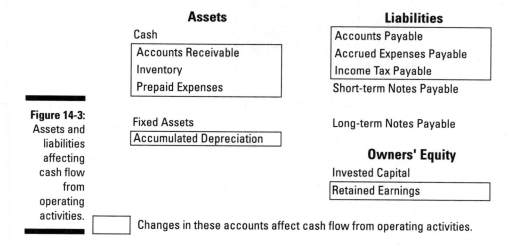

Figure 14-3: Assets and liabilities affecting cash flow from operating activities.

Note that *retained earnings* is highlighted in Figure 14-3. Profit increases this owners' equity account. Profit is the starting point for determining cash flow from operating activities. (Alternatively, a business may use the direct method for determining and reporting cash flow from operating activities, which I explain in Chapter 6.)

The cash flow from profit is determined as follows:

1. **Start with the accounting profit number, usually labeled *net income*.**

2. **Add depreciation expense (and amortization expense, if any)** because there is no cash outlay for the expense during the period.

3. **Deduct increases or add decreases in operating assets** because

- An increase requires additional cash outlay to build up the asset.
- A decrease means amount invested in the asset is reduced and thus provides cash.

4. **Add increases or deduct decreases in operating liabilities** because

- An increase means less cash is paid out than the expense.
- A decrease means more cash is paid out to reduce the liability.

You may ask: What about changes during the year in those balance sheet accounts that are not highlighted in Figure 14-3? Well, these changes are reported either in the cash flow from investing activities or the cash flow from financing activities sections of the statement of cash flows. So, all balance sheet account changes during the year end up in the statement of cash flows.

The manager should closely monitor the changes in operating assets and liabilities (see Figure 14-3). A good general rule is that each operating asset and liability should change about the same percent as the percent change in the sales activity of the business. If sales revenue increases, say, 10 percent, then operating assets and liabilities should increase *about* 10 percent. The percents of increases in the operating assets and liabilities (in particular, accounts receivable, inventory, accounts payable, and accrued expenses payable) should be emphasized in the cash flow report to the manager. The manager should not have to take out his calculator and do these calculations.

Controlling cash flow from profit (operating activities) means controlling changes in the operating assets and liabilities of making sales and incurring expenses: There's no getting around this fact of business life. There's no doubt that cash flow is king. You can be making good profit, but if you don't turn the profit into cash flow quickly, you are headed for big trouble.

Part V
The Part of Tens

The 5th Wave   By Rich Tennant

"I'm not familiar with auditing terms. What do you think that means?"

In this part . . .

This part contains two shorter chapters: the first directed to business managers, and the second directed to business investors and other outside readers of financial reports. The first chapter presents ten tips for business managers to help them get the most bang for the buck out of their accounting system; these ten topics constitute a compact accounting tool kit for managers. The second chapter offers investors ten tips regarding what they should keep in mind and what to look for when reading a financial report — to gain the maximum amount of information in the minimum amount of time.

Chapter 15

Ten Accounting Tips for Managers

*F*inancially speaking, business managers have four essential jobs:

✔ Score adequate capital from debt and equity sources

✔ Earn adequate operating profit on that capital

✔ Expedite cash flow from that profit

✔ Control the solvency of the business

How can accounting help make you a better business manager? That's the bottom-line question, and the bottom line is the best place to start. Accounting provides the financial information you need for making good profit decisions — and it stops you from plunging ahead with gut-level decisions that feel right but don't hold water after due-diligent analysis. Accounting also provides cash flow and financial condition information you need. But in order for accounting information to do all these amazing things, you have to understand and know how to interpret it.

Reach Break-Even, and Then Rake in Profit

Virtually every business has *fixed costs*: costs that are locked in for the year and remain the same whether annual sales are at 100 percent or below half your capacity. Fixed costs are a dead weight on a business. To make profit, you have to get over your fixed costs hurdle. How do you do this? Obviously, you have to make sales. Each sale brings in a certain amount of *margin,* which equals the revenue minus the variable expenses of the sale. (If your sales don't generate margin, you're in deep trouble.)

Say you sell a product for $100. Your purchase (or manufacturing) cost is $60, which accountants call the *cost of goods sold expense.* Your variable costs of selling the item add up to $15, including sales commission and delivery cost. Thus, your margin on the sale is $25: $100 sales price – $60 product cost – $15 variable costs = $25 margin. Margin is before interest and income tax expenses, and before fixed costs are considered.

Your annual fixed operating costs total $2.5 million. These costs provide the space, facilities, and people that are necessary to make sales and earn profit. Of course, your sales may not be enough to overcome your fixed costs. This leads to the next step, which is to determine your break-even point. *Break-even* refers to the sales revenue you need just to recoup your fixed operating costs. If you earn 25 percent average margin on sales, in order to break even you need $10 million in annual sales: $10 million × 25 percent margin = $2.5 million margin. At this sales level, margin equals fixed costs and your profit is zero (you break even). Not very exciting so far, is it? But from here on it gets much more interesting.

Until sales reach $10 million, you're in the loss zone. After you cross over the break-even point, you enter the profit zone. Each additional $1 million of sales yields $250,000 profit. Suppose your annual sales revenue is $4 million over your break-even point. Your profit (earnings before interest and income tax) is $1.0 million ($4 million sales over break-even × 25 percent margin ratio = $1 million profit). The main lesson is that after you cross over the break-even threshold, your entire margin goes toward profit.

Set Sales Prices Right

In real estate, the three most important profit factors are location, location, and location. In the business of selling products and services, the three most important factors are margin, margin, and margin. Of course a business manager should control expenses — that goes without saying. But the secret to making profit is making sales *and* earning an adequate margin on the sales revenue. (Remember, margin equals sales price less all variable costs of the sale.) Chapter 9 explains that internal profit and loss (P&L) reports to managers should separate variable and fixed costs so the manager can focus on margin.

In the example in the previous section, your sales prices earn 25 percent margin on sales. In other words, $100 of sales revenue generates $25 margin (after deducting the cost of product sold and variable costs of making the sale). Therefore, $16 million in sales revenue, for example, generates $4 million margin. The $4 million margin covers your $2.5 million in fixed costs and provides $1.5 million profit (before interest and income tax).

An alternative scenario illustrates the importance of setting sales prices high enough to earn an adequate margin. Instead of the sales prices in the previous example, suppose you had set sales prices 5 percent lower. Therefore, your margin would be $5 lower per $100 of sales. Instead of 25 percent margin on sales, you would earn only 20 percent margin on sales. How badly would the lower margin ratio hurt profit?

On $16 million annual sales, your margin would be $3.2 million ($16 million sales × 20 percent margin ratio = $3.2 million margin). Deducting $2.5 million fixed costs for the year leaves only $700,000 profit. Compared with your $1.5 million profit at the 25 percent margin ratio, the $700,000 profit at the lower sales prices is less than half. The moral of this story is that a 5 percent lower sales price causes 53 percent lower profit!

Don't Confuse Profit and Cash Flow

To find out whether you made a profit or had a loss for the year, you look at the bottom line in your P&L report. But you must understand that the bottom line does *not* tell you cash flow. Simply put, profit does not equal cash flow. Don't ever assume that making profit increases cash the same amount. Making such an assumption reveals that you're a rank amateur. Cash flow can be considerably higher than bottom-line profit, or considerably lower. Cash flow can be negative even when you earn a profit, and cash flow can be positive even when you have a loss. There's no natural correlation between profit and cash flow. If I know the profit number, I don't have a clue about the cash flow number because cash flow depends on additional factors.

Figure 15-1 shows an example I designed to illustrate the differences between sales revenue and expenses (the accounting numbers used to measure profit) and the cash flows of the sales and expenses. To keep it brief, only three expenses are shown: cost of goods sold, depreciation, and one total amount for all other expenses. (***Note:*** Reporting expenses this way in a P&L report is not adequate for managers and is not acceptable for income statements in an external financial report.)

Figure 15-1:
Comparing
cash
flows with
sales and
expenses
for the
period.

	P&L Report	Cash Flows	Differences
Sales Revenue	$5,000,000	$4,900,000	($100,000)
Cost of Goods Sold Expense	($3,000,000)	($3,225,000)	($225,000)
Depreciation Expense	($100,000)	$0	$100,000
All Other Expenses	($1,600,000)	($1,435,000)	$165,000
Bottom-line	$300,000	$240,000	($60,000)

Here are the reasons for the cash flow differences in Figure 15-1:

- ✔ Your accounts receivable (from credit sales) increased $100,000 during the year, so actual cash collections from customers were only $4.9 million during the year — a cash flow shortfall of $100,000.

- ✔ You built up your inventory $225,000 during the year, so your cash outlays for products were $225,000 higher than the cost of goods sold expense for the year.

- ✔ Depreciation expense is not a cash outlay in the period recorded; the cash outlay took place when the fixed assets being depreciated were acquired some years ago.

- ✔ Total cash outlays for other expenses were $165,000 lower than the amount of expenses recorded in the year, mainly because your accounts payable and accrued expenses payable liabilities increased during the year — you had not paid this amount of expenses by year-end.

Every situation is different, of course. I don't mean to suggest that cash flow is always lower than profit for the year. Suppose accounts receivable had remained flat during the year; your cash flow would have been $100,000 higher. If you had not built up your inventory, then . . . you get the picture. You must keep close tabs on the changes in the assets and liabilities that impact cash flow from profit. See Chapter 6 for more details.

Call the Shots on Accounting Policies

You may have heard the adage that war is too important to be left to the generals. Well, accounting is too important to be left to the accountants alone — especially when choosing which accounting methods to use. I'm oversimplifying, but measuring profit and putting values on assets and liabilities boils down to choosing between conservative accounting methods and more optimistic methods. Conservative methods record profit later rather than sooner; optimistic methods record profit sooner rather than later. It's a "pay me now or pay me later" choice. (Chapter 7 gives you the details on alternative accounting methods.)

I encourage you to get involved in setting your company's accounting policies. Business managers should take charge of accounting decisions just like they take charge of marketing and other key activities of the business. Some business managers defer to their accountants in choosing accounting methods for measuring sales revenue and expenses. Don't! You should get involved in making these decisions. The best accounting methods are the ones that best fit with your operating methods and strategies of your business. As the manager, you know the business's operations and strategies better than your accountant. Finally, keep in mind that there are no "default" accounting methods; someone has to choose every method.

Many businesses choose conservative accounting methods to defer paying their income tax. Keep in mind that higher expense deductions in early years cause lower deductions in later years. Also, conservative, income tax–driven accounting methods make the inventory and fixed assets in your balance sheet look anemic. Recording higher cost of goods sold expense takes more out of inventory, and recording higher depreciation expense causes the book value of your fixed assets to be lower. Nevertheless, you may decide that deferring the payment of income taxes is worth it, in order to keep your hands on the cash as long as possible.

Budget Well, but Wisely

When you hear the word "budgeting," you may immediately imagine a budgeting system at work — involving many persons, detailed forecasting, negotiating over goals and objectives, and page after page of detailed accounting statements that commit everyone to certain performance benchmarks for the coming period. In reality, all kinds of budgeting methods and approaches exist. You don't have to budget like IBM or a large business organization. You can do one-person limited-purpose budgeting. Even small-scale budgeting can pay handsome dividends.

I explain in Chapter 10 the reasons for budgeting — first, for understanding the profit dynamics and financial structure of your business and, second, for planning for changes in the coming period. Budgeting forces you to focus on the factors for improving profit and cash flow. It's always a good idea to look ahead to the coming year; if nothing else, at least plug the numbers in your profit report for sales volume, sales prices, product costs, and other expenses, and see how your projected profit looks for the coming year. It may not look too good, in which case you need to plan how you will do better.

The profit budget, in turn, lays the foundation for changes in your assets and liabilities that are driven by sales revenue and expenses. Your profit budget should dovetail with your assets and liabilities budget and with your cash flow budget. This information is very helpful in planning for the coming year — focusing in particular on how much cash flow from profit will be realized and how much capital expenditures will be required, which in turn lead to how much additional capital you have to raise and how much cash distribution from profit you will be able to make.

Be Sure to Get the Key Accounting Information You Need

Experienced business managers can tell you that they spend a good deal of time dealing with problems because things don't always go according to plan. Murphy's Law (if something can go wrong, it will, and usually at the worst possible time) is all too true. To solve a problem, you first have to know that you have one. Managers need to get on top of problems as soon as possible. A well-designed accounting system should set off alarms about any problems that are developing, so you can nip them in the bud.

You should identify the handful of critical factors that you need to keep a close eye on. Insist that your internal accounting reports highlight these factors. Only you, the business manager, can identify the most important numbers that you must closely watch to know how things are going. Your accountant can't read your mind. If your regular accounting reports do not include the exact types of information you need, sit down with your accountant and spell out in detail what you want to know. Don't take no for an answer. Don't let your accountant argue that the computer doesn't keep track of this information. Computers can be programmed to spit out any type of information you want.

Here are accounting information variables that should *always* be on your radar:

- ✔ Sales volumes
- ✔ Margins
- ✔ Fixed expenses
- ✔ Overdue accounts receivable
- ✔ Slow-moving inventory items

Experience is the best teacher. Over time, you discover which financial factors are the most important to highlight in your internal accounting reports. The trick is to make sure that your accountant provides this information.

Tap into Your CPA's Expertise

As you know, a CPA will perform an audit of your financial report; this is their traditional claim to fame. And the CPA will assist in preparing your income tax returns. In doing the audit, your CPA may find serious problems with your accounting methods and call these to your attention. Also, the CPA auditor will point out any serious deficiencies in your internal controls (see the next section). And, it goes without saying that your CPA can give you valuable income tax advice and guide you through the labyrinth of federal and state income tax laws and regulations.

You should also consider taking advantage of other services a CPA has to offer. A CPA can help you select, implement, and update a computer-based accounting system best suited for your business and can give expert advice on many accounting issues such as cost allocation methods. A CPA can do a critical analysis of the internal accounting reports to managers in your business and suggest improvements in these reports. A CPA has experience with a wide range of businesses and can recommend best practices for your business. If necessary, the CPA can serve as an expert witness on your behalf in lawsuits. A CPA may also be accredited in business valuation, financial advising, and forensic methods, which are specializations sponsored by the American Institute of Certified Public Accountants.

You have to be careful that the consulting services provided by your CPA do not conflict with the CPA's independence required for auditing your financial report. If there is a conflict, you should use one CPA for auditing your financial report and another CPA for consulting services. And, don't forget to ask the obvious question: Does the CPA have experience in providing the expert services? You might want to ask for names of clients that the CPA has provided these services to, and check out whether these businesses were satisfied.

Critically Review Your Controls Over Employee Dishonesty and Fraud

Every business faces threats from dishonesty and fraud — from within and from without. Your knee-jerk reaction may be that this sort of stuff couldn't possibly be going on under your nose in your own business. While waiting in an airport I once discussed fraud with a man who admitted that he had served hard time in the Nebraska State Penitentiary for embezzling $300,000 from his employer. He said that such a cocky attitude by a business manager presents the perfect opportunity for getting away with fraud (although he tripped up, obviously).

Without your knowing about it, your purchasing manager may be accepting kickbacks or other "gratuities." Your long-time bookkeeper may be embezzling. One of your suppliers may be short-counting you on deliveries. I'm not suggesting that you should invest as much time and money in preventing fraud and cheating against your business as do Las Vegas casinos. But every now and then you should take a hard look at whether your fraud controls are adequate.

Preventing fraud starts with establishing and enforcing good internal controls, which I discuss in Chapter 3. In the course of auditing your financial report, the CPA evaluates your internal controls. The CPA will report to you any serious deficiencies. Even with good internal controls and having regular audits, you should consider calling in an expert to assess your vulnerability to fraud and to determine whether there is evidence of any fraud going on.

A CPA may not be the best person to test for fraud — even if the CPA has fraud training and forensic credentials. A private detective may be better for this sort of investigation because he has more experience dealing with crooks and digging out sources of information that are beyond what a CPA customarily uses. For example, a private detective may install secret monitoring equipment or even spy on your employees' private lives. I understand if you think that you'd never be willing to go so far to defend yourself against fraud, but consider this: Someone committing fraud against your business has no such compunctions.

Lend a Hand in Preparing Your Financial Reports

Many business managers look at preparing the annual financial report of the business like they look at its annual income tax return — it's a task best left to the accountant. This is a mistake. You should take an active part in preparing the annual financial report. (I discuss preparing the financial report in Chapter 12.) You should carefully think of what to say in the letter to stockholders that accompanies the financial statements. You should help craft the footnotes to the financial statements. The annual report is a good opportunity to tell a compelling story about the business.

The owner/manager, president, or chief executive of the business has the ultimate responsibility for the financial report. Of course your financial report should not be fraudulent and deliberately misleading; if it is you can, and probably will, be sued. But beyond that, lenders and investors appreciate a frank and honest discussion of how the business did, including its problems as well as its successes.

In my view, Warren Buffett, the CEO of Berkshire Hathaway, sets the gold standard for financial reporting. He lays it on the line; if he has a bad year, he makes no excuses. Buffett is appropriately modest if he has a good year. Every annual report of Berkshire Hathaway summarizes the nature of the business and how it makes profit. If you knew nothing about this business, you could learn what you need to know from its annual report. (Go to its website at www. berkshirehathaway.com to get its latest annual report.)

Sound Like a Pro in Talking Your Financial Statements

On many occasions, a business manager has to discuss her financial statements with others. You should come across as very knowledgeable and be very persuasive in what you say. Not understanding your own financial statements does not inspire confidence. On many occasions your financial statements are the center of attention and you are expected to talk about them convincingly, including:

- **Applying for a loan:** The loan officer may ask specific questions about your accounting methods and items in your financial statements.

- **Talking with individuals or other businesses that may be interested in buying your business:** They may have questions about the recorded values of your assets and liabilities.

- ✔ **Dealing with the press:** Large corporations are used to talking with the media, and even smaller businesses are profiled in local news stories.

- ✔ **Dealing with unions or other employee groups in setting wages and benefit packages:** They may think that your profits are very high so you can afford to increase wages and benefits.

- ✔ **Explaining the profit-sharing plan to your employees:** They may take a close interest in how profit is determined.

- ✔ **Putting a value on an ownership interest for divorce or estate tax purposes:** These values are based on the financial statements of the business (and other factors).

- ✔ **Reporting financial statement data to national trade associations:** Trade associations collect financial information from their members. You should make sure that you're reporting the financial information consistently with the definitions used in the industry.

- ✔ **Presenting the annual financial report before the annual meeting of owners:** The shareowners may ask penetrating questions and expect you to be very familiar with the financial statements.

Chapter 16

Ten Tips for Reading a Financial Report

*Y*ou can compare reading a business's financial report with shucking an oyster: You have to know what you're doing and work to get at the meat. You need a good reason to pry into a financial report. The main reason to become informed about the financial performance and condition of a business is *because you have a stake in the business.* The financial success or failure of the business makes a difference to you.

Shareowners have a major stake in a business, of course. The lenders of a business also have a stake, which can be major. Shareowners and lenders are the two main audiences of a financial report. But others also have a financial stake in a business. For example, my books are published by John Wiley & Sons (a public company), so I look at its financial report to gain comfort that my royalties will be paid.

In this chapter, I offer practical tips to help investors, lenders, or anyone who has a financial stake in a business glean important insights from its financial reports. These tips also help anyone else with an interest in the financial reports of a business. See the sidebar "Sorting out financial report readers."

Get in the Right Frame of Mind

So often I hear non-accountants say that they don't read financial reports because they are not "numbers" people. You don't have to be a math wizard or rocket scientist to extract the essential points from a financial report. I know that you can find the bottom line in the income statement and compare this profit number with other relevant numbers in the financial statements. You can read the amount of cash in the balance sheet. If the business has a zero or near-zero cash balance, you know that this is a serious — perhaps fatal — problem.

Therefore, my first bit of advice is to get in the right frame of mind. Don't let a financial report bamboozle you. Locate the income statement, find bottom-line profit (or loss!), and get going. You can do it — especially having a book like this one to help you along.

Sorting out financial report readers

Shareowners and lenders have a direct stake in a business, of course. Quite clearly, they have important reasons to keep up with the information in its financial reports. In fact, they may have a duty to read its financial reports (such as the bank officer in charge of loans to the business, and investment managers of a mutual fund owning stock shares in the business). But many other people have a stake in a business and should consider looking in its financial reports. Consider the following examples:

✔ Employee retirement benefits depend on whether the business is fully funding its plans; employees should read the footnote discussing this issue (assuming the financial report is available to them).

✔ If you plan to make a large deposit on a new condo with a real estate developer, you should ask to look at its balance sheet to see whether the business is in financial trouble before you sign on the dotted line.

✔ People suing a business should focus on the items in the financial report that support their lawsuit against the business (such as misleading footnotes, for example).

✔ If you are considering moving into a retirement community that requires a large entrance fee you should read its latest financial report before writing the check.

✔ If you belong to a homeowners' association, you should review its financial statements to spot any serious problems.

✔ I read the annual financial report of my retirement fund manager closely because most of my retirement savings are in the hands of this organization (TIAA-CREF), in case you're interested).

✔ I shop regularly at Costco (a public company), so I glance at its financial report to check whether my annual membership fee is a good move.

Decide What to Read

Suppose you own stock shares in a public corporation and want to keep informed about its performance. You could depend on articles and news items in *The Wall Street Journal, The New York Times, Barron's,* and so on that summarize the latest financial reports of the company. Also, you can go to websites such as Yahoo! Finance. This saves you the time and trouble of reading the reports yourself. Generally, these brief articles and websites capture the most important points. If you own an investment portfolio of many different stocks, reading news articles that summarize the financial reports of the companies is not a bad approach. But suppose you want more financial information than you can get in news articles?

The annual financial reports of public companies contain lots of information: a letter from the chief executive, a highlights section, trend charts, financial statements, extensive footnotes to the financial statements, historical summaries, and a lot of propaganda. And you get photos of the top brass and directors (whoopee do!). In contrast, the financial reports of most private companies are significantly smaller; they contain financial statements with footnotes, and not much more.

So, how much of the report should you actually read?

You could read just the highlights section and let it go at that. This might do in a pinch. I think you should read the chief executive's letter to shareowners as well. Ideally, the letter summarizes in an evenhanded and appropriately modest manner the main developments during the year. Be warned, however, that these letters from the top dog often are self-congratulatory and typically transfer blame for poor performance on factors beyond the control of the managers. Read them, but take these letters with a grain of salt.

 Many public businesses send shareowners a *condensed summary version* in place of their much longer and more detailed annual financial reports. This is legal, as long as the business mentions that you can get its "real" financial report by asking for a hard copy or by going to its Web site. The idea, of course, is to give shareowners an annual financial report that they can read and digest more quickly and easily. And, condensed financial summaries are more cost effective.

In my view, the scaled-down, simplified, and shortened versions of annual financial reports are adequate for average stock investors. They are not adequate for serious investors and professional investment managers. These investors and money managers should read the full-fledged financial report of the business, and they perhaps should study the company's annual 10-K report that is filed with the Securities and Exchange Commission (SEC). You can go to the website www.sec.gov and navigate from there.

Improve Your Accounting Savvy

Financial statements — the income statement, balance sheet, and statement of cash flows — are the core of a financial report. To make sense of financial statements, you need at least a rudimentary understanding of financial statement accounting. You don't have to be a CPA, but the accountants who prepare financial statements presume that you are familiar with accounting terminology and financial reporting practices. If you're an accounting illiterate, the financial statements probably look like a Sudoku puzzle. There's no way around this demand on financial report readers. After all, accounting is the language of business. (Now where have I heard that before?)

The solution? Read this book. And when you're done, consider reading another book or two about reading financial reports and analyzing financial statements. Without undue modesty I can recommend my book *How To Read A Financial Report,* 7th edition (John Wiley & Sons).

Judge Profit Performance

A business earns profit by making sales and by keeping expenses less than sales revenue, so the best place to start in analyzing profit performance is not the bottom line but the top line: *sales revenue.* Here are some questions to focus on:

✔ How does sales revenue in the most recent year compare with the previous year? Higher sales should lead to higher profit, unless a company's expenses increase at a higher rate than its sales revenue. If sales revenue is relatively flat from year to year, the business must focus on expense control to help profit, but a business can cut expenses only so far. The real key for improving profit is improving sales. Therefore, stock analysts put first importance on tracking sales revenue year to year.

✔ What is the *gross margin ratio* of the business (which equals gross profit divided by sales revenue)? Even a small slippage in its gross margin ratio can have disastrous consequences on the company's bottom line. Stock analysts would like to know the *margin* of a business, which equals sales revenue minus *all* variable costs of sales (product cost and other variable costs of making sales). But external income statements do not reveal margin; businesses hold back this information from the outside world (or they don't keep track of variable versus fixed expenses.)

✔ Based on information from a company's most recent income statement, how do gross margin and the company's bottom line (net income, or net earnings) compare with its top line (sales revenue)? It's a good idea to calculate the gross margin ratio and the profit ratio for the most recent period and compare these two ratios with last period's ratios. If you took the time to compare these two ratios for a variety of businesses;

you may be surprised at the variation from industry to industry. By the way, very few businesses provide profit ratios on the face of their income statements — which is curious because they know that readers of their income statements are interested in their profit ratios.

One last point: Put a company's profit performance in the context of general economic conditions. A down economy puts downward pressure on a company's profit performance, and you should allow for this in your analysis (although this is easier said than done). In an up economy, a company should do better, of course, because a rising tide lifts all boats.

Test Earnings Per Share (EPS) Against Change in Bottom Line

As you know, public companies report net income in their income statements. Below this total profit number for the period, public companies also report earnings per share (EPS), which is the amount of bottom-line profit for each share of its stock. Figure 16-1 shows an example. Strictly speaking, therefore, the bottom line of a public company is its EPS. Private companies do not report EPS; however, the EPS for a private business is fairly easy to calculate — divide its bottom-line net income by the number of ownership shares held by the equity investors in the company.

The market value of ownership shares of a public company depends mainly on its EPS. Individual investors obviously focus on EPS, which they know is the primary driver of the market value of their investment in the business. The book value per share of a private company is the closest proxy you have for the market value of its ownership shares. (I explain book value per share in Chapter 13.) The higher the EPS, the higher the market value for a public company. And, the higher the EPS, the higher the book value per share for a private company. Now, you would naturally think that if net income increases, say 10 percent over last year, then EPS would increase 10 percent. Not so fast. EPS — the driver of market value and book value per share — may change less than 10 percent, or perhaps more than 10 percent.

Individual investors should compare the percent increase/decrease in total bottom-line profit over last year with the corresponding percent increase/ decrease in EPS. Why? Because the percent changes in EPS and profit can diverge. For public companies use its diluted EPS if it's reported. Otherwise, use its basic EPS. (I explain these two critical profit ratios in Chapter 13.) Suppose, for example, that profit (bottom-line net income) increased 10 percent over last year. EPS may not increase the full 10 percent. The business may have issued additional stock shares during the year, or it may have issued additional management stock options that get counted in the number of shares used to calculate diluted EPS. The profit pie may have been cut up into a larger number of smaller pieces. How do you like that? In doing this test you may find just the reverse. EPS may increase more than the 10 percent increase in bottom-line profit. The business may have bought back some of its own shares, which decreases the number of shares used in calculating EPS. This could be a deliberate strategy for increasing EPS by a higher percent than the percent increase in net income.

In summary, EPS doesn't necessarily move in sync with the profit performance of a business. A deviation in the change in EPS compared with the change in profit can hamper or boost market value or book value per share. Be prudent: Check the percent change in profit against the percent change in EPS. But be warned: You have to do this on your own because neither public nor private companies volunteer this comparison. Evidently they don't want to call attention to any disparity between the change in profit versus the change in EPS.

Tackle Extraordinary Gains and Losses

Many income statements start out normally: sales revenue less the expenses of making sales and operating the business. But then there's a jarring layer of *extraordinary gains and losses* on the way down to the final profit line. (I discuss extraordinary gains and losses in Chapter 4.) For example, a business may shut down and abandon one of its manufacturing plants and record a huge loss due to asset write-downs and severance compensation for employees who are laid off. A business may suffer a large loss from an uninsured flood. Or a business may lose a major lawsuit and have to pay millions in damages. The list of extraordinary losses (and gains) is a long one.

In these situations, there are two bottom lines: one for profit from normal, ordinary, ongoing operations; and a second for the effect from the abnormal, extraordinary, nonrecurring gains and losses. The final profit line is the net result of the two components in the income statement. (EPS is reported before and after the unusual items.) What's a financial statement reader to do when a business reports such gains and losses?

There's no easy answer to this question. You could blithely assume that these things happen to a business only once in a blue moon and should not disrupt the business's ability to make profit on a sustainable basis. I call this the *earthquake mentality* approach: When there's an earthquake, there's a lot of damage, but most years have no serious tremors and go along as normal. Extraordinary gains and losses are supposed to be nonrecurring in nature and recorded infrequently, or one-time gains and losses. In actual practice, however, many businesses report these gains and losses on a regular and recurring basis — like having an earthquake every year or so.

Extraordinary losses are a particular problem because large amounts are moved out of the mainstream expenses of the business and treated as nonrecurring losses in its income statement, which means these amounts do not pass through the regular expense accounts of the business. Profit from continuing operations is reported at higher amounts than it would be if the so-called extraordinary losses were treated as regular operating expenses. Unfortunately, CPA auditors tend to tolerate this abuse . . . well, up to a point. Investment managers complain in public about this practice. But in private they seem to prefer that businesses have the latitude to maximize their reported earnings from continuing operations by passing off some expenses as extraordinary losses.

Check Cash Flow Beside Profit

The objective of a business is not simply to make profit, but to generate cash flow from making profit as quickly as possible. Cash flow from making profit is the most important stream of cash inflow to a business. A business could sell off some assets to generate cash, and it can borrow money or get shareowners to put more money in the business. But cash flow from making profit is the spigot that should always be turned on. A business needs this cash flow to make cash distributions from profit to shareowners, to maintain liquidity, and to supplement other sources of capital to grow the business.

The income statement does not — I repeat does *not* — report the cash inflows of sales and the cash outflows of expenses. Therefore, the bottom line of the income statement is not a cash flow number. The net cash flow from the profit-making activities of the business (its sales and expenses) is reported in the statement of cash flows. When you look there, you will undoubtedly discover that the *cash flow from operating activities* (the official term for cash flow from profit-making activities) is higher or lower than the bottom-line profit number in the income statement. I explain the reasons for the difference in Chapter 6.

Businesses seldom offer any explanation of the difference between profit and cash flow. What you see in the statement of cash flows is all you get — no more. You're pretty much on your own to interpret the difference. There are no general benchmarks or ratios for testing cash flow against profit. I couldn't possibly suggest that cash flow should normally be 120 percent of bottom-line profit, or some other ratio. However, one thing is clear: Growth penalizes cash flow — or, more accurately, growth sucks up cash from sales because the business has to expand its assets to support the higher level of sales.

Cash flow from operating activities could be a low percent of profit (or even negative). This situation should prompt questions about the company's *quality of earnings,* which refers to the credibility and soundness of its profit accounting methods. In many cases cash flow is low because accounts receivable from sales haven't been collected and because the business made large increases in its inventories. The surges in these assets raise questions about whether all the receivables will be collected and whether the entire inventory will be sold at regular prices. Only time will tell. Generally speaking, you should be more cautious and treat the net income that the business reports with some skepticism.

Look for Signs of Financial Distress

A business can build up a good sales volume and have very good profit margins, but if the company can't pay its bills on time, its profit opportunities could go down the drain. *Solvency* refers to the prospects of a business being able to meet its debt and other liability payment obligations on time. Solvency analysis asks whether a business will be able to pay its liabilities, looking for signs of financial distress that could cause serious disruptions in the business's profit-making operations. Even if a business has a couple billion bucks in the bank, you should ask: How does its solvency look?

Frankly, detailed solvency analysis of a business is best left to the pros. The credit industry has become very sophisticated in analyzing solvency. For example, bankruptcy prediction models have been developed that have proven useful. I don't think the average financial report reader should spend the time to calculate solvency ratios. For one thing, many businesses massage their accounting numbers to make their liquidity and solvency appear to be better than they are at the balance sheet date.

Although many accountants and investment analysts would view my advice here as heresy, I suggest that you just take a quick glance at the company's balance sheet. How do its total liabilities stack up against its cash, current assets, and total assets? Obviously, total liabilities should not be more than total assets. Duh! And obviously, if a company's cash balance is close to zero, things are bad. Beyond these basic rules, things are a lot more complex. Many businesses carry a debt load you wouldn't believe, and some get into trouble even though they have hefty cash balances.

The continued solvency of a business depends mainly on the ability of its managers to convince creditors to continue extending credit to the business and renewing its loans. The credibility of management is the main factor, not ratios. Creditors understand that a business can get into a temporary bind and fall behind on paying its liabilities. As a general rule, creditors are slow to pull the plug on a business. Shutting off new credit may be the worst thing lenders and other creditors could do. Doing so may put the business in a tailspin, and its creditors may end up collecting very little. Usually, it's not in their interest to force a business into bankruptcy — doing so is a last resort.

Recognize the Risks of Restatement and Fraud

In 2007, the CEO of one of the Big Four global CPA firms testified before a blue-ribbon federal government panel on the state of auditing and financial reporting. He said that one out of every ten financial reports issued by public companies is revised and restated at a later time. If that's true, there's a 10 percent chance that the financial statements you're reading are not entirely correct and could be seriously misleading. An earlier study of financial restatements arrived at a much lower estimate. You'd think that the incidence of companies having to redo their financial reports would be extremely rare, but I have to tell you that financial restatements continue with alarming regularity.

When a business restates its original financial report and issues a new version, it does not make restitution for any losses that investors suffered by relying on the originally reported financial statements. In fact, few companies even say they're sorry when they put out revised financial statements. Generally, the language explaining financial restatements is legalistic and exculpatory. "We didn't do anything wrong" seems to be the underlying theme. This attitude is hard to swallow.

All too often the reason for the restatement is that someone later discovered that the original financial statements were based on fraudulent accounting. Frankly speaking, CPAs don't have a very good track record for discovering financial reporting fraud. What it comes down to is this: Investors take the risk that the information in financial statements they use in making decisions is subject to revision at a later time. I suppose you could go to the trouble of searching for a business that has never had to restate its financial statements, but, of course, there's always a first time.

Remember the Limits of Financial Reports

There's a lot more to investing than reading financial reports. Financial reports are an important source of information, but investors also should stay informed about general economic trends and developments, political events, business takeovers, executive changes, technological changes, and much more. Undoubtedly, the information demands required for investing have helped fuel the enormous popularity of mutual funds; investors offload the need to keep informed to the investment managers of the mutual fund. Many advertisements of financial institutions stress this point — that you have better things to do with your time.

When you read financial statements, keep in mind that these accounting reports are somewhat tentative and conditional. Accountants make many estimates and predictions in recording sales revenue and income, and expenses and losses. Some soft numbers are mixed in with hard numbers in financial statements. In short, financial statements are "iffy" to some extent. There's no getting around this limitation of accounting.

Having said that let me emphasize that financial reports serve an indispensable function in every developed economy. We really couldn't get along without financial reports, despite their limits and problems. People wouldn't know which way to turn in a financial information vacuum. Even though the financial air is polluted, we need the oxygen of financial reports to breathe.

Appendix

Glossary: Slashing Through the Accounting Jargon Jungle

● ●

*A*BC: The acronym for *activity-based costing,* which is a cost allocation scheme that allocates the cost of support functions in an organization (such as maintenance) based on the units of activity of the support function that are used by other departments and processes in the business.

accounting: The methods and procedures for identifying, analyzing, recording, accumulating, and storing information and data about the activities of an entity that have financial results, and preparing summary reports of these activities internally for managers and externally for those entitled to receive financial reports about the entity. A business's managers, investors, and lenders depend on accounting reports called *financial statements* to make informed decisions. Accounting also encompasses preparing tax returns that must be filed with government tax authorities by the entity, and facilitating day-to-day operating functions.

accounting equation: Assets = Liabilities + Owners' Equity. This equation expresses the fundamental duality, or two-sided nature, of accounting and is useful for explaining *double-entry accounting,* which uses debits and credits for recording transactions. It summarizes the balance or equality of an entity's assets and the sources of its assets, which fall into two categories: liabilities and owners' equity.

accounting fraud (also called *cooking the books*): The deliberate falsification or manipulation of accounting numbers to make the profit performance and/or the financial condition of a business appear better than reality. The term also applies to false or grossly inadequate disclosure in financial reports. But the main reference of this term is to misleading accounting methods designed with the intent to deceive. Accounting fraud can be very sophisticated and can escape discovery by the CPA auditors of a business. The incidences of accounting and financial reporting fraud, unfortunately, do not seem to have abated over the years. Accounting fraud is truly an embarrassment to the accounting profession. Accounting fraud is an unavoidable risk facing lenders and investors.

accounts payable: One main type of the short-term operating liabilities of a business, in which are recorded the amounts owed to vendors or suppliers for the purchase of products, supplies, parts, and services that are bought on credit. Generally these liabilities are non-interest bearing (although an interest charge may be added as a penalty for late payment).

accounts receivable: The short-term asset in which are recorded the amounts owed to the business from sales of products and services on credit to its customers. Customers are not normally charged interest, unless they do not pay their bills when due. The amount of this asset in a balance sheet is net of write-downs for uncollectible receivables (called *bad debts*).

accrual-basis accounting: Recording the financial effects of economic events when they happen, as opposed to simple cash accounting. Using accrual-basis accounting, revenue is recorded when sales are made (rather than when cash is received from customers), and expenses are recorded to match with sales revenue or in the period benefited (rather than when expenses are paid). The accrual basis of accounting is seen in the recording of assets such as receivables from customers, inventory (cost of products not yet sold), and cost of long-term assets (fixed assets) — and in the recording of liabilities such as accounts payable to vendors and payables for unpaid expenses.

accrued expenses payable: The generic term for liability accounts used to record the gradual accumulation of unpaid expenses, such as vacation pay earned by employees and profit-based bonus plans that aren't paid until the following period. *Note:* The specific title of this liability varies from business to business; you may see *accrued liabilities, accrued expenses,* or other account title. Generally you see the term *accrued* in the account title.

accumulated depreciation: The total cumulative amount of depreciation expense that has been recorded since the fixed assets being depreciated were acquired. In the balance sheet, the amount in this account is deducted from the original cost of fixed assets. The balance of cost less accumulated depreciation is referred to as the *book value* of the fixed assets.

acid-test ratio: An alternative name for the **quick ratio.**

adjusting entries: At the end of the period, these important entries are recorded to complete the bookkeeping cycle. These end-of-period entries record certain expenses to the period (such as depreciation) and update revenue, income, expenses, and losses for the period. *Note:* This term also refers to making correcting entries when accounting errors are discovered.

amortization: Traditionally in accounting this term applied to the allocation of the cost of an intangible asset over its expected useful life to the business, in the manner of depreciation accounting. However, in recent years amortization accounting has changed gears to an annual asset impairment approach instead of a predetermined schedule for writing down the cost of the asset. (*Caution:* In the field of finance and investments, amortization refers to the reduction, or pay down of the principal balance of a loan.)

asset turnover ratio: Annual sales revenue divided by total assets (at year-end, or the average total assets during the year). This ratio is used to judge the utilization of assets in making sales. It is also used as one component in the calculation of return on equity (ROE).

audit report: A three-paragraph (or longer) rather technically worded opinion issued by the CPA at the conclusion of an audit, which includes testing the reliability of the accounting system of a business and scrutiny of its financial report. The CPA's audit report states whether the financial statements and disclosures of the business are in conformity with applicable U.S. or international financial accounting and reporting standards. A so-called "clean opinion" is the best outcome of an audit; it means that the CPA auditor has no serious disagreements with the financial report of the business.

bad debt(s): The expense caused by a customer's failure to pay the amount owed to the business from a credit sale. When the credit sale was recorded, the accounts receivable asset account was increased. When it becomes clear that this debt owed to the business will not be collected, the asset is written down and the amount is charged to bad debts expense.

balance sheet: This financial statement summarizes the assets, liabilities, and owners' equity of a business at a moment in time. It's prepared at the end of every profit period (and whenever else it is needed). The main elements of a balance sheet are called *accounts* — such as cash, inventory, notes payable, and capital stock. Each account has a dollar amount, which is called its *balance.* But be careful: The fact that the accounts have balances is not the reason this financial statement is called a balance sheet. Rather, the equality (or balance) of assets with the total of liabilities and owners' equity is the reason for the name. This financial statement is also called the *statement of financial condition* and the *statement of financial position.*

book value (of assets and owners' equity): Refers to the recorded amounts on the books (accounting records) of a business, which are reported in its balance sheet. Often this term is used to emphasize that the amounts recorded in the accounts of the business are less than the current replacement costs of certain assets, or less than the market value of owners' equity.

break-even: The annual sales volume or sales revenue at which total margin equals total annual fixed expenses — that is, the exact sales amount at which the business covers its fixed expenses and makes a zero profit and avoids a loss. Break-even is a useful point of reference in analyzing profit performance and the effects of making sales in excess of break-even.

capital expenditures: Outlays for fixed (long-term) assets in order to overhaul or replace the old assets or to expand and modernize the long-lived operating resources of a business. Fixed assets is a broad category that includes land, buildings, machinery, equipment, vehicles, furniture, fixtures, and computers. These operating assets have useful lives from 3 to 39 (or more) years. The term "capital" implies that substantial amounts are invested for many years.

capital stock: The ownership shares issued by a corporation for capital invested in the business by owners. Total capital is divided into units of ownership called *capital stock shares.* In the old days, you actually got engraved certificates as legal evidence of your ownership of a certain number of shares. Today, *book entry* is the norm: Your ownership is recorded in the books, or records, of the registrar for the stock shares. A business corporation must issue at least one class of capital stock, called *common stock.* It may also issue other classes of stock, such as *preferred stock.*

cash flow: An ambiguous term that can refer to several different sources of or uses of cash. This term is often shorthand for cash flow from earning profit, or to me more correct **cash flow from operating activities** (see next entry). Some friendly advice: When using this term always make clear the particular source or use of cash you have in mind!

cash flow from operating activities: This important figure is reported in the first section of the statement of cash flows. It equals the total cash inflow from sales and other income during the period minus the total cash outflow for expenses and losses during the period. This cash flow number is higher or lower than the bottom-line net income of the business for the period, which is reported in its income statement. The sales revenue and expenses reported in the income statement are recorded using **accrual basis accounting.**

certified public accountant (CPA): The CPA designation is a widely recognized and respected badge of a professional accountant. A person must meet educational and experience requirements and pass a national uniform exam to qualify for a state license to practice as a CPA. Many CPAs are not in public practice; they work for business organizations, government agencies, and nonprofit organizations, or they teach accounting (a plug for educators here if you don't mind). CPAs in public practice do audits of financial reports, and they also provide tax, management, and financial consulting services.

common stock: The one class of capital stock that must be issued by a business corporation. It has the most junior, or "last in line," claim on the business's assets in the event of liquidation, after all liabilities and any senior capital stock (such as preferred stock) are paid. Owners of common stock receive dividends from profit only after preferred stockholders (if any) are paid. Owners of common stock generally have voting rights in the election of the board of directors, although a business may issue both voting and non-voting classes of common stock.

comprehensive income: Includes net income reported in the income statement plus certain technical gains and losses that are recorded but don't necessarily have to be included in the income statement. In other words, the effects of these developments can bypass the income statement. Most companies report these special types of gains and losses (if they have any) in a column in the *statement of changes in owners' (stockholders') equity* that is headed "accumulated other comprehensive income," or a similar title.

controller: The chief accounting officer of an organization. The controller may also serve as the chief financial officer (CFO) in a business or other organization, although in large organizations the two jobs are usually split.

cooking the books: A popular term for **accounting fraud**. This term should not be confused with the lesser offenses of **massaging the numbers** and **income smoothing**.

credits: see **debits and credits**

current assets: Includes cash plus accounts receivable, inventory, and pre-paid expenses (and short-term marketable securities if the business owns any). These assets should be converted into cash during one operating cycle or sooner.

Current liabilities: Short-term liabilities, principally accounts payable, accrued expenses payable, income tax payable, short-term notes payable, and the portion of long-term debt that falls due within the coming year. This group includes both non-interest-bearing and interest-bearing liabilities that must be paid in the short term, usually defined to be one year or less.

current ratio: One test of a business's short-term solvency (debt-paying capability). Find the current ratio by dividing a business's total current assets by its total current liabilities.

debits and credits: Accounting jargon for decreases and increases recorded in accounts according to the centuries' old scheme based on the *accounting equation*. An increase in an asset is a debit, and the ingenious twist of the scheme is that a decrease in a liability or an owners' equity is also a debit. Conversely, a decrease in an asset is a credit and an increase in a liability or an owners' equity is a credit. Revenue is recorded as a credit, and expenses are recorded as debits. In recording transactions, the debit or sum of debits must equal the credit or sum of credits. The phrase "the books are in balance" means that the total of accounts with debit balances equals the total of accounts with credit balances. (By the way, students have a hell of a time in learning debits and credits.)

depreciation: Allocating a fixed asset's cost over three or more years, based on its estimated useful life to the business. Each year of the asset's life is charged with part of its total cost as the asset gradually wears out and loses its economic value to the business. Either an *accelerated* method or the *straight-line* depreciation is used. An accelerated method allocates more of the cost to the early years than the later years. The straight-line method allocates an equal amount to every year.

dividend yield: Measures the cash income component of return on investment in stock shares of a corporation. The dividend yield equals the most recent (or trailing) 12 months of cash dividends paid on a stock divided by the stock's current market price. If a stock is selling for $100 and over the last 12 months paid $3 cash dividends, its dividend yield equals 3 percent.

double-entry accounting: Simply put, this term means that both sides of an economic event or business transaction are recorded, both the give and the take, as it were. In short, double-entry accounting means two-sided accounting. The *debits and credits* method is the bookkeeping means used to implement double-entry accounting. (See **debits and credits.**)

earnings before interest and income tax (EBIT): Sales revenue less cost of goods sold and all operating expenses — but before deducting interest expense and income tax expense (and usually, but not always, before extraordinary gains and losses). This measure of profit also is called *operating earnings, operating profit,* or something similar. The idea is to have a measure of profit independent of how the business is financed (debt versus equity) and separate from how the business is taxed on its profit.

earnings per share (EPS): Equals net income for the most recent 12 months reported, called the *trailing 12 months,* divided by the number of capital stock shares. Dividing net income by the actual number of shares in the hands of stockholders, called *outstanding shares,* gives the *basic EPS. Diluted EPS* equals the same net income figure divided by the sum of the actual number of shares outstanding plus additional shares that will be issued under terms of stock options awarded to managers and for the conversion of senior securities into common stock (assuming that the company has issued convertible debt or preferred stock securities).

extraordinary gains and losses: Unusual, nonrecurring gains and losses that happen infrequently and that are aside from the normal, ordinary sales and expenses of a business. These gains and losses, in theory, are one-time or rare events that can't be anticipated. But in actual practice many businesses record these gains and losses too frequently to be called *nonrecurring.* These gains and losses (net of income tax effects) are reported separately in the income statement. In this way, attention is directed to net income from the normal continuing operations of the business.

Financial Accounting Standards Board (FASB): The highest authoritative, private sector, standard-setting body of the accounting profession in the United States. The FASB issues pronouncements that establish *generally accepted accounting principles (GAAP).* **Note:** The federal Securities and Exchange Commission (SEC) also plays a dominant role in financial reporting by public companies in the United States.

financial leverage: Generally refers to using debt capital on top of equity capital. The strategy is to earn a rate of return on assets (ROA) higher than the interest rate on borrowed money. A favorable spread between the two rates generates financial leverage gain to the benefit of net income and owners' equity.

financial reports: The periodic financial communications from a business (and other types of organizations) to those entitled to know about the financial performance and position of the entity. Financial reports of businesses include three primary financial statements (balance sheet, income statement, and statement of cash flows), as well as footnotes and other information relevant to the owners of the business. Public companies must file several types of financial reports and forms with the Securities and Exchange Commission (SEC), which are open to the public. The financial reports of private businesses are generally sent only to its owners and lenders.

financial statement: Generally refers to one of the three primary accounting reports of a business: the balance sheet, statement of cash flows, and income statement. Sometimes financial statements are called simply *financials*. Internal financial statements and other accounting reports to managers contain considerably more detail, which is needed for decision making and control.

financing activities: In accounting, this term refers to one of three types of cash flows reported in the statement of cash flows. These are the dealings between a business and its sources of debt and equity capital — such as borrowing and repaying debt, issuing new stock shares, buying some of its own stock shares, and paying dividends to shareowners.

first-in, first-out (FIFO): A widely used accounting method by which costs of products when they are sold are charged to cost of goods sold expense in chronological order. One result is that the most recent acquisition costs remain in the inventory asset account at the end of the period. The reverse order also is acceptable, which is called the *last-in, first-out (LIFO)* method.

fixed assets: The shorthand term for the variety of long-life physical resources used by a business in conducting its operations, which include land, buildings, machinery, equipment, furnishings, tools, and vehicles. These resources are held for use, not for sale. Please note that *fixed assets* is an informal term; the more formal term used in a balance sheet is *property, plant, and equipment*.

fixed costs: Those expenses or costs that remain unchanged over the short run and do not vary with changes in sales volume or sales revenue. Common examples are building rent under lease contracts, employees paid on salary basis, property taxes, and monthly utility bills. Fixed expenses provide the capacity for carrying out operations and for making sales.

footnotes: Footnotes are the additional explanatory items of information attached to the three primary financial statements included in an external financial report. Footnotes present detailed information that cannot be put directly in the body of one of the financial statements. Footnotes have the reputation of being difficult to read, poorly written, overly detailed, and too technical. Unfortunately, these criticisms have a lot of truth.

free cash flow: This is largely a self-defined term that depends on what you want it to mean. Be cautious about this term because it has no uniform meaning. Some people use it as an alternative term for *cash flow from operating activities* — to emphasize that the business is free to do what it wants with this source of cash. This is not the only usage you see in practice, however. The person using the term may deduct certain amounts from the cash flow from operating activities. For example, capital expenditures during the period may be deducted from cash flow from operating activities to determine the remaining "free" amount of cash flow. To repeat, be careful when you run into this term.

generally accepted accounting principles (GAAP): The authoritative standards and approved accounting methods that should be used by profit-motivated businesses and private nonprofit organizations domiciled in the United States to measure and report their revenue and expenses; to present their assets, liabilities, and owners' equity; and to report their cash flows in their financial statements. GAAP are not a straitjacket; these official standards are loose enough to permit alternative interpretations.

goodwill: In accounting this term refers to intangible assets that have been purchased by a business, such as by buying an established brand name or buying a company for more than its market value. Only purchased goodwill is reported as an asset in the balance sheet. The cost of goodwill may or may not be amortized (charged off to expense over time). In the broader business sense, goodwill refers to the well-known and trusted reputation of a company. Goodwill in this usage is not found in the balance sheet. To be recorded and appear in the balance sheet of a business, goodwill must be actually purchased or acquired in the larger setting of a business combination.

gross margin (profit): Equals sales revenue less cost of goods sold expense for the period. Making adequate gross margin is the starting point for making bottom-line profit. There are other expenses below the gross margin line.

income smoothing: Manipulating the timing of when sales revenue and/or expenses are recorded in order to produce a smoother profit trend with narrower fluctuations from year to year. Also called *massaging the numbers,* the implementation of profit-smoothing procedures needs the implicit or explicit approval of top-level managers, because these techniques require the override of normal accounting procedures for recording sales revenue and expenses. CPA auditors generally tolerate a reasonable amount of profit smoothing — which is also called *earnings management.*

income statement: This financial statement summarizes sales revenue (and other income) and expenses (and losses) for a period and reports one or more different profit lines. Also, any extraordinary gains and losses are reported separately in this financial statement. The income statement is one of the three primary financial statements of a business included in its financial report and is also called the *earnings statement,* the *operating statement,* or similar titles.

internal (accounting) controls: Forms, procedures, and precautions that are established primarily to prevent and minimize errors and fraud (beyond the forms and procedures that are needed for record keeping). Common internal control are: requiring the signature of two managers to approve transactions over a certain amount; restricting entry and exit routes of employees; using surveillance cameras; forcing employees to take their vacations; separating duties; and conducting surprise inventory counts and inspections.

International Accounting Standards Board (IASB): The authoritative financial reporting standards-setting body for businesses outside the United States. The IASB and the Financial Accounting Standards Board (FASB) have been working together for more than a decade towards the adoption of world-wide accounting and financial reporting standards. However, this has proven to be more difficult than was originally imagined.

investing activities: In accounting this term refers to one of three classes of cash flows reported in the statement of cash flows. Mainly, these outlays are for major investments in long-term operating assets, typically called *capital expenditures.* A business may dispose of some of its fixed assets during the year, and proceeds from these disposals are reported in this section of the statement of cash flows.

last-in, first-out (LIFO): An accounting method by which costs of products when they are sold are charged to cost of goods sold expense in reverse chronological order. One result is that the ending inventory cost value consists of the costs of the earliest goods purchased or manufactured, which could be ten, twenty, or more years old. The actual physical flow of products seldom follows a LIFO sequence. The method is argued on the grounds that the cost of goods sold expense should be the cost of replacing the products sold, and the best approximations are the most recent acquisition costs.

lower of cost or market (LCM): A test applied to ending inventory that can result in a write-down and charge to expense for the decline in value of products held for sale. The recorded costs of products in inventory are compared with their current replacement costs (market price) and with net realizable value if normal sales prices have been reduced. If either value is lower, then recorded cost is written down to this lower value.

management (managerial) accounting: The branch of accounting that prepares internal financial statements and other accounting reports and analyses to help managers carry out their planning, decision-making, and control functions. Most of the detailed information in these reports is confidential and is not circulated outside the business. Management accounting includes budgeting, developing and using standard costs, and working closely with managers regarding how costs are allocated.

Manufacturing overhead costs: Refers to those costs that are indirect and cannot be naturally matched or linked with manufacturing particular products, or to a department, or to a step in the production process. One example is the annual property tax on a building in which a company's manufacturing activities are carried out. Production overhead costs are allocated among the different products manufactured during the period in order to account for the full cost of each product. In this way, manufacturing overhead costs are absorbed into product costs and remain in the inventory asset account until the products are sold.

margin: Equals sales revenue minus cost of goods sold expense and minus all variable expenses. (In other words, margin is profit before fixed expenses are deducted.) On a per-unit basis, margin equals sales price less product cost per unit and less variable expenses per unit. Margin is an exceedingly important measure for analyzing profit behavior and in making sales price decisions.

market cap: The total market value of a public business, which is calculated by multiplying the current market price per share times the total number of capital stock shares issued by the business.

massaging the numbers: It's also called earnings management or juggling the books, and includes the practice of **window dressing.** (See **income smoothing** and **window dressing.**)

net income: Equals sales revenue and other income less all expenses and losses for the period; also, any extraordinary gains and losses for the period are counted in the calculation to get to bottom-line net income. *Bottom line* means everything has been deducted from sales revenue (and other income the business may have) so the last profit line in the income statement is the final amount of profit for the period. Instead of *net income,* you may see terms such as *net earnings, earnings from operations,* or just *earnings.* You do not see the term *profit* very often.

operating activities: Generally this term refers to the profit-making activities of a business — that is, the mainstream sales and expense transactions of a business. In the statement of cash flows this term refers to one of the three classes of cash flows reported in this financial statement (the other two being *investing* and *financing* activities).

operating liabilities: Refers to the liabilities from making purchases on credit for items and services needed in the normal, ongoing operating activities of a business. The term also includes the liabilities that are recorded to recognize the accumulation or accrual of unpaid expenses in order to record the full costs of expenses for the period. (An example is accumulated vacation pay earned by employees that will not be taken until later).

owners' equity: The ownership capital base of a business. Owners' equity derives from two sources: investment of capital in the business by the owners (for which capital stock shares are issued by a corporation) and profit that has been earned by the business but has not been distributed to its owners (called *retained earnings* for a corporation).

pass-through tax entity: A type of legal organization that does not itself pay income tax but instead serves as a conduit of its annual taxable income to its owners. The business *passes through* its annual taxable income to its owners, who include their respective shares of the amount in their individual income tax returns. Partnerships are pass-through tax entities by their very nature. Limited liability companies (LLCs) and certain corporations (called *S corporations*) can elect to be treated as pass-through tax entities.

preferred stock: A second type, or class, of capital stock that is issued by a business corporation in addition to its *common stock*. Preferred stock has certain preferences over the common stock: It is paid cash dividends before dividends can be paid to common stockholders; and, in the event of liquidating the business, preferred stock shares must be redeemed before any money is returned to the common stockholders. Owners of preferred stock usually do not have voting rights, and the stock may be callable by the corporation, which means that the business has the right to redeem the shares for a certain price per share.

prepaid expenses: Expenses that have been paid in advance, or up front, for future benefits. The amount of cash outlay is entered in the prepaid expenses asset account. For example, a business writes a $60,000 check today for fire insurance coverage over the following six months. The total cost is first entered in the prepaid expenses asset account; then each month $10,000 is taken out of the asset and charged to expense. Prepaid expenses are usually smaller than a business's inventory, accounts receivable, and cash assets.

price/earnings (P/E) ratio: The current market price of a capital stock divided by its trailing 12 months' diluted earnings per share (EPS) — or its basic earnings per share if the business does not report diluted EPS.

product cost: Equals the purchase cost of goods that are bought and then resold by retailers and wholesalers (distributors). In contrast, a manufacturer combines different types of production costs to determine product cost: direct (raw) materials, direct labor, and overhead costs.

profit: A very general term that is used with different meanings. It may mean gains minus losses, or other kinds of increases minus decreases. In business, the term means sales revenue (and other sources of income) minus expenses (and losses) for a period of time, such as one year. In an income statement the preferred term for final or bottom-line profit is *net income.* For public companies, net income is put on a per-share basis, called *earnings per share.*

profit and loss (P&L) report: A popular title for internal profit performance reports to managers (which are not circulated outside the company). The term has a certain ring to it that sounds good, but if you consider it closely, how can a business have profit and loss at the same time?

property, plant, and equipment: The term generally used in balance sheets instead of **fixed assets.** (See **fixed assets.**)

proxy statement: The annual solicitation from a corporation's top executives and board of directors to its stockholders that requests that they vote a certain way on matters that have to be put to a vote at the annual meeting of stockholders. In larger public corporations, most stockholders cannot attend the meeting in person, so they delegate a proxy (stand-in person) to vote their shares *yes* or *no* on each proposal on the agenda.

Public Company Accounting Oversight Board (PCAOB): The regulatory agency of the U.S. federal government created by the Sarbanes-Oxley Act of 2002, which was enacted in response to fallout from a number of high-profile accounting fraud scandals that the CPA auditors of the businesses failed to discover. This board has broad powers over the auditors of public businesses.

quality of earnings: Generally used as cautionary term that raises questions about the net income reported by a business. The issue at hand is whether the accounting methods of a business are correct in the circumstances, and it raises the possibility that reported profit should not be relied on, or at least taken with a grain of salt.

quick ratio: Calculated by dividing the total of cash, accounts receivable, and marketable securities (if any) by total current liabilities. This ratio measures the capability of a business to pay off its current short-term liabilities with its cash and near-cash assets. Note that inventory and prepaid expenses, two other current assets, are excluded from assets in this ratio (which is also called the *acid-test ratio*).

retained earnings: One of two basic sources of the owners' equity of a business (the other being capital invested by the owners). Annual profit (*net income*) increases this account, and distributions from profit to owners decrease the account. The balance in the retained earnings account does not refer to cash or any particular asset.

return on assets (ROA): Equals profit divided by total assets and is expressed as a percent. *Caution:* There is not just one standard way of calculating this ratio. Different definitions of profit and total assets are used for different purposes. The general purpose for calculating ROA is to test whether a business is making good use of its assets, particularly relative to its cost of capital rate.

return on equity (ROE): Equals net income (minus preferred stock dividends if any) divided by the book value of owners' equity (minus the amount of preferred stock) and is expressed as a percent. ROE is a basic measure of how well (or poorly) a business is doing in generating earnings relative to the amount of owners' capital.

return on investment (ROI): In the field of finance this is a very broad and general term that refers to the income, profit, gain, or earnings for a period of time on the capital investment during that period, expressed as a percentage of the amount invested. Two relevant ROI ratios for a business are return on assets (ROA) and return on equity (ROE).

Securities and Exchange Commission (SEC): The federal agency that has jurisdiction and broad powers over the public issuance and trading of securities (stocks and bonds). Although it has the power to legislate accounting standards, the SEC has largely deferred to the *Financial Accounting Standards Board (FASB)*. The *Public Company Accounting Oversight Board (PCAOB)* is a quasi-autonomous branch of the SEC.

solvency: Refers to the ability of a business (or other entity) to pay its liabilities on time. The current ratio and quick ratio are used to assess the short-term solvency of a business.

statement of cash flows: One of the three primary financial statements of a business, which summarizes its cash inflows and outflows during a period according to a threefold classification: cash flow from operating activities, investing activities, and financing activities.

statement of changes in owners' (stockholders') equity: A supplementary statement (or schedule, if you prefer) to the three primary financial statements. Its purpose is to summarize changes in the owners' equity accounts during the year, including distributing cash dividends, issuing additional stock shares, and buying some of its own capital stock shares. Also, this statement reports changes in the *accumulated other comprehensive income* account, in which certain types of technical gains and losses are recorded that are not reported in the income statement.

variable costs: Costs that are sensitive to and vary with changes in sales volume or sales revenue. In contrast, *fixed costs* do not change over the short run in response to changes in sales activity.

window dressing: An accounting ruse that makes the liquidity and short-term solvency of a business look better than it really was on the balance sheet date. The books are held open a few business days after the close of the accounting year in order to record additional cash receipts (as if the cash collections had occurred on the last day of the year). This term generally does not refer to manipulating the timing for recording profit — which is called *income smoothing*). ***Tip:*** A reasonable amount of window dressing is not viewed as accounting fraud, but rather as "fluffing the pillows" (as my late father-in-law and businessman liked to put it).

Index

• D •